Colleges That Create Futures

50 Schools That Launch Careers By Going Beyond the Classroom

2016 Edition

By Robert Franek
and the Staff of The Princeton Review

PrincetonReview.com

nguin
Random
House

The Princeton Review
24 Prime Parkway, Suite 201
Natick, MA 01760
editorialsupport@review.com

Published in the United States by Penguin Random House LLC, New York, and in Canada by Random House of Canada, a division of Penguin Random House Ltd., Toronto.

ISBN: 978-0-8041-2608-3
ISSN: 2378-5837

Production: Best Content Solutions, LLC
Production Editor: Melissa Duclos-Yourdon

Printed in the United States of America on partially recycled paper.
9 8 7 6 5 4 3 2 1

2016 Edition

Editorial
Robert Franek, Senior VP—Publisher
David Soto, Director of Content Development
Kristen O'Toole, Editorial Director
Steven Koch, Student Survey Manager
Pia Aliperti, Editor

Random House Publishing Team
Tom Russell, Publisher
Alison Stoltzfus, Publishing Manager
Ellen L. Reed, Production Manager
Melinda Ackell, Managing Editor
Kristin Lindner, Production Supervisor
Andrea Lau, Designer

Contents

Acknowledgments

This book would not have been possible without the following individuals here at The Princeton Review and beyond, who contributed to making *Colleges That Create Futures* a reality: Kristen O'Toole, who was instrumental in the development of this title; Pia Aliperti, who shepherded the project to completion; and Scott Harris of Best Content Solutions and production editor Melissa Duclos-Yourdon, who transformed the various pieces of the manuscript into the book now in your hands.

A special thank you goes to writers Jason Bailey, Alex Dryden, Melissa Duclos-Yourdon, Sasha Fletcher, Jordan Foster, Laura Goode, Lincoln Michel, Katrina Otuonye, and Lucie Parker for their dedication in poring through surveys and interviews to produce the narratives of each school profiled. Thank you to our Student Survey Manager, Stephen Koch, who continues to work in partnership with school administrators and students alike. My continued thanks go to our data collections master, David Soto for his successful efforts in collecting and accurately representing the statistical data that we draw upon to create these college profiles.

Quite a few administrators, professors, and college alumni/ae kindly set aside time to speak with us about the experience at their institutions. We thank them for taking the time out of their busy lives to answer questions about the most meaningful experiences on their campuses. We commend you for your generosity in guiding the next generation of college applicants to find that best fit college that will transform them.

Robert Franek

Senior VP—Publisher

Author, *Colleges That Pay You Back* and *The Best 380 Colleges*

Introduction
Welcome to *Colleges That Create Futures*

Rest assured: every one of the fifty colleges in this guide offers a terrific education. But when it comes to getting the most out of college, the experiences you have outside the classroom are just as important as what you're learning in class. Every year, via our "College Hopes & Worries" survey (www.princetonreview.com/college-hopes-worries), one of the questions we ask college applicants and their parents is "What do you consider the biggest benefit of going to college will be?" Since 2010, when we first added the question to our survey, the plurality of respondents have seen the main benefit of a college degree as a potentially better job and higher income while the rest saw the education or exposure to new ideas as the major benefit. We see this point of view reflected on college campuses as well: At many schools, career services advisers begin to engage with students earlier in their time on campus, often in the first few weeks of their first year. These trends in career services aren't a result of colleges pressuring students to plan out their futures before they are ready—rather, colleges and universities are working to help students identify their interests, strengths, and passions, and use those to build the foundation of a meaningful career strategy.

Schools that empower students help them to discover practical applications for their talents and interests, oftentimes through experiences that complement or build upon their classes and coursework. Hands-on activities like internships, studying abroad, assisting with faculty research, and other experiential learning options give students the opportunities to apply their knowledge to authentic, real-world situations. Employers think so, too. According to PayScale.com, 69 percent of employers feel that hands-on or job specific training is an important or critical soft skill (other top five soft skills include: work ethic, teamwork, oral communication, and problem solving).[1]

What Is Experiential Learning?

You can think of experiential learning as learning by doing, but that's just half of it. Experiential learning is also applying what you already know (such as concepts and theories) to unfamiliar and variable situations. In some ways it's like the difference between learning Spanish vocabulary words in a classroom and trying to order local cuisine off a menu in Barcelona. Interacting with real Spanish speakers, who may talk faster and pepper their conversation with slang

---

[1] "Underemployment: What Employers Want," PayScale, Inc., accessed April 19, 2015, http://www.payscale.com/data-packages/underemployment/the-skills-gap.

and idioms, is a more authentic experience than learning Spanish solely in an American classroom.

Experiential learning is also a great way to find out what you like and what you don't. You love your biology and chemistry classes, but do you really want to go to medical school? An externship program shadowing a doctor for the day may convince you to sign up for the MCAT. Are your sensibilities better suited for an institutional software company or a scrappy environmental startup? Summer internships in both the corporate and non-profit worlds can give you a better idea of what fits you best. These types of activities are also chances to discover new interests and to develop talents and strengths, even in areas beyond your major—and more crucially, beyond your comfort zone. There's also a risk factor involved. The Association of Experiential Education explains that as experiential learning experiences require students to "take initiative, make decisions and be accountable for results," students may also "experience success, failure, adventure, risk-taking and uncertainty."[2] Just like in the real-world, you can't totally predict what the outcome of an experience will be—but no matter what you'll learn from it.

The final component of an experiential learning experience is reflection. What specifically did you learn through the experience? How could you apply what you've learned to other settings? Landing a great job after college means articulating your strengths and demonstrating their value to a potential employer. For example, upon reflection it will become clear that your work-study gig as a peer tutor in the Writing Center has strengthened your ability to break down complex material for others to understand (an experience you can reference when an employer is looking for someone with impeccable communication skills). Similarly, your role on the Solar Car Team finessed your technical skills as well as the ability to problem-solve as part of a team.

A Key of Terms

What kind of activities put the "experience" in experiential learning? We've compiled a short list of terms below to look out for on college websites and brochures (and you'll definitely seem them crop up in the profiles in this book). Here's a quick key you can refer to as you browse this book:

- **Cooperative Education (Co-op)** is a paid professional experience that a student completes for an extended period of time, often alternated with course work. For example, a student may work full-time for six months, followed by six months of classwork, and then repeat the pattern.

2   "What is Experiential Education?" Association for Experiential Education, accessed May 8, 2015, http://www.aee.org/what-is-ee.

- A **project** is an extended problem-solving activity either solo or in collaboration with a group. A few examples: a research-based thesis, works of art (plays, photography, or musical compositions), productions or performances (curating an exhibit or giving a recital), designing a prototype, or writing a computer program.

- An **externship** is a temporary job-shadowing program that allows students to get an introduction to a field or profession. These are typically short experiences anywhere from an afternoon to a few weeks. Externships can be a requirement for an academic course or an experience that students can seek out during winter or spring breaks.

- An **internship** gives you the opportunity to work for a company or non-profit organization for a limited amount of time, anywhere from a week to a semester. These can be paid or unpaid (though many schools have programs that will fund unpaid or lowly paid internships) and allow interns to learn more about a field of interest while completing tasks or projects alongside real employees.

- **Research** is a scholarly or artistic activity that produces new knowledge. On a college campus research experiences could run the gamut from working alongside your professor in a lab, writing a thesis, or completing a capstone project for your major.

- **Service-learning** combines a learning experience with community service. You are both seeking real objectives in a community while at the same time developing a greater understanding of community issues and skill-building on a personal level.

- **Student organizations** bring together students with a common interest in anything from sustainability to investment banking. Clubs are great places to do some good, have fun, and develop leadership and collaboration skills along the way.

- **Study Abroad** is a travel experience that combines academic, work, and cultural experiences.

We also think that unique community spaces, first-year programming (such as orientations and seminars), and other special places on campus like Oberlin College's Allen Memorial Art Museum (with its popular student docent education program) or the Student Shops at MIT (where students are trained to fabricate almost anything from scratch) are great sites to experiment and build skills. For example, the Residential Colleges at Rice University are completely student-governed, and students are assigned to one, even if they choose to live off-campus, for the entirety of their time in school. And at the College of Charleston, the First-Year Experience gets freshmen interested in their future career and academic options early-on and gives them a preview of what the college has to offer. We highlight these types of spots and experiences in the profiles when we can.

How We Produced This Book

To cull our list of the fifty colleges we feature in this book, we began with the pool of nearly 400 academically outstanding schools we profile in our guidebooks *The Best 380 Colleges* and/or *Colleges That Pay You Back*. From that core group of exemplary and highly diverse colleges, we worked to establish some parameters by which we could identify the schools that were not only academically first-rate but also first-rate at helping their students move on to successful and rewarding post-graduate chapters.

We narrowed our list to these fifty choices based on several factors. We looked at data from our own surveys of students and administrators, and we personally reached out to administrators, faculty, students and alumni at dozens of schools. We also sought feedback from our Princeton Review editors and test-prep experts who are on college campuses and have their ears to the ground about exemplary programs at various institutions.

In particular, we identified schools that reported a significant percentage of graduates pursuing further study, and colleges at which students we surveyed gave their schools high ratings in categories that ranged from career services and internship opportunities to community service and extracurricular engagement (more about how we conduct our student surveys follows).

Our interviews with administrators, faculty, and alumni at these schools generated a wealth of rich and useful insights about their campus facilities and programs. Among other things, we asked administrators to identify programs that they regarded as the most special on campus in terms of hands-on learning. We asked faculty to give us the scoop on the specific skills their students acquire by graduation. Finally, we asked alumni to share their assessments about ways their campus experiences shaped (or didn't shape) their career trajectories.

From that broad range of data, student and administrator surveys, and insightful feedback from current students, deans, professors, and alumni, we present our profiles of these fifty extraordinary colleges. We hope our profiles will give you a panoramic picture of how each of these schools prepares their students for careers that suit them and well into their futures.

About our Student Surveys for Our *Best Colleges* Books

Surveying tens of thousands of students on hundreds of campuses is a large undertaking. In 1992, when we published the first edition of our *Best Colleges* book, our student survey was a paper survey. Now all of our surveys are completed online. The average number of student surveys (per college) upon which our ranking lists are annually tallied is now 358 students per campus (and at some schools we hear from more than 3,000 students). Students submit surveys online from all schools in the book and they can submit their surveys at any time during the academic year at http://survey.review.com. (Our site will accept only one survey from a student per academic year per school—it's not possible to "stuff" the ballot box, as it were.) In addition to those surveys we receive from students on an ongoing basis, we also officially conduct surveys of students at each school in the book once every three years on average. And of course, surveys we receive from students outside of their schools' normal survey cycles are always factored into the subsequent year's ranking calculations, so our pool of student survey data is continuously refreshed

The survey has more than 80 questions in four main sections: "About Yourself," "Your School's Academics/Administration," "Students," and "Life at Your School." We ask about all sorts of things, from "How many out-of-class hours do you spend studying each day?" to "How do you rate your campus food?" Most questions offer an answer choice on a five-point scale: students fill in one of five boxes on a grid with headers varying by topic (e.g., a range from "Excellent" to "Awful"). Once the surveys have been completed and responses stored in our database, every college is given a score (similar to a GPA) for its students' answers to each question. This score enables us to compare student opinion from college to college and to tally the ranking lists. Most of the lists are based on students' answers to one survey question; some lists are based on answers to several survey questions. But all of our 62 ranking lists—covering career services, financial aid, campus facilities and amenities, extracurriculars, and more—are based entirely on our student survey results. Unless otherwise noted, the rankings referenced in the profiles in *Colleges That Create Futures* were reported in August 2015 in *The Best 380 Colleges* 2016 edition. To see all of our 62 ranking lists, or read more about our methodology, visit Princeton Review.com.

How This Book Can Help You

First of all, we hope that this book will give you an idea of all that is possible on a college campus. Some schools offer so many options and activities that you might need to do a little detective work to find that experience that is perfect for you and your interests. We believe these profiles will give you some pointers on where to look.

Second, we hope you'll benefit from the perspective of graduates from each institution. These alumni have had time outside of college to truly reflect on their experiences there. They've had their first entry-level jobs, their first promotions, and for the most part, are established on a career path. They can often pinpoint the experience in college that ignited their passion or gave them a leg-up when it came time to enter the job market. We talked to graduates who are entrepreneurs, business owners, politicians, writers and editors, scientists and engineers, consultants, doctors, and lawyers, and one thing is clear: College is what you make of it. If you want to hunker down and concentrate on your subject, you can do it there. If you want to try on internships in different fields—in social work one summer and in business the next—these schools will help you find the right internship programs. The opportunities are there, but you need to take the first step.

Most of all we hope you will use this book as a starting point. These profiles will give you a sampling of experiential education on each campus, but it is not the final word. There are many excellent choices, in addition to this curated list, for schools that make experiential learning a priority. And there are plenty of hands-on opportunities at each of these fifty schools that are not spotlighted in these pages. Check out other resources. Visit as many colleges as you can. Talk to the students at each college—ask what they love and what bothers them the most about their schools. Finally, form your own opinions about the colleges you are considering. At the end of the day, it's what YOU think about the schools that matters most, and that will enable you to answer that all important question: "Which college is right for me?"

The Schools

Arizona State University

P.O. Box 870112, Tempe, AZ 85287-0112
Admissions: 480-965-7788
E-mail: admissions@asu.edu
Website: www.asu.edu
Twitter: @asu, @FutureSunDevils

Introduction

With more than 60,000 undergraduates, Arizona State University is the largest college in the United States—and it has the amazing diversity, resources, and opportunities to match. The stats say it all: 5 campuses, 14 colleges and schools, 300 majors, 1,100 organizations, 7 libraries, 24,000 minority students, attendees from more than 130 nations, 7,500 graduates with internship experiences, 260 fully funded student startups, over 40 online degrees, and 3,000 stellar, research-enabling professors. (Oh, and 5 national baseball championships, 17 conference football titles, 13 trips to March Madness, and 2 national softball championships, as any spirited Sun Devil would tell you!)

With an immense student body and several campuses, one might fear ASU is a bit too big. Not at all, say its undergrads: "Students fit in easily as the university is extremely diverse and offers many . . . opportunities for people from different backgrounds, beliefs, and cultures," reports a business major. And according to one senior finishing up an exercise and wellness degree, ASU is all about "using a big school and a big campus to give students as many resources . . . as possible." A recent graduate sums it up succinctly: "Lots of students, but lots of opportunities to succeed."

Ultimately, these opportunities for success are what ASU is recognized for again and again. Spend an afternoon on any one of its sunny, warm campuses, and you'll witness busy students engaged in powerful, career-making projects both inside and outside of the classroom. At the downtown Phoenix campus, future journalists script, shoot, and edit footage at the Walter Cronkite School, while students in the research labs at the College of Nursing and Health Innovation tackle real issues like obesity and aging. Keep an eye on the skies at the Polytechnic campus, where students pursue degrees in aviation, build working robots in the Engineering program, and craft user-friendly products in the X-Lab. At the West campus in northwest Phoenix, you might spot students in the Mary Lou Fulton Teachers' College exploring the effects of games on learning or preparing to explore science education in Costa Rica. And then, of course, there's the main campus in the heart of Tempe, where 55,000 students converge for unprecedented opportunities in state-of-the-art research labs, arts centers, and athletic facilities. Amber Wutich, professor of anthropology in the School of Human Evolution and Social Change, offers one student scenario for the kinds of opportunities ASU undergrads have access to: "Here's an example of a common pathway for a student in global health. In freshman year, she is passionate about healthcare but hasn't settled on a career path. During her time at ASU, she joins a research lab, goes on a study abroad, conducts research in another country, learns a foreign language, learns to collect survey data, learns to analyze qualitative and quantitative data, completes an Honors Thesis, and presents her findings at a national conference. Upon graduation, she might decide to get a job immediately as a data analyst, continue her education by earning a master's in public health, or join AmeriCorps to further develop her skills in community health care."

Arizona State University recently reinvented itself as a model for a New American University—a research-oriented, interdisciplinary learning institution where innovation and discovery pave the way for public good. One of the university's most telling tenets? To measure its success not by who it excludes, but who it includes and those students' successes. If this open and egalitarian approach doesn't make you feel immediately welcome, check out some of the other exciting, cutting-edge programs and services that ASU offers to support the accomplishments of its hard-working and energetic students.

Barrett, The Honors College

For especially motivated young scholars looking for a more intimate university experience, there's the nationally praised Barrett, The Honors College: "[Barrett] is a small, close-knit community, while ASU has all the perks of going to a large university," says a student, studying psychology and philosophy. Honors students follow any of the available degree programs throughout the university, adding specialized Honors courses to their schedules and completing an Honors thesis project. With more National Merit Scholars than MIT, Duke, Brown, Stanford, or the University of California—Berkeley, Barrett is a powerhouse for students looking for a challenge—and for individually tailored coursework and seminars, job and internship opportunities, study abroad programs, and access to 1,800 Honors faculty across all ASU colleges. Barrett is recognized as one of the nation's top producers of prestigious Fulbright Scholars, and its students regularly progress to graduate programs at top-tier and Ivy League schools.

Walter Cronkite School of Journalism and Mass Communication

When it comes to immersing students in rich, real-world experiences outside of the classroom, ASU's journalism school is truly headline-worthy—in fact, its state-of-the-art facility in downtown Phoenix and its game-changing, hands-on philosophy have landed it in the pages of both the *New York Times* and the *Times of London*. Named after the one and only anchor Walter Cronkite (who worked closely with ASU and annually presented an award there until his death in 2009), the School offers a dazzling array of first big breaks—for aspiring camera operators, investigative journalists, and sports reporters alike. "Walter Cronkite School of Journalism and Mass Communication is the best of its kind," one proud student declares to us.

Each night, Cronkite News students create a broadcast that reaches millions of viewers through Arizona PBS. In addition, News21 journalists-in-training produce focused, long-form multimedia investigations into critical issues, while students in the brand-new sports journalism program report on topics such as, say, the MLB's nearby spring training. Plus, a dedicated Washington D.C. bureau covers government action as it happens on Capitol Hill. Meanwhile, communication majors in the New Media Innovation and Public Relations Lab work to create real solutions for real clients—all of which looks fantastic on résumés.

Ira A. Fulton Schools of Engineering

Students in ASU's Ira A. Fulton Schools of Engineering can get a jump-start on what their careers need most: experience solving real-world problems—and often for well-respected industry partners scouting for new hires, to boot! Through the popular iProjects program, students team up in interdisciplinary groups with an enthusiastic faculty member to develop products for corporate sponsors, while the Engineering Projects in Community Service (EPIC) pairs students with nonprofits to engineer products for the common good.

After a semester or year spent prototyping, manufacturing, and finessing their projects, students present their work at the annual Innovation Showcase, an inspiring show-and-tell for student-produced projects. One software engineering major describes his ASU experience as all about "making cool things that matter." What better way to prepare for a lifetime doing just that?

Meanwhile, the engineering school's Fulton Undergraduate Research Initiative (FURI) provides funding and mentorship for hands-on lab work, independent research, and even travel to conferences. An annual symposium provides a perfect spot for undergraduates to showcase their work and engage with their peers and potential employers. "I was already working on research, but FURI made everything more goal-oriented and formal," says one biomedical engineering major. "I liked having an event to work toward where I was able to have a poster and share my work and results."

Entrepreneurship

Innovation may be a buzzword these days, but ASU's commitment to supporting the next generation of entrepreneurs is way more than a passing trend. Through the ASU Incubator, students can secure the mentorship, training, and even office space necessary to grow the seeds of big ideas into full-fledged startups that create real economic, social, and environmental change. Projects with real legs progress to the Edson Student Entrepreneur Initiative program, which provides up to $20,000 in seed financing. The results? Over the past three years, Edson teams have raised more than $2 million in external funding, created 150 jobs, and filed more than thirty patents. Projects range from software that predicts how successful a medical procedure will be for a specific patient to a barrel that helps people transport and purify water—all meaningful, innovative contributions and excellent work experiences, too.

Likewise, over at the InnovationSpace students from the Fulton Schools of Engineering, the W.P. Carey School of Business, the Herberger Institute for Design and the Arts, and the School of Sustainability link up in the same creative studio to develop products that are both useful and sustainable. Teams of students from these schools, who might be studying industrial design, visual communication design, business, engineering or sustainability, join together for a senior-year capstone project to complete a "real-world, development project." Together they brainstorm, research, problem-solve, and ultimately produce a prototype. The school explains, "Put simply, we seek to create products that are progressive, possible and profitable. At the same time, they must have a meaningful impact on the daily lives of ordinary people." Dr. Prasad Boradkar, the director of the program, says that some students launch their own ventures after graduation, and that "many have mentioned that their time in InnovationSpace was transformative for their careers." The program's primary goal, he says, "is to ensure that students leave not just with a set of skills, but also new ways of thinking about how their disciplines can help change the world. "

Thunderbird School of Global Management

Business students eager to get out into the big wide world and put their new skills into practice should look no further than the Thunderbird School of Global Management. We've named it a Best Business School (along with ASU's W.P. Carey School of Business), and the program has nearly 70 years' experience equipping young leaders with the language smarts, intercultural instincts, and business acumen needed to play key and ethical roles on a global stage. Thunderbird hosts students from more than 60 nations and boasts an alumni network of 40,000 professionals around the world. It's perfect for students who know to start networking now.

In addition to rigorous coursework (including classes in Arabic, Chinese, and Spanish), the School requires an international internship and a senior capstone project that serves as an online portfolio for prospective employers. And when it comes time to rub shoulders with those employers, the School's Career Management Center puts on recruiting events, offers job search tools, and helps with resumes, mock interviews, and career coaching.

Changemaker Central

A core feature of ASU's mission is empowering students to contribute to the public good—to shape their curiosity and education into a lifetime of civic service. Those contributions begin at Changemaker Central, a dedicated facility that matches students up with volunteer programs, community service projects, social entrepreneurship, and service learning that best suits their passions. Annually, Changemaker Central hosts Devils in Disguise, the largest day of service at ASU, put on by and for students. On this day, thousands of students make a difference in their communities—and have a blast doing it—at different volunteer sites. The center also acts as a gateway to socially minded career opportunities, such as AmeriCorps, Peace Corps, and Teach for America.

And for those students with exceptional track records of community service, there's the Leadership Scholarship Program—a generous, four-year scholarship awarded to twenty-five incoming freshmen annually—and the Spirit of Service Scholars Program, which recognizes up-and-comers in the world of public service. Yesenia Barraza, founder of YB Company LLC, was a scholarship recipient ASU. She tells us, "I knew I wanted to major in business. ASU has a top-rated business school, and it immediately attracted me to it. . . . I was fortunate to be part of the Leadership Scholarship Program that allowed me to be the first in my family to attend college." After graduating from the Barrett, The Honors College and the W.P. Carey School of Business with a degree in accountancy (and a minor in Spanish), she returned to W.P. Carey for her master's degree in taxation.

Faculty

Arizona State University's faculty have some serious bragging rights. The teaching roster lists two Nobel laureates, four Pulitzer Prize winners, twenty-five Guggenheim fellows, one MacArthur fellow, thirteen members of the National Academy of Sciences, and sixty-six fellows of the American Association for the Advancement of Science—just to name a few. Noted faculty members include Donald Johanson, who discovered the 3-million-year-old fossil Lucy, and Gloria Feldt, women's rights advocate and *New York Times* bestselling author.

Like the students, professors are drawn to the university's immense offerings and commitment to practical, hands-on learning. "People come to ASU—whether as faculty or students—because we are passionate about pushing new frontiers: in cutting-edge sciences, in new ways of learning in and outside the classroom, in transforming our communities through service," Dr. Amber Wutich of the School of Human Evolution and Social Change tells us. "We have the resources of an enormous university, but also enjoy close relationships built through collaboration, respect, and common work to achieve a shared vision."

This enthusiastic commitment to learning doesn't go unnoticed by the students. A nursing major tells us, "The professors at ASU are so knowledgeable and experienced in their respective fields. Many have won numerous awards. The best part is … all of my professors have truly wanted me to succeed. They were available, helpful, and truly cared that I learned." A student of computer information systems adds, "[My professors] bring the materials to life by sharing with us their personal experiences."

Plus, ASU's professors echo and admire the university's inclusive charter: "There is little to no sense of entitlement but rather a strong work ethic among a large portion of our students, which makes ASU a rewarding place to work and collaborate with students on their educational journey," notes Amy Ostrom, a professor of marketing in the W. P. Carey School of Business.

Alumni/ae

ASU has a fascinating list of noted alumni—from news anchor Christine Devine to fashion designer Kate Spade, and from NFL pro Pat Tillman to former PepsiCo CEO and president Craig Weatherup. But its major merit is its scope: There are more than 350,000 active ASU alumni worldwide. That's a lot of potential networking contacts! The school spirit extends well past graduation date, with an engaged alumni network that hosts events, provides resources for the job hunt, and upholds ASU's traditions—like "whitewashing the A" on Tempe Buttes, which has been going strong since the 1930s. Jeffery Labelle, a professor in the Fulton School of Engineering, can easily rattle of the impressive accomplishments of his 200-plus Fulton Engineer mentees. He told us about his many MD/PhD candidates, interns with Mayo Clinic Rochester, and his Whitaker, Fulbright, and Flinn Foundation award winners. He boasts, "Two have been College Researcher of the Year award recipients at ASU's Barrett, the Honor's College; and one was named to the Barrett Top 25 Alumni to Watch list."

> ❝ *ASU did a wonderful job helping me gain access to people who have impacted my career in ways I could never have imagined.* ❞

Alumni are connected by their love of all things ASU (including popular Sun Devil tailgating sessions), but also by a deep appreciation for the skills that their education has provided them. As Yesenia Barraza puts it, "I became a member of the Alumni Association the very same time I bought my cap and gown." "ASU did a wonderful job helping me gain access to people who have impacted my career in ways I could never have imagined," reports Graham Rossini, Vice President of Special Projects for the Arizona Diamondbacks. In particular he credits a three-year internship as a Baseball Operations Intern with helping him to launch his career. He explains, "I was able to use this experience and transition into full-time employment as Director of Baseball Operations at ASU as soon as I graduated. The experience working for a nationally-ranked college baseball program allowed me to immediately apply the principles I was learning in my business classes." A student of the engineering division chimes in: "I believe that students graduating from ASU are known for their can-do attitude, ability to learn anything, [and] their rigor." Which just goes to say: ASU graduates are good company to be in.

Babson College

231 Forest Street, Babson Park, MA 02457
Admissions: 781-239-5522
E-mail: ugradadmission@babson.edu
Website: www.babson.edu
Twitter: @babson, @babsoncollegeUG, @babsonalumni

Introduction

It wouldn't be an exaggeration to say that Babson College, which offers a Bachelors of Science degree in business and a wide variety of concentrations, wrote the book on teaching entrepreneurship. In fact, the school invented its own methodology, called Entrepreneurial Thought and Action®, which balances a deep understanding of business fundamentals with action, experimentation, and creativity. Frequently topping The Princeton Review's ranking list of Top Entrepreneurial Programs for undergrads, the college has a stellar rep for business, and the students know it. "I really wanted to study business, and I knew Babson had the best hands-on curriculum. Every student graduating from Babson has taken part in running a business, [has] a background in all aspects of business (law, accounting, marketing, finance, organizational behavior, etc.) and [gets] exposure to an international community," one student tells us.

But Babson also understands that an entrepreneurial spirit knows no "artificial barriers between disciplines." Along with the academic divisions that you might expect from a business school, like marketing and finance, is a liberal arts focus that you may not: History, society, and the humanities all have a place in a Babson education. In fact, the school says that part of its job is to show budding entrepreneurs how liberal arts skills "play into businesses of all types and sizes."

The school, which hosts over 2,100 undergraduates from more than 70 countries, works hard to create a sense of community through its unique living learning housing, Greek life, and over 160 student clubs and organizations. All of these activities keep students engaged in life at Babson, and complement the school's holistic approach to business education. A current business major explains, "Babson is about teaching students innovative and creative ways to apply their entrepreneurial knowledge to real world situations." An emphasis on preparing students for the real world is at the core of Babson's curriculum, which includes an opportunity for students to start their own businesses and network with working professionals.

Babson also stresses the importance of civic engagement. One business administration major tells us, "Babson College attracts creative, hard working, extremely passionate individuals that want to turn their passions into businesses or excel in their industries while always acting for the betterment of society." Through its involvement with various nonprofits in the community Babson focuses on creating entrepreneurs who know what it means to give back.

Foundations of Management and Entrepreneurship

Students we surveyed all agree that Babson's standing in entrepreneurship drew them to the school, a rep that is due, in part, to the internationally recognized yearlong immersion course, Foundations of Management and Entrepreneurship (FME). The program attracts many students to the College, including alumnus Ross Beyeler, the founder of Growth Spark, who was "immediately hooked" on the idea of starting a business his freshman year.

In the FME program, first-year students working in teams of ten are loaned $3,000 by the university to launch their own business under the tutelage of two dedicated faculty members. Students learn the ins and outs of entrepreneurship, marketing, accounting, organizational behavior, information systems, and operations, as well as the integrated role these functions have in a business.

As part of their work, students also establish a partnership with a local social services agency. The team donates eighty hours of community service to their partner agency and all the profits from their business after paying back the college's initial loan. Students have supported a variety of organizations this way, including Special Olympics, Habitat for Humanity, Cradles to Crayons, Boys and Girls Club, and the Greater Boston Food Bank. Since 1999, FME businesses have donated more than $430,000 to local charities.

The value of this award-winning course is clear. Dr. Candida Brush, chair of the Entrepreneurship Division at Babson, explains, "Because of this signature learning experience, our freshmen are 'changed' because they have entrepreneurial skills by the end of their second semester." Students recognize this value as well. "I compare my education to what my peers are receiving at other schools,

❝ Our freshmen are 'changed' because they have entrepreneurial skills by the end of their second semester. ❞

and feel very confident that I'm more than prepared to compete in the working world," a business administration major confides.

This preparation has real effects on Babson students. Brittany Lo, who graduated in 2014 and founded Beautini by B.Lo, tells us, "I entered Babson wanting to have my own company, but then thought a corporate job in marketing would be safer to start with. However, since Babson provided me with so many opportunities to try new things like starting a business with the support of many valuable resources and people to help guide me, I was able to bypass my initial career move and go directly in the path I wanted to pursue. I had a full time job offer with L'Oréal but was able to turn it down and pursue my dream with my startup after receiving investment (some from the Babson community)."

Center for Women's Entrepreneurial Leadership (CWEL)

Founded in 1999 and originally called the Center for Women's Leadership, the CWEL has sponsored projects on women in family business, women's business centers, and women of color entrepreneurs, and has published the *Top 100 Woman-Led Businesses in Massachusetts* publication. The CWEL partners and collaborates with the Forté Foundation; Supporter of Springboard Enterprises; Federal Reserve Bank of Boston on GEM Women data; The Commonwealth Institute on Women CEOs; Association of Women's Business Centers on WBC impact; Center for Women's Business Research on Symposia for Women Entrepreneurs of Color; Ernst & Young's Young Entrepreneurial Winning Women Competition; and the Center for Women's Business Research, among others, to work toward advancing women in entrepreneurship.

In addition to putting on various events throughout the year, the CWEL sponsors the CWEL Scholars Program, which offers events and coaching to undergraduate women and includes milestones for each year they are in school; the Women Innovating Now Lab, which provides twenty women each year the chance to launch entrepreneurial ventures; and mentoring events during which undergraduates can meet with successful business women leaders.

The Coaching for Leadership and Teamwork Program (CLTP)

Started in 1997, CLTP is closely tied to Babson's undergraduate curriculum, with a focus on building self-knowledge and empowering students to help shape their personal development. Students take CLTP sessions during their Foundations of Management and Entrepreneurship course in their first year, and again in the capstone Strategic Problem Solving (ASM) class, typically taken junior or senior year.

In the program, students work with coaches—consisting of alumni, parents, graduate students, and staff with experience in industries such as entertainment, finance, insurance, retail, and travel—to complete exercises dealing with ethics and problems that businesses encounter. Once they have completed the cases, students meet with their coaches to receive feedback, though they aren't graded on their work. The program exemplifies Babson's commitment to providing real world experiences that students will be able to draw upon once they graduate.

A Strong Sense of Community

Providing the foundation for its innovative course work is Babson's strong sense of community. On this front and others, the school takes student input seriously. One business major tells us, "The administration really puts their money where their mouth is and involves students in virtually every aspect of how the school is run on a day-to-day basis as well as heavily involving them in shaping the future strategy of the institution." The school's living learning communities, which were originally proposed by students, are evidence of this commitment to student involvement. As one business management major explains: "After freshman year, you can apply for a special interest living area . . . For example there's [the] investment banking tower, Habitat for Humanity tower, the Greek towers, the Asian Pacific Association tower, [and] the ONE diversity tower."

Beyond these residential communities, students at Babson have found many other ways to get to know their peers. "The Greek community is so close-knit and supportive, as is my freshman class! I know almost everyone's name! It is so easy to get involved if you want to because everyone is so open and friendly!" one business management major enthusiastically tells us. Another reports, "In my freshman year I've been elected to a two-year leadership position, joined a sorority, been active in a great service club, started a business as a REQUIREMENT for one of my classes, and over the summer I'm going to be traveling abroad to teach entrepreneurship in Ghana and Rwanda!"

Students agree that the sense of community at Babson, in and beyond the classroom, is strong. "Classes are small in order for more of a personal interaction. In addition, they really encourage group projects; therefore by the end of your career at Babson you have probably worked with more than half of your graduating class," says an accounting major. The school puts it this way: "Rugby players, debaters, journalists, scuba divers, musicians, and astronomers—each member of the undergraduate school is unique and brings their own perspective to Babson." Students historically report that the atmosphere at the school is incredibly open and welcoming, and is full of opportunity.

This sense of community extends to the faculty as well. Dr. Candida Brush, chair of the Entrepreneurship Division, tells us, "We are ONE faculty (liberal arts and humanities and business). Faculty teach across grad and undergraduate schools, and faculty from all parts of the school engage in service activities together. I came from a very large university, and I never even saw people from history or math. At Babson, we all work together."

Real World Experience

Babson's commitment to real world experiences extends outside the classroom as well. Freshmen can start off with Babson's Externship Program, which offers one- to five-day job-shadowing experiences that provide students with an opportunity to observe professionals on the job. While the program is not for academic credit, and students are not compensated, it does allow them to develop strong and valuable connections with alumni and business organizations.

Babson also offers Management Consulting Field Experience (MCFE), which connects Boston-area organizations with talented Babson students who work as consultants to address a current business challenge. Students work on projects for both profit and nonprofit organizations, and an award is granted to the most successful MCFE for a nonprofit organization. Students gain valuable experience while providing your local organization with creativity, insights, and results.

Skill-building happens at various centers and institutes on campus as well. At BabsonARTS, a space where the campus community enjoys films, lectures, and performances, students can build skills in teamwork, project management, visual literacy and public speaking through workshops, master classes, and student-run performances. Students who want to use their entrepreneurial chops to make a difference should check out Babson's Social Innovation Lab where "new concepts in social innovation are prototyped, evaluated, and proved in real-world contexts." And the Stephen D. Cutler Center for Investments and Finance trains future investment bankers by allowing select students to manage a portion of the Babson College endowment.

A Global Perspective

Babson understands that graduates who want to compete in today's business climate need to be prepared with a global education. To that end, Babson has partnered with Global Experiences to provide high-quality customized international internships abroad. Global Experiences offers internships in disciplines including but not limited to: accounting, business, marketing, fashion, finance, human resources, and information technology.

Whether or not students participate in Global Experiences, though, they will be getting an international education at Babson. A business management major tells us, "At Babs, we have something like 27 percent international students, which is so amazing because you get to interact with all the different cultures, make great friends all over the world, and learn how to work with people from different areas of the world in a business environment." Many of the other students we surveyed agree that the diversity on Babson's campus is one of the school's biggest assets.

Natalie Taylor & Grossman Scholar Programs

Though they are all studying business, Babson students aren't only concerned with making money. In fact, students appreciate the school's overall commitment to civic engagement. As one business major explains, "My school is about entrepreneurship, and many people think that it's all about money but it's so much more than that. It's about being innovative and finding ways to do something differently and that includes helping people." Another student majoring in environmental sustainability, marketing, and entrepreneurship agrees: "The focus on sustainability, social entrepreneurship, and global responsibility shown by faculty and staff (including the Dean of the Undergraduate School) demonstrates great leadership and care for our world."

Among the many opportunities for civic engagement offered under the Bernon Center for Public Service at Babson, the Natalie Taylor & Grossman Scholar Programs recognizes and rewards Babson students who have demonstrated a commitment to service, community engagement, and social responsibility. Students accepted into the program participate in 4-credits of capstone classes including one independent study, and complete 200 hours of community service.

Current Natalie Taylor and Grossman scholars are working on projects teaching entrepreneurship to underprivileged schools in Boston as part of the Lemonade Day project; building homes with Habitat for Humanity in El Salvador; and providing shelter to abused children on the Cape Verde Islands, in partnership with a Babson alumna.

Faculty

Students who took part in our survey all agree that while the academics at Babson are challenging, the engaging and invested professors make all their hard work worth it. Babson employs 254 full- and part-time faculty, and has a student faculty ratio of 14:1. Faculty are available to students during office hours and beyond, and students often run into their professors in the shared lunchroom areas and other collaborative spaces around campus. A computational mathematics and finance major tells us, "I've never had a teacher who doesn't know me by name. My largest class ever was 60 students, [and] my marketing professor invited me to Thanksgiving dinner at her house last year." A business major agrees: "Professors know your name and devote [the] majority of their classes to discussion."

Seventy-three percent of Babson's full-time faculty hold a doctoral degree or its equivalent, but that doesn't mean professors here are stodgy academics with no knowledge of what happens in the real world of business. On the contrary, the Babson students we surveyed all appreciate the faculty's real world experience. One business major highlights his appreciation for "professors [who] actually practice and have background in the subject which they teach." Polina Raygorodskaya ('08), co-founder and CEO of Wanderu.com (her third business) tells us, "I chose Babson for its strong reputation in business as well as the amazing professors there that actually had their own multimillion dollar companies or were previously CEOs of massive corporations. I wanted to learn firsthand from people that ran companies in the past."

Alumni/ae

Many of the students we surveyed cite Babson's strong alumni and recruiting networks and their excellent job prospects as the main reasons they chose to attend Babson. Graduates are in good company. Arthur Blank, co-founder of The Home Depot, Daniel Gerber, founder of Gerber Baby Foods, and Roger Enrico, former chairman of DreamWorks Animation SKG, Inc. are all counted among prominent Babson alumni, and more recent grads have founded or co-founded an impressive roster of businesses like NatureBox and Zumba Fitness. A student in business management boasts, "Ninety-nine percent of Babson students either have a job or are pursuing higher education six months after graduation. In this economy . . . that's fantastic!" In fact, students' stellar ratings of career services at Babson combined with PayScale.com's median starting and mid-career salary information earned Babson a top ten spot on The Princeton's Review's 2015 ranking list for Best Career Placement, which was reported in the 2015 edition of our book *Colleges That Pay You Back*. The Career Development office hosts many industry spotlight events (accounting, finance, and more) and even has fifteen or so "employers-in-residence" each semester. Just like professors, these employers hold office hours so that students get can one-on-one time for résumé critiques or mock interviews with the boss. Students can hobnob with representatives from Ernst & Young and Fidelity Investments, just to name a few.

Even once they are employed, Babson graduates remain committed to the school community. Speaking to us about his continued involvement with the school, Ross Beyeler, founder of Growth Spark, tells us, "I'm actually a mentor in the summer venture program. I've been doing that since I graduated, probably a year after they started the program. And I participated in the Coaching for Leadership and Teamwork program, where you go back and mentor a student. I have certainly done business with Babson students and professors. I've maintained a relationship with some of the professors. I go to reunion events, . . . [and] I've guest lectured for a few classes in the undergrad and MBA programs." Beyeler has also hired several Babson graduates, which speaks to the strength of this alumni network. When asked about Babson graduates' reputation in the real world, he says, "There is a get-it-done attitude that Babson students have that people really appreciate, especially in the startup world where there are often no clear answers. You have to work hard, explore a lot of different options, and be willing to take risks. At Babson, [those qualities] are just inherent in our DNA."

❝ There is a get-it-done attitude that Babson students have that people really appreciate, especially in the startup world where there are often no clear answers. ❞

Bryn Mawr College

101 North Merion Ave, Bryn Mawr, PA 19010-2899
Admissions: 610-526-5152
E-mail: admissions@brynmawr.edu
Website: https://www.brynmawr.edu
Twitter: @BrynMawrCollege

Introduction

Bryn Mawr isn't just known for its stellar education, rigorous academics, highly talented and driven students, and ambitious faculty. It's also home to one of the most beautiful campuses in the United States. Founded by Quakers in 1885, Bryn Mawr has grown into an impressive institution of higher education. Only four miles outside of Philadelphia, the suburban campus is a small hideaway from the city with 135 acres where 1,300 students learn and explore. On this campus, sustainability is a social justice issue.

❝ A Bryn Mawr woman is someone who fights for others as well as herself. ❞

Bryn Mawr was originally created as a place for women to have access to intellectual training and the chance to do original research, a privilege that was only extended to men at the time. Due to these efforts, the school has created a strong community of women (and some men in the graduate school), who have benefited from this exploratory, thoughtful philosophy of education. An alumna told us that "a Bryn Mawr woman is someone who fights for others as well as herself. She is thoughtful about the world around her and utilizes all her strengths to accomplish really phenomenal goals."

The students we surveyed were nearly unanimous that Bryn Mawr's close-knit campus community was a huge factor in their decision to attend. Many said they wanted a more individualized college experience—they wanted to be active leaders on campus and develop a close group of like-minded connections. A sociology major explained, "I like to get involved in school and take up the opportunities presented before me. During my sophomore year I was treasurer for Mujeres, our Latina affinity group on campus. Being a part of the group exposed me to other Latinas on campus and provided me with a sense of familiarity." Bryn Mawr is also known for being inclusive and comes in at number four on The Princeton Review's 2016 ranking list for LGBTQ-Friendly schools.

Of her students, Tamara Davis, chair of the biology department says, "I love their level of curiosity, and I love the fact that no matter what I give them to do they rise to the occasion. They're good students and it's so much fun to work with them." Bryn Mawr is also part of the Tri-College Consortium with Haverford and Swarthmore Colleges, which means that even with a small enrollment, students have access to more students—and more resources—in the surrounding area.

For her part, alumna Cara Petonic told us, "I remember coming to the admitted students' weekend and meeting my potential peers and thinking, 'This is exactly where I want to be. This is where I need to be.' My choice boiled down to all of the different opportunities available to me at Bryn Mawr." With the right tools and the right attitude, there's little these students can't handle.

Getting Started

Sometimes students coming in from high school feel like they need to wade into college first before they dive in. At Bryn Mawr, the students immediately delve into academics and start developing projects. Dr. Davis said, "Right from the beginning in our introductory curriculum we want students to be thinking about synthesis and application to new scenarios. Another thing that is really important—and I've heard a lot of students in their senior year talk about the value of—is their ability to read the primary literature."

The College also encourages students to speak up. Students who do well at Bryn Mawr "have the capacity to work pretty independently, but who also understand that they do work in groups." The most involved students at Bryn Mawr are self-motivated, eager to participate, and willing to discuss topics in conversation. The professors here are also intent on creating a happy and helpful environment for their students.

How do incoming students feel about their professors? Petonic said she was drawn to her formerly improbable math major because of her professors at Bryn Mawr and "the incredibly supportive environment that they create for their students." And from what we hear, this is not a rare occurrence. Dr. Davis told us, "In our labs the faculty . . . really try to do fresh, current, innovative experiments." The professors really do make a difference, and their push to include their students and take their ideas to heart makes for a collaborative atmosphere that engages the students in their own education.

Undergraduate Research

Part of this push is related to the research program. For example, each summer, the college provides forty summer science research stipends for students to do full-time research over the course of the summer with faculty members in the sciences. The Hanna Holborn Gray Undergraduate Research Fellowships fund fifteen independent research projects in the humanities or humanistic social sciences. Even more students are funded through the Undergraduate Dean's Office or faculty grants. Many students use their summer experiences as the basis for their senior thesis projects, so they're already getting a head start on what's coming up next. Another option during the school year is the Mellon Mays Undergraduate Program, which seeks to increase the number of minority students pursuing graduate work in the arts and sciences. Each year, five juniors and five seniors receive stipends through MMUP, allowing them to conduct several hours of research each week. Dr. Davis told us that the benefits of a research experience as student are "huge." She explained, "In my opinion the most important thing a student can do with their undergraduate career is to get involved in some sort of research experience. . . . They are going to be drawing information from different courses and applying that knowledge to the practice of conducting research. I know that doing that kind of work forces our students to think in a more sophisticated way."

Cara Petonic, the first young alumna appointed to Bryn Mawr's Board of Trustees, currently works in higher education consulting in Philadelphia. She was impressed by how her professors went out of their way to prevent "this fear that there is only one right answer" and let students know that "there may be a number of different answers or a number of different ways to get to an answer." Petonic's research experiences, including a senior thesis on knot theory, gave her the opportunity "to stand side by side with my professor, face difficult questions, and tackle them together." She felt that her entire liberal arts experience, including majoring in math and minoring in dance, helped her develop skills, such as analytical and critical thinking, logic, and reasoning, that equipped her to succeed in business school.

360° Course Clusters

360° is an "interdisciplinary experience that creates an opportunity to participate in a cluster of multiple courses." By application only, 360° clusters are a "great way to explore new topics, subjects and skills," as the College points out. The courses in these clusters are all related, so the students are given an opportunity to invest in one topic for an extended period.

One of the most exciting aspects of the program is the opportunity for non-traditional classroom experience. Through their courses students travel (recent cohorts have gone to Cuba, Belize, China, Ghana, and the United Arab Emirates), shadow experts in the field, or take part in project work, field placement, or lab research. Upcoming clusters include topics based on China and the Environment (a combination of philosophy, history, and economics); Arts of Resistance (education, English, and political science); and Climate Change: Science and Politics.

The Honor Code

Bryn Mawr's academics are seriously engaging, but the College goes out of its way to make sure the students are taken care of. In 1892, Bryn Mawr allowed students to set their own rules and regulations for enforcing rules on campus. This is commonplace now, but Bryn Mawr was the first institution of higher education with an SGA to let students make these rules, and enforce them, too. Along with the ever-developing Honor Code, students get to set the standards for how they want to be treated on campus. In a bold extension of the golden rule, part of the Honor Code reads: "Although we entered into a community that existed before our arrival, we recreate the community through our participation." With a school with a history like Bryn Mawr's, a lot changes in 130 years. The Honor Code begins with "personal integrity" and "mutual respect" and includes a Dean's Panel, academic resolutions, and following the code of other campuses.

One of the benefits of SGA: Students have self-scheduled exams. This ensures that exam week isn't a jumble of marathons with a draining, random order. Students are allowed to do what everyone does in real life: Decide what your priorities are, organize your time and prepare accordingly. This way, exam week isn't so haphazard. It's a simple way for students to showcase their knowledge acquired over the semester—the entire point of final exams.

The Q Project

In addition to a dedicated Writing Center, where students polish their skills in public speaking and written communication, Bryn Mawr houses a Q Center on campus as part of the Q Project, the College's initiative to prepare students "to solve the complex challenges of our increasingly quantitative world." The Q Center supports the development of "mathematical, logical, and statistical problem-solving skills" that are required across the curriculum. Trained mentors at the Center "[seek] to assess and address unintended gaps or weaknesses in a student's preparation for introductory and more rigorous forms of math and science study," according to the school. "The goal of the Q Center is to help to develop quantitative skills, competency and confidence in every student, making it possible for her to maximize her potential in whatever her field of study." In fact, the Q Project is emblematic of Bryn Mawr's mission to produce students who are more than capable of navigating the surprises of the working world. Cara Petonic offered an example from her own career trajectory: "I first went into finance right after college. I didn't have any formal finance training. I had taken two economics courses, and I was a pure mathematician by training. However, I leveraged the lifelong skills I gained at Bryn Mawr to overcome the challenge of a steep learning curve."

Faculty

Bryn Mawr's faculty consists of 212 full-time and part-time members, including 126 women, and thirty-five minorities. Among them, 189 hold a terminal degree in their field. The College has cultivated this large group of scholars to maintain an 8:1 student to faculty ratio, ensuring the amount of individualized attention each student receives on campus.

Dr. Davis said, "We engage such a large proportion of our students in research. That makes a huge difference because…we're strategizing, and problem-solving and celebrating the research successes together. I feel personally that I've developed many close relationships with my students over the years." Faculty members have ample opportunity to rethink and modernize Bryn Mawr's educational goals. And this goes a long way toward reinvigorating the student experience overall. For example, a redesigned introductory biology lab curriculum expanded the number of majors "because the students found it so exciting. I think that the autonomy has allowed the faculty to be very fresh and forward thinking in the development of experiences that our students enjoy."

LILAC (Leadership, Innovation, and Liberal Arts Center)

Applicants should add this to their list of great Bryn Mawr attributes: The College has "an outstanding record in placing students in graduate and professional schools" in addition to connecting graduates to other promising career opportunities. Many of these opportunities come from hubs like LILAC, which combines a range of options for students on campus through avenues such as civic engagement, career development and the alumnae network. The result is "a completely integrated center, where students can get answers to their questions from a variety of different perspectives," Petonic said. LILAC's workshops and programming also emphasize exploration—these students aren't just headed down one particular path. In fact, Dr. Davis described some of the diverse career trajectories biology students in her department have taken—from medicine and law to the biotech industry. One former student worked on a dairy farm in Russia and is now in veterinary school. Another student wants to be a veterinarian for lab animals, and other students are pursuing professional degrees in public health and epidemiology. "In terms of alumnae networking and career offerings Bryn Mawr is a phenomenon," Petonic added.

Alumnae Network

Bryn Mawr has a lot to be proud of, especially its alumnae. Drew Gilpin Faust ('68) is the 28th President of Harvard. Dorothy Klenke Nash ('22) was the first U.S. woman to become a neurosurgeon. Sari Horwitz ('79) won the Pulitzer Prize in Journalism (three times) and Katharine Hepburn, Academy Award-winning actress, graduated from Bryn Mawr in 1928. The Katharine Houghton Hepburn Medal is named after her mother, who also attended Bryn Mawr, Class of 1900. This year, the 2015 Katharine Houghton Hepburn Medal was awarded to U.S. Supreme Court Justice Sonia Sotomayor. The honor "recognizes women who change their worlds. . . . Award recipients are chosen on the basis of their commitment and contributions to the Hepburn women's greatest passions—civic engagement and the arts." Graduates' careers are also supported by a designated member of Bryn Mawr's Alumnae Association via webinars as well as group sessions and coffee chats hosted at different cities. (Unsurprisingly, this person works closely with LILAC, understanding that someday those students will be in touch with her.)

As Bryn Mawr explained, the College connects women, "to ideas, to opportunities, to one another, and to the world." When students get to the campus, they just know it's a perfect fit. A current double major in biology and economics said, "Everything about it felt right. The people here, the classes, the professors, the social life, and the community all fit into my idea of an ideal college experience."

City University of New York—Hunter College

695 Park Ave, New York, NY 10065
Admissions: 212-772-4000
Email: admissions@hunter.cuny.edu
Website: hunter.cuny.edu
Twitter: @Hunter_College

Introduction

> 66 *The city is our campus, and it's up to you to use it to the fullest.* 99

For many New Yorkers seeking a top-notch college degree, Hunter College, located in Manhattan's Upper East Side, offers the best, most affordable option around. Hunter's 16,000-plus students choose from more than seventy undergraduate programs, but regardless of their areas of concentration, all Hunter students are encouraged to have broad exposure to the liberal arts: "Hunter is all about bringing people from all different parts of the word together in one place to learn from one another and to be exposed to almost every subject imaginable to help one find their true calling in life," says one sophomore. Another student says, "I can honestly say I feel that my academic experience is as challenging and enriching as that of my good friends at Ivy League schools." Of course, being located in the heart of New York City is also a boon for these students. As one political science major boasts, "It's nearly impossible not to find stuff to do, no matter what your tastes are. The city is our campus, and it's up to you to use it to the fullest."

Muse Scholar Program

Hunter definitely capitalizes on its prime New York City location via the Muse Scholar Program, a four-year honors program for artistically talented students. Dara Meyers-Kingsley, the director of the program, tells us that Muse students have "opportunities all four years to engage in creative practice" including all arts disciplines (visual and performing arts, film / media and creative writing) as well as via "access to internships and to professionals in the arts and culture fields." A yearlong course called Exploration in the Arts initiates them into the program in which students visit museums and galleries, attend dance, musical, and theatre performances on and off Broadway, as well as at other venues like Lincoln

Center and Carnegie Hall. The course has a writing critique component as well as "time for creative practice and work-shopping" tied to the performances they are seeing. For example, a class period prior to attending a dance performance is devoted to movement and choreography and taught by graduate students in Hunter's Arnhold Graduate Dance Education Program. Other core requirements are similarly geared toward the particular interests of Muse Scholars. When they take a required English composition course, for example, "the professor knows the Muse students come in with artistic talents and interests and has tweaked their . . . reading and writing assignments accordingly." An annual Muse Arts Showcase (which includes an art exhibit and evening performance) allows dancers, opera singers, and creative writers alike to show the Hunter campus "what they can do." Though most Muse students end up majoring in the arts, this is by no means a requirement. Ms. Meyers-Kingsley tells us, "They major in media and music, English literature, psychology, accounting, history, art history, biology, environmental studies, geography, sociology, theatre, and film. Two or three are pre-med."

Academic and Career Advising

Muse Scholars have access to an extensive advising network and numerous professional development opportunities. Ms. Meyers-Kingsley is each student's Faculty Mentor for all four years ("I'm their life coach it feels like!") and there is a special full-time academic advising team dedicated to Muse students. Many of the college's cultural partners, who offer students discounted tickets to performances and internships, are also brought into the classroom to talk about career paths. Ms. Meyers-Kingsley explains, "There are so many different ways to participate and work in the arts and cultural world. [Our students] may have been to the Met to see paintings once on a school trip, but they don't have a sense of the entire world behind the scenes that makes it run—accountants, conservators, marketers, fundraisers, educators, and curators. I make that part of my mission as well: to open their eyes to all the ways to engage with the arts and potentially work in the arts someday." As the program originated in 2011, Ms. Meyers Kingsley told us that her first graduates (who were ahead of schedule) are now in graduate school, one at Columbia studying art history and the other at St. John's University studying education. Her third graduate is working for the Decorative Arts group at Christie's, the international auction house where she had completed an internship while in school.

And Muse is not alone. Other themed communities that, like Muse, offer merit scholarships for incoming freshmen, include: the Roosevelt Scholars Program (public policy and civic affairs), the Yalow Scholars Program (pre-health or scientific research), the Athena Scholars Program (philosophy and literature), and the Nursing Scholars Program.

Chinese Flagship Program

One of only twelve in the nation, Hunter's Chinese Flagship Center, funded through the U.S. Department of Defense's National Security Educational Program, aims to create global professionals. Graduates of the program will have language and cultural skills miles ahead of those gained by the typical major or minor in Chinese. "It's actually a program requirement that students must live, study and work in China for one year after their language proficiency reaches advanced level," Professor Der-lin Chao told us. Dr. Chao is the director of the Chinese Flagship Center project at Hunter and head of the Chinese literature and language division. She says, "Very few language programs prepare their students up to a level that permits them to take college-level content-based courses with local university students, and to work capably in a Chinese-speaking environment." This highly advanced and accelerated curriculum seeks to get students to the "superior/professional level" of language proficiency by graduation, even if the student enters college with no Chinese learning background. And for employers, the appeal of these students goes beyond their professional language skills. Dr. Chao explains, "They become fluent in Chinese culture and civilization. Through language training, community service, internships in the United States, and internships in China, they find they are capable of working and communicating effectively with global customers and partners. We are truly preparing our students for global professional careers." The program invites a number of global professionals from the legal, medical, business, marketing, and education fields to speak with the students because "they not only need professional language skills but solid professional knowledge to succeed," Dr. Chao tells us. But, like any college students, not everyone has specific career goals right from the start. "For those students who need time to explore," Dr. Chao explains, "professionals from different fields [show] students different career possibilities."

Real World Experience

Students spend a significant amount of time interacting with Chinese communities during the course of their study. "Hunter is fortunate to be able to take advantage of New York City's rich Chinese cultural resources," Dr. Chao tells us. Flagship students interact with "organizations in the local Chinese community in Chinese," including "community-based non-profit organizations, senior centers, clinics, schools, banks" and other organizations. They also complete summer internships "sponsored by organizations such as Asia Society, Museum of Natural History, or businesses that are relevant to their major and career goals." Students who have reached advanced proficiency in Mandarin spend their final "capstone" year in China, "taking courses with Chinese students in a local university and interning at a Chinese company or organization." And by their final year a lot of doors have opened for Language Flagship students: "Because of their outstanding language skills, our students find that they are given serious jobs during their internships and make real contributions to their places of work."

Undergraduate Research

Students say that they love that Hunter provides them with lots of opportunities for research. According to the school, over 1,000 undergraduates engage in self-directed and faculty led research every year. Many students pursue multiple lines of research, and even find opportunities to research in wildly different fields over multiple years of their undergraduate careers.

STEM majors have fifteen federally and privately funded research initiatives on campus to choose from, which are all bundled together into Hunter's Science Mathematics Opportunity Network, thanks to a $1.25 million grant from the National Science Foundation. These programs range from The Quantitative Biology Project, where "students receive training and mentoring by a multidisciplinary team of research scientists and have access to competitive scholarships, national bioinformatics workshops, and internships," to AstroCom NYC, which pairs students "with long-term mentors to work with peers on real astrophysics research." There are also a number of programs specifically targeted to women, minority groups, and low income students, which help these populations gain access to cutting edge research and resources that will help them pursue graduate degrees.

But STEM majors don't get all of the attention when it comes time to dole out funding. Recognizing that funded research opportunities are vital to students in all fields, Hunter has developed the Undergraduate Research Initiative "to provide funded research experiences for Hunter undergraduates outside the STEM disciplines—areas where federal funds to support such activities are scarce," the school says. These faculty-student research collaborations pursue both academic and creative projects that can take them everywhere from the library stacks to the costume studio. And students say "the accessibility to a wide variety of NYC internships and research" is one of the school's greatest strengths. Humanities and social sciences students join their peers in the STEM fields every year for Hunter's Undergraduate Research Conference. In the last three years, student participation in the conference has nearly doubled, which is representative of the growing number of resources Hunter provides and the administration's efforts to widen the range of disciplines that have access to undergraduate research opportunities.

Presidential Student Engagement Initiatives

Like many of the CUNY institutions, Hunter College is primarily a commuter school. Fortunately, there's still plenty of camaraderie among these undergrads. Indeed, students say, "Hunter encourages student interaction through Student Government-run parties and other student-run activities." And many undergrads are quick to take advantage of the numerous "great events, visiting authors and scientists, [and] guest lectures" happening around campus." To further support student-faculty interactions outside of class, the President's Student Engagement Initiatives are handcrafted programs that address the particular needs of Hunter students and the opportunities available in New York City. As one student tells us, "Nobody lives on campus at Hunter so it isn't the same as I imagine other schools are. Most people that attend school at Hunter work part- or full-time, have apartments, pay bills, and go to school full time." Because "on-campus" activities are one of the primary ways that schools connect students with their faculty, Hunter had to get a bit more creative (read on!).

Co-Curricular Initiative

The Co-Curricular Initiative allows Hunter students and faculty to get to know one another through excursions or field trips that the school pays for. Through these ventures students might get a chance to develop their skills in the field, like the geography students who went on an overnight trip to Black Rock Forest to introduce them to field methods in soil science, ecology and water quality sampling and to promote camaraderie among faculty and students. Or, like the German 101 class that went to the Guggenheim Museum to tour works of contemporary German artists, including 20th century painter Wassily Kandinsky, they might get a broader understanding of the cultural and artistic influences within a language they are studying. Students in a theatre production course who were working on a production of Chekhov's *Uncle Vanya* even got to enjoy a Russian restaurant on West 54th Street where they discussed the play while learning about Russian food and culture.

Student-Faculty Research Initiative

Another part of the Presidential Student Engagement Initiative, the Student-Faculty Research Initiative, provides opportunities for students to collaborate with their professors on important research. Students get to have one-on-one access to their professors, which includes perks like learning to use advanced scientific equipment or developing and implementing research methodology. In the past such efforts have included work designing methodology to sample and measure the heavy metal content of rainwater collected at Hunter College's weather station and address related questions of metal accumulation in soils and plants on Hunter's green roof. Students have even joined in on important medical research in teaching hospitals, like two chem majors who worked alongside a Hunter College chemistry professor and a professor of biochemistry and chemistry at Weill Cornell Medical College to conduct x-ray crystallography of a protein that is showing promise as a possible target for drug therapy for aggressive breast cancer that doesn't respond to conventional treatment.

These initiatives allow faculty and students to interact in ways that would be impossible to engineer in the classroom. Hunter College tells us that these close interactions mean students benefit from more "mentoring, advising and a collaborative spirit that encourages students to see new possibilities for themselves and their futures." One current student enthuses: "The professors are what have made my experience here so incredible! . . . Perhaps most encouraging, they bring to the table their vast experiences in their field of expertise and have never hesitated to educate on what to expect when we are outside of the classroom, often offering a practical aspect to what in many classrooms are strictly academic discussions."

66 *The professors are what have made my experience here so incredible!* **99**

Hunter Hawks out in the World

Hunter was once the academic home to luminaries like Gertrude Elion, winner of the National Medal of Science and the Nobel Prize and the first woman named to the National Inventors Hall of Fame, and Antonia Pantoja, the social activist, civil rights leader and founder of Boricua College. Hunter's Career Development Services truly does a tremendous job for its students. Undergrads have the opportunity to attend a variety of career panels throughout the year, featuring guest speakers and assorted alumni from a number of industries. Hunter also presents students with many chances to attend different career expos. There, undergrads are able to network, learn about specific corporations and career fields and discover potential job openings. Naturally, the college also works hard make the most of its New York City location. Each semester, Hunter invites companies to campus to meet with students regarding internships, part-time jobs and entry-level positions. Undergrads can attend recruiting events in a number of areas: social services, public affairs, film and media, financial services, scientific research, and more. The College also provides career mentoring for students connecting them to the impressive range of successful Hunter alumni.

Claremont McKenna College

888 Columbia Avenue, Claremont, CA 91711
Admissions: 909-621-8088
Email: admission@cmc.edu
Website: claremontmckenna.edu
Twitter: @CMCNews

Introduction

As part of The Claremont Colleges, Claremont McKenna College has the intimacy of a small liberal arts college with the institutional resources of a major research institute, and "because campus life is very integrated across the [colleges] there is enough variety to keep students engaged." It is good that CMC students are "very concerned about extracurriculars and building their résumés through internships and other opportunities," as one student told us, because their choices are abundant. Its eleven research centers and institutes offer students "unmatched internship and professional world opportunities" and a wide selection of faculty-led research opportunities. Some of these research efforts have created major intellectual resources used by academics all over the country, like the Miller-Rose Initiative Database that tracks every voter initiative in the United States and provides analysis of court cases challenging them. Students benefit from academics that are "very rigorous . . . but the way professors present information makes it clear and applicable." Students choose classes from twelve CMC departments, along with a variety of departments from the other Claremont Colleges, and have the option to pursue accelerated, joint, and dual degrees. "However, there is more to a college education than going to class," one student reminded us. "CMC develops well-rounded and passionate individuals who are ready to go into the real world and succeed. This may be one of the only places in the country where you can ski and go to the beach in the same day. There are always people playing pick-up sports games, throwing a Frisbee or laying out in the beautiful sunshine."

> **❝ CMC develops well-rounded and passionate individuals who are ready to go into the real world and succeed.❞**

It seems that everything is available right around campus—and in some ways it is. As one of the country's largest, most diverse and economically active states, California provides students with an endless supply of opportunities.

Students don't even have to leave the state to rub elbows with top corporate executives during the Silicon Valley Networking Trip, and they can engage in groundbreaking research at the Rose Institute for State and Local Government, which has spent the last thirty years developing and revolutionizing how local and state economic, political, and demographic data is collected and analyzed. Here are a few of the opportunities available in and around campus.

Information Technology Advisory Board

CMC has a big footprint in Silicon Valley companies, and they use their alumni relationships to great effect. Through the Information Technology Advisory Board, or ITAB, CMC students have access to "executives working in the technology field, who have a special interest in advancing the importance of technology at CMC." ITAB's flagship program is the Silicon Valley Networking Trip, a week-long trip to meet with companies and CMC alums in Silicon Valley for "students who have demonstrated an interest in management leadership in the computing or technology corporate arena." While learning about the various career possibilities in technology fields, students also "gain exposure to job opportunities in technology" and begin networking and establishing relationships with CMC alumni, who often hold high positions in these companies. Many of the biggest technology firms have been represented at the event, including Apple, Google, Electronic Arts, Microsoft, and a number of Silicon Valley startups, including ones founded by CMC alumni. Each company represented provides private meetings with corporate executives who are CMC alumni, a presentation about the company and the work it does, and time for students to ask questions of the presenter. The students attending these meetings have usually done some research into the companies and can ask probing, relevant questions about the company, its markets, and emerging industries that the company might be taking an interest in. The questions and answers session is certainly one way that students can distinguish themselves and demonstrate their value to these corporate executives.

The companies also provide a panel of young employees, who talk about their roles in the company and represent different departments like marketing, sales, software engineering, and operations. Students are also given a tour of the company's facilities and talk with recruiters to discuss career opportunities. According to the school, "the goal is for these relationships to evolve into summer internship and full-time job opportunities for CMC students in the Silicon Valley," and often times that is exactly what happens. Through the Silicon Valley Networking Trip, students have secured internships at top companies and startups alike, and they have been sent all over the world. The program does a great job matching students up with employers based on their skills and interests. While the companies are based in the Silicon Valley, the school doesn't just bring economics majors. Everyone from politics to philosophy joins in, including one international relations student who was sent to Bangalore, India by Infosys. But beyond the direct benefits students get from jobs or internships, the experience is a great way to learn about the structures and needs of various companies and practice the art of networking—an ever more important skill in today's interconnected job markets.

Because there is a great mix of large companies and small, nimble start-ups represented at the networking trip, students interested in entrepreneurial opportunities get a chance to learn from founders with different strengths and approaches. A current environment, economics, and politics major told us, "The focus on developing students to succeed in the real world—there is a very strong focus on skills such as networking and learning to interact in a business context. There are also numerous internship and recruiting opportunity to support students."

Research Institutes

CMC has eleven different research institutes or centers, and each focuses on a different academic field or research objective. The purpose of these programs is to provide CMC students with graduate-level research opportunities in nearly every field so that they are well prepared for graduate school or the job market.

The Financial Economics Institute offers student research analyst positions in the summer and during the school year that allow students to work closely with faculty on their research projects. These positions allow students to get a lot of exposure to the research process: typically students will work (paid!) six to ten hours a week during the semester or thirty-seven hours a week during the summer sifting through annual reports and corporate filings, financial databases, biographical directories and analyzing the data they compile. In the past students have collaborated with faculty on empirical research projects that examines the effect different kinds of stock options have on shareholder value, evaluate the risk management style of different firms, and measure the impact of university governance structure on endowment performance." The Financial Economics Institute also offers fellowships for juniors and seniors interested in asset management and investment management, which provide fellows a significant amount of "financial support and research experience."

With a tremendous store of financial and economic resources, including the coveted "Bloomberg Terminal," the Financial Economics Institute is a one-stop-shop for students in finance, economics, and related fields to complete their research projects. In addition, the Financial Economics Sequence of classes, under the auspices of FEI, provides students who are looking forward to careers in finance or to graduate school with rigorous, quantitative-focused curriculum that is designed to complement the Robert Day Scholars program in the school of economics and finance. However, in line with the college's mission of a liberal arts education, the Financial Economics Sequence is available to any student regardless of major field. After completing the coursework, students use the resources of the institute to complete a major research project and completion of the Sequence is noted on the student's transcript to indicate a high level of proficiency in the field.

Robert Day Scholars

Within the School of Economics and Finance, the Robert Day Scholars Program provides students with leadership development opportunities. Students attend workshops and meet with business and government leaders to learn about management techniques and offer insights into their industries or fields. Students network with alumni and friends of CMC in the business community to where they develop personal contacts and get job and internship leads, and they also take part in planned visits with potential employers to discuss business and industry needs. A current student confided that "the focus on cultivating leadership skills" at CMC was a major factor in their choice to attend.

Rose Institute of State and Local Government

Few colleges have entire programs devoted to state and local policy, but the Rose Institute has been studying—and shaping—local and state policy in one of the countries largest and most diverse states for over three decades. The Rose Institute, founded by lawyer, business leader, and activist Edessa Rose, has a history of breaking new ground and even "developed the nation's first comprehensive statewide demographic and political database." Since then, the institute has be a leader in demographic analysis, redistricting research, political and environmental studies, and most major political events in California—including a "complex and delicate study of South Central Los Angeles during the 1993 Rodney King riots" commended by the Ford Foundation, according to the college. And since its inception, "the Institute committed itself to conducting research with faculty-student teams." Today the Rose Institute provides students "a hands-on opportunity to take on real-world policy problems under the guidance of leading experts in their respective fields."

Hardly anywhere else in the country can undergraduates get this kind of exposure to cutting edge, practical research into major political events. Students involved in the Rose Institute's research opportunities "have contributed significantly to the Institute's survey research programs, providing high-quality interviewing services, assisting in data presentation, and often playing key roles in analysis. Today, all Rose Institute students are trained in GIS, survey research, fiscal analysis, and legal and regulatory analysis." For anyone wanting to pursue a career in politics or in government, these are certainly skills that will get a foot in the door.

The Rose Center conducts a huge number of research efforts, including a joint venture between the Rose Institute and CMC's Lowe Institute for Political Economy called the Inland Empire Center. The Inland Empire is a metro region east of LA that has, despite being the country's 14th largest metro area, been subject to shockingly few political and economic analyses. The Inland Empire Center, established in 2010, seeks to change that. Through another of its research efforts, the Miller-Rose Initiative Database, the Rose Center shifts focus away from California and onto the country as a whole. "Originally developed by Dr. Ken Miller of Claremont McKenna College and student researchers as the empirical basis for Dr. Miller's book *Direct Democracy and the Courts*," the college explains, the Initiative Database tracks every ballot initiative in the country, from 1904 to 2013, and also tracks post-election challenges to voter passed initiatives. It has served as an invaluable resource for political science researchers nationwide and is indicative of the valuable and lasting research opportunities available to CMC students.

Faculty

An incredible student to faculty ratio of 8:1 means that students get unparalleled access to professors who "are absolutely incredible. They lecture with enthusiasm and facilitate meaningful and interactive classroom discussion." Students say they have a genuine interest in getting to know you as a student and more importantly as a person. They are known for their "[willingness] to Skype on the weekends to answer questions," and one student told us, "I have lunch with many of my professors at the dining hall throughout the week." Some even arrange for "a class dinner at the athenaeum or at their home." Students "leave almost every class with an excitement about the subject" and find that their professors are "interested in assisting with any sort of independent research a student might be interested in pursuing" as that excitement develops.

Life after Claremont McKenna

Claremont McKenna comes in at number three on The Princeton Review's 2016 ranking list for Best Career Services. So it's fitting that alumni find themselves in the highest ranks of business and government, including as the CEOs of Trust Company of the West, Abercrombie & Fitch, Toys "R" Us and as head of European Markets at Goldman Sachs. CMC has also produced leaders in government, like Montana State Governor Steve Bullock and former California Congressman David Dreier, a 32-year veteran of Congress and longtime Chairman of the House Rules Committee. A current literature student informed us that at CMC "most people here are highly motivated, entrepreneurial people that will find success in their future whether it be on Wall Street, Capitol Hill or with their own start-up." A rock-solid network with "amazing alumni contacts" makes those aspirations a reality. Through their alumni career contacts database, the Career Services Center makes it fairly simple for current students to connect with alums working in industries of interest. Even better, Mentor Connect allows students to find an accomplished alum and enlist him or her as a mentor. In fact, "some older students do tend to branch out more and spend time with alumni in Los Angeles" where they gain valuable insights into life after CMC and further access to the "extensive and helpful alumni network." Beyond alumni, CMC's robust internship database allows undergrads to search through a myriad of interesting opportunities. One student sums up the Claremont experience: "The opportunities and resources of professors, study abroad, internships, career services are unsurpassed, yet the balance of academics and social life is very balanced." With all of these outlets, it's no wonder CMC grads are so successful. Claremont McKenna comes in at number two on The Princeton Review's 2015 ranking list for Best Internship Opportunities and number twenty-seven on the list of the Top 50 Colleges That Pay You Back. Both rankings were reported in the 2015 edition of our book *Colleges That Pay You Back.*

> **❝ Most people here are highly motivated and entrepreneurial.❞**

College of Charleston

66 George Street, Charleston, South Carolina 29424
Admissions: 843-805-5507
E-mail: admissions@cofc.edu
Website: cofc.edu
Twitter: @CofC

Introduction

A liberal arts and sciences college on the Atlantic coast, College of Charleston is the thirteenth oldest institution of higher education in the country, and six of its founders either signed the Declaration of Independence or helped craft the United States Constitution. It "has a beautiful campus with a wonderful staff that is always there to help you" and where students say they take pride in "expressing yourself through your education." A typical student "is trying to break out of the mold and be seen as who they really are." Greek life at CofC is nearly as old as the modern Greek state, but it "is different at CofC as it seems less exclusive and all different sororities intermingle." When they take a break from school work, students enjoy the sights in Charleston and "love to go to the beach nearby or walk to the waterfront." As a sea-grant and space-grant university, CofC offers "a wide range of courses and majors in a variety of fields as well as research opportunities with professors who lead active lives as research scientists in off-campus labs." It supports a vibrant leadership program and a student-run financial investment outfit that looks and feels like a top-tier Wall Street operation. CofC also boasts a first-year program that thoroughly integrates freshmen into the academic community, providing them with everything a great undergraduate institution can offer: compelling seminars taught by experts, study-abroad opportunities, undergraduate research, and built-in support systems. One student told us that even "as an out-of-state student, I did not find it difficult to fit in freshman year."

Welcome to Freshman Year

The College of Charleston has done away the traditional "University Life 101" that so many colleges and universities require their freshmen to take. We talked to Dr. Christopher Korey, the director of the CofC's revamped First-Year Experience, and he told us that, instead of a "transition to college course" that lacks academic content and student enthusiasm, CofC offers First-Year Experience courses that give freshmen a chance to interact with professors who are experts in their field, participate in dynamic learning communities, and step into the academic community with some of the college's brightest upperclassmen as mentors. Freshmen even have the option to spend some time studying abroad. The broad range of FYE possibilities have a few common themes: They get students interested in their future career and academic options early-on, help them make connections among academic disciplines, and give them a preview of what the college has to offer.

First-Year Seminars

Students choose from either a First-Year Seminar or a Learning Community. First-Year Seminars are topic-based classes taught by some of the college's best faculty. The topics covered in these seminars are similar to what seniors might find in their senior level capstone, but these are specially designed with freshmen in mind. Past seminars have included intriguing topics like, "Genetics and Society," where students learn about genetic science and its potential social, ethical, and legal implications; "Ernest Hemingway in the Hispanic World," a literary class that focuses on Hemingway's Spanish and Cuban work; and "The Science of Secrecy," a class that explores secret messages from the Rosetta Stone to present day cryptography. All freshman schedules are often filled with intro classes—as they should be. These classes give students the fundamentals they need to enjoy more advanced topics. But the First-Year Experience seminars give freshmen a taste of the rich coursework that their academic careers have in store for them, while providing a bit of a respite from survey classes that cover a broader range of issues in less detail.

Learning Communities

The other FYE option is participation in a Learning Community, classes that combine the efforts of two professors who are experts in two separate fields into one interdisciplinary experience. Dr. Korey told us that these classes are particularly good at connecting students to faculty and for getting students to begin thinking about career options. For example, the course "Measuring the Impact of Tourism in Charleston" connects faculty in hospitality and tourism management and in mathematics. Charleston is a top international tourism destination, so faculty bring in local business leaders to discuss how they use statistics to measure and capture tourism revenue. The class takes outings to local businesses, including a cruise line, to further study the tourism sector. These connections to local business leaders can lead to internships or even jobs for interested students, Dr. Korey told us. Other learning communities include "Biology and Chemistry for Pre-Med Majors," for students who have a career track in mind from the start, and "Gateway to Neuroscience," a class that combines molecular and cell biology with psychology for students interested in neuroscience. Whether they choose a seminar or a learning community, FYE students also participate in a Synthesis

Seminar where they learn valuable transition-to-college skills while discussing their classes with an upperclassman who is a top student in the subject. This gives students a convenient way to get perspective and advice on the challenges and opportunities of college life—especially because everyone in the Synthesis Seminar is also a freshman.

First-Year Study Abroad

Dr. Korey told us that as an extension to the FYE program, students are able to take a weeklong study abroad class in the spring. These often dovetail with a student's seminar or learning community—for example, students studying "Genetics and Society" in a fall seminar might investigate "Genetics and Ethics in Berlin," or follow in the footsteps of Charles Darwin in "The Natural History of the Galapagos." But no matter what they choose, these mini study away experiences show students the value of study abroad and provide them with connections that they might rekindle later. Dr. Korey told us about one such student who took the "UK Soccer Experience" class as a freshman, meeting with managers and marketing personnel from different English soccer clubs, including Nottingham Forest Football Club. The following year, as a sophomore, he interned with a local soccer club to get a sense of a career in sports management. Now, as a junior, he is studying abroad at the University of Nottingham and he was able to leverage his experiences into an internship in the community outreach program of the same Nottingham Forest Football Club he first visited as a freshman. When he gets back he will help run "Charleston Kicks," a new youth outreach program being developed by the organizer of the FYE Study Abroad Programs, Dr. Bruce Fleming, at CofC and Nottingham Forrest FC. "He has closed the loop," Dr. Korey said, "between his first year experience, internship, study abroad, and now."

First-Year Study Research

❝ The school caters mainly to undergraduates, allowing for a great support system in your first year. ❞

There are a number of other ways that the First-Year Experience program at the College of Charleston lowers the threshold for entry into the academic community, such as the First-Year Research program, where students rotate through the different campus research labs to get a sense of which one they might want to join later. Dr. Korey added that "the program supports more casual interactions between faculty and students that can lead to increased academic engagement." These are some of the reasons why students told us "the school caters mainly to undergraduates, allowing for a great support system in your first year" and "making the first year as pleasant and smooth as possible."

School of Business Investment Program

Students told us that "because [CofC] is not a very large school there are more opportunities for hands-on learning and one-on-one instruction." Well, it doesn't get any more hands-on than this: School of Business students are applying the theory they learn in class to the real world—and it is paying dividends. The Investment Program looks and feels just like a Wall Street firm: Students manage two portfolios of investments and build relationships with local, regional, and national investment communities. The program operates just like a top-tier investment firm, complete with market analysts; Europe, U.S., Asia, and Latin America economists; an accountant and an operations manager; and asset managers covering the whole spectrum of financial instruments and investment classes (derivatives, ETFs, fixed income, private equity, and real estate). They even have an audio/visual specialist. All the while, they are learning to work as a team under the same conditions that they will be subject to when they enter the workforce. They also work with an advisory committee of seasoned investment and business professionals who have many years of experience as corporate executives and close ties to the College. These motivated students also have leveraged their experience with the Investment Program to intern as junior analysts at major firms analyzing global equity markets, study in language immersion programs, and secure internships at corporate law firms. When they graduate, these students will not only have a host of soft and hard skills for a competitive résumé, but they will also be able to list details about the portfolios they have been managing as an undergraduate.

Higdon Student Leadership Center

Another community-building entity on campus, the Higdon Student Leadership Center (which celebrated its ten-year anniversary in 2015) offers students a number of different leadership development opportunities from "one-time workshops to a whole six-day immersive experience," according to the Center's director Michael Duncan. Signature programs run the gamut from retreats—including a Cougar Excursion retreat for incoming freshmen—conferences, lectures, networking events with community leaders, and a Leadership Certificate Program.

One option, Leadership CofC, offers a monthly all-expenses-paid outing for students to meet with local leaders while they learn about a diverse range of leadership approaches, network, and develop their own group dynamic and communication skills. "They're able to get some real world experience from people who are out there leading beyond the College of Charleston," Mr. Duncan said. Another, The Institute, a weeklong event run by the not-for-profit leadership development company LeaderShape®, is an activity-based retreat through which up to sixty students participate in "team-building [experiences that teach] the concepts of trust, communication and group problem solving." Mr. Duncan revealed that the experience is "all about developing a passion and learning to lead with integrity. . . . It's a very intensive process that ends with a blueprint for action. They've identified a vision—whether it's in their own major, life, community, or anticipated career—and they've come up with an action plan to get to that vision." This "highly interactive program" pulls students out of their comfort zones and gets them to interact in a variety of group sizes and activities that creates a diffuse learning environment where "everyone is a teacher and everyone is a leader," according to the Center.

Leadership Certificate Program

Students looking for greater leadership growth can opt into the Center's Leadership Certificate Program at any point during their college career. Over the course of three or four semesters, students who pursue the Leadership Certificate Program customize their own leadership development by combining a number of the Center's offerings (leadership roles through other organizations on campus like an orientation intern or an officer position in a student club also can count as credit toward the certificate). A capstone project completes the experience. Mr. Duncan said, "Students have to create what we call a leadership artifact. Something like a blog or picture book that details their leadership development across the two to three years they've been in the certificate program and what they anticipate taking beyond the College of Charleston from those experiences." The Center also holds a workshop series that explores topics such as servant leadership theory, social change, community health, and various leadership models. Students pursuing a Leadership Certificate are also encouraged to find other events, lectures, and educational opportunities that develop leadership skills that they can add to their leadership portfolios—which shouldn't be too tough, because students are proud that "there are [so] many opportunities for leadership and volunteering" on campus.

> **❝ We define leadership beyond just holding a title. ❞**

As Mr. Duncan explains, the Leadership Center programming is truly focused on demonstrating "life skills." He said, "We try to get at leadership beyond a positional model. It's a set of characteristics and traits that a person can identify, learn, develop, and strengthen over time. We define leadership beyond just holding a title." According to an alumni survey cited in the Center's 2013-2014 annual report, 100 percent of the 150 alumni who participated in multiple Center-sponsored events during their time at CofC reported they have been able to apply what they learned at the Center to aspects of their life post-college.

Faculty

With a student-to-faculty ratio of 15:1, "class sizes are small enough to have a personal relationship with the professors in your major. Having this relationship makes learning significantly more enjoyable and memorable." Many of them are experts in their fields and they "are all actively engaged in their classroom and love student involvement both inside and outside of the classroom." Students said that the professors there "make you feel like an individual." One theatre major told us that her professors "are wonderful and very supportive. They are always trying to find opportunities for their students." Beyond being terrific teachers, the 500-strong members of the CofC faculty are quite distinguished in their fields. Among their ranks include past and present Fulbright, Guggenheim, and MacArthur fellows, a CAREER award winner from the National Science Foundation, a Grammy Award nominee, a Drue Heinz Literature Prize recipient, and a recipient of a Henry Dreyfus Teacher/Scholar Award.

Life after CofC

Prominent CofC alumni include Arlinda Locklear, the first Native American to argue in front of the Supreme Court; Nafees Bin Zafar, a two-time Academy Award-winning software engineer; and James B. Edwards, former Governor of South Carolina and U.S. Secretary of Energy. Young alums are making a splash out in the world as well. Among them are writer and actor Orlando Jones '89; boxer Lucia McKelvey '00; conservation biologist and filmmaker Justin Jay '08; and water quality specialist Cheryl Carmack '14. (You can read profiles of the stellar faculty, alumni, and current students alike at: cofc.edu/featureprofiles.) The college maintains an active network of alumni, who are more than willing to support the school as mentors and to advise students on career opportunities. The Alumni Association even offers a number of scholarships, including the Student Alumni Association Leadership Scholarship and those designed to help CofC students attend graduate school. Students say the College has "a great environment for networking," and, as a current history major confides, "Networking is really big here and a lot of doors can be opened for you if you mingle with the right people." With this impressive bunch, the alumni network seems like a great place to start.

The College of William & Mary

Office of Admissions, P.O. Box 8795
Williamsburg, VA 23187-8795
Admissions: 757-221-4223
E-mail: admission@wm.edu
Website: www.wm.edu
Twitter: @williamandmary, @WM_Admission

Introduction

The College of William & Mary is big on legacy. Situated in colonial Williamsburg, Virginia, the school was chartered in 1693 making it the second oldest college in America. It's also second only to Harvard (and tied with Yale) in turning out U.S. presidents. Today, W&M is lauded as one of eight "public Ivies"—public schools that offer just as stellar of an education as their pricier Ivy League counterparts. The university hosts five main schools: Arts and Sciences, the Mason School of Business, the School of Education, the Law School, and the School of Marine Science. Together, they offer more than forty undergraduate programs and more than forty graduate and professional degree programs to a student body that self-describes as "eclectic and quirky and definitely warm and welcoming," according to one psychology/linguistics major.

According to most TWAMPs (clever student shorthand for "typical William & Mary person"), the unofficial student motto might be "work hard, play hard." The student body balances a passionate if frenetic load of ambitious coursework, community service, and club or sports team memberships. And then there's the usual collegiate hang sessions in dorm rooms and at events put on by the popular Alma Mater Productions (AMP). "Even if you're not a partier, you will have no trouble finding a fun event to attend, such as classic movie showings, dance concerts, karaoke, slam poetry, campus-wide scavenger hunts, campus golf, and so much more," says a business student.

Students still converge daily inside the nation's oldest college structure, the beautiful Sir Christopher Wren Building, and stroll the gorgeous, 1,200-acre grounds of the traditional redbrick campus—part of which have been lovingly restored to their eighteenth-century glory. Popular hangouts include the university quad, charmingly dubbed the Sunken Garden, and the nearby woods and scenic Lake Matoaka. Its natural beauty alone is an inspiration to many: "I wanted a small school for the benefit of small classes and student and faculty interaction. My last requirement was grass, which William & Mary has plenty of," one kinesiology student half-kids.

But above all, William & Mary's main appeal is its intimate community and rigorous academics. It comes in at number forty-five on The Princeton Review's 2015 ranking list of the Top 50 Colleges That Pay You Back (reported in our book *Colleges That Pay You Back*), and W&M attendees consistently list its passionate professors, nurturing administration, and tight-knit, curious student body as major strengths that help prepare them both inside and out of the classroom. "[It's] a place to call home and engage my mind," one English major declares. Here are some programs and offerings to be aware of, should you decide to make it your collegiate home, too.

Interdisciplinary Study

Ask around, and you'll hear that this school is all about engagement across tons of disciplines: "Everyone has diverse interests and does many different activities, but we all unite with our passion to learn," shares an international relations major. So it's fitting that one of the university's big initiatives is helping students fuse their various interests into individualized study—which is sure to come in handy when students must devise their own routes after college. Within Arts and Sciences, students can team up with a faculty sponsor to craft a self-designed interdisciplinary major, or opt for one of more than ten existing interdisciplinary degrees. Many of these more structured programs (like Africana studies, environmental science and policy, and medieval and renaissance studies) actually came into existence because of student demand. Meanwhile, over at the Mason School of Business, undergraduates can tailor an Individual Program of Study that allows for study abroad, research projects, leadership experience, and more than one emphasis within the business program or in conjunction with Arts and Sciences.

❝ This is perhaps the single thing which W&M does best: meaningful undergraduate student research with the intensive mentorship of faculty.❞

Research & Scholarship

Despite the word "college" in its name, William & Mary is actually a university. The school explains, "Part of what makes us a university is that we make more than our share of a university's contributions to the creation of knowledge—otherwise known as research and scholarship." As Dr. Lu Ann Homza, professor of history, attests, "This is perhaps the single thing which W&M does best: meaningful undergraduate student research with the intensive mentorship of faculty. Such experiences can occur at any time in a typical undergraduate career, from freshman through senior years." In fact, it's quite possible for undergraduates to leave as published authors in peer-reviewed journals.

In addition to capstone experiences within many of the majors, about 10 percent of seniors undergo research projects though the Department Honors Program, which gives them the opportunity to complete an extended research project (over two semesters) under the mentorship of a faculty adviser. Students write up their findings in a thesis, which they will orally defend at an annual Honors Colloquium at the end of the semester. The Charles Center even offers a "kickstarter" through which students can raise funding for their thesis projects. There are summer research options as well as student-faculty research. Dr. Homza enumerates a few recent projects: "We have professors in Biology who routinely supervise students in testing for mercury contamination in Virginia rivers; professors in Sociology and Hispanic Studies who take students to the Arizona-Mexico border to study illegal immigration; professors in Anthropology and Geology who sponsor students on field trips to Hawaii and Oman. Yours truly takes groups of undergraduates to Pamplona, Spain, over Spring Break to allow them to read legal cases from the seventeenth century, which are held in state archives. In March 2015, a professor in German Studies led ten undergraduates along the Rhine River in Germany to explore the migration routes of medieval Jews."

William & Mary's accessible size means that it can provide research opportunities for undergraduates that other schools fill with graduate students.

Student Life

William & Mary's 6,000-strong undergraduate body are a busy crew—and with 400-plus student organizations that range from sketch comedy to a cappella, hip hop to ultimate Frisbee, each student quickly finds a group. "Everyone has a place here—all of us have some sort of gift—it's a lot like going to school at Hogwarts," jokes one biology major, name-checking the famed school from the Harry Potter series. A whopping 85 percent of W&M students participate in an on-campus recreational program (which includes more than forty sports teams) and, all in all, there are thirty fraternities and sororities and more than sixty community engagement groups. Beyond contributing to a rich and active student life, these opportunities push students into leadership roles beyond the classroom—a major indicator of future success. (And a great way for this proudly nerdy group of students to meet and have some much-needed fun.)

But extracurriculars aren't the only way this university instills leadership in its already devoted and conscientious student body. If you've set foot on its campus, you probably didn't get far without hearing about its honor code—and rightfully so. The first in the nation, W&M's honor code is a pledge that all students must take to ensure academic honesty and on-campus safety. "[With] the honor code comes a community of trust—students are not afraid to leave their books and laptops unattended in the library for hours at a time," a linguistics major says. Plus, the university's policy of self-determination allows residents to create their own rules about visitation, noise, and the use of community spaces, while students all over campus annually give feedback on policies ranging from athletic concerns to parking appeals. "William & Mary places great value and trust in its student leaders. They are asked to participate in the governing of the community in a variety of ways," reports one government alumna. And a former student body president cites student government as one of her most valuable college experiences: "It gave me opportunity to champion causes, develop my public speaking skills, and learn to become an effective leader . . . Student government taught me how to put myself in the shoes of my constituents—or today my clients. It became about 'us' not 'me.'"

A Fresh College Curriculum

For the entering class in fall 2015, William & Mary rolled out a new general education curriculum designed to help students explore various academic disciplines and make meaningful connections between them, as well as expand their perspectives on the world and provide active, inquiry-based learning that breaks students out of their comfort zones—and out of their classrooms. This game-changing strategy is the brainchild of the university's excellent, dedicated professors. Says Dr. Eugene Tracy, chair of the physics department, "The recent curriculum overhaul . . . [was] led by the faculty through a long series of committee discussions, open meetings, deliberation, and debate. The administration played a supporting role, and once the faculty decided what we wanted to do, they help us to make the new curriculum a reality."

For incoming freshmen, this means enrollment in two classes (COLL 100 and COLL 150) that immediately ground them in the university and its incredible resources, challenge them to the rigors of college-level study, and sharpen their communication skills. In later years, students are asked to step outside the university setting and interact with different cultures or environments, and then participate in a capstone experience by, say, problem-solving in an applied setting or creating entirely original scholarship. "It is sometimes said that an education is what you need when you encounter a problem your skills didn't equip you to handle," one professor wisely notes. This updated, all-new curriculum is designed to provide just that support and personal development to students.

Sharpe Community Scholars

For freshmen looking to jumpstart careers in activism, there's the Sharpe Community Scholars, a program hosted by the Charles Center for Academic Excellence that combines academic study with community engagement. Each year, between sixty and seventy-five incoming do-gooders enroll in specialized coursework and commit at least five hours a week to outside research, mentorship, collaboration, and action that benefits others—and that prepares them for a lifetime of service to the greater good. "There are some skills that are better learned through practice and experience than just a professor lecturing," reports a recent grad. "For me, I've been able to realize my own abilities and interests in terms of service, and how I can work toward making a stronger community."

But passion for giving back extends well beyond first-year studies. Often through the Office of Community Engagement, students at William & Mary complete more than 30,000 hours of community service each year, and an amazing 70 percent of students volunteer—two feats that have landed the school on the President's Honor Roll for Service six years in a row and counting. In fact, William & Mary has been recognized as one of the top producers of Peace Corps volunteers over the last decade. "Our students are working now to make the world a better place rather than waiting until graduation," one international relations/environmental studies student proudly remarked.

The Washington Office

William & Mary's main campus is just a few hours' drive from bustling Washington, D.C., but for young policy-makers eager to begin careers in the political sphere, it's impossible to get close enough to our nation's capital. Enter the university's Washington Office—a satellite campus that offers housing, classes, internships, networking opportunities, and guided "behind-the-scenes" looks into D.C.'s dynamic advocate, governmental, and international institutions. This setting is perfect for a student body that one sociology major describes as constantly "thinking about local, state-wide, and national politics and issues."

Cohen Career Center

William & Mary is committed to helping students thrive long after they've tossed their graduation caps—and that support begins at the Cohen Career Center. Here, freshmen and sophomores can sign up for MACE (My Active Career Exploration), a six-week non-credited course that helps them navigate majors and scope out potential career paths. Students can also test career options in the wild via a variety of internships in the Williamsburg community. These opportunities let students develop valuable skills and forge key connections while working seven to ten hours a week. (Plus, those who work unpaid internships may apply for a $4,000 stipend from the Cohen Career Center Internship Fund—a rare but most excellent offering among universities.)

"There are numerous resources for finding jobs and internships, as well as networking," a theater/business major noted, while a government student listed William & Mary's "strong resources for [a] career after college" as one of the university's core benefits. That's no doubt in part to the steady flow of alumni whom the Center invites to share their experiences and offer advice to soon-to-be graduates, as well as the employers that routinely visit to chat up students about their chosen fields.

In addition to the usual career-counseling sessions, the Center also provides access to online job-search tools, such as Vault, CareerShift, and Focus. And, for liberal arts and science majors looking to boost their business smarts, the Center sets up targeted symposiums, workshops, and competitions so all students feel ready for the job market—whether their course of study lands them in the art studio, the science lab, or the corporate boardroom.

Faculty

With more than 600 full-time faculty members at William & Mary, the student-to-teacher ratio clocks in at an awesome 12:1—one of the lowest in the nation—and an impressive 85 percent of classes have fewer than forty students. But the student-faculty relationship is about more than nice numbers: "The professors here are frequently the nation's and world's leading figures in their field," shares one linguistics/government major. "They are nothing short of inspiring." And with former faculty members like George Wythe (the nation's first law professor, who schooled the likes of Thomas Jefferson) and William Barton Rogers (founder of a little school called the Massachusetts Institute of Technology), it's no surprise that William & Mary continues to draw top-tier researchers and scholars.

Despite their high standing, W&M professors are also incredibly approachable and enthusiastic about their work in the classroom—an opinion echoed by pretty much the entire student body. "Professors at W&M are dedicated to both teaching and research... They conduct their own research (and gladly share research opportunities with undergraduate students), yet still find time to be extremely accessible to ensure that you get a quality education," reports a student of biology and Chinese. Turns out all this respect is a two-way street: "What I am most proud of is when I go to faculty social events, and hear my colleagues brag about their students," says Dr. Tracy. "We are amazed by them, and want to help them succeed."

Alumni/ae

> **❝ The College has provided me with both the personal development and professional network to set me on the path for a successful career. ❞**

William & Mary has been cranking out incredible graduates since its doors opened in 1693. Three American presidents (Thomas Jefferson, James Monroe, and John Tyler) once roamed its halls, as did Speaker of the House Henry Clay and U.S. Supreme Court Chief Justice John Marshall. All in all, sixteen signers of the Declaration of Independence attended the university. Not surprisingly, this track record of excellence is one of the university's main appeals today. A recent graduate from the government department told us, "It was important for me to attend a school with a strong historical tradition. I wanted to constantly be surrounded by the inspiration of those who had come before me." More recently, its exceptional alumni include Robert Gates, former U.S. Secretary of Defense; NASA astronaut David M. Brown; Emmy- and Tony-award winning actress Glenn Close; and Emmy-award winning host of *The Daily Show*, Jon Stewart.

Once graduates have sprung out into the real world, the alumni network can prove a valuable resource in job hunting. "The College has provided me with both the personal development and professional network to set me on the path for a successful career," says one former student body president. "Already in . . . my career, I have been extended opportunities from alumni of the College that have placed me on my current trajectory. It is the shared experiences of academic rigor, extracurricular passions, and commitment to service that allow alumni to have confidence in each other."

Columbia University

116th Street and Broadway, New York, NY 10027
Admissions: 212-854-2522
E-mail: ugrad-ask@columbia.edu
Website: www.columbia.edu
Twitter: @Columbia, @CC_Columbia, @CUSEAS

Introduction

Columbia University was founded in 1754 as King's College by royal charter of King George II in a schoolhouse at Trinity Church, in what is now part of Lower Manhattan. After the American Revolutionary War, King's College was renamed Columbia College in 1784, and in 1896 it became Columbia University in the City of New York, with the undergraduate liberal arts school retaining the name Columbia College. In 1897, the campus was moved from Madison Avenue, its third location, to its current spot in Morningside Heights, where it occupies more than six city blocks, and around 36 acres. In 1919, Columbia College instituted "Contemporary Civilization," the oldest course in its famed Core Curriculum, a set of common courses required of all undergraduates devoted to developing critical dialogues not just with classic texts, but amongst the students themselves.

Additionally, Columbia comes in at number five on The Princeton Review's 2016 ranking list for Best College Library, and number fifteen on the Great Financial Aid list. Students report that Columbia offers the "perfect medium of an urban school with a stunning campus," which allows them "to choose whether they want to take advantage of the urban setting or just stay on campus and have a more traditional [college] experience." One example of the benefits of going to college in Manhattan is Columbia's Arts Initiative. Founded in 2004, the Arts Initiative allows Columbia students, faculty, and staff to attend cultural events across New York City; benefit from ticket discounts to movies, plays, and other events; visit, for free, thirty museums throughout the city; and connect with each other through vibrant arts programming.

A Focus on Community

With over 500 student clubs and activities on campus, it is hard for students not to find somewhere to fit in, be it on one of the thirty-one Division I athletic teams, the dozens of club and intramural teams, the thirty-some Greek organizations, one of the several dance clubs or thirteen a cappella groups, the organic

> **❝ I look out for young Columbians and do anything I can to give them a boost out in the world. ❞**

food cooperative, a mock trial team, or the Varsity Show (alumni of this longstanding performing arts tradition include Oscar Hammerstein II '16, Lorenz Hart '18, Richard Rodgers '23, and I.A.L. Diamond '41). There is, in all likelihood, an activity, a group, a set of unforgettable peers and companions, for nearly everyone. And, if you were wondering if the Columbia community extends beyond graduation, Brian Yorkey, alumnus and Tony and Pulitzer Prize winner, states, "I—and I suspect this is true of every Columbia grad—look out for young Columbians and do anything I can to give them a boost out in the world."

Columbia College

Columbia College is "a smaller college inside a larger university system which affords both an intimate academic experience and a broad exposure to a diverse, never-dull community. Every Columbia College student and alumnus/a reads the same Great Books and discusses universal ideas through the Core Curriculum," alumnus Wah Chen, who is founding partner of a real estate development company, told us. With over 100 majors and concentrations, Columbia College offers students the opportunity to delve deeply into the humanities, social sciences and natural sciences. In addition to their majors and/or concentrations, students can also pursue a pre-professional track, the Combined Plan program with Columbia Engineering, the Columbia-Juilliard Exchange, or an accelerated graduate program.

Core Curriculum

Columbia's Core Curriculum happens to be legendary. The curriculum is made up of a set of common courses required of all undergraduates, regardless of their choice in major. The communal learning—with all students encountering the same texts and issues at the same time—and the critical dialogue experienced in small seminars are the distinctive features of the Core. This arrangement means that students are gaining exposure to literature, philosophy, history, music, art, writing, and science—course work that may build upon pre-existing interests or introduce students to new ones. One current student tells us, "I am big on the sciences, and I knew that if I did not attend a school that had a core curriculum all I would take are science classes. With Columbia's core, I am able to have a more holistic education." One of the oldest Core courses, and one that all freshmen take, is the Literature Humanities course. Essential reading—texts that have never left the syllabus—include Dante's *Inferno* and Homer's *The Iliad* and exemplify the goals of the Core to explore "foundational texts" and "enduring documents" while honing essential skills such as logic, creative thinking, and argument. The College says, "Ask Columbians about the value of their Columbia education and the Core is likely to be the first thing they will mention." Many of the student's we surveyed also praised the University Writing course: Rather than approaching writing as an innate talent, the course teaches writing as a unique skill that can be practiced and developed. A computer science major testifies that their University Writing professor "would meet with me one on one, on multiple occasions, for each paper so I [could] produce the best material I possibly could. That sort of dedication really helps you grow." Alumnus Wah Chen adds that he was grateful for this liberal arts foundation when he went on to business school: "[It is] extremely valuable insofar as giving individuals a framework from which to make everyday judgments like 'What is right, what is just, and how can I contribute?' across all possible career fields. Expertise can be learned later, but judgment is developed in college."

A Global University

Seventeen percent of Columbia's students are international; over 150 countries are represented on campus; there are about 50 languages available to study at Columbia, and roughly 180 are spoken by New York City residents. Furthermore, there are more than 200 study abroad programs available to students through Columbia's Office of Global Programs. In addition to those, there are summer programs, fellowships, and global field studies that are part of classes or research projects. Columbia also has a network of Global Centers in places such as Mumbai, Beijing, and Paris and special programs at universities like Oxford and Cambridge. Then there's the Columbia Experience Overseas program, which enables students to have summer internships abroad in places like Istanbul and Singapore, among many others locales.

And you don't even have to leave campus to participate in international issues. Approximately twenty World Leaders Forum events happen each year, bringing newsmakers to campus for lively dialogue (past participants have included Ban Ki-moon, Vladimir Putin and the Dalai Lama.) Columbia could easily be considered a global university in the world's most international city.

Presidential Global Fellowship

Being a first-year does not preclude students from taking advantage of Columbia's tempting global opportunities. In fact, the Presidential Global Fellowship funds trips for undergraduates that take place during the summer after their first year. Global Fellows have a fully-funded experience (a scholarship covers the program fee for a Columbia study abroad program and a stipend covers round-trip airfare plus living expenses) that is enhanced with specialized advising focused on academic and career. The goal is that when Presidential Global Fellows return they will be equipped to make the very best use of the Columbia's global networks on campus and beyond. Advising sessions and other program requirements are set with this goal in mind. In fact, one requirement of the program is for fellows to meet with President Bollinger to discuss topics related to globalization. On how many college campuses can students say that access to the President is a built-in experience?

Columbia Engineering

An incredible 50 percent of Columbia undergraduates major in science or engineering. Founded in 1864 as the School of Mines, and officially re-named The Fu Foundation School of Engineering and Applied Science (SEAS) in honor of the late Chinese philanthropist Z.Y. Fu, who gave the school $26 million to bring the best and brightest faculty and students to Columbia Engineering in 1997, Columbia Engineering is the nation's third oldest engineering school. While SEAS is home to a long history of invention and innovation, New York City is arguably the world's most impressive example of built environment from skyscrapers to the subway system. There's no better place to study engineering and applied science. Offering professional-level course, hands-on design projects, and research and internships both in New York City and around the world, Columbia Engineering affords students a broad experience (students also get to engage in the Core Curriculum and can choose from over twenty liberal arts minors).

Student Research Involvement Program

Columbia actively encourages student involvement in faculty research, and for Columbia Engineering students, opportunities span across all nine engineering departments. The Student Research Involvement Program (SRIP) was designed to enable engineering students to participate with 400-plus positions reserved for engineering undergraduates. Students can find information on specific research opportunities through an online portal, after which they may find themselves working on mathematical models for HIV prevention funds in Sub-Saharan Africa or on a design for a lightweight, inexpensive, and human-friendly robotic arm. Students who participate in summer research programs at Columbia or elsewhere have the opportunity to showcase their work at the Undergraduate Summer Research Symposium (a great place to hone those presentation and communication skills as well!).

Special Work Spaces

Doers and makers have access to plenty of design spaces on campus that will help them turn their ideas into something tangible. Graduating entrepreneurs can take advantage of a co-working space with seventy-one seats for young alumni (including Columbia Business School entrepreneurs). And the CU Maker Space welcomes current students (as well as Columbia faculty, staff, and post-docs) to use its space as a resource "for projects, hobbies, building prototypes or just trying something new." Most of the equipment you'll need is housed there as well, including 3D printers, a laser cuter, sewing machines, power tools and woodworking equipment as well as supplies like solder and glue. Student challenges such as the Columbia Venture Competition offer project opportunities and prize money to fund early-stage ventures.

Real-World Experience

At some colleges, students are prone to describe their campus as a "bubble," a bit disconnected from the world outside the Ivory Tower. At Columbia, a vibrant undergraduate community is fully integrated with the larger research, university and the major metropolis beyond. The internship, research and cultural opportunities for students in New York City are limitless. Students attend the symphony, opera and theater and visit the Metropolitan Museum of Art with their courses. The university itself holds 600 different patents from work conducted by faculty members and students. Its hundreds of labs, led by pioneers in the field, conduct nearly $1 billion of annual research in the sciences, humanities and social sciences. Over 200 research centers and institutes, including several interdisciplinary centers, are shaping public policy and enhancing technology around the globe. The campus culture encourages collaboration: between students and faculty, between disciplines and departments, and between the campus and the surrounding world

Faculty

With faculty like Martin Chalfie, recipient of the 2008 Nobel Prize in Chemistry; or Jeffrey Sachs, the director of The Earth Institute, Quetelet Professor of Sustainable Development, and professor of health policy and management at Columbia, (in addition to being special adviser to United Nations Secretary-General Ban Ki-moon); or Core professor and 2012 Guggenheim Fellow Christia Mercer, Columbia can safely boast of a broad, accomplished, and world-renowned faculty, whom students testify are actively engaged with not only their education, but well-being. Students feel that "in small classes, all professors are interested in getting to know their students," while, "in larger

❝ So often, when I read the backflaps of biographies of my favorite authors, Columbia was mentioned. ❞

lectures, if you make the effort, professors will also be thrilled to get to know you." Regardless of how many people are in the room, Columbia faculty do everything they can to connect the students to the material at hand.

Alumni & Careers

Students and alumni have had various reasons for attending Columbia, including the people ("Everyone I met who had attended Columbia was cool, interesting, smart, different"), the talented graduates ("So often, when I read the backflaps of biographies of my favorite authors, Columbia was mentioned"), the location ("It was in New York City" home to "the culture, the events, the variety, the internship and job potential, and many other things I felt were within my grasp"), and the classes ("The relatively small class size was something that really attracted me and I wanted to have a more diverse and unique experience"). And after graduation, they'll be welcomed into a network of 60,000-plus undergraduate alumni. In terms of Columbia's reputation and what it can do for its graduates, Mike Brown Jr., founder and general partner of Bowery Capital, feels that "students graduating from Columbia College have had a rare opportunity due to proximity to take a number of internships, external project opportunities, and see New York City in a very different way from most other students around the world. They have a strong sense of self, a genuine curiosity about them given their NYC experiences and exploration, generally a strong work ethic, and finally strong interpersonal skills."

When it comes to career support, Columbia's Center for Career Education hosts 415 yearly events, programs, and workshops, and reports facilitating 5,087 on-campus interviews. Recent graduates surveyed by Columbia the fall after they graduated reported that 65.4 percent were employed, 20.5 percent had gone on to graduate school, and 10.6 percent were still looking. Aspiring doctors take note: Columbia boasts an 82 percent admit rate for medical school—almost twice the national average—not to mention a 91 percent admit rate for MD/PhD programs. According to PayScale, the median reported income among graduates of Columbia College and the Fu Foundation School of Engineering and Applied Sciences is $62,700. Columbia came in at number thirteen on The Princeton Review's 2015 ranking list for the Top 50 Colleges That Pay You Back, which was reported in the 2015 edition of our book *Colleges That Pay You Back*.

DePauw University

P.O. Box 37, Greencastle, IN, 46135-0037
Admissions: 765-658-4800
E-mail: admission@depauw.edu
Website: www.depauw.edu
Twitter: @DePauwU, @DePauwAdmissions

Introduction

Serious-minded students are drawn to DePauw University for its "small classes," "encouraging" professors, and the "individual academic attention" they can expect to receive. The fundamental elements of a DePauw education focus on preparing students to think critically, wrestle with complexity, and to write and communicate effectively. How do they do it? A low student-to faculty ratio (currently 10:1) and a curriculum that asks their students to take courses across all disciplines.

DePauw has historically been particularly committed to connecting this core liberal arts philosophy with strong preparation for life after graduation. The Fellows Programs (Management Fellows, Media Fellows, Science Research Fellows, and Environmental Fellows) connect the liberal arts to experiential opportunities (including both research and internship experiences) in management and business, media and journalism, the hard sciences, and sustainability and the environment. More recently, the addition of the Hubbard Center for Student Engagement (made possible through a gift in 2013) has made it possible to significantly expand career planning and student advising to better and more deeply prepare students for their post graduate plans.

Professors lead small, discussion-based classes and hold their students firmly to high academic standards. So be prepared to pull your "fair share of all-nighters," students say. Beyond stellar professors, DePauw's other academic draws include "extraordinary" study-abroad opportunities and a "wonderful" alumni network great for "connections and networking opportunities." Alums also "keep our endowment pretty high, making it easy for the school to give out merit scholarships," along with need-based aid, which undergraduates appreciate. DePauw emphasizes life outside the classroom, too. The school operates several fellowships to support independent projects by high-achieving students, and four out of five DePauw students will complete a professional internship during college. Winter Term, a month long interterm, sends many students abroad while allowing others to undertake research or creative projects. Arts and culture are at the forefront of campus life; the performing-arts center was recently renovated, and events like the school's annual ArtsFest allow students and invited artists to exhibit or perform for the campus and community. Beyond the frats and sororities, which are indeed plentiful on campus, "there is always a theater production, athletic event, or organization-sponsored event going on," and popular bands occasionally perform on campus. To cap off the experience, the city of Indianapolis is forty-five miles away for internships, externships, or just to "watch a good movie."

A Focus on Community

The Greek scene is pretty big at DePauw, with 77 percent of the student body joining fraternities and 63 percent joining sororities. DePauw is no Animal House, however, with the Greek life here reportedly "promot[ing] not only social activities but also philanthropic events." There are 119 student organizations, 13 honor societies, and 10 religious organizations in addition to 23 varsity teams. The typical DePauw student is "driven." They "have all had multiple internships, international experience, and [have held] some type of leadership position." Though these folks may seem "overcommitted," they "always get their work done." For those who don't fit this mold, don't fret; most students seem to be "accepting of the different types" of people on campus. Diversity on campus is augmented through the school's partnership with the Posse Foundation, which brings in urban (though not necessarily minority) "students from Chicago and NYC every year." These students are described as "leaders on campus" and "take real initiative to hold their communities together."

Fellows Programs

The four Fellows programs on campus are further ways for students to build community and find their "intellectual home." Designed for students who share similar academic interests, these programs offer multiple hands-on experiences on top of course work. Students can take part in semester-long internships or research experiences and frequent opportunities to engage with leading scholars and industry leaders on and off campus. Several of the students we surveyed credited acceptance into one of the Fellows Programs as their reason for choosing DePauw. Here's a quick rundown of what makes each Fellows program unique:

Management Fellows

Blending a traditional liberal arts curriculum with real-world experiences in business and entrepreneurship, the Management Fellows Program also includes a full-time, semester-long, credit-bearing business internship. More than 700

Management Fellows have successfully completed internships in a wide variety of companies across the United States and around the world, gaining valuable experience in finance, consulting, sales and marketing, strategic planning, and investment banking. Graduates of the program have accepted positions after graduation with Accenture, BMO Harris Commercial Bank, Cancer Treatment Centers of America, Cummins Inc., Deloitte & Touche, Eli Lilly and Company, Epic Systems Corporation, GE Oil & Gas, Golfstat, KA+A, Milhaus Development, Walker Information, WebLink International, and West Monroe Partners, among others. Current students are currently interning at BBDO, Eli Lilly, Guardian Life, Road2Argentina, and Ronald McDonald House Charities, among other business and non-profits.

Media Fellows

Combining classes with hands-on experience, the Media Fellows Program trains students in the theory and practice of media. Media Fellows benefit from semester-long, off-campus media internships at sites such as *The Today Show*, *The Colbert Report*, the White House, *USA Today*, and C-SPAN; a robust speakers series that brings students face-to-face with professionals from premier media and governmental organizations; and resources like the Pulliam Center for Contemporary Media, a living laboratory where students gain experience in radio and television production, newspaper and magazine publishing, and multimedia for the web. A current Media Fellow told us that the program "has allowed me to take this semester to do a full-time off campus internship for academic credit. It's also given me access to speakers and networking opportunities that will become even more valuable as I approach graduation. Also, it's great to be able to take a semester off campus and still graduate in four years. DePauw's flexible course requirements make it easy to do so."

As for the Pulliam Center for Contemporary Media, its resources include WGRE radio (the oldest originally 10-watt college FM radio station in the U.S.), *The DePauw Newspaper* (the oldest college newspaper in Indiana), D3TV Student Television studios, *A Midwestern Review* (a national literary magazine), *The Cauldron* monthly (a student magazine), as well as general video, audio and still photographic production, teleconferencing, word processing and large-scale audio-visual presentations.

Science Research Fellows

An honors program for outstanding students interested in studying science and getting significant hands-on research experience as an undergraduate, Science Research Fellows begin learning and experiencing authentic scientific research in a wide variety of disciplines from their very first year. SRF students go on to major in chemistry, biochemistry, physics, biology, kinesiology, computer science, geosciences, mathematics, or psychology. They collaborate with DePauw faculty in summer-long, on-campus research, and they experience research internships at leading facilities across the globe.

As for what the program directly entails: Preparation for thoughtful and productive scientific research begins with the fall semester course "Understanding Science" and continues with the spring semester course "Research Methods," and while there are no SRF requirements during the summer following the first year, research opportunities do exist for interested students. In the summer following the second year, students join the lab of a science faculty member for a collaborative ten-week summer research experience. All students present their findings in a poster session at an open-university forum in mid-fall. Depending on the outcome of the research, students may have opportunities to present their research at regional, national and/or international conferences, or work with faculty members to publish results in a professional journal. In their third year, students complete an additional research experience, generally in the summer, but students may also choose a semester long internship for academic credit. This is followed by a capstone seminar in the fall of students' senior year.

Environmental Fellows

The Environmental Fellows Program is a four-year honors program for students who are interested in addressing the complex, interdisciplinary environmental challenges facing humanity today, and is designed to complement a student's academic pursuit of any major that DePauw has to offer. During the first year, Environmental Fellows will participate in an environmentally focused first-year seminar. Fellows will also attend monthly luncheon discussions with faculty members, professionals, and their upperclassman colleagues. Sophomores will begin the process of fulfilling the summer-long or full semester field experience component of the program. This experiential learning opportunity could take the form of research with faculty, internships, or off campus study. As juniors, Environmental Fellows are expected to continue developing and exercising collaborative leadership skills by creating a junior leadership project. This will involve assuming responsibility for planning environmentally themed co-curricular events and activities to take place during the year. Finally, seniors will take part in a capstone seminar that will call on them to integrate all the aspects of their environmental education. Upon graduation, seniors will have completed six environmentally focused courses—three in the humanities and social sciences and three in the sciences. Plus, each semester, Environmental Fellows will have attended special lectures, luncheons, and seminars sponsored by the Environmental Fellows Program and other organizations on campus.

Honor Scholar Program

The DePauw Honor Scholar Program is open to students of all majors who show unusual promise and commitment to the development of the life of the mind. Each year a small number of carefully selected first-year students are invited to participate in the program and the special opportunities it presents. In their first year, Honor Scholars take two special seminar courses. During their remaining three years, students take three interdisciplinary seminar courses. These seminars focus on a wide variety of topics, and allow students to investigate issues in the natural sciences, socials sciences, and humanities. Honor Scholars read, discuss, and write about both classic and cutting-edge sources in a small group setting, working closely with professors. During their last two semesters at DePauw, Honor Scholars pursue independent work under the direction of a faculty thesis adviser and a committee of two or more additional faculty members, culminating in an Honors thesis.

But being an Honor Scholar implies more than formal academic study! There are countless opportunities for Honor Scholars to mix socially and informally with one another and with members of the faculty and alumni. Above all, the program provides an opportunity to be part of a group that seeks to find in its college education an incredibly intensive and stimulating intellectual experience.

Extended Studies

In the 1970s, DePauw developed a month-long term between the first and second semester. This Winter Term has made experiential learning a central element of a DePauw education. From short-term study abroad experiences and global service trips, to unique independent study experiences, short-term internships, or research opportunities with faculty, Winter Term has helped DePauw students explore opportunities that will shape their careers after DePauw. Today, Winter Term has been joined by similar programs in May and in the summer months within DePauw's Extended Studies Program, but the mission and purpose is much the same: creating opportunities for DePauw students to connect their liberal arts education with the world at large.

Career Prep

The Kathryn F. Hubbard Center for Student Engagement connects students with applied learning opportunities that enhance their liberal arts education by promoting curiosity, intellectual challenge, and self-reflection. The Hubbard Center strives to empower all students to be thoughtful decision-makers, culturally aware, and socially responsible citizens who can articulate their values,

> **❝ The campus is full of energy right now with changes the administration is bringing and a new accessibility President Casey provides to the student body. ❞**

interests, and skills while actively leading lives of purpose. The Hubbard Center provides information, resources and advising in the areas of service, study abroad, national fellowships, pre-professional advising, internships and career development—including opportunities over Winter Term, May Term, or the summer. This integrative approach enables DePauw students to tie the many threads of their liberal arts experience together in meaningful ways that enhance their employment and graduate school opportunities. With so many programs designed specifically to offer hands-on experience via internships and research projects, DePauw has the area of real-world experience pretty much covered. DePauw students "are very focused on getting their degrees and [landing] really good jobs." Considering that the average starting salary of recent grads is $46,600 (according to PayScale.com), we'd say they're achieving their goals. This is no doubt due to DePauw's "amazing" resources to help students find internships, job leads, and alumni mentors. To begin with, undergrads love to highlight the "alumni database [which is teeming with] successful people." Additionally, students can scour TigerTracks, an internal site that allows undergrads to search for jobs and internships listed specifically for DePauw students. The Hubbard Center also offers some really unique programs beyond the traditional résumé workshops and mock interviews. For example, collaborating with Indiana University's Kelly School of Business, DePauw offers the Liberal Arts Management Program, which teaches how businesses (from for-profit companies to entrepreneurial start-ups) are created and how they function. The insight gleaned from programs like this is enormous.

Faculty

As for the faculty and administration at DePauw, an English Writing major said: "The campus is full of energy right now with changes the administration is bringing and a new accessibility President Casey provides to the student body. The professors, like at any school, are mixed ... Fortunately I've had more fantastic professors than so-so professors, and the truly dedicated and exceptional ones make up for the bad professors. They are frequently accessible and several care about the students both in the classroom and outside the classroom. My overall academic experience has been challenging and time consuming but excellent. I've taken advantage of the liberal arts by exploring many subjects, and the experiential learning through off-campus study, internships, and Winter Term is top-notch."

In the liberal arts tradition, DePauw's faculty members are expected to be teacher-scholars, exemplifying a commitment to teaching while also advancing their own scholarship. It is not uncommon to regularly see faculty members attending events on campus (athletic events in which their students are competing) or musical events at which their students are performing. Students often meet with faculty members at Starbucks or in the faculty member's office.

Through a robust faculty development program, faculty are also encouraged to include undergraduate students in their own research. A few examples of faculty accomplishments (many of them related to their work with students) include the following: a professor who included students in his research about heart regeneration in zebrafish; a DePauw biology professor who served as a CDC infectious disease responder during an outbreak of Ebola in Uganda; a former English professor whose work formed the basis of the HBO hit "True Detective"; and yet another English professor whose work regularly appears in *Esquire*.

Alumni/ae

The Tigers are an extremely talented bunch. Notable alumni include Bill and Scott Rasmussen, founders of ESPN; Ben Solomon, whose work as *The New York Times* Middle East Correspondent on the Ebola outbreak in Liberia won the Pulitzer Prize; Angie Hicks, founder of Angie's List; Tim Solso, the Chairman of the Board of General Motors; famed fiction writer Barbara Kingsolver; Ford Frick, Commissioner of Major League Baseball from 1951 to 1965; NASA Astronaut Joseph P. Allen; and 44th Vice-President Dan Quayle. A 2014 graduate in political science admits that the "strong alumni network" was a huge factor in making DePauw her alma mater. And more than a few of the current students we surveyed cited DePauw's unofficial motto "Uncommon Success." Overall, a music education major summed up, "DePauw does a great job instilling pride in its students and preparing them for careers in the real world."

66 *DePauw does a great job instilling pride in its students and preparing them for careers in the real world.* **99**

Drew University

36 Madison Avenue, Madison, NJ 07940
Admissions: 973-408-DREW
Email: cadm@drew.edu
Website: www.drew.edu
Twitter: @DrewUniversity

Introduction

With 1,356 undergraduates attending its College of Liberal Arts, Drew University offers a wide range of programs to its diverse student body. Drew "is about creating an environment where a student of any gender, race, religion and sexual orientation can receive a good education," a German and history major told us. Another student we surveyed agreed: "Drew has a lot of diversity; walking across campus you see people from all types of different backgrounds than you." Beyond this demographic diversity, the school excels—thanks to its well regarded programs in theatre and the sciences, and its array of real-world work experiences—at "helping you achieve any dreams you have, from being the next big Broadway star to being the President of the United Nations," as one economics major put it.

Tuition, room, and board for the academic year 2015–2016 totals $58,224. Despite the sticker price, many of the students we surveyed explained that, due to generous financial aid and scholarships, Drew turned out to be much more affordable than many other schools. One psychology major told us, "Drew, although extremely expensive, provided a great financial aid package, which surpassed that of nearly all the other colleges I was accepted to," while another student explained, "I received over half of the cost of tuition." According to its website, the university awarded over $30 million in grant assistance during 2014–2015, with the average student receiving $27,000 in grants and scholarships. In return for their investment, students have access to highly-ranked programs, resources in New York City and all over the world, real-world research opportunities with faculty mentors, and an involved alumni network. All of this translates to a lot of opportunities for Drew students at a relatively low cost.

Location

Drew's 186-acre wooded campus in Madison, New Jersey is within walking distance of the Madison train station, with direct service to New York City's Penn Station. Students take advantage of this easy access to Manhattan for both recreation and cultural enrichment. "New York City is only an hour away by train, so it's perfect for a day trip on the weekend," a women's and gender studies major told us, while an English literature major explained, "I got to perform my poetry in NYC under a professor's invitation."

Thanks to the school's proximity to New York City, the city also becomes a classroom for students, through programs such as the Semester at the United Nations, Semester on Communications and Media, Semester on Contemporary Art, and the Wall Street Semester.

Professor Marc Tomljanovich, chair of the Department of Economics and Business, runs the Wall Street Semester, and explained what students selected to participate do during the two days each week they spend in New York. "Each day is split up into two parts. The mornings are lecture-based, during which I teach them about the historical, structural and institutional aspects of financial markets. More specifically, the semester is split into four main themes—bonds and bond markets, stocks and stock markets, the role of regulators in financial markets, and financial derivatives. The afternoons are experiential-based, and tied into the morning's lectures. For example, if I am talking about bond markets in the morning, we will go visit a bond trader from Barclay's in the afternoon. If I am discussing the risk structure of interest rates in the morning, we will head over to Moody's or S&P in the afternoon. The point of the afternoon is so that students get the practical viewpoints to augment (or contradict) the morning's information."

❝ Thanks to the school's proximity to New York City, the city also becomes a classroom for students.❞

Fatima Diallo, who graduated in 2013, credits her involvement in the United Nations Semester with helping her to secure a job after graduation. "Due to my semester at the UN with Drew, I was able to get an internship with the UN Wider network which led to another two internships at UN-Habitat and the UN Millennium Campaign. The latter then turned into a consultancy position after graduation."

Top-Ranked Theatre Program

Drew comes in at number nine on the The Princeton Review's 2016 ranking list for Best College Theater, and its theatre program, which benefits from the university's close proximity to Broadway, is what draws many students to Drew. The program affords students opportunities for writing, workshopping, reading, producing and performing across all field including acting, directing, playwriting, design, tech, stage management and choreography. Through the Robert Fisher Oxnam Visiting Artist Program, Drew has invited actors Olympia Dukakis and Pat Carroll; playwrights Wendy Wasserstein, David Ives, Romulus Linney and Joyce Carol Oates; and Broadway fight choreographer Rick Sordelet, among others to teach regular courses and master classes at the university.

Drew provides financial support to students interested in the theatre as well, including The Presidential Scholarship for outstanding work in the theatre pre-Drew (similar scholarships exist in the other arts and non-arts disciplines); The Vincent and Genovina Porcelli Scholarship, which supports juniors who have made substantial contributions to theatre at Drew; The President's Award in Theatre, given to seniors who have exhibited exemplary dedication to Drew theatre and contributed superior work; The Robert Fisher Oxnam/Ensemble Studio Theatre Award in Playwriting, to support professional readings of student plays and residencies with the Ensemble Studio Theatre in New York City to further develop plays; The Joe Patenaude Internships, which support theatre internships; and The Garden State Arts Center Foundation Thomas H. Kean Scholarships, which support a New Jersey resident studying and working in theatre.

As part of its theatre program, Drew offers a London Semester that offers access to organizations like the Royal National Theatre, the Royal Shakespeare Company and West End theatres, and a Theatre Semester, participation in which has led to job offers for many students. Theatre students who are looking to get a head start on their careers can also take part in full-time internships with established Off-Broadway or local major regional companies.

Psychology Major

The psychology major at Drew provides students with the support and opportunities to develop real-world research skills. "The professors in the science and psychology department are simply amazing. They make sure to get to know you individually and often guide you towards fulfilling opportunities," one neuroscience major told us. For example, psychology students at Drew have presented papers at the Tri-Collegiate Psychology Research Symposium, a conference that Drew organizes with two other area universities, as well as the following regional and national conferences: The Meeting of the Association for Psychological Science, 2015; The Meeting of the Society for Personality and Social Psychology, 2014; The Meeting of the Eastern Psychological Association, 2012, 2013, 2014, 2015; and The Annual Meeting of the Society for Neuroscience, 2011, 2013. Along the way to such accomplishments, students complete writing-intensive laboratory classes that provide research experience, a community-based psychology course, directed research in a faculty member's lab, and other advanced research opportunities.

Programs For Budding Scientists

Science-minded students will appreciate the Research Institute for Scientists Emeriti (RISE), which was recognized with a Merck Innovation Award for Undergraduate Science Education. Through this program, believed to be one-of-a-kind, hundreds of Drew students have conducted research with senior scientists in state-of-the-art labs which have recently undergone extensive renovations. Through RISE, students have access to state-of-the-art, analytical instrumentation typically found only at Tier 1 research universities, including liquid chromatography and mass spectrometry (LC/MS) for separating and identifying components of a mixture and high-field nuclear magnetic resonance spectrometry (NMR) for determining molecular structures.

Through the Drew Summer Science Institute (DSSI), students of science receive a stipend and housing for the summer to work one-on-one with a faculty mentor on a real-world research project. During the summer, DSSI students meet to discuss their projects on a weekly basis, and then present their results to the Drew community at the annual Fall Poster Session. Recent projects completed by DSSI students include "Analysis of Environmental Risk Assessment of Toxins in Fish: Food Security Implications for Inuit"; "Analysis of Eye Movements to Biological Motion"; and "Modeling Atmospheric Aerosols: Ozonolysis of Surface Adsorbed Vanillin in the Presence and Absence of Light."

Other Real-World Learning Experiences

Theatre, psychology, and science majors aren't the only students at Drew who benefit from real-world work experience. The university has cultivated relationships with employers in the region, which afford students internship opportunities that often lead to post-graduate employment. The long list of companies where students have interned include Bank of America, Morgan Stanley, Lincoln Center, CBS Sports, CNN, the Audubon Society, HarperCollins, the New York City Police Department, Planned Parenthood, Revlon, Johnson & Johnson, and many others. "I even got an amazing internship at Sony Music," an English literature major told us. Additionally, the Thomas H. Kean Summer Internship Program provides a stipend to support students' completion of a full-time political science or international relations–related summer internship. Alumnus Thérèse Postel told us, "If it wasn't for this scholarship, I couldn't have interned on a political campaign in New York City that eventually helped me land my first job with New York City Council."

Drew students also have an opportunity for real-world learning through the Center for Civic Engagement. Through the center, Civic Scholars attend seminars, perform internships, and take community-based classes that connects students' academic interests with their work in the community. For example, one Civic Scholar majoring in art history completed an internship with the Museum of Early Trades and Crafts, studied abroad in Italy during her junior year, held a summer internship with the Arnot Art Museum in Elmira, NY and worked as a coordinator with Drew's Arts and the Common Good program. Other scholars have worked with Jersey Battered Women Services, an after-school program at the Morristown Neighborhood House, and the Borough of Madison, New Jersey. Khemani Gibson, class of 2014, was a Civic Scholar and explained how the program ultimately "provided me with the skills I am now using to better serve my community in Orange, NJ with a local non-profit."

Center for Global Education

In addition to organizing the previously mentioned semesters in New York City, the Center for Global Education offers Drew students the opportunity to study abroad, something nearly 50 percent of students choose to do. One English literature major we surveyed "went to Paris and London to study urban culture and space." Other students have the option to study with partnering colleges and universities in Morocco, Brazil, South Africa, Israel, and Spain, to name just a handful of locations. Students also have the opportunity to pursue summer projects abroad, again emphasizing Drew's focus on experiential learning. During the summer of 2015, for example, Drew students performed hands-on archaeological field research in Ecuador, developed anthropological field research studies on race and ethnicity in Bahia, Brazil, researched the energy industry and its impact on the economy and the environment in Wyoming, and explored public health in the Republic of South Africa by studying and working in hospitals, herbal clinics, healing centers of several faith traditions and indigenous religious shrines.

These global experiences lead to even closer relationships between faculty and students. Professor Tomljanovich described trips he took with students "to London and Dublin to study global financial markets . . . to Brussels and London to learn about the economics of European integration" and to Tokyo "to compare and contrast U.S. and Japanese business goals, strategies and corporate cultures. . . .I can honestly now say I've been around the world with them." Dr. Lillie J. Edwards, the founding director of the Pan-African Studies program agreed: "PANAF has taken students to Africa almost every year during my twenty-three years at Drew. . . they have also gone to Egypt with Drew's Middle East Studies Program, to Cuba with the Spanish Department and to Brazil with the Anthropology Department."

Faculty

As evidenced by the small class sizes and the faculty mentoring program, Drew's philosophy emphasizes a close relationship between students and faculty. The school's 9:1 student-faculty ratio, and its commitment to hiring faculty who are passionate about teaching and the undergraduate experience help turn this philosophy into reality, leading students in our survey to frequently cite the faculty as Drew's biggest strength. An economics and mathematics major told us, "The professors are generally very accessible outside of class. Not only will they provide help in their own courses, but they will also discuss your interests in the field, their personal research, and future career options." A chemistry major agreed, explaining,

> 66 *Within my major, I feel like part of a family. All of my professors know me and I think truly care about my performance.* 99

"The professors at Drew are always eager to help the students, whether during class or outside of class. The professors have helped me understand the material by working with me one-on-one." Professors are supportive outside the classroom as well. "They also seem genuinely interested in helping us improve as students and human beings, and in getting to know us as maturing adults," a psychology major reported, while an English literature major wrote about the close relationship she has developed with her professors: "My professors have really encouraged me to pursue the most out of my education here. One provided me with the opportunity to read my original poetry in NYC with distinguished poets. Another has influenced my decision to write a senior thesis. Within my major, I feel like part of a family. All of my professors know me and I think truly care about my performance." Finally, a neuroscience major told us, "The greatest strength of this school is how supportive administration and faculty are. A lot of them tend to be like family to students."

Patrick McGuinn, associate professor and chair of the political science department told us, "A number of faculty have incorporated various forms of experiential learning into their regular courses." For example, Associate Professor McGuinn himself offers "Social Policy and Inequality in America," a community-based learning course in which "students surveyed over one hundred local food pantries, social service organizations, and municipal governments to determine the kinds of food assistance that is being provided to those in need in Morris County and indemnity where gaps in access to food exist." Dr. Edwards, speaking of PANAF, told us: "Several of the faculty in our program direct major off-campus initiatives. Professor Kesha Moore (sociology) directs NJSTEP, a program that takes the Drew classroom into men's and women's prisons, and Professor Lisa Brennan (theater) co-directs a Newark project in which Drew students help middle school students write and produce plays." Beyond their care and concern for their students, Drew faculty are award-winning scholars in their fields, deeply engaged in their own scholarly research and professional pursuits.

Alumni/ae

Several students in our survey cited the alumni network as one of the school's strengths. Not surprisingly for a top-ranked theatre school, this network includes alumni who attended the Yale School of Drama, Carnegie Mellon University and the Royal Academy of Dramatic Art and the London Academy of Performing Art in England, and worked for organizations like CBS-TV, the Paper Mill Playhouse, the Shakespeare Theatre of New Jersey, *The Late Show with David Letterman*, and the Eugene O'Neill Theatre. Students pursuing careers in business or finance also benefit from alumni connections created through the Wall Street Semester. According to Professor Tomljanovich, alumni actively network with students, provide job shadowing opportunities, and help students secure full-time employment. Through their donations, alumni have also established "The Fund"—real money that Drew students can invest.

Outside of these programs, alumni are involved with students' lives in a variety of ways. Khemani Gibson, for example, has worked as a counselor for Educational Opportunity Scholars, a program he was involved in as a student as well. Thérèse Postel explained her continued involvement with Drew students: "I am in close contact with the Political Science and International Relations Department until this day and often send job and internship opportunities to the school when I come across them. I've mentored several students who are interested in a career in international affairs. Drew is working, again, to build its alumni network and make it stronger. Over the past few years, I've attended some really great Drew events in New York City."

Duke University

2138 Campus Drive, Box 90586, Durham, NC 27708
Admissions: 919-684-3214
Email:undergrad-admissions@duke.edu
Twitter: @DukeU

Introduction

Around 6,500 undergraduates share an expansive campus, which, according to one graduate, is "stunningly beautiful.... The chapel, in particular with its tolling bells, towering stained glass windows, and piping organ still leaves me in awe. The campus also houses the gardens, which [become] a popular spot to feed the ducks, sunbathe, or just hike through to see the flowers." The campus is located in Durham, North Carolina, a small city without being "as overwhelming as a large city like New York or Los Angeles."

Marvin Marcelin, a 2009 grad, told us that he, too, "was particularly drawn to the beautiful scenic venues Duke had to offer," but that after visiting with the student body he "was blown away by the discussions Duke students had amongst themselves, with faculty, and the community. There was a sense of intellectual fullness amongst the students," he said, "that intrigued me, and there was a sincere desire to make connections with others in a deep and meaningful way. I wanted to be part of a diverse community that enjoyed participating in meaningful discussions where students were able to see different perspectives on any given topic."

Duke is known for putting that academic vigor to work through its service-based learning programs and degrees that allow students to design a personalized education. The university told us that it "views education not only as a gateway to personal development, but also as a pathway for improving society." And their students agree. Jin-Soo Daniel Huh, another 2009 grad, this time in poli-sci and public policy, said he "was impressed by the high caliber of academics and the focus it had on applying knowledge in service to society. . . Duke fosters an environment where you are able to develop your academic interests and also your personal interests . . . through experiences like activities, internships, and hands on learning. As a result, I left Duke with a strong academic background and leadership skills."

Duke grads can "go virtually anywhere in the country and find other people who [are] passionate about Duke and [understand] the caliber of the individuals who graduated from [this] institution," Marvin told us. Here are a few of the ways that Duke students have developed personally and professionally from the university's experiential and student-directed education.

Service Learning at Duke: One student's process

Marvin Marcelin graduated in 2009 as a psychology major with minors in biological anthropology and anatomy, and a certificate in human development. He spent three years teaching and is currently training to be doctor of podiatry at Temple University. We had a chance to ask Marvin about his experiences at Duke, and he told us that the service-based learning, whether it took the form of creating a dropout prevention program or volunteering at medical facilities and nursing homes, helped him develop his career and discover his professional interests. Here is what he had to say:

"I was heavily involved in the service-based learning components that were offered. For example, I took education courses where I learned different teaching techniques in a classroom setting, and implemented those techniques while tutoring middle school students in an after school educational setting. I took human development courses where I learned the various stages of development ranging from infancy, adolescence, pre-teen, teenager, young adult, adult, up to the elderly stages of life. As a Duke student, I had the opportunity to observe what I learned in the classroom and apply them to real-life settings such as elementary schools, middle schools, and nursing homes.

"My most valuable experience I had in college stems from the experiences I gained during my Independent Study. With the help of one of my Duke professors, I was able to develop an intervention strategy to improve the problem of dropping out among middle school students. Throughout the span of a semester, I traveled to a nearby middle school and implemented a program that helped students set goals for themselves. My professor gave me the reins of my project and allowed me to take charge. This experience allowed me to think critically, showed me the importance of working together in a real life setting, and gave me an opportunity to leave a lasting impression in the lives of others.

"After graduating from Duke, I became an educator in the School District of Philadelphia. I was able to implement the lessons I learned while at Duke, and I was able to inspire middle and high school students to work hard in school and set worthwhile goals that will guide them towards one day becoming successful professionals. My time at Duke has showed me that I have a strong interest in teaching and providing service to others."

Customized Degrees

With fifty-four majors, fifty-two minors, and twenty-one certificates that can be combined in any way, Duke students certainly have a lot of options. Some of Duke's specialized majors are designed to be completed as "co-majors" in conjunction with another field of study. When these degrees are paired with experiential learning requirements, such as the global health co-major, students effectively carve out a specialized niche in their field. The school told us that "more than 80 percent of Duke students go beyond their major to obtain a second major, a minor, and/or a certificate." However, these options provide something beyond variety. They help students probe a subject and really figure out what it is that interests them the most.

Becca Ward '12, a public policy major who now works as a legislative aid for a U.S. senator, explained how this process affected her career: "I have always known I wanted to work in the environmental conservation/protection space, but it was a nebulous idea when I matriculated. While I am still trying to find my exact path, Duke gave me insight into different perspectives and concentrations within conservation and public policy influence the way I approach my job everyday."

Duke offers ways for students to further customize their education and degree beyond the established majors. Ana Homayoun ('01) raved about one such opportunity: "One of the greatest opportunities Duke gave me was the chance to be a Program II major. Program II is a self-designed curriculum where a student is allowed to design a curriculum around a personal interest. At the time mine was International Health Policy. I took classes in the graduate school and at UNC School of Public Health, and it was quite interesting in so many different ways. But the most important thing it taught me is that there is no one pre-set path to success, and there are ways in which you can create your own blueprint for success. Duke gave me the opportunity to be an entrepreneur of sorts when it came to shaping my education, and I took that confidence in starting a business shortly after graduation."

Duke encourages students to become the authors of their own educational and career paths, which students at Duke take very seriously. This collective sense of agency and self destiny has a powerful effect. "In aggregate sense," Becca Ward explained, "the opportunity to be surrounded by so many incredibly

> **❝ Duke gave me the opportunity to be an entrepreneur of sorts when it came to shaping my education, and I took that confidence in starting a business shortly after graduation. ❞**

passionate and intelligent peers and advisers helped me understand that there is no right or standard path, and inspired me to be brave and unapologetic about forging my own."

DukeEngage

DukeEngage is another way that Duke allows students to customize their education and gain practical experience through socially conscious efforts. "This is a program where students identify an opportunity to provide a service anywhere in the world and Duke will help fund your travel, immunizations, lodging, etc.," alumnus Jin-Soo Daniel Huh told us. "DukeEngage also provided training that prepared us to perform service in communities. Students can go as individuals or professors will sponsor groups to work on a project. I had the opportunity to go to Mali and work with an international development group and help measure the impact the schools they were building in rural areas were having on the communities." DukeEngage service projects last a minimum of eight weeks and take place in seventy-eight countries around the world. Thanks to an endowment from The Bill and Melinda Gates Foundation and the Duke Endowment, the program has covered the cost of 2,800 students since its 2007 inception. "It was an incredible opportunity to apply the skills I had developed in class in a tangible way," he added. "To do this with the financial support and programmatic support of Duke made it an even more meaningful experience."

This is an exciting time for DukeEngage: by 2017, when current incoming students will be thinking about service-learning opportunities, Duke expects to be funding 600 students every year and further developing partnerships in the US and around the world.

The Futures Duke Creates

Everyone we talked to said that Duke's experiential learning not only advanced their career, it helped them know how to make satisfying, empowering career decisions. Jin-Soo Daniel Huh told us, "Duke emphasizes learning . . . in order to give back to society. That is something I value greatly about Duke. I had that desire coming into Duke and Duke continued to shape this desire. I am now in education working with schools in high poverty urban settings and I can directly trace this to my experience at Duke."

He continued, "My time at the Sanford School of Public Policy . . . did a great job of teaching mindsets and critical thinking skills that are applicable to pretty much every field. In my current job, I work with schools to think through how we can better leverage technology to personalize learning to help students of all backgrounds and ability level learn. I know that the combination of Duke's commitment to serving society and fostering critical thinking skills have led me to be successful in my career."

He also told us that Duke graduates can look forward to joining a well connected community all over the country. "We are also known to have a real pride for our university. Basketball games and, more recently, football games are rallying points for our alumni. When it comes to Duke-UNC basketball games, you know the local Duke bar in every city is going to be filled with alumni in Duke blue." Ana Homayoun agreed that Duke alums benefit from their peers, who are often known to be "solid, smart, dynamic, and ambitious. Every time I hear a colleague or person talking about a Duke grad, they are describing someone who is engaged and willing to give back, and in general, someone who is enthusiastic, fun to be around, and collegial. All great qualities."

Alumni/ae

Prominent alumni like Elizabeth Hanford Dole, a former president of the American Red Cross, and Benjamin Chavis, Jr., civil rights activist and former executive director of the NAACP exemplify Duke's commitment to leadership and service. And that is a nice group to join. A current biomedical engineering student told us, "Duke has a very strong alumni network, which makes for great connections when coming out of school and looking for opportunity all over the globe in the professional world."

Part of the value of a Duke degree lies in these extensive alumni networks. Alumni connect and collaborate through two primary channels: through groups that focus on particular regions of the world, which can be a huge help when moving to a new community, and through "affinity groups," such as the Duke Global Health group or the Women as Leaders group. Becca Ward is currently in a mentoring program through the Duke Politics and Policy group, and she told us "I am constantly amazed at the supportiveness and warmth of the Duke alumni network." Since the 2008 economic downturn, grads in the Young Alumni group have been able to check out "a series of online conversations with knowledgeable Duke alumni to answer questions relating to 'what to do now,'" according to the university. Leave it to a university that focuses on leadership and service to produce alumni networks that are so consistently helpful.

Faculty

Members of Duke faculty are among the most respected in the world. While they are public intellectuals who hold appointments in the National Academy of Sciences and provide expert testimony to the United States Congress, they "are [also] committed to giving students the individual attention that pushes them to excel. . . . Undergraduates, even in their first year, interact with senior faculty on a regular basis," the school told us.

A 8:1 faculty to student ratio certainly means that Duke students can get plenty of face time with their professors. But Duke encourages these interactions further with "programs like 'FLunch' where a student can invite their professor to lunch at the college's expense, and have an hour-long chat about their classes, their experiences & future plans, as well as hearing about what the professor does," Dr. Mohamed Noor, a professor of biology told us. A casual, hour-long chat with a world expert and free lunch? Who could say no? Based on the success of FLunch, "Duke recently also started 'FINvite' to have students and professors have longer interactions such as a group dinner and games at a dorm or going out to a restaurant," Dr. Noor explained. "I've participated in many of these each semester, and the interactions they stimulate are great . . . those are some of the kinds of interactions that make me love my job."

Dr. Noor explained how these relationships strengthen over time and told us that, "students who've worked directly on research with me are like family . . . they come to our lab meetings, have regularly scheduled meetings to go over their research progress, and join the lab social network. These undergraduates often operate, in effect, like starting PhD students, often leading to publication of research, too."

Faculty gain valuable perspective from these interactions as well, which helps them when it comes time to make decisions about the curriculum. Duke faculty, Dr. Noor told us, enjoy a great deal of control over the curriculum. "[We] are currently involved in a committee that is reimagining what general education requirements we offer to all Arts & Sciences undergraduates, and our committee is thinking about the impact not just about 'classes' but also about the totality of student experiences—undergraduate research, study abroad, even extra- or co-curriculars."

Franklin & Marshall College

P.O. Box 3003, Lancaster, PA, 17604-3003
Admissions: 877-678-9111
E-mail: admission@fandm.edu
Website: fandm.edu
Twitter: @FandMCollege, @fandmadmit

Introduction

Once a week on the Franklin & Marshall campus, a liberal arts school in south central Pennsylvania, there is a block of time when no classes are scheduled and the college community of about 2,300 students and 175 faculty come together for a special event. The college told us that "this common gathering time, used for lectures, topical discussions, projects and other community gatherings was designed to promote the involvement of all members of the college in meaningful intellectual exchange and to broaden the reach of the liberal arts experience." The notion of the college as a community that gathers inside and outside of the classroom epitomizes the F&M experience.

Caitlin Krutsick, Class of 2012, didn't know much about F&M before she got there, "but on the [college] tour," she told us, "I remember feeling so at home walking around the campus and thinking that was what college was supposed to feel like." Caitlin said that she was impressed by the collegiality of the two House Deans leading a panel discussion on proposed changes to the College Houses, F&M's community learning system. "They were very willing to stay and answer prospective students' questions, and made me feel that I would be valued as a member of the F&M community if I chose to attend that school." But it was an email from a member of the F&M volleyball team, which Caitlin would later join, that cinched it for her. "Any institution whose students are willing to go that extra mile to reach out to prospective students has developed a community and culture that anyone would want to be a part of."

From its interactive learning/living design, to the 10-week long intensive summer research session that is sure to produce more than a few publications co-authored between students and faculty every year, F&M fosters amazing faculty-student relationships. Students also benefit from an extensive and well-connected alumni network—especially prominent in government, politics, and medicine. Here are a few of the ways that F&M creates an intimate and personalized educational experience.

Interactive Living

Instead of typical freshman dorms, F&M sorts freshmen into five distinctive "Houses." The Houses, which include rooms for seminars and dynamic common areas that function as meeting rooms and performance stages, "are designed to be a third space between the classroom and the residential experience" where "students [engage in] intellectual [activity] close to where they live," Stephen Medvic, professor of government, told us. F&M assigns students to their house based on the "interest they express for their first-year Connections course, a seminar-style learning environment." Connections offers everything from the standard fare of music composition and genetics, to more exotic options, like Civil War fictions, and Zeno's paradoxes, according to the school (more on "Connections" below).

Each house has its own distinct personality, complete with a "crest" designed by the house's founding residents, and each "receives a substantial annual budget that students may spend on social programs, décor, academic and community activities, special projects and more," according to the school. "Students disburse these funds through House governments that draft their own constitutions." The houses become a space where academics and social life mingle, where students use house funds to host dinners with artists and business leaders, produce plays and faculty-student publications, throw yard-sales to raise money for local nonprofits, and conduct research with faculty. Houses even inspire distinctive academic communities, such as the Junto Society, modeled after Benjamin Franklin's group of the same name, where members present papers they have written "on a topic of public interest and current debate for discussion by all members," or the Marshall Fellows Program, a kind of lab where "students think about and prepare for post-graduate opportunities," according to the college.

Caitlin Krutsick was a Junto member, and she told us, "After presenting your paper, the entire group of faculty and students discussed the paper and asks questions of the author about what he or she had found in the research. I wrote my paper on 'Big Ag' and how agribusiness affects the food in our supply chain, and therefore, our health. It was a rewarding experience to be able to dive into a topic outside of my major, and to hear from peers about topics that interested them. Sharing in dialogue often offers the best learning experiences, and Junto certainly shows the value of opening doors to have those conversations."

Faculty don't live on-site, but "[they keep their offices there] and teach classes over there, they come over to show a film in the evening," Dr. Medvic told us. "We are an active faculty so we are on campus not just to teach . . . but we're in our offices a lot even when we're outside of office hours. Students pop in all the time, if something occurs to them or they're walking down the hall. . . Students can pop in if they're nervous about job prospects or career choices." This is the kind of truly personal attention that is only available at a small college and that F&M has gone to great lengths to curate. Professor Kimberly M. Armstrong, a 26-year veteran in the Spanish department, said, "It is very hard to not have a relationship with a professor. My son is finishing his first year at a large university, and *not* one of his professors knows his name. I know the names of all the students who are in my classes by the end of the first week in class."

As a result, "[students] become a lot more independent," Dr. Medvic told us. "We pride ourselves on begin a rigorous, demanding school. A lot of times freshman get here and they're smart, they're capable, they're hardworking, but they just get overwhelmed right off the bat. And they should kind of feel that way. They won't have their sea legs yet. That means that they need direction figuring out how to stabilize everything, how to manage the workload, and how to find themselves." The F&M community works as a wonderful stabilizing force, so that by the time they leave, "they find an identity. They become much more independent when they leave here."

Making Connections

The F&M "Connections Curriculum" serves as the framework for the college's educational philosophy and embodies the spirit of a liberal arts educations: to explore how different fields relate to and inform one another while developing expertise in particular areas. In two phases—Connections 1 and Connections 2—the program first initiates students into the academic world through critical analysis, research, writing and civil debate. The rigor with which F&M develop these fundamental skills mean that grads really stand out in any field. Katie Rouff-Ward, Class of 1999, told us, "The curriculum at F&M was intense, and I had to work really hard, [but] F&M taught me how to write. I'm in finance now and I do not write that much, but when I do people are impressed." In the second Connections phase, students explore a wide array of subjects in the liberal arts and practice analyzing problems from multiple perspectives before selecting their major and concentration.

Many students develop personalized double- or joint-majors and can even design their own special studies major to fit their specific academic interests. This allows the school to award a huge variety of interdisciplinary degrees, like the "business, organizations and society-environmental studies" joint major or a "consumer behavior" special studies major. Students also pursue a rich variety of experiential learning opportunities, including internships, community-based learning programs, independent study, and faculty-led research.

In one such program, the Hackman Summer Scholars program, students receive "a stipend for sticking around here in the summer, living in Lancaster, and doing research with a faculty member," according to Dr. Medvic. It is a great time to capitalize on the relationships students build with faculty during the school year. The 10-week program allows students to focus on a specific problem and may even provide them with the opportunity to co-author a "publication in a peer-reviewed journal. Some students have had as many as six co-authored publications from their F&M research . . . and 40 percent of faculty publications are co-authored by students," the school tells us. In addition, 65 percent of students take one or more classes where they work one-on-one with faculty members. As a result, students develop even closer relationship with the faculty. Dr. Medvic explained, "We know our students very well. We interact with them a lot outside of the classroom. We have them over, especially our seniors who are graduating. We are mentoring them. Sometimes they are our research assistants. Essentially, we're friends by the time they are seniors."

Learning by Doing

66 I was involved in a student-run finance portfolio through the finance department. We were given a set amount of money from an alum and we are able to manage it. 99

A major component of the F&M educational philosophy is "learning by doing." Katie Rouff-Ward told us about some of the experiential learning opportunities she took part in throughout her F&M career. "I was involved in a student-run finance portfolio through the finance department . . . We were given a set amount of money from an alum and we were able to manage it." This experience put her in a good position to take on more responsibility when she moved on to internships at two different banks, including one that focused on investing, that ultimately helped her land top jobs in the financial industry. "I ended up getting a job with Prudential Investing through Career Services. Prudential had an accelerated management development program and that really launched my career. They came to F&M, and they hired two of us. It was twenty-eight college just-grads from all over the country. We did internships at Prudential and then at the end of the program we could pick where we wanted to be." And that wasn't the only opportunity; according to Katie, "a lot of companies came to campus. I was going to an interview every other day."

Katie told us that "the career services department has been completely revamped now" and has taken on new roles as the Office of Student and Post-Graduate Development (OSPGD), where she is involved as an alumna. OSPGD starts working with students the moment they walk in the door to develop fundamental career skills, like networking and financial literacy. It helps students secure internships and interviews with potential employers. "They have a boot camp for all seniors, where they do role plays, they work on interview skills, and resume writing," Katie told us. Sixty-one percent of students complete at least one summer internship during their time at F&M, and high-level alums like Katie are a huge support.

Caitlin Krutsick told us about two internships that she secured through the college and that helped her start her career at a policy think tank in D.C.: "The first was during the summer between my sophomore and junior years. I found an internship opportunity to work in the law office of an F&M alumnus through the alumni network database. His law firm was small, so my internship involved a lot of substantive work that I'm sure interns at large, corporate law firms would not get to have. Additionally, this alum was a commissioner for his township, so I also had the opportunity to do work for him in that capacity and gain exposure to local government operations."

Dr. Medvic told us that the government program that Caitlin studied in is one of the college's largest, with "a long and storied history of connecting people into the practical world of politics and governing." And part of that history is the Wise internships, "which give students a stipend [that pays for living expenses so that they can take an unpaid internship] and [. . .] live in D.C. or Harrisburg, the capital of Pennsylvania, to do work in government, politics, or something related to public affairs."

The college also has a robust selection of service learning opportunities that partner students with organizations that like the School District of Lancaster, where students volunteer as tutors, and "community-based learning courses that [work] with refugees," Dr. Medvic told us. These classes and opportunities help students discover interests they didn't know they had and connect with careers that can put those interests to work. "A lot of students," Dr. Medvic said, "learn that they are interested in criminal justice or the legal profession by taking a Public Health Course." The community-based learning class called Problem Solving Courts or Drug Courts "is kind of a joint effort between government and biology." Part of the public health major, the class is taught by a local judge, and "students [engage] with the local problem-solving court [through visits and interviews] with people who have gone through the system. It's a field that most of them never even thought of that maybe someday they want to be a judge or some kind of advocate in that system."

Faculty

Professor Armstrong told us that the faculty is deeply connected with the curriculum and professors have devoted years of careful study, planning and revision to developing a new Connections Curriculum, which, she said, has nearly completed its first year. "It has been an intensive and collaborative process that has been guided by faculty, not by the administration of the college . . . The faculty have the primary responsibility for creating, implementing and assessing the curriculum at F&M, and we take that charge very seriously."

They take their responsibility as academics seriously, too. The college told us that a "typical year would see more than $1 million in [faculty] grants, ten books, and seventy-five to one hundred peer-reviewed articles." With a student-faculty ratio of 9:1, intense contact with this stellar faculty is the biggest pull for most students. Professor Armstrong gave us a wide-angle overview of what that relationship looks like:

"By the second week we know who is fearless during class discussions and who needs a little bit of prompting. By the third week, we know who has been keeping up with the reading and homework. By the fourth week, we know who the strong and weak writers in the class are. We encourage those who need extra help to visit us during office hours. We send emails to students to encourage them to see us before the next paper so that we can discuss their topics. We recognize those students that are showing a talent for our disciplines and begin advising them about other classes that they might find interesting. We advise them and we talk to them about study abroad. We meet with them over coffee to discuss graduate school. For those students who have proven to be curious and smart and really responsible, we invite them to work with us on our research. These relationships are the hallmark of an F&M education."

Alumni/ae

F&M graduates have a reputation for their positions particularly in government, and count among their ranks Mary Schapiro, former chair of the U.S. Securities and Exchange Commission, Ken Mehlman, past director of the White House Office of Political Affairs and former chair of the Republican National Committee, members of the U.S. Congress as well as top aids, such as Kenneth Duberstein, who was President Reagan's Chief of Staff. "Our alumni are very committed and loyal to the college," Dr. Medvic told us, and that plays a huge role in integrating students into the job market. Caitlin Krutsick, for example, told us that an internship experience she had in the Office of U.S. Senator Bob Casey Jr. after graduating was "enhanced through alumni who also worked in that office." Caitlin also regularly attends D.C. networking events and hosts F&M externs whenever she can. "Particularly in Washington, D.C.," she said, "I think F&M has created an extensive alumni network full of successful and hardworking individuals that gives graduating students credibility as they go out in search of employment."

Dr. Medvic agrees that the opportunities for connections are huge. "It's easy to connect a student with an alum. If a student is interested in working for a non-governmental organization on hunger, for example, and I don't know somebody in the field, my colleagues and I are bound to find somebody who is doing some kind of related work and we connect them to that alum, who will 99 times out of 100 say they can give them an internship or some leads."

The George Washington University

2121 Eye Street, NW, Washington, DC 20052
Admissions: 202-994-6040
E-mail: gwadm@gwu.edu
Website: www.gwu.edu/undergraduate-admissions
Twitter: @GWadmissions, @GWtweets

Introduction

Named after America's first president, The George Washington University does indeed trace its roots to that famed founding father. When George Washington died, he left money for the creation of a national institution of higher education in the nation's capital of Washington, D.C. In 1821, Congress acted to create a university that, to quote GW, fulfilled "George Washington's vision of an institution in the nation's capital dedicated to educating and preparing future leaders." A mid-sized private university, GW's main campus sits right in the heart of D.C. in the Foggy Bottom neighborhood. GW has around 9,950 undergraduates and 15,000 graduate students. In fact, the university and its students view the city of D.C. as their campus. The White House, the National Mall, the Lincoln and Washington memorials, and other sites are only short walks away. There are foreign embassies and various government buildings around every corner. The university says GW "utilizes Washington, D.C., as an extended classroom unlike any university, where faculty members often hold classes in the U.S. Capitol, the Newseum, or the Folger Shakespeare Library."

As the university is located so close to the halls of power and centers of diplomacy and politics, it will come as no surprise that the school boasts one of the most politically active campuses in America. In fact, GW comes in at number one on The Princeton Review's 2016 ranking list for Most Politically Active Students. "There are a few students that hate politics, but they are definitely in the minority," one student says. Demonstrations and political campaigns are common on and off campus. As one recent alumna put it, students here "are known for being smart, internationally minded, and politically savvy." Students come to campus looking to change the world, and the university aims to create leaders that will shape futures. George Washington is a great choice for students who want a school with "a great reputation and a diverse student body" according to one recent alumna. The school attracts many international students as well as students from all sorts of areas and backgrounds in the United States. Current students confirm the school is "extremely diverse" and "essentially breeds you in professionalism from the very beginning."

A Culture of Service

Given its location, it's no surprise that GW is the kind of college that attracts students who want to change the world. Service and real-world engagement are a major part of GW's student culture—right from the very beginning. Each year GW hosts its annual Freshman Day of Service and Convocation event officially welcoming the incoming class in a day filled with engaging speakers and service projects throughout D.C. And this commitment to service grows during students' four years: Last year, students, faculty and staff logged a record 403,146 hours of community service. But it's not all work, all the time at GW: The university has several programs to engage students in events in and around Washington, D.C., including cultural and performing arts, professional sporting events, D.C. cook-offs, cultural celebrations on the National Mall, and D.C. neighborhood festivals and street markets. Freshmen are introduced to all this and more at Colonial Inauguration or CI, as it's called. Students and, if desired, their families gather on campus to meet with professors and other staff to get oriented and gain a jump-start on their social networks and relations to faculty. CI ensures that students will be prepared for the challenges and opportunities in the years ahead.

Columbian College of Arts & Sciences

With 53 majors and 61 minors to choose from, the Columbian College of Arts and Sciences is the intellectual and creative backbone of GW. Yet perhaps few majors are as popular or celebrated as political science. Students who have interests in politics and government will love the combination of rigorous academics, real-world expertise, and location by the United States government. As one student told us, "What political science major would pass up the chance to go toe to toe with protesters every week at the rallies outside the White House and Congress?" The political science department has over forty full-time professors. According to the school, "The majority of political science majors take advantage of being located in the nation's

❝ What political science major would pass up the chance to go toe to toe with protesters every week at the rallies outside the White House and Congress?❞

capital: Many students intern with members of Congress, the White House, NGOs, embassies, lobbying groups, and federal agencies. The department also offers five combined bachelor's/master's programs in political science, legislative affairs, public administration, public policy, and political management." If politics is your passion, there may be no better school than GW.

Elliott School of International Affairs

Another set of politically-minded students can be found at the Elliott School of International Affairs. This school, which is located right across the street from the U.S. Department of State, instructs about 2,000 undergraduates in four different majors: Asian studies, Middle Eastern studies, Latin American and Hemispheric studies, and international affairs. The international affairs major is then itself differentiated into about a dozen concentrations such as "Conflict Resolution," "Global Public Health," and "International Economics." The faculty is filled with foreign affairs professionals who can bring real-world experience into the classroom. The school encourages first-hand experience with other cultures, and a whopping 81 percent of Elliott School students study abroad during their time at GW.

School of Media and Public Affairs

Politics is hardly the only area at GW where future leaders are being trained. Within the School of Media and Public Affairs, faculty and students are working with various media platforms and creating innovative new work for the world. The Center of Innovative Media calls itself "a 21st Century Incubator for New Forms of Communication, Public Affairs, and Hands-On Learning." Examples include The Documentary Center, which teaches classes in documentary film making to both undergrads and graduate students and Planet Forward, which was featured on PBS, and is "a social network where creative and innovative ideas addressing global challenges are featured, discussed, and evaluated."

STEM and the Arts

When it comes to STEM-related fields and the arts, GW has been literally breaking new ground. Just opened in the beginning of 2015, GW's Science and Engineering Hall (SEH)—now the largest academic building dedicated to these fields in the nation's capital—is a brand-new, 500,000 square-foot complex that houses four specialized labs and many other spaces that will serve as the academic home for thousands of students. Working with some of the nation's most influential scientific organizations on discoveries and breakthroughs that impact everyone's lives, GW students and professors conduct original research in animal behavior, environmental engineering, nanotechnology and more. GW also recently expanded its arts education portfolio, becoming the new home of the Corcoran School of the Arts and Design, the only professional college of art and design in Washington, D.C. Plus, the brand new George Washington University Museum and The Textile Museum houses 20,000-plus artifacts from its collections, linking audiences, scholars and other cultural organizations, as well as creating numerous opportunities for learning and research.

Internships

Students come to GW to get involved, and there is no better way to do that than getting an internship in D.C. In fact, GW comes in at number one on The Princeton Review's 2015 ranking list for Best Schools for Internships, which was reported in the 2015 edition of our book *Colleges That Pay You Back*. No matter what your major, the city provides near-endless internship opportunities. From technology and health to the arts, non-profits and, yes, politics, GW students have literally thousands of options, and have landed coveted gigs with hundreds of illustrious organizations, including Discovery Communications, the National Institutes of Health (NIH), NASA, Google, and *The New Yorker*. Plus, through GW's Knowledge in Action Career Internship Fund (KACIF), students can earn grants up to $3,000 to offset an unpaid internship. A recent alumna, Elizabeth Edwards, explained what her own internship meant to her: "I had an incredible internship with the Victory Fund my sophomore year, which ultimately led to a staff position working on the Presidential Appointments Project, which helped give members of the LGBT community a voice in the government through the identification of LGBT professionals for presidential appointments by the Obama administration." Students regularly cite "opportunities for internships" as a major strength of the school. Professor Isabelle G. Bajeux-Besnainou, associate dean of undergraduate programs and professor of finance, said, "One of the many strengths of GW is the engagement of students in their community and their ability to leverage GW's location for internship opportunities in particular." With so many government agencies, major non-profits, and global institutions situated in D.C., students here can train for the future alongside the leaders of today.

Study Abroad

Studying and working in the nation's capital is not the only way GW helps train future leaders. The school has an acclaimed study abroad program and comes in at number seventeen on The Princeton Review's 2016 ranking list for Most Popular Study Abroad Program. GW students study abroad in over 375 programs in more than 60 countries around the world. According to the school, fully 50 percent of undergraduate students participate at some point in the study abroad program in their GW career. Plus, GW students' financial aid packages travel with them to approved programs, ensuring that cost is not a barrier to studying abroad. The university says its "academic success is built on the philosophy that learning does not—and should not—end at the edge of campus." The expansive study abroad program ensures that the learning doesn't just stop in the city either, but rather draws from the whole world. Among the most popular destinations for undergraduates are the United Kingdom, China, France, Italy, Chile, and Argentina.

Faculty

George Washington has a student to faculty ratio of 13:1, and boasts 2,226 faculty members, including 942 full-time and 1,284 part-time faculty members. Approximately 92 percent of full-time faculty members have the highest degree in their field. A little over 40 percent of professors are female and just under 20 percent of faculty members self-identify as minorities. According to the school, "GW's mission of educating citizen leaders is embodied by its renowned faculty, spread throughout ten colleges and schools, who can seamlessly blend theory and practice." The D.C. location gives students access not only to highly qualified professors, but also guest speakers of the highest caliber. One political science major gave a telling example: "I not only took a class on globalization and comparative politics, but then was able to go to a university event which featured Secretary of State Clinton and Secretary of Defense Gates as the speakers which gave further perspective to the issues I was studying." Professors here are passionate about both teaching and their fields in the real world. The university points out that the faculty here "is conducting groundbreaking research that not only creates new knowledge but also transforms policy that affects people in their daily lives. From Professor James Foster developing groundbreaking theories on global poverty and Dr. Akos Vertes's research efforts to thwart biochemical terror attacks to Dr. Sara Rosenbaum, who has literally written the book on the American health care system, GW often works directly with the world's top academic, industry and policy leaders at the forefront of discovery."

Life after GW

Since George Washington sits in the nation's capital surrounded by the institutions of government, it is no surprise that many notable alumni have gone into politics. The school boasts two former secretaries of state: John Foster Dulles and Colin Powell. First lady Jacqueline Kennedy Onassis attended the school and even has a dorm named after her. Several U.S. senators are alumni, including Mike Enzi from Wyoming, Harry Reid from Nevada, Mark Warner from Virginia, and J. William Fulbright from Arkansas. That is the same J. William Fulbright who created the Fulbright Program. Alumni from outside of politics include actress Kerry Washington, celebrity chef Ina Garten, and NBA coach Arnold "Red" Auerbach. To this day, the university continues to produce leaders and thinkers who go forth and help shape the world. GW alumni number more than 270,000 strong in more than 150 countries around the world, creating a vast network that current students can tap into. Plus, many illustrious companies and organizations, from Apple and Citigroup to the Smithsonian Institution, come to campus to recruit GW's best and brightest. Overall, 55 percent of 2014 graduates who participated in the graduation survey were employed within six months of graduation, and 21 percent were admitted to graduate school.

Gettysburg College

300 North Washington Street, Gettysburg, PA 17325-1484
Admissions: 717-337-6300
E-mail: admiss@gettysburg.edu
Website: www.gettysburg.edu
Twitter: @gettysburg, @GburgAdmissions, @GBurgCareers

Introduction

It should come as no surprise that Gettysburg College, in such close proximity to the ground where Lincoln delivered his Gettysburg Address, should place such a strong emphasis on leadership. Gettysburg's curriculum stresses the themes of multiple inquiries, integrative thinking, communication skills, and finally, informed citizenship—themes underscored by the college's emphasis on preparing global citizens. The curriculum was designed in large part by the faculty, who felt that "instead of the traditional sense of breadth and depth, [Gettysburg should] also stress interconnectedness and multidisciplinarity."

❝ Life at Gettysburg is focused on the community as a whole. ❞

Gettysburg offers their freshmen a series of first-year seminars called the Burg program. First-year students take field trips, screen films, sponsor speakers, and hold discussions that merge coursework, current events, and personal interests. They also live together in themed residence halls along with student taking similar first-year seminars. While the principle seems rather simple, Gettysburg finds that Burg participation increases opportunities for conversation with faculty and staff, intellectual discussions outside the classroom, diverse peer interactions, and attendance at campus lectures and cultural events. During orientation, first-year students, together with faculty, staff, upperclassmen, and local community members, participate in the First-Year Walk. Now a time-honored campus tradition, this walk recreates the 1863 walk to the Gettysburg National Cemetery that Gettysburg College students took with Abraham Lincoln on the day he delivered the Gettysburg Address. The first-year class hears a distinguished speaker deliver the Gettysburg Address and remarks just a few feet away from where Lincoln gave his speech.

But the Burg program is only the beginning. Here is a sampling of Gettysburg's distinctive programs that encourage students to enhance their leadership skills and make the most out of their involvement both on campus and in the community.

The Garthwait Leadership Center

A biology major notes, "Life at Gettysburg is focused on the community as a whole. We're really into diversity, equity, and inclusion, and further exploring what those words actually mean." These thoughts tend to echo throughout the student body, one that is "active in the community, interested in many different things, willing to share their passions, and supportive of their peers." With a strong alumni network, and many networking opportunities through the Garthwait Leadership Center, Gettysburg does its best to show you that graduation does not mean that this community will leave you behind. As a new department within the college's College Life Division, the GLC has enhanced a tradition of leadership at Gettysburg, helping students and alumni recognize their potential as leaders and their responsibility to serve. It offers an individualized leadership certificate program that serves as a strong connection to integrating and articulating one's leadership experience within the context of a career plan, and, through collaborative partnerships across the institution, creates intellectual and experiential opportunities for students and alumni to develop leadership skills.

Leadership Training

To begin with, the Emerging Leaders Retreat is an annual leadership experience designed for first-year and sophomore students who are interested in developing their leadership knowledge and skills. The program, which is delivered off campus, is designed to provide a rich learning experience regardless of whether or not you hold a formal leadership position.

Then there's the Leadership Institute: a semester-long, seminar-style leadership experience which explores leadership through social justice issues and culminates with a week-long immersion project at the end of the spring semester at an off campus site. The intent of the program is to illustrate the potential that individuals have to create and attain positive and sustainable social change in the world today. The program has partnered with the Center for Public Service and the Eisenhower Institute to coordinate an experience to challenge participants to think critically about civil rights and leadership and to act intentionally in addressing the social injustices of the 21st century, by taking participants through an intensive, yet exciting journey in which historic examples of leadership in the 1950–1960s American Civil Rights movement and the legacy of President Eisenhower are examined, specifically through the Little Rock Nine. The program consists of learning workshops, lunch discussions, social issues dialogues, one-on-ones with the leadership mentors, and an all-expenses paid immersion trip to Abilene, Kansas and Little Rock, Arkansas. The Leadership Institute's goal is to equip participants with tools to actively challenge the social injustices through both an individual and a unified voice, and of course modeling the way for the present and future generations.

Mentorship

And, for those concerned with their future today, the Alumni Mentor Retreat is an annual leadership experience for seniors who are interested in learning from alumni about how to apply the knowledge and skills they have learned at Gettysburg after graduation. The retreat helps participants reflect on their Gettysburg leadership experience through meaningful conversation with several successful alumni. Participants identify ways to apply the skills learned in college that will empower them to achieve success in the workplace, graduate study, their family, and their community.

Emphasizing its commitment to a strong sense of community, the GLC offers recent graduates the Young Alumni Leadership Program. A mentoring experience for individuals interested in developing their leadership ability, young alumni who apply for the program are assigned a mentor who supports and challenges them to develop and implement a personal leadership plan, designed to broaden their leadership ability, and demonstrating that the Gettysburg experience does not end after graduation.

Additionally, this year Gettysburg has excitedly announced the Women's Leadership Track of the Leadership Certificate program, offering participants the opportunity to develop their leadership skills and explore issues related to women.

The Eisenhower Institute

The college's close distance to Washington, D.C. provides students with an all-access-pass to leading policy makers through the college's Eisenhower Institute. Honoring the legacy of Dwight D. Eisenhower, the Eisenhower Institute is a distinguished center for leadership and public policy that prepares successive generations to perfect the promise of the nation.

A distinctive program of Gettysburg College, the Institute has offices in the heart of the nation's capital and in the historic Gettysburg home once occupied by Dwight and Mamie Eisenhower, and combines top-level dialogue among policy-makers with a premier learning experience for undergraduates, and is home to both resident and non-resident fellows that have expertise in a variety of fields, including energy, nuclear nonproliferation, foreign relations, Middle East affairs, U.S. politics, the U.S. presidency, economics, international security, and environmental sustainability.

Students may participate in semester-long programs through the Institute, ranging from Inside Politics with EI's Expert-in-Residence Kasey Pipes, Strategy and Leadership in Transformational Times with Susan Eisenhower, and Women in Leadership with Jennifer Donahue, the Public Information Officer for the Supreme Judicial Court of Massachusetts, to their year-long Undergraduate Fellowship program. Each of these experiences offers unparalleled access to Washington insiders and lessons in leadership with an eye to politics, advocacy, and public policy.

The Civil War Institute

Being just a mile from the historic battlefield where Lincoln delivered his unforgettable address, Gettysburg's Civil War Institute uses an interdisciplinary approach to engage diverse audiences in a dialogue about the Civil War. It offers an undergraduate minor in Civil War Era Studies, the Gettysburg Semester (an entire immersion semester in Civil War studies at Gettysburg), and provides numerous educational opportunities for Gettysburg College students such as the Civil War Institute fellows program and the Brian C. Pohanka Fellowships, as well as assisting students with internships and other professional opportunities in the National Parks, preservation agencies, heritage tourism associations, and the museum community at large. Gettysburg even offers a unique minor in Civil War era studies, which is enhanced by the CWI's hands-on programs.

The Sunderman Conservatory

look no further than The Sunderman Conservatory of Music as evidence of Gettysburg's strong offerings in the arts. A conservatory embedded in a rich intellectual community, Sunderman is, according the college, "a place of synergy and energy, of concertos and calculus, symphonies and science, history and harmonies, gamelan and German." An exceptional faculty of artists and scholars, and opportunities that range from residencies with internationally-renowned guest artists and lecturers each semester to musical experiences abroad for a semester or a summer make Sunderman one of the most distinctive undergraduate music options available. Gettysburg College offers a Bachelor of Music in Performance, a Bachelor of Music Education, and a Bachelor of Arts with a Major in Music with the option for a double major. Additionally, the Conservatory benefits from the college's proximity to major metropolitan areas like D.C., New York City, Philadelphia, and Baltimore with expert faculty and a robust artist-in-residence program.

Real World Experience

> **❝ Our students travel with us off campus to observe the heavens, take part in world-class experiments at national laboratories, and present research at huge conferences. ❞**

Gettysburg College is one of only four liberal arts colleges that landed on The Princeton Review's 2015 ranking list of the Best Schools for Internships, which was reported in the 2015 edition of our book *Colleges That Pay You Back*.. The GLC, Eisenhower and Civil War Institutes all provide multiple real world experiences with practiced professionals, giving students a leg up, and a hand to guide them along the way. Dr. Sharon Stephenson, Professor and Chair of Physics, notes that "[our] students travel with us off campus to observe the heavens, take part in world-class experiments at national laboratories, present research at huge conferences. Teach for America hires our students, our Fulbright students work to teach science to kids in Cameroon, others teach peace through basketball in South Africa."

Faculty

Gettysburg's more than 190 faculty members boast an impressive record of achievement as teachers and as scholars. Nearly 100 percent have a doctorate or the highest degree in their field. The faculty is the living embodiment of the Gettysburg experience of a devotion to leadership within the community at large. A prime example is English professor Chris Fee, who stepped up when the state cut funding for a crucial after-school elementary program. He worked with other administrators on campus and the local community to provide limited financial support to transport student volunteers to and from the elementary school, in addition to providing a healthy after-school snack for the children. (The program has continued as a part of Dr. Fee's class on rural poverty, offered each spring semester.) And of the nearly 600 sections of courses offered, just over 70 of them consist of classes allowing 30 or more students. In fact, nearly 400 sections contain fewer than 20 students.

Dr. Stephenson notes, "Faculty come to Gettysburg College because we believe in the mission of liberal arts education. We believe that the intellectual life creates better citizens and also that the intellectual life extends beyond the classroom. We spend LARGE amounts of time outside of class with our students." Dr. Stephen Gimbel, chair of the philosophy department, says, "The students who do well at Gettysburg are those who keep from trapping themselves in a narrow band of intellectual experience. We take the notion of liberal arts seriously.

Einstein played his violin daily, kept active in politics, and read philosophy. We see education not as a narrow set of training exercises, but as a set of interconnected experiences—curricular and co-curricular—that allow students to shape themselves into broad and well-rounded people who can bring multiple lenses to see the world around them."

Alumni/ae

In terms of their graduates, "what is fascinating is the wide range of paths they take. We have some who take traditional routes like graduate school or law school, but we have airline pilots, FBI agents tracking down fraud in war zones, acupuncturists, members of the clergy, Teach for America and Peace Corps members, archivists and librarians, people working to feed the hungry and helping abandoned animals," says Dr. Gimbel. A recent alum notes that students choose Gettysburg "for the sense of community and individualized attention it offered as a small college; for its strong writing program with accomplished writers on faculty; for the opportunity to participate in music programs at the Sunderman Conservatory as a non-major; and for the internship and externship experiences offered through its alumni network."

Harvey Mudd College

301 Platt Boulevard, Claremont, CA 91711
Admissions: 909-621-8011
E-mail: admission@hmc.edu
Website: www.hmc.edu
Twitter: @harveymudd

Introduction

Harvey Mudd College, one of the premier engineering, science, and mathematics colleges in the country, educates engineers, scientists, and mathematicians who are leaders in their fields and who understand the impact of their work on society. It's a mission that resonates with Harvey Mudd students, who appreciate the school's unique combination of STEM disciplines and liberal arts requirements. One mathematical and computational biology major values the "broad education in the sciences as well as in non-technical subjects. And the opportunity to learn in the company of some of the greatest people ever." Harvey Mudd offers a Bachelor of Science with majors in biology, chemistry, computer science, engineering, mathematics, physics; an Independent Study Program; off-campus majors; and joint programs in chemistry and biology, computer science and mathematics, and mathematical and computational biology.

Harvey Mudd is a small school, with only 800 students (one engineering major who took our survey referred to the school as "the most interesting place you have never heard of"), but as a member of The Claremont Colleges, it provides students with many more resources and class options than its size would suggest. "I have the chance to study world class engineering as well as be able to take art classes on the other campuses, which is a rare thing to have access to in an engineering college," another engineering major explained.

With its curriculum that affords a broad perspective on STEM disciplines, an honor code enforced by students, and stellar opportunities for undergraduate research, Harvey Mudd provides students with the autonomy and real-world experiences that they need to succeed after college.

The Common Core

Harvey Mudd requires a unique combination of coordinated courses in all the STEM disciplines—biology, chemistry, computer science, engineering, math and physics—as well as classes in academic writing and critical inquiry. The Core gives students a solid foundation in STEM courses and highlights the relationships between them. Not surprisingly, this focus on STEM disciplines attracts science-minded students. "Mudd is basically a school of science nerds, and being around people who think like-mindedly to me was important in my college decision. I love that at Mudd I can make a science joke and the people around me get it, and I love that everyone is as dedicated to science, and as hard working as I am," a mathematical and computational biology major told us.

Harvey Mudd isn't just about STEM classes, though. In keeping with its mission to educate scientists who understand the implications of their work on society, Harvey Mudd also requires one quarter of students' coursework be in the humanities, social sciences, and the arts. The students certainly appreciate this approach. One undeclared major explained, "Given how much groundbreaking work is being done in interdisciplinary fields, I liked the idea of a sort of 'liberal sciences' degree—one where I'd really be getting breadth before and while digging into one particular subject." Another student agreed, explaining that the school "has a good math and science program, but also ensures its students are educated in the humanities and social sciences." "I wanted a strong liberal arts education AND a strong STEM education, and Harvey Mudd was one of the few places where I could have both," a physics major explained. The faculty designed the Core, and any revisions to the curriculum require full faculty approval.

Of course, this broad focus leads to quite a lot of work for students. One mathematical and computational biology major went so far as to call the school "horrifyingly challenging at times." At the same time, the majority of students we surveyed recognized the value in all that hard work. "The brutal work fosters an extremely collaborative environment where people focus not on the grade they get but the learning behind it," a student double majoring in economics and engineering told us. The Academic Excellence program—which trains upperclassmen to lead workshops helping first years and sophomores with the Core curriculum—is a perfect example of this kind of supportive community.

Students and graduates alike recognize the value of Harvey Mudd's emphasis on hard work. Glen Hastings, the Business Operations Manager at Facebook, who graduated in 1993 with a BS in Chemistry, explained how his time at Harvey Mudd impacted his career: "My career trajectory was shaped by Mudd initially through the specific jobs that I had immediately post-graduation which leveraged the chemistry and engineering that I learned at Mudd. Subsequent to that, the elements of hard work, intellectual curiosity, and the confidence to learn that were fostered at Mudd shaped my decision to go to business school, transition to consulting, and then move on to strategy and analytics at Yahoo and Facebook."

The Honor Code

66 My career trajectory was shaped by Mudd initially through the specific jobs that I had immediately post-graduation, which leveraged the chemistry and engineering that I learned at Mudd. 99

The students we surveyed raved about the strong community at their school. "The professors are friendly and are truly interested in helping, and the students are always ready to take a break from their own studying to make sure you understand a concept you are struggling with," a computer science major informed us. Other students describe the community as "close knit" and "incredibly welcoming," while one engineering major explained, "I love the Mudd community. Everyone is so welcoming and the environment is very cooperative. I really enjoy that I can work with other students on anything, and that the professors are so readily available. Everyone is there to help each other succeed, and it shows!"

Faculty, as well, appreciate the close-knit community at Harvey Mudd. Dr. Kerry K. Karukstis, chair of the Chemistry Department and the Ray and Mary Ingwersen Professor of Chemistry, told us, "The collaborative environment that exists among students and between faculty and students enhances both the teaching and learning enterprises. Being part of a faculty community that values collegiality and shared governance is an enormously energizing experience."

Part of what has created such a strong community at Harvey Mudd is its Honor Code, an important aspect of student self-governance at the school. The Honor Code is a pledge all students take when entering the College to act as responsible individuals, to conduct themselves with honesty and integrity both personally and academically and to respect the rights of others. Students are also given leadership positions in the school related to the Honor Code, serving as judiciary board chair, disciplinary board chair, appeals board chairs, appeals board representatives, and honor board representatives. Many students, including one computer science major we surveyed, cited the honor code as among the schools biggest strengths, and a double mathematics and computer science major told us, "With the honor code, everyone trusts one another and not only that— they care about one another." This code, Dr. Karukstis informed us, "enable[s] students to develop the values associated with ethical scientific conduct."

The Claremont Colleges

Harvey Mudd is one of five liberal arts colleges and two graduate schools that share academic and administrative resources as part of The Claremont Colleges. While students appreciate Harvey Mudd's small size and the close relationships with classmates and faculty that it promotes, they are also grateful for their college's participation in the consortium, which affords the school the resources of a much larger college. "Even though the [school] is small, there are four other undergrad colleges and two other grad schools all next to each other (often across the street), so we still get the feel of a 'mid-size' college," a computer science and mathematics major explained. One undeclared major explained his reasoning for attending Harvey Mudd: "I wanted to attend a small school, and I like . . . access to classes/programs at the other Claremont Colleges."

The resources available to students within the consortium are considerable. Students at Harvey Mudd are able to take classes at any of the colleges (including select courses at the Claremont Graduate University), enjoy meals at each of the seven dining halls, and have access to four fitness centers and five swimming pools. All five of the colleges in the consortium share adjacent campuses, so walking between the schools takes no more than fifteen minutes. Outside of classes, The Claremont Colleges regularly host concerts, guest lecturers and speakers, cultural events, art exhibits, film screenings, career fairs, plays and sporting events that are open to students from all of the colleges, and over half of the clubs and organizations at the colleges are open to all students.

Research Opportunities

As a strictly undergraduate institution, Harvey Mudd offers research opportunities that many students wouldn't expect to find until graduate school. "It is an undergraduate institution, so the focus is all on undergrads. We get all the research positions, on-campus jobs, etc.," a computer science and mathematics major told us. An engineering student cited the "small community [and] lots of research opportunities," as the main reasons he chose to attend the school. After just one year of coursework, students have the opportunity to become full research collaborators, working directly with faculty rather than graduate students or post-docs.

Students also may pursue paid research opportunities through the Summer Undergraduate Research Program, during which they partner with faculty to explore a topic of mutual interest. Roughly 200 students—a quarter of the student body—take part in the summer program. Beyond these optional experiences, the college also requires either a capstone research or Clinic Program experience, providing all students with real-world research or design experience.

In the Clinic Program, juniors and seniors work in small groups with a faculty adviser in partnership with a corporate client. Students work together to present solutions to real-world, technical problems for their client. These projects run from September through May, and involve 1,200 to 1,500 hours of work, giving students valuable experience before graduation. It is no wonder that many students identified the "many opportunities for students to do research or pursue internships" as a major asset.

Faculty

There are eighty-nine tenured or tenure track faculty at Harvey Mudd, all of whom hold PhDs or an equivalent degree in their fields. The school's small size leads to a 9:1 student to faculty, a benefit that isn't lost on the students we surveyed. A chemistry major told us, "I wanted to go to a small school where I could really interact with professors," while a mathematics and computer science major cited "close contact with professors" as a key strength of the school.

Beyond being available, faculty members at Harvey Mudd really care about their students. "Undergraduate education is our No. 1 priority, and everything we do is student-centered. We pride ourselves on close student-faculty interactions both in the classroom and beyond," Dr. Karukstis said. Students agree. "The professors at our school are all excellent and are all incredibly smart, and are always willing to help you if you come in with questions or even just want to chat. The professors are part of the reason why Harvey Mudd is so great and successful," a physics major told us, while a computer science major added, "The professors at Harvey Mudd are enthusiastic and truly care about their students. They aren't just interested in delivering facts; in addition, they relate concepts to their real-world applications, showing students how the material they learn now can be used in their future work." Finally, an undeclared major shared, "The professors are extremely competent, knowledgeable, and successful at what they do. But even more than that, they are jumping at the opportunity to help students and are the most helpful and kind people I've ever met. I'm blown away by the quality of my courses and amazed by how much I've learned in a single semester."

The faculty at Harvey Mudd is 62 percent male and 38 percent female, which is one of the highest percentages of female professors at any STEM-focused school in the United States. The college puts a high value on encouraging diverse students to pursue STEM fields. The student body is nearly gender balanced with 46 percent female and 54 percent male students. The computer science department faculty worked together in 2006 to redesign the computer science curriculum to make it more engaging and supportive of women; in the four years after these changes were made, the percentage of female computer science majors at Harvey Mudd jumped from 10 percent to 40 percent, the highest of any co-ed college in the nation. Harvey Mudd now averages about 40 percent female computer science majors annually.

Alumni/ae

Graduates from Harvey Mudd are hard working and adaptable team members, and potential employers know it. Mr. Hastings relayed to us something he'd been told by a fellow Harvey Mudd graduate: "If you have an MIT grad and a Caltech grad on a team, you have two smart people. If you add a Mudder, you have much more than three smart people. The Mudder simply makes the team better than the sum of its parts."

The school says that 60 percent of Harvey Mudd seniors enter the workforce after graduation and close to 40 percent go on to graduate school. For every major offered at Harvey Mudd, the Office of Career Services provides career monographs to show the relationship between major and career. Students can see at a glance what employers have hired Harvey Mudd graduates within their major, what job titles have been secured, and where graduates have been accepted to graduate school. (Take a look at: www.hmc.edu/career-services. The diversity of career paths may surprise you.)

Mr. Hastings, who majored in chemistry, valued the real-world experience he gained through summer research, the Clinic Program, and working as a student grader. Students we surveyed also mentioned work grading and tutoring as valuable experiences during their undergraduate careers. Beyond the experiences they gain during college, students can also rely on an active alumni network once they graduate. "There are a number of alumni at my company and in the Silicon Valley and I often attend social events in the area. I currently do not recruit students, but I set up the alumni LinkedIn group and assist the career services office with networking and outreach," Mr. Hastings told us.

Haverford College

370 Lancaster Avenue, Haverford, Pennsylvania 19041
Admissions: 610-896-1350
E-mail: admission@haverford.edu
Website: www.haverford.edu
Twitter: @haverfordedu

Introduction

❝ You come to school, and Haverford gets you to ask yourself: What am I passionate about, and how am I going to fulfill that passion?❞

With its close proximity to the busy metropolis of Philadelphia and its small student body—enrollment is approximately 1,200—Haverford embodies a friendly community that encourages its students to not only dream big but to achieve big things. Founded in 1833 by the Religious Society of Friends, the school is no longer affiliated with a religious institution but its Quaker roots still show. As award-winning playwright Ken Ludwig, a 1972 Haverford alumnus, puts it, Haverford students are "known for their tremendous integrity and good fellowship. I think we acquired some strong Quaker virtues at Haverford—regardless of our personal religions—that never left us." The Quaker values of intellectual freedom and tolerance still resonate at Haverford, where students take charge of their own academic future and are encouraged to work collaboratively with each other and with the dedicated faculty. In keeping with the close-knit feel of a small liberal arts school, the majority of the courses at Haverford are taught seminar style, rather than as larger lectures, to foster intellectual debate and discussion. From anthropology to physics, there are academic pursuits available to satisfy a wide range of interests. "You come to school, and Haverford gets you to ask yourself: What am I passionate about, and how am I going to fulfill that passion?" a recent alumna tells us. While there's a drive among the student body to do great things both in the classroom and beyond, one political science major underscores that "Haverford has a way of changing all of us, quietly reminding us that the way forward is not through others, but with others, and that personal drive and ambition is fully compatible with an unhesitating desire to help others."

Academics

Haverford is known for its rigorous academics. As one student, major still undecided, puts it, "Haverford is all about academic integrity. Students are there to learn, not to compete with one another." A liberal arts education encourages students to learn from not just one but many disciplines, and it's this school of thought that drives Haverford's curricular requirements. All students must take a one-semester or year-long writing seminar as freshmen, a course that will serve as a foundation for their later studies, whether in the hard sciences or the visual arts. Since Haverford recognizes that the world is ever-expanding and the school wants its graduates to be prepared to meet challenges outside the comforts of the Pennsylvania campus, all students are also required to complete two semesters of college-level study of a language other than English by the end of junior year. For students eager to take advantage of one of Haverford's study abroad programs, it's the perfect opportunity to explore a new country and learn a new language at the same time. Every student at Haverford, regardless of major, is enabled to complete a senior thesis, which represents the culmination of his or her time at Haverford and, since there is no graduate program at Haverford, often gives students the opportunity to conduct graduate-level research while still an undergrad, under the supervision (and with the encouragement), of the faculty. Senior theses range from the hard sciences, such as tracing the origins of antibiotic resistance, to the humanities, where students have applied their linguistic training to parsing the J.R.R. Tolkien's languages in The Lord of the Rings series and studied the role of working women during the Second World War. Balancing strong academics with the school's progressive ideals, one psychology major says that "Haverford values academic excellence with a strong emphasis on social justice and mutual respect between students and professors." The professors, many of whom are on a first-name basis with their students and often host dinners at their on-campus houses, also cite this shared respect between students and faculty. Says one Haverford chemistry professor, "I learn new things all the time through interacting with my students, and that is certainly also the case for many of my non-science colleagues, whose scholarly interests are always enriched through interacting with inquisitive, hard-working, and critical Haverford students."

The Honor Code

One aspect of Haverford life, both social and academic, that sets it apart from other colleges is the Honor Code. Students and administrators are quick to point out that it's not a set of rules—that, in fact, is the antithesis of the Honor Code—but rather "an articulation of ideals and expectations emphasizing genuine connection and engagement with one another, and the creation of an atmosphere of trust, concern, and respect." Instituted in 1896, the Honor Code is one of Haverford's oldest traditions and one that is founded, like so much else at the college, on mutual respect. It is completely student-run and is re-ratified each year by the student body. The students are also in complete control of the school's $400,000 activities budget and all decisions on how and when to spend the funds are voted on by consensus; students don't just have a vote at Haverford, they have *the* vote. The Honor Council is comprised of sixteen Haverford students, four from each class, who are elected for either semester- or year-long terms. The council meets once a week and students may email questions and concerns to be discussed during those meetings directly to the council, as well as potential violations of the Honor Code. Unique features under the Honor Code system include take-home, self-timed exams. As one biology major puts it, the Honor Code "allows for an incredibly trusting and comfortable environment where the students are trusted to be honest and have good values. The final exams are all self-scheduled or take-home, and when students take in-class tests, the professor leaves the room, trusting the students to be honest." This fosters an environment not of cutthroat collegiate competition but of intellectual curiosity and debate. A 1981 Haverford graduate in molecular biology who's currently a doctor working for a biopharmaceutical company, credits the "rigorous academic experience" at his alma mater and says that Haverford graduates are known for their "high integrity as a result of the four years of honor code self-governance."

The College Consortium

Haverford students have the opportunity to take advantage of not only all the academic offerings at Haverford but also to sign up to take classes at the three other nearby institutions that make up a four-college consortium called The Quaker Consortium: Swarthmore, Bryn Mawr, and the University of Pennsylvania. This allows students to retain the "small town" feel of Haverford while enjoying the "big city" opportunities available to them through classes, internships, and other out of the classroom experiences offered at consortium schools. All students participate in the Tri-College Consortium—Haverford, Bryn Mawr, and Swarthmore—meaning that everyone is able to take classes at all three of these "sibling schools" and the students at each often collaborate and engage in friendly competition, particularly in an annual event known as the Tri-Co Hackathon, a two-day marathon of brainstorming and computer coding. Participants are split into 10 teams who race feverishly through 48 hours—and countless slices of pizza—to devise new software, or mobile apps, to tackle everything from cleaner air to a more user-friendly course guide for Tri-College students. More than 2000 students cross-registered at Haverford and Bryn Mawr—the latter is only a mile from the Haverford campus—and there are 2.5 billion shared volumes in the colleges libraries. This particularly close relationship between Haverford and Bryn Mawr is affectionately known as the "Bi-Co," short for Bi-College, and allows students who cross-register—a very common occurrence as evidenced by the fact that it has its own term and nickname—to live on either campus and eat at the dining hall of their choosing, either at Haverford or Bryn Mawr, along with more academic decisions, like where to pursue their major.

In cooperation with the nearby University of Pennsylvania, Haverford offers two degree partnership programs that allow students to complete both their bachelor's and master's degrees on an accelerated schedule. In the first, known as the 4+1 Bioethics Program, students study for four years at Haverford, where their receive a bachelor's degree, followed by one year at Penn's Bioethics Program in the Perelman School of Medicine, where they receive a Master's in Bioethics (MBE). This combined program means streamlined admission for qualified Haverford students to Penn's prestigious Perelman School straight from undergrad. The 4+1 Engineering Program, requires students to complete four years of study at Haverford, where they'll earn a Bachelor of Science, followed by one year at Penn, where they'll earn a Master's of Engineering. Haverford is the first liberal arts school to enter into such an arrangement with an Ivy League engineering program.

Academic Centers

Haverford is home to three academic centers: the Center for Peace and Global Citizenship (CPGC), the John B. Hurford '60 Center for the Arts and Humanities (HCAH), and the Marian E. Koshland Integrated Natural Sciences Center (KINSC). The mission of the CPGC is to integrate innovative scholarship and civic engagement both inside the classroom and out in the world at large. Founded in 1999, the CPCG strives to provide opportunities for students during the academic year as well as during the summer, along with maintaining a network of social justice resources and running a campus café. A 2008 Haverford graduate in political science stressed the importance of one of her summer CPGC grants, a program that she explains has grown since her time at Haverford: "Twenty people were given a grant to intern with some sort of social justice oriented non-profit or company that really can't afford to offer a paid internship. Haverford didn't want us to lose the opportunity to take that internship, so they would fund it for you." A current Growth and Structure of Cities major echoes the importance of CPGC funding, adding that the "Center for Peace and Global Citizenship funds dozens of students for international and domestic internships related to social justice every year and sponsor conferences, faculty and student research regularly . . . it has allowed me to finance internships that I would not have been able to do on my own."

The Hurford Center supports the artistic ambitions of Haverford students and staff through art exhibitions, performances, lectures, symposia, writing and reading groups, artist residencies, and other visual and cultural programming. In an attempt to bring a more diverse culture to the Haverford campus, the HCAH reaches out to a wide range of artists and performers. HCAH gives students and faculty the time and space to host lectures and seminars, as well as exhibits and art residencies, which are organized by faculty and supported by the HCAH's Exhibitions and Mellon Creative Residency Programs. Exhibitions range from explorations of Latin American destructivism to a workshop on making your own 'zine.

In keeping with the interdisciplinary tradition that forms the backbone of Haverford, The Marian E. Koshland Integrated Natural Sciences Center (KINSC) does for scientific inquiry what HCAH and CPGC do for the arts and social justice, respectively. A place for students and faculty with an interest in the natural sciences to come together, the KINSC encourages Haverford students to pursue scientific questions beyond the classroom. The departments that make up the KINSC—astronomy, biology, chemistry, computer science, mathematics and statistics, physics, and psychology—get supplemental support from the center in order to facilitate interdisciplinary dialogue and collaborations, both within the sciences themselves and between other departments throughout the college. As with the other academic centers at Haverford, with which the KINSC cooperates, the KINSC helps fund student projects that take them outside the confines of Haverford to explore larger scientific questions that may have a more global impact.

Faculty

The experience at Haverford is designed to maximize the amount of time students spend in direct collaboration with faculty. In fact, 61 percent of faculty live on campus. This close proximity means that faculty attend their students' concerts, art shows, and athletic events and that the majority of students will get asked over for dinner at some point during their time in school. A professor of chemistry says, "As the Faculty Athletic Representative, I often talk to students about their most recent games or how their teams are doing, and I attend many on-campus athletic events. I run an active research group that includes students from all levels, and we have regular group meetings that are either in the Science Center or at my house." From this handy vantage point, what kind of student does well here? One professor answers, "Close interaction with faculty helps to identify students' interests and acumen for specific areas and kinds of problems, but students who are able to begin to think about these things for themselves get the most out of our very personalized academic system. My hope for all of my students is that they will learn to 'follow their own noses' into challenging and interesting areas for them; many of our most successful students have some sense of how to do this soon after they arrive on campus." And a professor of biology, adds, "The students here are incredibly bright, intellectually and technically fearless, and idealistic. If a student is curious and deeply interested, they will enjoy being at Haverford."

Life After Haverford

With so many choices of majors and opportunities to take courses at neighboring schools, it's no wonder that some of the only unifying characteristics of Haverford alumni are that they are prepared and successful. Ken Ludwig, a 1972 double major in English and music theory and composition, credits his time at Haverford—where he wrote librettos for school shows and studied Shakespeare—with his success in graduate school—he went on to earn degrees from Harvard (where he studied under Leonard Bernstein) and Cambridge. Ludwig knew that Haverford was the right place for him after his first visit to the campus: "In addition to having the best academics I had ever seen [it] was a very human place—a caring place—where I would feel happy." While Ludwig's career trajectory can be traced back to his time at Haverford, other graduates found themselves taking advantage of Haverford's myriad liberal arts offerings, trying their hand at numerous careers before deciding on something that might not have even crossed their minds without certain experiences they had during college. One political science graduate from 2008 underscores how much her undergraduate experience at Haverford meant to her in her post-college life, particularly when she found herself following a different path than she originally envisioned for herself: "The best part of the Haverford experience is that is allows you to be malleable. A liberal arts degree doesn't say that this person has to do one thing: I've gone from being a teacher, to academic consultant, and now a business development manager for a big corporation. My experience has let me be nimble."

❝ The students here are incredibly bright, intellectually and technically fearless, and idealistic.❞

Hobart and William Smith Colleges

629 South Main Street, Geneva, NY 14456
Admissions: 800-852-2256
E-mail: admissions@hws.edu
Website: http://www.hws.edu/
Twitter: @HWSColleges

Introduction

❝ I did not want to be a number in a classroom; I wanted to be a person. ❞

Located in the Finger Lakes region of New York, Hobart and William Smith Colleges provide students with a small and incredibly supportive community; there are 2,421 undergraduates attending the Colleges, where the average class size is 18 students. Students love the sense of inclusiveness at HWS. As one geoscience major told us about her reasons to attend HWS: "I did not want to be a number in a classroom; I wanted to be a person." "As soon as I got on campus it felt like 'my people' were here," a sociology major added. Students who are attracted to HWS include those who are interested in developing their own approach to their education, as the school's popular interdisciplinary curriculum allows. They are also willing to make a commitment to community service: The Colleges report that 100 percent of students engage in some kind of community service, service learning, or community based research. In the 2013–2014 academic year, HWS students completed more than 80,000 hours of service, and in 2014 the Colleges were listed for the fifth consecutive year in the President's Higher Education Community Service Honor Roll by the Corporation for National and Community Service (CNCS).

What kind of student does well here? The faculty we spoke to were unanimous that, in the words of Dr. Jack Harris, "we work with students where they are." This is a school that specializes in community, ensuring no student is lost "but rather nurtured and mentored." Dr. Harris, a professor of anthropology and sociology, told us, "I have often felt that any school can do well with bright independent achievers, and we have many of those." Still, he added, "We certainly excel in motivating the bright high school underachiever." Dr. Nan Crystal Arens, an associate professor in geoscience added: "I've seen lots and lots of academic misfits really thrive here. These are students who may not find a natural habitat in the classroom, in traditional clubs or on a sports team. If they connect with a faculty or staff member—which happens a lot—they get the individualized nurturing they need to set them on fire."

Small Classes Foster Community

The HWS students we surveyed unanimously raved about the small class sizes and the sense of community that is fostered by the Colleges. One media and society major told us, "The small class sizes have motivated me to do better work and take more initiative with my education [to make] my future career become a reality." A public policy major commented on the campus vibe, explaining, "HWS fosters such a tight knit, supportive community. It feels like home." This supportive community is created right away, in part through the First-Year Seminars that all first-year students take. Seminar topics vary each year, as do the professors who teach them, which means the class discussions are always fresh. These classes, with topics like rock music, monsters in America, and French culture, are small at around fifteen students, and they lay the groundwork for close relationships between students and faculty that continue throughout the students' college careers.

Outside the classroom, HWS fosters a sense of community by engaging students in the decisions of the Colleges. One writing and rhetoric major told us, "HWS gives every student a personal experience, and no one is left out of the important conversations that happen on our campus." These important conversations happen in a number of places, including the HWS Board of Trustees, where Student Trustees, elected by their classmates, are voting members. Students also have a voice in their community via the Hobart Student Government and the William Smith Congress, which represent student interests across a number of committees on campus.

Learning Communities

Building on the First-Year Seminars that all students take, Learning Communities are available to students who would like a more immersive first-year experience. The first-years who opt in to these communities live together, take classes together (usually the first-year seminar plus a related introductory course), and attend lectures and field trips together. For example, first-year students in the intensive year-long Sustainable Living Learning Community will first take the First-Year Seminar, "Consuming the World," four sections of which are taught by four different professors. Students then remain in their sections through the spring to extend their learning. Dr. Thomas Drennen, chair of environmental studies and professor of economics, explained a bit more about the experience: "There are four professors and small fourteen to fifteen person seminars twice a week. Then once a week we all come together with a common purpose to watch movies, to go on field trips, to work on our new farm [Fribolin Farm, just a mile away], and to initiate sustainability projects on campus. It's really hands-on."

According to HWS, students who participate in Learning Communities tend to have higher GPAs, a smoother transition to college life, and higher overall satisfaction with their college experience. Dr. Drennen offered an explanation, stating, "The students in the this program are going to know forty-five other students and four faculty members, and they're going to know them well. They are going to feel connected from day one."

Interdisciplinary Curriculum

Hobart and William Smith Colleges are proud of their interdisciplinary curriculum, and students appreciate the freedom this unique approach affords them. "You have the freedom to design your own educational experience," one international relations and political science major told us, echoing the feelings of many students in our survey. The curriculum is designed around eight learning goals focused on communication, critical thinking, quantitative reasoning, scientific inquiry, artistic expression, cultural understanding, ethical judgment and action, and an understanding of differences and inequalities. As the school explained, "Students work with faculty advisers to design a program of study that both meets their interests and fulfills the degree requirements." Students easily recognize the value of such a curriculum. A writing and rhetoric major told us, "HWS is a strong academic institution that truly promotes educational growth and real learning. The interdisciplinary nature of the liberal arts is highlighted, and I know that my education here is worth something"; while a mathematics and economics major expressed gratitude for the "interdisciplinary education for a world which requires being able to think from many different perspectives."

HWS's purposefully interdisciplinary approach affects faculty as well as students. For example, Dr. Thomas Drennen has been the chair of economics and is now the chair of environmental studies. Does it seem strange that the chair of one department could be chair of another? Dr. Drennen says, not at all. "My area is: How do you solve environmental problems? I think that to do that you have to understand economics," he explained. "We're trying to make students understand what it means to be interdisciplinary." Meanwhile Dr. Jack Harris offered this assessment of the school's approach: "I describe HWS as a 'culture of yes'—if a faculty member wants to try something new it is generally encouraged. There are so many examples—just look at our interdisciplinary offerings, or the different international programs (such as in Vietnam) that have sprouted from faculty initiatives. We often do the same for students, enabling them to create individual majors, and going out of our way to stretch the boundaries of learning."

The Center for Community Engagement and Service-Learning (CCESL)

HWS and its students are serious about serving their community. According to Dr. Jack Harris, "over 60 percent of our students take service learning courses and are civically engaged." CCESL helps organize their efforts through the Geneva Partnership, a sustained and engaged relationship with the city of Geneva, New York—the school's hometown. Through this partnership and the Geneva 2020 collective impact initiative, the HWS community provides assistance in three areas affecting Geneva's children: graduation rates, career and college readiness, and literacy. Beyond this partnership, the Colleges told us, "Students participate in regularly scheduled Days of Service in which they volunteer in the surrounding area with the common purpose of giving back to the greater Geneva community. Past Days of Service activities have included working at the Special Olympics, providing trail maintenance on the Ontario Pathways, spreading wood chips on a playground in Seneca Lake State Park and visiting with residents at the Clifton Springs nursing home. On their first full-day at HWS, students of the incoming classes participate in a Day of Service during First-Year Orientation."

> **66** *A well-rounded citizen must contribute to his or her local community AND the global community, and in doing so will find that the two aren't so different.* **99**

Students also have the opportunity to participate in the Compass Program, in which they "explore options for local, national and international volunteerism; reflect on the ways service connects to coursework; create sustainable programs that merge community needs with students' academic and personal interests and abilities; and embark upon a lifelong commitment to justice and social consciousness." HWS even allows for community-based projects to count toward students' majors, through their Community Based Research program in which students work with a community partner and faculty sponsor to explore an important community issue. The students who participated in our survey value these opportunities to impact the local and global community. One undeclared sophomore told us, "A well-rounded citizen must contribute to his or her local community AND the global community, and in doing so will find that the two aren't so different." According to a geoscience and environmental studies major, "Hobart and William Smith Colleges is about community—Geneva, New York in the smallest sense of the word and defining what it means to be a global citizen in the biggest sense of the word."

A Global Education

Given HWS's commitment to community—both local and global—it will perhaps come as no surprise that study abroad opportunities are incredibly admired among students. The Colleges, through its Center for Global Education, offer nearly 50 study abroad destinations on six continents. These opportunities help to define HWS students. "What comes to mind when I think of HWS is community. The student body creates an inclusive community that leads lives of consequences. Students study abroad, volunteer in the local Geneva community, help with sustainability issues on campus, get involved in various clubs and sports," a biochemistry major told us. Faculty appreciate the opportunities as well, as Dr. Nan Crystal Arens explained: "The opportunity to teach whole semesters abroad as a faculty member was a major factor influencing my decision to come to HWS. I've led three of our semester-long off campus programs and it is wonderful to participate in the transformation that happens during these experiences." All of this international experience impacts class discussions back in Geneva as well. "Classes bring in current materials, and given that more than 50 percent of students go abroad, conversations are diverse and global," a geoscience and environmental science major reported. (According to the Colleges, 60 percent of all students actually study abroad.)

HWS takes its commitment to providing a global education even further through its Charles H. Salisbury Summer International Internship Stipend, which provides three students with financial support of up to $20,000 to pursue an international internship experience in a location of the student's choice (examples of past destinations include London, Singapore, Rome, Hong Kong, Sweden, Peru, India and South Africa). According to the Colleges, "By supplanting classroom education with internship experience, students gain a practical understanding for the demands and rewards of future careers."

Centennial Center for Leadership (CCL)

Given the Colleges' motto, "Preparing students to lead lives of consequence," HWS stresses the importance of leadership skills. Through the CCL, the Colleges offer services in four key areas: leadership development, community leadership, entrepreneurial leadership, and global leadership. CCL hosts a leadership certificate program, fellowships, a three-day leadership institute, a series based on leadership discovery, and speakers who engage with students in café style discussions. Through The Stu Lieblein '90 Pitch Contest and the idea accelerator program HWS IdeaLab, students also have opportunities to showcase their ideas for businesses, organizations, products and services. Dr. Nan Crystal Arens explained to us the value of these various programs: "There are many opportunities to exercise leadership with a variety of groups and on a variety of scales.

What I like about this approach is that students get to try things in the complex environment of real people and real organizations and sometimes fail."

The Salisbury Center for Career, Professional and Experiential Education

HWS is proud of its career center, which offers a range of services to students. Many of the students who took our survey cited career services as one of the school's biggest strengths. One architectural studies major gives HWS credit for "providing academic and career services that the students are interested in." A Spanish and Hispanic studies major agrees, listing among the colleges' strengths "community service opportunities, career services resources for jobs and internships, and research opportunities with professors." The Colleges structure career services in a four-phase program called Pathways. Through this program, the Colleges explained, "students research careers, spend time with professionals, take behind the scenes tours of various professions and find internships and jobs." Students in good academic standing who complete the Pathways program are guaranteed an internship, usually completed over the summer between junior and senior year. The Colleges will even provide a stipend to students whose internships are unpaid. In addition to the Pathways program, the HWS career center also provides job shadowing opportunities, on campus speakers, and a career connection program offered in major cities across the country that gives students a behind-the-scenes look at a variety of industries.

Faculty

HWS boasts an 11:1 student-faculty ratio, allowing them to maintain those small class sizes that so many students applaud. An impressive 98 percent of full-time faculty have PhDs or other terminal degrees. Faculty are "very knowledgeable about their subject in addition to enthusiastic and willing to teach," an economics major told us. Other students, however, are even more impressed with their professors' accessibility. A media and society major stated, "Professors are always accessible, and a good number of them reach out to their students as opposed to simply expecting students to take initiative for help. They easily become friends with students and keep in touch with and mentor them after graduation." A public policy major agreed: "The professors are the people who make this place come alive. They are more than just teachers shouting at you from the front of the classroom. I have been fortunate enough to dine with them, meet their families, become friends with them and get to know them on a very human level."

Students aren't the only ones who appreciate the camaraderie with faculty members. Dr. Jack Harris shared with us how beneficial this is to faculty as well, stating, "Faculty work with students (without additional compensation) on honors projects and independent studies. Each sports team has a faculty mentor who communicates to faculty about the team and encourages us to come out and cheer. Students work with faculty on community projects, in the school system and community theater. I often meet with students at my home, which is near campus, and we have gone camping together as a class, gone out for Vietnamese food, and had potluck dinners at my home. The Provost even provides a stipend for each class to do these out of the classroom activities."

Alumni/ae

In addition to their close relationships with faculty, HWS students also benefit from engaged alumni and alumnae. "Alums are always happy to help out graduates and current students in any way possible," an environmental studies major told us. Dr. Jeremy T. Cushman, who graduated in 1996, provided an example of such extensive alum engagement: "While completing my medical training I attended college fairs on behalf of the institution, interviewed prospective students, and served as a resource for students contemplating a career in medicine. Since moving less than an hour away from my alma mater nine years ago, I am often on campus giving guest lectures or career services and leadership talks, I am the Medical Director for their campus first response program, and I frequently attend many campus events. I have had students take independent study courses with me, and I have served as a member and officer of the Hobart College Alumni Association and get to interact with my fellow alumni and students on campus on a regular basis."

Alumni and alumnae are perhaps eager to give back to HWS because they credit the Colleges with preparing them for successful careers. Dorothy Wickenden, the executive editor of *The New Yorker*; *Glee* co-creator Brad Falchuk, and Abigail P. Johnson, the president and CEO of Fidelity Investments are all counted among prominent HWS grads. Aloysee H. Jarmoszuk, class of '98 and currently the chief of staff for University Development and Alumni Relations at New York University explained, "I was very involved in student government and held a work study post in the William Smith Deans Office, both of which . . . helped prepare me for post-college life." Dr. Cushman agreed, stating, "The leadership experience I gained while at Hobart and William Smith no doubt built my skills and confidence to take leadership roles in Medical School, and certainly now in my career in Emergency Medicine. There is no doubt that the foundation on which I now operate was set during my time at Hobart."

Lehigh University

27 Memorial Drive West, Bethlehem, PA 18015
Admissions: 610-758-3100
E-mail: admissions@lehigh.edu
Website: www.lehigh.edu
Twitter: @LehighU

Introduction

With an undergraduate student population of just under 5,000, Lehigh University rests on a 2,358-acre campus in eastern Pennsylvania dotted with wooded areas and boasts some of the most advanced research facilities in the world. Lehigh strikes a good balance between small college experience and big university opportunity. As one computer science and business major told us, "The size is perfect. It is small enough to see familiar faces every day, but big enough to always be meeting new people." Lehigh explains that its size "allows us to be nimble and agile in developing some unique curricula." What types of opportunities make Lehigh stand out? Students and alumni alike highlighted the multi-year undergraduate research projects shepherded by one-on-one faculty attention, fully funded international internships, a specialized relationship with the United Nations, and a new mountaintop educational facility that puts students in charge, to name a few.

At Lehigh, students chart their own course with an emphasis on experiential learning opportunities that don't just teach skills but help students discover what they want to do with their education. The university told us that its "Career Services works closely with students to develop multiple career-related experiential opportunities prior to graduating. Sometimes these experiences can solidify one's choice of major, or creates an opportunity to explore for another career field that might be a better fit."

For Ashley Pritchard, who is a project manager at the Friedrich Naumann Institute in Myanmar, this support and encouragement was one of her most valuable experiences at Lehigh: "I was an undergraduate student with no idea what I would major in, and Lehigh gave me the support and guidance I needed not only to find my way, but also to maneuver between colleges. While at Lehigh, I took courses in the Business School, Engineering, and Arts & Sciences and explored my interests with professors and academics who helped me map where I could utilize my learning after graduation. In the end, I managed to pick up a major and/or minor from each! Most schools do not offer this opportunity or flexibility and certainly didn't offer the support."

> **❝ We're smart. We work hard. And we have a lot of personality.❞**

Through study abroad and internship opportunities, Pritchard, who double majored in economics and political science and minored in engineering, explained, "[I was] awakened to a larger world—and one that I would later go on to explore myself! My best experiences at Lehigh were those that taught me the life lessons that have distinguished me from other colleagues 'in the real world,' and provided me with the opportunity to excel in my professional career." Ashley Miller, an accounting and finance alumna, adds, "We're smart. We work hard. And we have a lot of personality. There's a likability factor, which in your career is huge when it comes to knowing how to carry yourself in different social situations or being able and willing to get in front of clients and build new relationships. Lehigh alumni have the confidence to do that from day one."

Presidential Scholars Program

While all colleges and universities recognize students who achieve high GPAs, Lehigh distinguishes itself by providing every student who attains a 3.75 or higher with a fifth year of study tuition free. The Presidential Scholars program, which includes a summer and two academic semesters following degree completion, can be used for any kind of scholarly, artistic, or career project, emphasizing Lehigh's commitment to student-driven learning. The school explains that "this benefit is intended to give students an opportunity to pursue a second undergraduate degree, pursue a graduate degree, or undertake an advanced project of a scholarly or creative nature (e.g., a thesis, a portfolio of artwork, a design project, a field or laboratory research project) that does not lead to a degree." With employers increasingly demanding more and more from new hires, the free fifth-year at Lehigh could help a résumé stand out from the crowd. And because the year can include anything from a summer studying self-assembling nanomaterial in the largest electron microscope lab in the United States to immersion in the sculpture studio, the program benefits a diverse group of students and their career interests.

Partnership with the United Nations

In 2006 Lehigh became the sixth university in the world to be recognized by the United Nations as a Non-Governmental Organization (NGO). This allows "Lehigh students to attend UN conferences and private briefings, intern with UN NGO offices worldwide and host ambassadors and UN officials on campus," which, for the last three years, has included campus visits from the UN

Secretary General, according to the university. Lehigh students also serve as Youth Representatives, "fully sanctioned and accredited by the United Nations," the university explained. Youth Representatives work with a wide array of national and international organizations, such as Lawyers without Borders, The Peres Center for Peace in Israel, The Center for Public Health in Nigeria, and the Darfur Rehabilitation Project in Sudan. These students receive unparalleled, hands-on training as they "attend conferences, workshops, and sessions pertaining to the NGO's cause, and report back critical details or UN action," and the organizations they serve greatly benefit the Youth Representatives' support.

An organization as large as the United Nations offers opportunities for every kind of student with every kind of interest. Lehigh explains that students who have served as UN interns have worked as "speech writers, social media marketers, UNESCO researchers, NGO relations staff members, and designers of globally viewed briefings." Lehigh also offers classes and experiential learning opportunities in a wide variety of fields that leverage this exposure to the United Nations, whose headquarters in New York City is only a two-hour's drive from campus. Journalism majors have shadowed United Nations correspondents; education students can learn about the roles of NGOs in education policy; while marketing students engage in UN commissioned social media research.

> ❝ My first internship upon graduating from Lehigh turned into a full-time job working for the United Nations due, in great part, to Lehigh's connections. ❞

Programs like these can launch careers. Ashley Pritchard told us, "My first internship upon graduating from Lehigh turned into a full-time job working for the United Nations due, in great part, to Lehigh's connections."

International Business and Scholarship

Designed to specifically investigate international business, economics and public policy, these programs allow students to develop a particular course of inquiry over a substantial period with one-on-one faculty mentoring, and offer a feast of additional opportunities, such as internships, scholarships, travel, and publication. One of the Lehigh's most compelling international offerings is the Martindale Student Associates Program.

Each year the Martindale Student Associates Program takes a select number of juniors on a paid 10- to 12-day exploration of global economics and public policy through study in a particular country where, the school told us, "they meet and interview business and government leaders and other policy-makers." After completing their fact-finding mission, Martindale Student Associates spend the following academic year conducting additional research on campus and working closely with a Lehigh faculty member to write an academic report of their findings. Their report is then published in the Martindale Center's undergraduate research journal, *Perspectives on Business and Economics*. Associates also enjoy membership at the Martindale Center, where they spend their senior year "taking part in conferences, as well as meeting and talking with leading figures in government, business, finance, and academia who come to the Center as visiting scholars," according to the school.

From Lab Table to Mountaintop

Housed within an old, industrial facility on top of a mountain, The Mountaintop Project certainly looks unlike any other university classroom. Inside a factory relic of industrial-age titan Bethlehem Steel, old distillery vats have been repurposed for aquaponics, where tillabia swim among the roots of crops; 3D printers build exoskeletons aimed to help children relearn movement after illnesses like stroke; and outside students compost some 450 pounds of the school's food waste for fertilizer. Here, students across disciplines are offered near complete academic freedom without the constraints of assignments, grades, or a pre-set curriculum, to answer "open-ended problems." The university explains that, from the project's inception in 2013, "students were given the liberty to define the scope of their projects, to take risks intellectually, to make mistakes, and to change course. . . . Faculty mentors focused on coaching and supporting students in the process of discovery. Not only were students able to collaborate with fellow students on their multidisciplinary teams, but they were also able to brainstorm with students from other projects and turn to any faculty member for guidance."

Students investigate problems and come up with their own, innovative solutions—an invaluable skill in any industry—and this work is already making an impact. The group working on the pediatric exoskeleton has consulted with Good Shepherd Rehabilitation Hospital, and the group developing fertilizer has expanded their efforts to other initiatives across campus, including sustainability internships. The Mountaintop program has seen great success since its inception two years ago, and already the administration is working on ways to scale it up so more students and faculty can take part. (To see more of the Mountaintop projects, visit lehigh.edu/mountaintop.)

The Mountaintop Project's philosophy aligns perfectly with the student-driven research ethos of Lehigh. An engineering student told us that "research driven classwork" was one of the key factors that brought her to Lehigh. A chemical engineering and biotechnology student further explained, "Professors usually tend to give out 'open-ended' projects instead of homework, which greatly enhances understanding of the material. For example, for my Senior Chemical Engineering design course, I designed a chemical plant on my own—I was free to do it any way I wanted, so there was no clear cut way as to how to do it. Another example involved a picture of cells that my professor took in her lab and we were supposed to figure out what is wrong with them—bringing a new dimension to our learning and understanding the concepts covered in class."

Dr. Michael Spear, assistant professor in the Department of Computer Science and Engineering, told us, "The research opportunities at Lehigh are fantastic, the resources are top-notch, and the students (graduate and undergraduate) with whom we research are exceptional. . . . In the lab, Lehigh undergraduates are able to perform at such a high level, and contribute directly to significant published research."

Faculty

Members of Lehigh's dedicated faculty have been named an Outstanding Science Teacher Educator of the Year by the Association for Science Teacher Education, have received the J. James R. Croes Medal at the American Society of Civil Engineers' Global Engineering Conference, an Alfred P. Sloan Research Fellow in Chemistry, and ranked 34th worldwide in terms of impact to the international business literature by Management International Review. And that was just in 2014. Lehigh faculty have numerous awards and lauded publications, including ten recipients of the National Science Foundation CAREER Awards, described by the NSF as its "most prestigious awards in support of junior faculty who exemplify the role of teacher-scholars."

But that doesn't go to their heads. An English and political science major told us "I have always felt respected by my professors," whose classes "allowed me to study what I loved and also step out of my comfort zone from time to time." That might be because, as Dr. Spear explains, "faculty and students see each other as teammates. . . . As faculty, we know that our position relative to our students is not a consequence of intellectual superiority, but of greater experience." Dr. Georgette Phillips, Dean of the College of Business, adds that, in the CBE, "faculty are always finding out about what kinds of jobs people are interested in and putting students in touch with people they might know in the industry in terms of networking. I've not seen a limit to faculty interest." The faculty-student relationship often extends post-graduation: Dr. Phillips says, "Years go by and faculty can still talk about this student or that student or students can come back and the faculty member will not only remember them but probably have some embarrassing stories to tell about them! It's a wonderful relationship."

Alumni/ae

Lehigh counts Peter D. Feaver, National Security Council member in the Clinton and Bush administrations; Lee Iacocca, former chairman of Chrysler; and numerous members of the United States congress and state governors among its distinguished alumni. And, Catherine Engelbert (an '86 grad in accounting), CEO of Deloitte LLP, has the distinction of becoming the first female CEO of a Big Four firm.

Luckily for Lehigh students, Career Services "maintains partnerships with alumni and company partners," the university told us, "[who] hold events, including Mock Interview Days, Résumé Marathon, etc., where the companies send representatives to campus to support our programs. Alumni support is huge here at Lehigh, and our Lehigh alumni family of over 75,000 is a wonderful resource for our institution to draw upon." Events like the Conference of Accounting Professionalism draw professionals from each of the "Big Four" firms and other companies to campus for a weekend of panels and workshops. Alumna Lauren Miller, who participated in the event as an undergrad and is now a partner at Ernst &Young, told us: "You would rotate into an employer's workshop on things like public speaking, the importance of relationships, the importance of teaming, etc. It was a really a day to help you network but also to gain some soft skills and really understand what firms are looking for and how to improve on those skills."

Alumna Ashley Pritchard credits the Lehigh alumni network with shaping her career trajectory: "[If] you ask me now what I should have paid attention to when I was 17 and applying for college, it would have been Lehigh's outstanding career services and alumni relations.... It was through Lehigh's alumni networks and Career Services that I received my internships, feedback on résumés and how to present myself in interviews, and ultimately, the stepping point of my career."

Alumnus Bill Gross, who graduated in 1998 with a degree in mechanical engineering, is now Engineering Program Manager for a multinational technology and engineering firm; he told us, "I liaise with Lehigh's Career Services Department to recruit, interview, and guide students from campus to corporate opportunities, such as co-ops and internships. . . . Lehigh students are typically known for being particularly sharp, adaptive, technical leaders. [They] have the benefit of diverse and broad campus experiences, in addition to the strong academics, so they are ready for the chaos of a large matrixed organization and can ultimately lead and succeed in such an environment." Lauren Miller agrees. She said, "Lehigh trains you. We worked hard there, but they also got us ready for day one coming into the real world. . . . Half the reason I'm a partner at Ernst & Young is probably because of my education and the training I got a Lehigh." Now as a campus recruiter for her company, she actively seeks Lehigh graduates as new hires. "I recruit them off campus, and they go right on my team. Everyone at the firm knows that those are the people I want to work for me."

Marist College

3399 North Road, Poughkeepsie, NY
Admission: 845-575-3226
E-mail: admission@marist.edu
Website: marist.edu
Twitter: @Marist, @maristadmit

Introduction

On the banks of the Hudson River, Marist College is constantly striking the perfect balance between a liberal arts campus and a high-tech university system, providing the tools and resources of a world university and the access and personality of a small institution. "Marist College has the perfect location," one marketing student told us. "Its position between New York City and our state's capital makes the students available for internships while thoroughly involved in classes." But its more scenic location in Poughkeepsie, New York grants students some quiet from the big urban centers while providing "the surrounding [Mid-Hudson Valley] to do ecology research," a biology major added. "So," students say, "we get the best of both worlds." The College also has a branch campus in Florence, Italy that offers pre-college, freshman year, full-year, and graduate opportunities to earn a degree. Academically, "Marist students are highly focused on studies throughout the week. Between classes and clubs, Marist students are VERY busy." Marist students take their community involvement very seriously, too, and "many Marist students are socially and environmentally conscious, often taking part in fundraisers and other benefits for different causes."

> 66 *Marist College has the perfect location between New York City and our state's capital.* 99

Marist strikes the same kind of balance between aesthetics and power: Students rave about its "beautiful buildings and landscape," which, thanks to a decades long partnership with IBM, are all wired to a "zSeries 900 mainframe that provides a level of computing power ordinarily associated with large research universities and Fortune 500 companies," according to the school. This relationship with one of the world's oldest and largest technology firms "provides the unique opportunity for Marist students, faculty, and IT staff to work collaboratively with IBM research and development staff on various emerging technology initiatives," and might have something to do with the success of Marist's computer science program, "which includes a renowned concentration in game design & programming," Dean of Admissions, Kent Rinehart told us.

For entertainment, students can either look to the outdoors and spend an afternoon "hiking one of many trails, visiting the Vanderbilt mansion, FDR library, or the Walkway Over the Hudson, exploring a quirky nearby town like New Paltz, Beacon, or Rhinebeck," or hop on an express train to New York City, where students enjoy "$25 Broadway tickets." Students in the well-known fashion design and marketing program can also pop down to Manhattan for fashion week and see their industry's most popular and influential event unfold.

❝ All student organizations on campus are required to hold community service hours as part of their club charter.❞

Civic engagement is an integral part of the Marist ethos and one way that the college "[creates] a sense of community and an environment that supports service initiatives," in the words of one Marist communications major. Dean Rinehart told us that the school derives its educational and service philosophy from the Marist Brothers, whose Catholic order was founded on the principles of higher human values, dedication to service, and excellence in education. Under this banner, "all student organizations on campus are required to hold community service hours as part of their club charter," and Campus Ministry, the college's largest club, directs weekly community service initiatives, Dean Rinehart said. With over eighty campus organizations clocking services hours, Marist has developed a culture of "incredible involvement with the local community," according to one accounting major that we surveyed. This also translates into incredible leadership and management opportunities for students.

Service Learning

Marist has several programs that help students integrate service into their educational experience, whereby, as a criminal justice major told us, "Marist provides a quality educations with a strong emphasis on making connections and giving back to the community." One such program is the Center for Civic Engagement and Leadership, or CCEL, which aims to develop leadership skills by helping students get involved with local community organizations. Through programs like the Tarver Summer Internships, named after community leader and civil rights activist, Marie Tarver, CCEL teaches students how to be creative and independent while working alongside existing organizations toward a common goal. These paid internships require students to design and execute a project in coordination with a faculty member, who serves as a mentor, and a community organization, which provides the infrastructure for the student's project. Students have a wide degree of latitude when developing their project, but they must select a community partner from an approved list of organizations from the Hudson River Valley. In consultation with their mentor and the local organization's director, interns identify key issues their work will address and how the project's objectives align with the strategic goals of the organization.

Experiences like these help students manage multiple lines of communication and develop strategies to integrate their ideas into existing action networks—increasingly important skills as the world becomes more interconnected, and resources, including institutional infrastructures, more limited. Through the internship, students learn how to develop actionable plans, coordinate resources, measure effects, and present their results to the campus community.

Dahley Turner, a 2014 Tarver Intern, with the help of her mentor, associate professor of social work Daria Hanssen, developed a youth intervention program in association with an organization called Liberty Partnership Program, or LPP. LPP is a local initiative sponsored by Marist and funded by the New York State Department of Education to help at-risk high school students develop skills that will help them succeed in college and their careers. LPP works with the local school districts and has extensive access to at-risk students. Dahley worked with the director of LPP to develop and implement "a self-confidence building curriculum" and devised a method to measure the intervention's impact through pre- and post-assessments, according to the college. She then prepared a report on the intervention's findings to the campus community.

The program makes it easy for students to devote an entire summer to their project because the internship includes free campus housing during the summer, three free tuition credits, and a significant stipend. By devoting all of their time to the project, students get a more realistic idea of what full-time project coordination and development feels like, and it helps them develop follow-through skills while granting them a sense of project ownership.

Leadership

In addition to the leadership skills that students develop through experiences like Dahley Turner's, Marist has a robust leadership development program. The Emerging Leaders Program offers students a series of workshops, lectures, and activities that cover everything from basic leadership skills, like effective evaluation and feedback, to specific leadership plans, such as leadership during a transition or how to deal with poor performance or low participation within an organization. The program is free to students, and the college offers a certificate to those who complete five or more programs. The college has recently added the Raymond A. Rich Institute for Leadership to its repertoire of leadership programs. Endowed by the industrialist Raymond A. Rich, the Institute for Leadership is housed on a historic estate about ten miles north of campus. The institute helps students develop "communication, interpersonal, and social skills necessary to lead complex organizations in a global setting," according to Dean Rinehart, by establishing campus residencies for leaders from government, corporations and nonprofits, hosting leadership conferences, and providing students with workshops. The institute aims to "encourage potential leaders to become better at motivating others through consideration and persuasion, and to foster dedication to a better social and economic environment," Dean Rinehart told us.

Influence and Decision Makers

Marist offers a range of experiential opportunities that have captured the attention of its "politically involved, bright students." For students interested in anything to do with media, politics, government, public policy, activism, or foreign affairs, Marist offers ways to intern, study abroad, and research at home. Undergraduate researchers work with faculty members as part of a team, and can participate in case study competitions requiring intensive research and presentation among a national audience. Away from campus, students have the opportunity to pursue three distinct programs that combine research, scholarship, and practical work experience in every field from local government to international relations.

Marist in Manhattan

The Marist in Manhattan internships allow students to get practical experience in the worlds of art, fashion or media. Students get college credit for interning with top companies and complement their on-the-job experiences with group activities, lectures, and networking opportunities. A broad range of options means there is room for just about any interest. Past interns have worked at CNN, NBC News, and Comedy Central's *The Colbert Report* as well as at other media outlets, museums, presses, and fashion houses.

Washington Semester

Marist students also prize the "help [they get] with obtaining internships outside of New York state," an international business student said. Two programs that get students away from The Empire State to explore the political machine at the national and international levels—one in D.C. and the other in London. Through the Washington Semester Program, hosted by the School of Professional and extended Studies at American University, Marist students study and work with other undergraduates from around the globe. Here, too, students attend class and work as interns, but during their Washington Semester, Marist students will also "have the option of choosing to conduct an in-depth research project using Washington, D.C. as a laboratory of information or to take an elective class from [American University's] hundreds of offerings to fulfill an academic requirement," according to American. Students gain access to the program's extensive network of organizations for internship opportunities and resources that help with résumés, cover letters, and interview prep. For their seminar, students get to choose from a variety of concentrations, like sustainable development, global economics, journalism and new media, and public health, each with its own niche within the Capitol. A unique set of resources comes with each concentration. For example, students in the sustainability concentration have, in the past, visited the USAID and met with World Bank communications director, Angelica Silvero.

In London

On the other side of the Atlantic, in association with the London School of Economics and Political Science, Marist students in the Hansford Scholars Program follow the same model of study and internship as they discover the British political system. Students engage in academic work that includes classes, guest lectures, and supervised research, and work as interns with "an NGO, a government department, a lobbying group, or in the Houses of Parliament themselves." They also get to take a four-day trip to Edinburgh to learn about Scottish politics and to Oxford to learn about the history of elections. With the recent Scottish independence referendum and British Parliamentary elections, this is a great time to learn about the political systems of our British and Scottish cousins. Travel enthusiasts take note: Marist also has a branch campus in Florence, Italy.

Marist Institute for Public Opinion

Any student interested in government or public policy knows that the pollster is the campaign manager's best friend. Marist students have a privileged opportunity to put their finger on the pulse of America and learn the challenges of polling. One student told us that being "home to the Marist Poll" was one of the college's greatest strengths. The Marist Institute for Public Opinion conducts the Marist Poll, a long-established and well-respected poll used by journalists and analysts around the world. In 1978, it became the first survey center embedded in a college to engage undergraduate students in the business of survey research. Students participate in every aspect of the dynamic polling process, which "[allows] them to weave political science, computing, communications, marketing, and psychology into an interdisciplinary learning experience," according to the college. Through the institute students have access to "employment, internships, conferences, and seminars with leading journalists, pollsters, and government officials." Because the Marist Poll covers a wide range of issues on local and national scales, students are sure to find work relevant to their interests.

But the Marist Institute for Public Opinion should appeal to more than just political science students. As polling is used in nearly every social science and is a huge component of marketing, the institute offers great opportunities for students to work on something bigger than a class project. It also gives students a chance to see how polls are constructed and interpreted, and students are likely to explore how concepts of behavioral economics, like message framing and anchoring, work in a real-world context.

Life After Marist

Students agree that Marist "prepares you for the professional world, with the help of great alumni." Marist alumni include prominent international business figures like Mike Buckley, vice president of Global Business Communications at Facebook, and political commentators, like Bill O'Reilly. "The network of Marist alumni is very strong and willing to give back to the school," a communications and Spanish major told us. The school also has developed a way for students to directly access and even search through that network. The Alumni Career Network "contains hundreds of names of individuals who are willing to be contacted by fellow alumni and current students about career choices and paths," according to the school. This "alumni network is more than eager to help current students" with job leads and internship opportunities.

Faculty

> **❝ I have gotten a great liberal arts education without even being in a liberal arts field. ❞**

Because the student to faculty ratio is 16:1 and "classes are capped at about twenty-five," students are "able to develop a personal relationship with [their] peers and professors." Student interactions with their professors are "overwhelmingly positive. I have gotten a great liberal arts education without even being in a liberal arts field," a journalism major told us. "They know how to give value from seemingly unvaluable things." Students benefit from the experience of their professors, who "are usually very influential" and can "relate topics to real life. And equally important, Marist "professors do a really good job with keeping the students engaged" with academics and community work because they "are brilliant and captivating to listen to," and "they care about their students and want to help them in and out of the classroom."

Massachusetts Institute of Technology

77 Massachusetts Avenue Room 3-108, Cambridge, MA 02139
Admissions: 617-253-3400
E-mail: admissions@mit.edu
Website: mit.edu
Twitter: @mit

Introduction

Massachusetts Institute of Technology, the East Coast mecca of engineering, science, and mathematics, "is the ultimate place for information overload, endless possibilities, and expanding your horizons." The "amazing collection of creative minds" includes enough Nobel Laureates to fill a jury box as well as brilliant students who are given substantial control of their educations. The essence of Massachusetts Institute of Technology is its appetite for problems. Students here tend to be game-changers, capable of finding creative solutions to the world's big, intractable, complicated challenges. A chemical engineering major says that "MIT is different from many schools in that its goal is not to teach you specific facts in each subject. MIT teaches you how to think, not about opinions but about problem-solving. Facts and memorization are useless unless you know how to approach a tough problem."

While MIT is a research university committed to world-class inquiry in math, science, and engineering, MIT has equally distinguished programs in architecture, the humanities, management, and the social sciences. No matter what their field, almost all MIT students get involved in research during their undergraduate career, making contributions in fields as diverse as biochemistry, artificial intelligence, and urban planning. "Research opportunities for undergrads with some of the nation's leading professors" is a real highlight for students here. The school also operates an annual Independent Activities Period during the month of January, during which MIT faculty offer hundreds of noncredit activities and short for-credit classes, from lecture and film series to courses like Ballroom Dance or Introduction to Weather Forecasting. (Students may also use this period to work on research or independent projects.) Students are frequently encouraged to unite MIT's science and engineering excellence with public service. Recent years have focused on projects using alternative forms of energy, and machines that could be used for sustainable agriculture. MIT's D-Lab, Poverty

Action Lab, and Public Service Center all support students and professors in the research and implementation of culturally sensitive and environmentally responsible technologies and programs that alleviate poverty.

Inherent qualities to the quirky student body at MIT are verve and curiosity. The "stereotypical student [who] looks techy and unkempt...only represents about 25 percent of the school," a current student told us. The rest include "multiple-sport standouts, political activists, fraternity and sorority members, hippies, clean-cut business types, LARPers, hackers, musicians, and artisans." Extracurricular options range from "building rides" (recent projects have included a motorized couch and a human-sized hamster wheel) "to partying at fraternities to enjoying the largest collection of science fiction novels in the United States at the MIT Science Fiction Library." Students occasionally find time to "pull a hack," which is an ethical prank, like changing digital construction signs on Mass Ave to read "Welcome to Bat Country" or building a "life-size Wright brothers' plane that appeared on top of the Great Dome for the 100th anniversary of flight." Luckily, "there actually isn't one typical student at MIT," students here assure us. "The one thing students all have in common is that they are insanely smart and love to learn. Pretty much anyone can find the perfect group of friends to hang out with at MIT."

66 *I wanted to be surrounded by dreamers and architects of the future.* **99**

In fact, it can be downright inspiring to be around all that talent. An aerospace engineering student told us, "Being among such intelligent professors and students has changed my perspective on what I can achieve in the future." A current student studying computer science said, "I wanted the best engineering education out there. I wanted to be surrounded by dreamers and architects of the future. I love the tireless energy of fellow MIT students and their insistence on not settling."

The Freshman Experience

"As soon as you arrive on campus," students say, "you are bombarded with choices." All of a sudden you have "access to an amazing number of resources, both academic and recreational," not to mention the "research opportunities for undergrads with some of the nation's leading professors." There's an "energy" on campus that can be inspiring for sure, but MIT also wants to make sure no student gets overwhelmed or overlooked in the transition from high school to the fast-paced environment at MIT. Here's a quick rundown of a few ways MIT makes first-years feel welcome.

Freshman Advising Seminars

These seminars are academic courses with a twist. Your professor is also your adviser. Courses in digital and darkroom imaging or an immersion into start-ups and entrepreneurship bring together advisees in one course. Don't expect to see quizzes or p-sets here (though you do receive college credit). The school says these classes are completely different in "size, style of learning and pace" from other courses at MIT and are meant for adviser and advisees to know each other as people, "not just as student and teacher." They are also a fantastic way to experiment in a new subject by looking into the intersections between engineering and art (and designing, say, a display in the MIT Museum) or to get a jumpstart on Chemical Engineering with like-minded first-years.

First-Year Learning Communities

Another route for freshmen is to opt into one of the first-year Learning Communities, which are a great way to make smaller communities, within the larger campus community, right off the bat. You can choose between four communities, which bring together students of common interests: You'll take a several classes together, have freshman advising together, and socialize at special programs like pizza parties or weekly lunches. In the Terrascope Community, for example, students are tasked to explore problems related to the environment and sustainability (a recent class worked to design an environmentally friendly plan to feed the planet for a decade.) Students do field work together over spring break (in locales like Sirsi, India), and produce a series of radio programs about the overall experience. And in the Concourse Community, students take small, seminar-style versions of some of their core requirement classes together (in both science and the humanities) as well as Friday seminars that bring guest faculty across the disciplines for a behind-the-scenes look at "how different disciplines think." Most communities have facilities on campus with study areas, kitchens, and lounges for meeting up between classes. Students often say that these communities are the best part of freshman year.

Independent Activities Period

Between fall and spring semesters, Independent Activities Period (IAP) is a special term that runs through January and is a chance for students to do, well, whatever they want. Students, faculty, staff and alums can all propose IAP activities, including "how-to sessions, forums, athletic endeavors, lecture series, films, tours, recitals and contests," according to MIT. Student can pick and choose how they will participate, and, in essence, are the architects of their IAP experience. A hypothetical schedule might put you in a Cocktail 101 class on Mondays, led by MIT alumni and local bartenders, on Tuesdays you might intern in the marketing department for a 3-D printing company, and on Wednesdays you could take one-off courses like a leadership session on "how to run a meeting" or a

Mediterranean cooking class. Finally, you might cap off your schedule with a for-credit phys ed course like rifles for beginners or figure skating. MIT also offers study abroad courses during IAP such as a Spanish language course in Madrid.

Edgerton Center

Named after beloved MIT professor, engineer, and inventor Harold "Doc" Edgerton, the Edgerton Center is a special space on campus—full of workspaces, machinery, and hands-on training programs—for all kinds of makers. It's a place to skill-build, create prototypes, or just get advice for self-initiated independent projects (there are lots and lots of curious and motivated students at MIT) or for projects for credit. Here you might find students in one of the three Student Shops learning to fabricate the parts of a flashlight from scratch and working with 3-D printers or over in the Strobe Lab learning the fundamentals of high-speed imaging. Edgerton is also the hub for many of the student teams on campus such as the Solar Electric Vehicle Team, which designs 100 percent solar powered cars to race in long distance competitions, and the MIT Robotics Team, which enters and designs for a variety of competitions in the field of robotics.

Public Service

MIT is positively brimming with opportunity and resources. One student puts it bluntly: "MIT has dough. If you want to do something, there are a million and one ways here to get funding." But MIT also places a premium on social responsibility, and hosts a few unique spaces on campus doing just that.

D-Lab and J-Pal

Housed on MIT's campus, D-Lab is a global network of innovators "trying to improve the lives of people living in poverty." D-Lab academic courses and projects are all tied to real-world communities, and students are asked to draw upon their math, science, engineering, social science and business skills to tackle very real global problems. Conceived in 2003 as a research center within the MIT Economics Department, the Abdul Latif Jameel Poverty Action Lab, or J-Pal, has grown into a global network of partners who "are driven by a shared belief in the power of scientific evidence to understand what really helps the poor, and what does not," according to the Center. J-Pal headquarters still remain on the MIT campus, where researchers work on issues as diverse as "boosting girls' attendance at school, improving the output of farmers in sub-Saharan Africa, racial bias in employment in the United States, and the role of women political leaders in India."

The Public Service Center

The Public Service Center facilitates hands-on service learning opportunities for members of the MIT community through fellowships, grants, internships, and trainings. There are many programs going on at any given time at the PSC, but one of particular interest to incoming first-years may be the Freshman Urban Program. This pre-orientation event acclimates incoming first-years to campus and the surrounding community by giving them of a preview of "who's who and what's where" with five days of service projects in Boston and Cambridge. Past projects have included an elementary school clean-up, gardening with CitySprouts, or working with a local rescue mission, all alongside MIT upperclassmen. Participants get a first look at the resources that will help them become leaders on campus as well as the issues affecting the surrounding community. Plus it sets them up for future participation in CityDays of service, CityWeeks, which organizes Alternative Spring Break event in Cambridge, or Four Weeks for America, a pre-cursor to a Teach for America-like experience. The Public Service Center helps students connect their academic interests and strengths to service opportunities and become leaders no matter their discipline or area of study.

Entrepreneurship

MIT's approach to entrepreneurship is fresh and inclusive. One way that everyone from freshmen up to graduate students can get involved is through the MIT Global Founder's Skills Accelerator. If you think you've got a great idea, round yourself up a team of MIT talent and apply to be a GFSA founder. Select teams with "an interesting idea or proof of concept focused on creating impactful, innovation-driven startups" are given start-up capital (up to $20,000), office space, and a stipend along with mentorship and other helpful resources, all with an eye to eventually pitching their concept to investors at Demo Days in San Francisco, Boston, and NYC. Other funding streams on campus are the MIT $100K Entrepreneurship Challenge, a series of competitions designed to help students accelerate over the course of an academic year; the MIT Global IDEAS challenge, an invention competition put on by the Public Service Center; or the Legatum Fellowship for incoming or current MIT students "who demonstrate the potential to create innovative, sustainable, and for-profit enterprises that promote prosperity in low-income countries." Of course, in addition to competitions and the dozen or so student organizations on campus focused on entrepreneurship, there is a top-notch advising network facilitated by the Center for MIT Entrepreneurship. Students meet first with a Peer Advisor (student leaders on campus who hold meetings and office hours), and then have the option to meet with Entrepreneurs in Residence (full-time Center staff with different areas of expertise like business strategy, brand development, or fundraising), as well as Professional Advisors (industry experts across the country who donate their time and know-how to intrepid MIT inventors. An impressive collection of courses complete the picture and are taught by both faculty and practitioners.

Faculty

MIT doesn't hide away their talented professors in research labs or in upper-level only courses. A student majoring in computer science told us: "Eric Lander, leader of the Human Genome Project, and Ron Rivest, the 'R' in RSA encryption, and other legends are teaching freshmen. I have walked into professor's labs and stuck up conversation without previous appointment. Professors are human here and you are treated like a human too." "Legends" at MIT, past and present, include eight-one Nobel Prize recipients, four Pulitzer Prize winners, thirty-nine recipients of the National Medal of Science, two recipients of the National Medal of Technology and Innovations, and two winners of the Millennium Innovation Prize. There are sixty-five Guggenheim Fellows, five Fulbright Scholars, and twenty-two MacArthur Fellows among current faculty and staff.

Life After MIT

MIT's alumni network is rock solid. A computer science student said, "You hear all these stories of successful products and companies and hacks coming out of MIT, and next thing you know, you're working on the penultimate story." MIT graduates found companies like Bose and Harmonix, they invent things like the first ever computer game or Technicolor film, and host popular radio shows like Car Talk. The dedicated Global Education and Career Development "seeks to empower" students and alumni by taking a holistic approach to career services. A few offerings (among many) include career counseling and mock interviews, study abroad informational sessions, and graduate school advising. Frequent career fairs connect undergrads with potential employers (and the Career Fair Online Workshop will help you make the most of your time with them) or you can also peruse job and internship listings on CareerBridge. Students definitely get a hand-up from the impressive alumni network, and the surrounding areas of Cambridge and Boston abound with tech and research companies, offering students abundant opportunities for networking and internships. According to the school, the top industries for graduates are computer technology, consulting, and finance, while the top employers are Google, Apple, Oracle, Accenture, and Boeing. In 2014, the school reports, students found jobs through on-campus recruiting and MIT-sponsored job listings (21 percent), received full-time job offers based on an internships (19 percent), found jobs through career fairs (19 percent) or through networking (18 percent). Another 32 percent went on to graduate school. MIT comes in at number two on The Princeton Review's 2015 ranking list for Best Career Placement, which was reported in *Colleges That Pay You Back*.

Middlebury College

14 Old Chapel Rd., Middlebury, VT 05753
Admissions: 802-443-3000
E-mail: admissions@middlebury.edu
Website: www.middlebury.edu
Twitter: @Middlebury

Introduction

A small liberal arts college in Vermont with roughly 2,450 undergraduates, Middlebury's curriculum emphasizes critical thinking, rigorous analysis, problem solving across disciplines, and clear communication. A current student and environmental studies major sums up the school's mission well: "teaching students how to think both analytically and creatively in order to benefit the broader world." "[The school] has a great academic reputation for creating well-rounded students rather than narrowing you down to only studying one specialty," a biochemistry major we surveyed explains. A psychology major adds that this approach "allows you to develop these skills in whatever subject/s [you are] most passionate about."

Passionate and interested students thrive at Middlebury, where "students are creative, smart, motivated, and intellectually curious," Professor of Economics Jessica Holmes explains. "They ask insightful questions and are genuinely interested in understanding the answers. My students inspire me every day with their passion, enthusiasm and desire to make a difference in this world." Not surprisingly then, graduates of Middlebury go on to do big things. "Middlebury alumni certainly have a reputation in the real world. We're seen as uncommonly gifted, quirky, fierce, systems oriented thinkers who tackle some of society's hardest problems head on. Whether through campaigns, the arts or the private sector, Middlebury alumni have a deep sense of commitment to many important fights," Pier LaFarge, co-founder and CEO of SparkFund and 2010 graduate, tells us.

Middlebury prepares students for such success through its unique combination of top-rated academic programs, international experiences, leadership opportunities, mentoring, and career support.

Environmental Leadership

With the oldest undergraduate environmental studies program in the country, launched in 1965, it's no surprise that many of the students we surveyed mentioned this program and more generally the school's environmental efforts as two of its biggest strengths. LaFarge explains the strengths of this program in more detail: "I was drawn to the Environmental Studies program because of its commitment to system thinking. I was able to focus on both Policy and Economics, but without sacrificing an exposure to hard science, literature and geography. Climate change is a systems problem, and it can't be fully understood, or tackled, without developing a systems approach. Middlebury overall, and the environmental studies program in particular, provide students with a powerful framework for analyzing our societies' greatest challenges from a systems perspective."

Beyond this specific program, "environmental issues are very important to students," a Middle Eastern studies major reports. The school has acknowledged that interest and has responded with programs that both improve the environment and enrich the students. For example, the Middlebury School of the Environment, which is in session in the summer, began last year and places a special focus on leadership skills. The school also built, at students' urging, a biomass plant, which has cut the college's use of high carbon #6 fuel oil by more than one million gallons per year.

Students also pushed for more local food to be served in the dining halls, resulting in Middlebury signing onto the Real Food Challenge, a national campaign, and pledging that by 2016, 30 percent of food purchased by Middlebury's Dining Services will meet specific criteria, including that it be local (within 150 miles), ecologically sound, and farmed under fair working conditions and with humane animal treatment.

Top-Notch Language Programs

The Environmental Studies program is not the only well-regarded academic program at Middlebury. "I know Middlebury's the best for language study, and that's what I knew I wanted to study," an international politics and economics major told us. Middlebury offers courses in ten modern Eastern and Western languages: Arabic, Chinese, French, German, Hebrew, Italian, Japanese, Portuguese, Russian, and Spanish. Several students we surveyed mentioned the strength of Middlebury's Chinese program, while another Middle Eastern studies major tells us, "I wanted to study Arabic, and Middlebury's languages are renowned—for good reason."

In addition to language courses offered during the school year, the Middlebury Language Schools offer immersion instruction in eleven languages in the summer, during which the campus transforms into a multilingual community. The languages are the same as throughout the academic year with the exception of Korean, which was offered for this first time in summer 2014. Middlebury students take advantage of this intensive program in order to prepare to study abroad.

A Global Education

Given the school's focus on languages and summer study offerings, it is perhaps no surprise that more than 50 percent of Middlebury students study abroad. Most students do so through the Middlebury Schools Abroad, located in sixteen countries and thirty-seven cities. All of the study abroad programs usually include opportunities for students to have an internship or other volunteer experience. Students may also take advantage of The Middlebury Institute of International Studies at Monterey, California, which offers integrated degree programs in significant internationally focused areas, allowing college students to earn a BA and MA in a total of five years.

Even students who remain on Middlebury's campus are given an international education. The college is well-known for its major in international and global studies, which blends disciplines and provides students with a deep understanding of a specific geographic region. One Japanese major tells us that Middlebury's "position as a leading International Relations school put me at an advantage in connecting my various international interests," while an international studies major explains: "Middlebury is committed to cultivate future leaders who are passionate about environmental and social issues and ready to effect positive change in the world."

Outside of the major, Middlebury demonstrates this commitment through the Rohatyn Center for Global Affairs, which works with Middlebury faculty to create co-curricular programming such as lectures by distinguished scholars and professionals, annual symposia and conferences, and a student internship program.

A Focus on Entrepreneurship

Students on our survey applauded Middlebury for its "emerging focus on creativity and entrepreneurship," as one environmental studies major puts it. Alumnus Pier LaFarge was able to capitalize on this focus during his time at the school. "At

> **❝ At Middlebury, I learned the most important lesson of my career: I love to build things.❞**

Middlebury, I learned the most important lesson of my career: I love to build things. Whether it was starting campaigns with the Sunday Night Group, or organizing events and building infrastructure for student engagement with the outdoors through the Mountain Club, I realized that what I'm most committed to is the simple act of building systems that can shape the world and help solve difficult problems. Middlebury provided the perfect context to gain early experience at a small scale, and that experience has directly shaped my interest in entrepreneurship."

Middlebury provides these early experiences in entrepreneurship through several innovative programs. For example, during its month-long January term (or J-term) students can enroll in "Middlebury Entrepreneurs," a course which requires students to move quickly from idea to company launch with hands-on mentoring both from professors and visiting entrepreneurs and investors. At the conclusion of the course, students compete with their classmates in a pitch competition. To enroll, students must submit a business proposal.

Middlebury also runs the Center for Social Entrepreneurship, which provides students with funding, training, and opportunities to achieve social impact. For example, alumna Emily Nunez, the co-founder of Sword and Plow, a company that recycles former military gear such as tents into attractive bags, started her company while still at Middlebury with the help of a $3,000 grant she won in the Center's annual MiddChallenge competition.

The center is one facet of Middlebury's Programs on Creativity and Innovation (PCI). Through PCI, Middlebury also offers Midd Ventures (a student organization that fosters the entrepreneurial spirit on campus), MIDDSTART (a micro crowd sourcing fundraising site created and maintained by Middlebury College for student projects), Davis Projects for Peace ($10,000 grants from Projects for Peace for summer projects that promote peace), and the New Millennium Fund (a fund that pays half of the employer's cost for internships for students who wish to work for Vermont-based start-ups, small companies, non-profits or NGOs.

MiddCORE

Another J-Term course, "MiddCORE," is an intense mentor-driven leadership and innovation program that builds skills and confidence with collaborative and experiential learning. Through frequent challenges, students gain experience in leadership, strategic thinking, and numerous other skills.

Professor Holmes, who is also the director of MiddCORE, explains the program in more detail: "This four week (160 hour) program is for students who want to develop the skills, experience and confidence to be successful in life and work. Through mentor-led, hands-on workshops, students learn skills in teamwork, innovation, trial-and-error exploration, networking and practical problem-solving. The program is highly collaborative and students work closely with each other and more than forty mentors from varying fields and professions. During the program, students participate in several strategic partner challenges, working with peers to solve actual business problems posed by mentors. They also work on their own to develop a new product or service or a new way to address a social problem. Graduates leave MiddCORE with a strong foundation of leadership and innovation skills that prepare them for future successes: they're ready to solve problems, ready to perform as part of a team, ready to persuasively communicate their ideas and ready to have an engaged and meaningful life."

The Center for Careers and Internships (CCI)

Middlebury is committed to creating student leaders, and then helping them to launch their careers after graduation. CCI helps with that process, providing students with career counseling through all four years. CCI also helps students obtain hundreds of internships in numerous fields and supports 250 students every summer with funding for unpaid internships. CCI staff bring alumni to campus for panels on specific industries and work with employers to identify job openings. Through CCI, numerous alumni volunteer to serve as resources to students seeking information about a particular profession.

Faculty

Middlebury faculty are leading experts in their fields, authors of scholarly and popular books, and winners of grants, fellowships, and national and international prizes. A number of faculty write opinion pieces published by leading media outlets such as the *New York Times*, *The Atlantic*, CNN.com, the BBC, NPR, and the *Washington Post*. They also provide reporters with comments on current issues for news stories. All of this expertise, though, doesn't mean that faculty aren't interested in their students. With a 9:1 student-faculty ratio, and an average class size of 19, Middlebury students have the opportunity to form close relationships with their professors. "Several of my professors have given out their cell phone numbers after particularly difficult lectures to make sure that students can figure things out (as long as they don't call too late) and it's very common to be invited to your adviser's house for . . . dinner at least a few times per semester," an environmental studies major tells us. A sociology and anthropology major agreed, stating, "Students are able to visit professors, even outside of office hours! I have a very high level of contact with my academic adviser. We work out together, have multiple meals per week, and he has successfully recommended me for internships at AT&T and Princeton University."

Professor Holmes confirms that the Middlebury faculty values these interactions as much as students do. "Faculty at Middlebury choose to work at Middlebury because we value the interactions and personal connections we have with our students. The most rewarding part of my day is the one-on-one meetings with my students where we discuss research, share ideas, explore future careers and new opportunities. To know I have made a difference in a student's life is the fuel that keeps me going. I am not alone. Many faculty members collaborate with students on research, supervise independent projects or theses, help students find internships, and socialize outside of class by inviting students to their homes for dinner or by attending student shows, athletic events, etc. That is the joy of a small, residential liberal arts college like Middlebury."

Alumni/ae

Middlebury alumni are conscious of the valuable skills they acquired during their undergraduate years. For example, a recent survey of alumni by the school focusing on MiddCORE, highlights the program's value to Middlebury graduates. Professor Holmes informed us that "94 percent felt MiddCORE gave them the skills to be confident in the workplace, 98 percent could approach strategic challenges in new, creative ways, 91 percent thought MiddCORE was one of their most important undergraduate experiences and 79 percent felt MiddCORE opened their eyes to new career pathways."

Given this appreciation for their undergraduate programs, it's not surprising that alumni remain involved with the school. An economics major we surveyed cites the "family-like alumni" as the main reason for choosing the school, while Professor Holmes expounds on the alumni connection from her perspective. "I am in contact with many of my former students. They often check in when they want to go back to school or change jobs, get married, have children, or are coming back to town for reunions. A good number send me news articles that remind them of something we discussed in class—I love those emails as it means they retained material from class, years after graduation."

Finally, alumnus Pier LaFarge details his continuing involvement with the school. "The college network is a core part of my personal and professional networks, and I continue to benefit from the support and mentorship of professors, staff and administration. I'm active as a fundraiser in the alumni network, SparkFund has hired more than a dozen Middlebury alumni as full-time staff or summer fellows, and will keep hiring more as we grow. The college has been very supportive of SparkFund, inviting me back to speak to students and through programming at the Center for Social Entrepreneurship."

Northeastern University

360 Huntington Avenue, 200 Kerr Hall, Boston, MA 02115
Admissions: 617-373-2000
E-mail: admissions@neu.edu
Website: northeastern.edu
Twitter: @chooseNU, @AlumniNU

Introduction

Near many of Boston's cultural centers, the Northeastern University's campus is host to over 13,000 undergraduate students representing 126 countries, two subway stations, and a signature co-op program. A finance major tells us, "[Northeastern] has the perfect combination of city and campus life and the co-op program is amazing," while a journalism student points out that "the Museum of Fine Arts is down the street, the Red Sox are around the block and Boston's best bars are down the corner. There is something for everyone in Boston and at Northeastern."

Students and employers alike have increasingly been taking notice of Northeastern because of its stellar cooperative education programs and its top-tier research. One political science major tells us that "Northeastern has grown to be competitive with all of the other schools in the Boston and Cambridge areas . . . and I've heard of a number of companies who would choose Northeastern graduates over other graduates in the area because of their unique cooperative experiences."

Karim Sabbidine, a 2014 business administration grad with dual concentrations in finance and marketing and a minor in law and public policy, agrees that these opportunities pay huge dividends. "I chose Northeastern because I wanted to attend an institution in which I could get a practical education matched with an equally excellent academic program. The co-op program provided me with a year and a half of full time work experience that has been invaluable to my professional life. I wanted to be in a diverse city with a vibrant international community. Northeastern provided both the venue and population for all my hopes."

Northeastern is great for self-starters and career minded students. The Huskies we talked to agreed that the student population was diverse and that "every Northeastern student is ambitious and determined. Having the co-op program gives us focus sooner than most schools and it helps us to see what we want to do post-college a lot sooner," as one journalism student puts it.

Experiential Learning at the Core

The university tells us that, "cooperative education/experiential learning is our flagship program." And that flagship leads a global armada. All students complete at least one semester of experiential learning—cooperative learning, community service, or global study—integrated into their coursework, so nearly every part of the Northeastern educational apparatus is designed to maximize the value of experiential learning opportunities.

Northeastern describes their educational philosophy as a dialogue between the classroom and the jobs market that "integrates rigorous coursework with real-world experience, requiring students to apply their classroom learning in professional environments where the challenges—and the stakes—are real. That not only arms students with the problem-solving and teamwork skills they will need for any career path—starting with the ability to learn and adapt in the unfamiliar setting of the workplace—it also gives our students entirely new perspectives on their field of study that they bring back to the classroom, enriching their future learning in class."

Cooperative Education

Cooperative education is at the heart of a Northeastern's learning philosophy. With 95 percent of students participating in at least one semester of cooperative learning, it is by far the most popular experiential learning program at the school, and Northeastern has one of the highest levels of co-op participation in the country. So it is no wonder that within nine months, 90 percent of graduates are employed or in graduate school, and 85 percent of those working have careers within their field of study.

The high participation rate also means that Northeastern benefits from the economy of scale. Northeastern can efficiently provide resources that smoothly integrate cooperative learning into the curriculum. That means resources that students directly interact with, like co-op councilors and visa specialists, and ones that work behind the scenes, such as the "Center for Advancing Teaching and Learning through Research," which "[assesses] the efficacy and learning value of our co-op program, to determine what we can do better," according to the school. And because co-op learning can take students anywhere from across campus to across the globe, Northeastern offers resources to help students find housing, stay connected to home, navigate transportation while away, and integrate experiential learning opportunities into their academic and career goals when they return.

Students also benefit from the broader options and increased exposure to the job market. Co-op is available in every major and employers know it—nearly

3,000 companies here at home and abroad employee Northeastern undergraduate students. Northeastern's global co-op programs operate in 114 countries in conjunction with a wide variety of organizations and multinational corporations, so environmental science students can work on sustainable development in Bolivia, and computer science majors can study digital animation at Toonz Animation India. Northeastern also offers hundreds of Presidential Global Scholarships every year that defray the extra cost of international co-ops. A select number of Presidential Global Scholars are also awarded substantial fellowships to aid in their continued global scholarship.

It is not uncommon for a Northeastern student to spend three semesters in co-op education with different employers or even in different fields. Getting a feel for a particular line of work certainly gives students the tools to succeed in the future, but it also helps them find out if they even like that line of work. Karim Sabbidine tells us, "I came to Northeastern thinking that I wanted to become an investment banker. Having done investment co-ops I came to the realization that I wanted to be in a different line of work, specifically the legal field. I structured my co-ops to lead me to that goal and I am now currently in law school." The ability to engage in a many different lines of work helps students like Karim find their true passion before they hit the job market, which could save years of frustration and regret.

Karim was also able to realign his co-op's strategic goals because cooperative learning is fully integrated into the Northeastern advising system. Both through classes that integrate cooperative experiences and through co-op advisers, students can chart their academic and career futures based on their developing interests. That is why the co-op program is such a big pull for career minded students. One political science major tells us, "In an uncertain economy, the world-class co-op program really gives students a leg up in finding a career." In fact, Dr. Thomas Webster, chair and professor of chemical engineering, tells us that "a majority of our students will get job offers from the company they co-op for."

Northeastern students enter co-ops already armed with a proactive attitude because this philosophy of experiential education penetrates into the classroom. Dr. Webster also explains how "Northeastern's programs are built on learning by doing, which is great for engineering. We are the leaders in cooperative education (where almost all of our students complete three six-month rotations at companies, hospitals, or in university research labs) to practice what they learn. But our experiential learning is more than that. In all of our courses, we have students learn by doing. Studies show that learning is enhanced when it is active (conducting a lab, co-oping at a company, completing an experiment) than passive learning (taking notes off of power point slides, etc.). Teaching is fun

> **66** *Northeastern's programs are built on learning by doing, which is great for engineering.* **99**

at Northeastern because of this and our students are much more engaged, helping them learn and helping them decide what career path to take in life. There are no classes in chemical engineering in which students sit there and only take notes (and fall asleep)."

Service-learning courses

Northeastern fully integrates service-learning into the classroom with specialized classes that "require students to undertake and execute an actual community service project related to the specific subject of the course," the administration tells us. In many of these classes students will interact with community service partners in the Boston area, like the AIDS Action Committee or Project Adventure at Boston Children's Hospital. But some service-classes, like those offered through the Social Enterprise Institute, take service-learning abroad. These classes usually address a social problem in a global context, such as "gender inequality, financial exclusion, climate vulnerability, environmental degradation, water access, disease, illiteracy, human trafficking, food insecurity," according to the Social Enterprise Institute. In one such class, "Social Entrepreneurship and Sustainable Development in India," students, "working alongside local counterparts in government, private sector and the social sector, [design], develop and test innovative solutions to improve existing systems and help local partners achieve sustainable development," according to the course description. In these programs students also develop field research skills to investigate and design solutions for social problems.

Venture Accelerator

> **66** *Northeastern alumni are innovators and entrepreneurs.* **99**

Not all career preparation involves a job search—Northeastern also hosts an impressive array of entrepreneurship initiatives. One civil engineering student tells us that when looking around at the student body you find people with a "breadth of interests and lots of entrepreneurs." The school echoes that sentiment, explaining, "Students with a passion for entrepreneurship thrive at Northeastern in what is a robust ecosystem of passionate students from all majors working closely with faculty and alumni mentors from industry." Karim Sabbidine tells us about one program that is making a big difference for a lot of students. "Northeastern alumni are innovators and entrepreneurs," Sabbidine says, "through the help of IDEA, Northeastern's campus accelerator, many students have launched their own businesses and watched them flourish financially and socially."

IDEA is a student-run, student-founded venture accelerator, and it demonstrates how seriously Northeastern takes feedback and suggestions from students. IDEA exists because in 2009 six undergraduates went to the dean of the business school and said that Northeastern entrepreneurs needed support. Since then the program has provided more than half a million dollars in non-equity funding and helped launch 30 companies. The program provides students from across the university, as well as alumni and faculty, "with coaching, mentoring, in-kind services, business planning framework, and the opportunity to apply for gap funding," according to the university. "Last year, it had 150 active ventures in its portfolio," and it is one of the reasons Northeastern has ranked in our top ten programs for undergraduate entrepreneurship education. Some of the potential benefits include up to $1,000 in prototype funding, an investor network that has helped students connect with angel investors and venture capital, and service partners that provide legal, accounting, marketing, and backend services.

Chart Your Own Path

Students are granted a large degree of academic flexibility through interdisciplinary degrees and the PlusOne programs that allow students to pursue a bachelor's and master's degree in five years. Students can design their own major by combining existing majors into an interdisciplinary degree that investigates an emerging field of study or bridges two disciplines, such as "computer science and game design, interactive media and music technology, and mathematics and media and screen studies," the university explains.

The PlusOne program allows high achieving students to apply up to sixteen credits to both their undergraduate degree and a graduate degree. Beyond saving time and money, the PlusOne program is also a guaranteed way to get into one of the Northeastern graduate programs. PlusOne master's degrees are available through the colleges of computer and information science, engineering, science, health science, and social science and humanities, with a variety of specializations within each college.

Faculty

With a 13:1 student to faculty ratio, professors have time to treat students individually and, as one political science major tells us, find additional resources for any interested students. "My professors all come from a variety of backgrounds, have fascinating research projects, and love to teach. They always organize extra lectures, speakers, and events for students who are really interested in the course. Ultimately, my professors want me to succeed and that's awesome." It also helps when those "extras" involve industry connections and job leads. A communications major tells us that by forging these kinds of bonds with faculty, students reap huge benefits: "They will do anything in their power to help you with a job."

Aptly, the school that preaches hands-on education provides faculty with the reins. According to Dr. Thomas, the faculty maintain extensive control over the curriculum and "try very hard to lower the separation between faculty and students." They "have weekly tea times and other get-togethers to establish an environment where students experience a friendly environment [and get] to ask questions about anything. It is only through this 'family' environment that students can excel in active learning."

Alumni/ae

The well-connected and involved alumni are one of Northeastern's greatest assets. Karim Sabbidine tells us about the school's Empower campaign, a major funding, mentoring, networking operation, where he is "currently attempting to recruit 155 donations from my graduating class of 2014 in addition to helping the Northeastern Fund in any capacity." Empower helps students connect with alumni like Joe Fleming, '70 and '71, who chairs Specialty Pharma Inc., and Chris Ford, '73, the founder, former chair, and CEO of American Renal Associates. Together they founded a campus organization known as health Science Entrepreneurs that helps develop startups. The organization connects student inventors and entrepreneurs with an extensive network of industry experts and corporate officers, and it is available to them as long as they need it. Fleming and Ford also serve as advisers in the university's newly launched Venture Mentoring Network. The Empower Campaign has branches in every college and department and roots in decades of industry leading alumni. Other famous alumni include Napster founder Shawn Fanning and poet Martín Espada.

Oberlin College

101 North Professor Street, Oberlin, OH 44074
Admissions: 440-775-8121
E-mail: college.admissions@oberlin.edu
Website: www.oberlin.edu
Twitter: @oberlincollege, @oberlin_news, @obieadmissions

Introduction

If you're looking for an open-minded, incredibly inclusive, equality-embracing, and socially mindful college, look no farther than Oberlin: They proudly invented the category. Established in 1833, Oberlin College was the first in the nation to adopt a policy to admit African American students, opening their doors in 1835—an amazing thirty years before the Emancipation Proclamation and more than 120 years before Brown v. Board of Education made segregated education illegal. Unsurprisingly, the college was also the first to go (and stay) co-ed; the school accepted its first female students in 1837 and they graduated in 1841 as the nation's first women with baccalaureate degrees.

Today, that spirit of social responsibility and respect for all is as palpable as ever on Oberlin's campus. A major in East Asian studies told us that Oberlin is "a community that participates in conversations about social justice and activism on a daily basis" and that's devoted to "building an educated student body with a heightened awareness of racial, socioeconomic, and environmental issues that exist in today's society." An environmental studies/jazz trumpet major added, "Most people are very engaged in what they do, whether that be music or political activism or neuroscience. There are a lot of politically conscious, left-wing students here." With testimonies like these, it should be no surprise that the school landed on our 2005 roundup of Colleges with a Conscience. Likewise, Oberlin comes in at number five on The Princeton Review's 2016 ranking list for LGBT-Friendly schools. And thanks to sustainability initiatives on campus, Oberlin is also profiled in The Princeton Review's 2015 *Guide to 353 Green Colleges*. (When you visit, check out the environmental studies center's parking lot—it's roofed with a massive 336-panel solar array.)

All these feel-good, freethinking, granola-crunching vibes have a major payoff: They create a fantastic learning environment for students (or Obies, as they like to be called!). The college is divided into two divisions, the College of Arts and Sciences—which boasts forty-seven degree programs—and the

Conservatory of Music, the oldest continually operated music school in the nation, which offers eight undergraduate majors and access to 1,500 musical instruments. This unique mix of scholars and musicians results in a community that's sensitive and appreciative of the arts—and with a nationally respected art museum on campus and 500-plus (mostly free!) performance events going down each year, it's not hard to see why.

While its inclusive legacy is large, Oberlin is actually quite small—it has just under 3,000 students and its acceptance rate is 30 percent, making it a pretty choosey private school in a town of just under 10,000 people. This intimate setting, however, means that students really dig in to all that Oberlin has to offer: "We have strong academics and so many extracurricular and enrichment opportunities going on. There are SO MANY lectures and guest speakers . . . on campus!" one biology major proclaimed. "Many people are concerned that the town of Oberlin is too small, but it and the campus have so many opportunities that I'm rarely ever bored," said a peace, politics, and conflict studies major.

> **❝ One of our responsibilities is to make sure students see all the different outlets for what [their] major can do. ❞**

And what about life after Oberlin? "The liberal arts degree prepares you to do everything, but a liberal college doesn't often model everything," says an art history faculty member and Oberlin alum Erik Inglis. "One of our responsibilities is to make sure students see all the different outlets for what [their] major can do." This means that Oberlin students are continually encouraged to make their own ways—to use their rich, rigorous liberal arts training to connect with their passions and go forth to be the good they want to see in the world. Here are some programs and benefits that help them make that happen—and that could help you make it happen, too.

Winter Term

Give many college students the option of taking January off from school, and they'll gladly hop a bus back home for a few weeks of free food and laundry. Not so much at Oberlin, where the beloved winter term gives students the opportunity to pursue interests that aren't listed on the usual course schedule. Without actual classes, students can devote all their time and energy to one special project, which can be completed as a solo or group endeavor, pitched by students or faculty, conducted on campus or elsewhere in the world.

From hand-making paper to overhauling one's personal fitness regimen, from recording radio programs in El Salvador to working at a socially responsible investment firm through the Business Scholars Program, winter term is designed to give students the chance to focus on something that matters to them—or try out something they think might matter to them. "I use winter term as a time to express some creative part of myself that is not as well nurtured as it should be during the academic year," wrote an African studies/sociology major on the Oberlin student blogs (read more at: blogs.oberlin.edu). And a math/creative writing major wrote, "There will never again be a time in my life when I can drop everything for four weeks and do whatever I want without having to worry." Plus, being able to conceive of, line up, and execute a month's worth of fruitful, self-directed work is inarguably a fantastic experience for the working world—regardless of what month of the year you do it in!

> **❝ I use winter term as a time to express some creative part of myself that is not as well nurtured as it should be during the academic year.❞**

Experimental College

If you're at Oberlin, chances are you've got a passion—and you're itching to share it with your peers. Enter the Experimental College (or the ExCo, as it's called), where students, faculty, and members of the great community teach fascinating classes that are off the beaten path from most university curriculum. Sample courses include children's literature, rock climbing, ceramics, Japanese cinema, and understanding police brutality. Established in 1968, the program is run by students, which helps them learn how to become powerful instructors and gives them leadership skills for life after school.

Plus, students can earn credit for both taking and teaching ExCo classes, which are also open to the general public. "You can take a course on the Pokémon Trading Card Game and have it show up on your transcript. ExCos are truly a uniquely Oberlin experience," a studio art major and blogger for Oberlin wrote.

Allen Memorial Art Museum

Not all colleges can count a nationally ranked art museum as a major facility, but then again, Oberlin isn't just any college. The Allen Memorial Art Museum is considered on par with museums at Harvard and Yale, and it boasts 14,000 works of art—some of which students can rent for five dollars a semester. You read that right: In the dorm rooms of Oberlin students, original works by Renoir,

Picasso, and Dalí hang on the walls next to the usual Jimi Hendrix and *Pulp Fiction* posters. This is one school that trusts its student body!

Beyond being a beautiful place to take in the works of the Dutch Masters for free, the Allen Memorial Art Museum is a huge draw for students interested in pursuing museum work as a career. There's the Student Docent Program, which introduces students to the theory of museum learning, trains them in leading guided tours, gives them exceptional access to the collection, and exposes them to a variety of practical careers within the museum world, often inspiring them to become curators or art educators. "[The] museum … is a place where students can get all sorts of experience as undergraduates," Professor Erik Inglis told us. "Which then means that when they are applying to … grad school or internships, they really have more experience than students from other schools. You can go through any museum of significance in the United States and find Oberlin grads."

Oberlin Student Cooperative Association

This mega-liberal, socially minded college is famous for its co-ops: community living residences in which students define a house's purpose, set up rules, keep budgets, cook meals, and pitch in on chores—and make massive strides in developing independence, responsibility, and cooperation. OSCA boasts eight co-ops for various student identities (such as vegetarian, interfaith, and first-generation) and spots are typically awarded by lottery.

There's also a financial benefit: Co-op members get three square meals a day and access to a fully stocked kitchen for less than the usual college dining program. Plus, if the co-op overall is thrifty, members may even get a refund! OSCA also proudly takes on neat projects—like making their own granola, tofu, bread, and yogurt. "Cooking and cleaning together makes for one of the tightest bonds of friendship you can think of," an Oberlin blogger and communications major wrote of Harkness, the school's famous and self-identified hippie co-op. "[And] learning to respect the space you are living in is an incredibly valuable experience."

Creativity and Leadership Program: Entrepreneurship at Oberlin

Oberlin may seem like a hippie's haven, but that doesn't mean it's not keeping up with the entrepreneurial spirit of our times. "As a word that describes money-centric capitalists, yes, entrepreneurship has always been a little antithetical to Oberlin's values," blogged one two-time LaunchU participant and the current

Creativity & Leadership Program fellow. "As a skill set and state of mind, however, it defines nearly everything that makes Oberlin what it's proud to be today." The Creativity and Leadership Program offers loads of mentorship and funding opportunities—in the case of the LaunchU accelerator, up to $45,000 in funding. Held during winter term, LaunchU is a three-week boot camp that helps students develop business models and hone pitches to venture capitalists at its annual pitch competition. LaunchU participants receive ongoing support from Oberlin alumni—in the form of venture coaching and connections to industry experts and investors, for example. Students of all stripes can participate: There's a venture track for those with the next big tech ideas, social track for nonprofit visionaries, and small business track for innovators in the performing arts, food, and so forth.

For those students who aren't quite in pitch mode yet, there's the Ignition Fund, a smaller grant that will help them take their ideas to the next level. And for conservatory students, the Flint Initiative Grants are music-specific endowments that allow them to dream up big new artistic endeavors. Creativity and Leadership programming also offers workshops that coach students through the various application processes.

Examples of ventures include a startup that provides a solar-run education platform to schools in developing nations, which they then use to hold interactive video sessions; an indie record label and collective; a running app that pairs up the best music for your workout; and a Moroccan rug collective that gives back to weavers back in Africa.

Bonner Center for Service and Learning

Each year, 63 percent of Oberlin students rally to contribute more than 100,000 hours of community service through the Bonner Center for Service and Learning, a college organization that teams up students, faculty, community partners, and alumni to solve pressing problems. Students frequently work within the community of Oberlin or the greater Northeast Ohio area, but in recent years they've also spread their good work to more than thirty countries, too. Opportunities include acting as Ninde Scholars to mentor students attending Oberlin City Schools (often so they can be the first in their families to attend college) and joining AmeriCorps as part-time members through the Bonner Leader Program to work on initiatives in public health, the environment, veteran issues, education, and clean energy, to name a few.

For fifteen incoming freshmen who are especially passionate about kicking off lifetimes of community service, the center offers the Bonner Scholars Program, a generous, four-year scholarship initiative that requires several hours of weekly community service and participation in seven weeks of summer volunteer programs. "I'm a Bonner Scholar and it's quickly turning out to be one of the most rewarding decisions I've made since coming to Oberlin," one computer science major blogged. "I work at America Reads and the Du Bois Fraction Club right now and I love both sites."

There's also the Dalai Lama Fellows Program and Projects for Peace, competitive scholarship programs that reward and facilitate cross-cultural, inter-faith, and conflict-reducing projects at home and abroad.

Faculty

At Oberlin, students enjoy lots of one-on-one time with professors and find most of their classes to be cozy, personal sessions—the official student-to-professor ratio is 9:1. There are only five classes with more than 100 seats, and of Oberlin's 900 classes, 700 have fewer than twenty students. Small classes are nice, but they're even nicer given the exceptional caliber of the college's faculty. "The professors are top-notch, enthusiastic, encouraging, and willing to work with you," shared a biology major. "I can't imagine having gotten a better education anywhere else."

The most powerful indicator of the faculty's lasting effect on its students is the life-long relationships that it often fosters. "I always tell them, I can guarantee them twenty years of advice," said a neuroscience professor Lynne Bianchi. For a graduate headed out into the real world, that's an invaluable resource—and a generous, committed professor!

Oberlin faculty pride themselves on teaching students how to think, not what to think, in preparation for a lifetime of engagement. The faculty also encourage determination and drive, but rarely competition: "Oberlin students never talk about their GPA. . . . You could brag about how hard you work, but you can't brag about how good you are. And I think that's healthy," reported Professor Inglis. But ultimately, it's all about finding that passion: "For me, one of the great things about Oberlin is that Oberlin genuinely encourages students to do what they love: It's both tremendously and intellectually liberating and pragmatically useful." Professor Bianchi agreed: "Our students tend to want to be the best for themselves, but not to be better than someone else. So while they are working on doing their best they are also helping their classmates along the way."

Obies in the World

Oberlin's bright, political, self-starting students often find themselves in the spotlight—from suffragist Lucy Stone to creator of the HBO drama *Girls* Lena

Dunham, from winner of the Nobel Prize in Literature Sinclair Lewis to Jad Abumrad and Robert Krulwich (both halves of popular podcast *Radiolab*). Established in 1840, Oberlin's alumni association counts 40,000 members, and current students regularly get to meet their more senior counterparts to hear how their education shaped their careers: "Alumni are a way to show students, 'This is what I did at Oberlin and this is where I am now,'" said Professor Bianchi. "Oberlin alumni tend to want to give back because they so appreciate their experience here." Oberlin grads have yet another good thing going for them: Since 1920, more have earned PhDs than those from any other undergraduate college in the United States.

Overall, as one current student shared, Oberlin is a place where "every student can have the undergrad experience for which he or she is looking." This sentiment meshes perfectly with the series of questions that Professor Inglis told us he always asks of his new advisees: "What *might* you want to be doing in five years? Why do you want to do it? How can you explore whether you *really* want to do it? And how can we help you think about doing it?"

Pitzer College

1050 North Mills Avenue, Claremont, CA 91711-6101
Admissions: 909-621-8129
Email: admission@pitzer.edu
Website: www.pitzer.edu
Twitter: @pitzercollege

Introduction

Pitzer College in Southern California is a liberal arts school that celebrates the ingenuity of its students and strives to be on the cutting edge of new ideas. Since its inception in 1964, Pitzer students and faculty have directed the college's mission, values and practices,"[embracing] interdisciplinarity in teaching and learning, creative and cooperative classroom experience, and community governance, encouraging every voice to be heard equally and fully." Pitzer is one of The Claremont Colleges, a consortium of five undergraduate schools and two graduate schools. Membership grants Pitzer students the individual attention, freedom and support of a small, liberal arts college while gaining access to the libraries, research facilities, and educational network resources usually enjoyed by larger institutions.

With a "quirky" student body and an inclusive environment "where students are free to be themselves," Pitzer is a great choice for anyone with an independent spirit. In particular, it attracts students with an interest in social and environmental justice, sustainability, or community action. Because Pitzer places a premium on student innovation and ideas, students can easily create personalized majors tailored to their passions. But students also have a voice in the college community at large. Pitzer affords its students a greater level of influence and participation in college governance than almost any other school. Students actually help set the requirements for every academic degree the college offers and aid in the establishment of new academic divisions because they serve on most college committees and on the College Council. The central legislative body for the school, the Council is instrumental "in setting institutional priorities and shaping academic and student life," according to the college website.

Pitzer's emphasis on social and environmental action means that there are plenty of opportunities for hands-on learning. More than 75 percent of Pitzer grads have studied abroad, and the college has dedicated experiential learning programs that allow students to explore environmental resource management, tropical ecology, sustainable agriculture, urban studies, public policy and vaccine research, and more.

Student Driven Academics

Pitzer produces active, engaged graduates by placing their students at the helm of their educational careers. Unlike colleges that have pre-set criteria for each major with little room for individual control, Pitzer provides a set of educational goals that students use, in cooperation with their adviser, to create an academic plan with "an individualized program of study which responds to the students' own intellectual needs and interests." Students can choose from any of Pitzer's four-one majors or any major offered by another Claremont College that is not available at Pitzer. In addition, students may create their own Combined Major, which borrows elements from two majors to generate a specialized, interdisciplinary major. But for those who want to carve out an even more specialized space for themselves, Pitzer has a third option called a Special Major. Special Majors are for students who wish to pursue a line of academic inquiry that is not covered by any existing major. The student is responsible, in collaboration with at least two members of the faculty, for developing the title and purpose of the Special Major and for establishing the intellectual coherence and the academic guidelines for their Special Major.

An Asian studies graduate of 2013 told us this kind of autonomy and interdisciplinary study was a huge pull. "I really liked and appreciated the fact that you had the option to design your own major, that there was no strict set of courses you had to take, but rather had the option to take many courses within different disciplines, many of which overlapped with other disciplines which allowed for a truly interdisciplinary experience."

Agents of Change

In addition to the premium it places on a student-guided education, Pitzer's curricular structure also weaves in elements of its social justice mission. Katie Purvis-Robert, professor of chemistry and environmental science, told us that students who do well at Pitzer are "curious and want to change the world." Student engagement is a huge part of Pitzer culture all the way down to its curriculum. All students, regardless of major, fulfill a Social Responsibility Objective through community service, community-based fieldwork, or a community based internship. Many Pitzer classes help to fulfill this requirement by pairing theory with practical, community-based application. In fact, Kathy Yep, assistant professor of sociology and Asian American studies, was awarded a Carnegie Foundation Faculty Fellowship for service-learning courses that "focus on facilitating students' analytical skills . . . by exploring social theories such as Pierre Bourdieu's social reproduction or Chandra Mohanty's feminist genealogies through collaborations with communities-at-large," according to the school's website. Collectively these students have gained thousands of hours of experience in cooperation with "community partnerships [ranging] from after-school tutoring programs in underserved communities to first-generation college student retention efforts at the Claremont Colleges and adult literacy work with immigrant communities," the school's website explained.

In addition, every student explores a topic of special interest within their major through at least two disciplines and two cultural perspectives. Students collaborate with their academic advisers and are encouraged to be innovative in their approach. Through social engagement and multifocal study, students are able to test, reevaluate, and fine-tune what they've learned in the classroom while gaining an appreciation for what Pitzer calls "the ethical implications of knowledge and action."

Study Abroad Programs

❝ My semester abroad was the most valuable experience I had in college. The Pitzer in Botswana program was life changing.❞

With sixty programs to choose from, study abroad is hugely popular at Pitzer. The Institute for Global Local Action "helps students integrate their learning from study abroad experiences with local community engagement." For Sayjal Waddy, a 2007 sociology major, studying abroad was a transformative experience. "My semester abroad was the most valuable experience I had in college. The Pitzer in Botswana program was life changing. Through that program I lived in a rural village for a month with no electricity or running water. In that month I learned that I was stronger than I realized. I spent the rest of my time working in orphanages throughout the country." Experiences like Sayjal's run deep in Pitzer's institutional memory. A history major from the Class of 1975 told us that "a clear grasp of their role as agents of change, here and abroad; a devotion to social-justice causes; a commitment to making the world more habitable, green, and just" are the defining characteristics of Pitzer graduates.

The college also operates a semester long study abroad program in Costa Rica through the Firestone Center for Restoration Ecology. Located near the Hacienda Baru Reserve, the Firestone Center is a former lowland rainforest that was cleared for cattle farming during the 1950's and 1960's. Today Pitzer College manages the land through restoration ecology and sustainable forestry efforts. Students take classes in topical and human ecology where they study "critical interactions between humans and the natural world" and gain hands on experience in the study of tropical ecosystems, according to the program's description.

Engaged Parent and Alumni Networks

This may be the time when students are looking forward to getting away from their parents and exploring the world on their own, but when it funds internships, establishes international medical research partnerships, and hosts career shadowing and entrepreneurial opportunities, the Pitzer parent network is the last place to run away from. Pitzer places a premium on early career preparation, so it makes sense parents and alumni share those values and want to get involved. Pitzer told us that they "[emphasize] to students and their parents that Pitzer students need to begin the career planning process early in their academic careers. Career Services has worked closely with the Admissions office to reach students and families during the college application and decision process . . . to reach students as early as possible."

A culture of parent involvement at Pitzer has helped to develop some fantastic career programs, like the Winter Break Shadowing Program, the Pitzer Internship Fund, the Institute for Entrepreneurship, as well as extensive research opportunities. Pitzer explained the rationale behind this early intervention to us: "The earlier that students begin preparing to tell their story (résumé writing, cover letter writing), building relationships (networking with alumni, parents, peers), exploring their interests (researching career paths, shadowing, work experiences), and building their skills (internships, research experiences), the better they will be at making good career decisions and having an executable career plan at graduation."

Ferré/Marquet Vaccine Research Center

At the Ferré/Marquet Vaccine Research Center students can join members of the faculty and the local community in the quest to improve healthcare in developing countries. Established in 2008 through a gift from Dr. Francois Ferré and Dr. Magda Marquet, the parents of 2011 alumnus Alexandre Ferré, the Vaccine Research Center provides excellent opportunities for anyone interested in groundbreaking biomedical research with the potential to affect millions of lives. It also lives up to Pitzer's ethos of global/local action, social responsibility, and cutting edge ideas. In collaboration with the University of Botswana, Pitzer faculty, students and community members work to "develop cost-effective vaccine production and address urgent health issues in southern Africa."

The Research Center's pilot project, the development of a cattle vaccine that protects against a common and debilitating disease, reflects Pitzer's multi-focal approach. While its researchers develop multiple vaccines and conduct clinical trials (with promising results!), the program is also addressing a problem that has plagued vaccine delivery in southern Africa for years: the need for continuous refrigeration. The Center is developing vaccines that can be produced safely anywhere in the world and transported as a dried powder, thus eliminating the need for a "cold-chain" from production at a centralized lab to injection in the field. This method of examining all of the components of a problem is a reflection of Pitzer's social responsibility mission to understand the full implications of academic endeavors. This approach helps account for the success of its research programs, which Pitzer tells us "garnered over $750,000 in external science funding to support faculty-student research" in the 2013-14 school year alone.

Funding the Unfunded Internship

Internships are a great way to gain experience in an industry and to network with employers looking for new talent. However, when an increasing number of those internships offer little or no pay, they aren't viable options for many students. Here is where the Pitzer Internship Fund comes in. The school explained, "Through the generosity of alumni and parent donors, Pitzer provides summer internship funding to students who find and secure summer internships that would otherwise be unpaid or very low-paid. Many students may not be able to create or accept internship opportunities that support their future career plans and enable them to explore potential career paths unless they are able to receive complete or partial funding for their internship experience." Funding a program like this is easier with a strong parent and alumni network that is willing to give back. One 2013 graduate we interviewed benefited from an internship while studying at Pitzer and now sits on the Alumni Board where he leads the pillar for alumni giving (He explained that the board has four pillars that each have responsibilities for engaging alumni.) As a student, it's nice to have someone in your corner who knows firsthand the benefits of a career experiences outside of the classroom.

Pitzer Institute for Entrepreneurship

PIE is an entrepreneurship program with a social conscience. While it is a brand new program, it is seemingly inevitable development from a school that places so much emphasis on student ideas and action. The administration told us that, at its core, "PIE encourages and empowers student to 'turn their ideas into actions' through programs and workshops. PIE aims to educate students about the concept of entrepreneurship (with an emphasis on social impact) and to teach entrepreneurial skills that will benefit students in preparation for conventional careers or for starting their own ventures."

Just as importantly, "PIE will connect students with alumni and parent entrepreneurs for mentoring purposes," giving students the exposure to success and confidence to turn their ideas and actions into lasting change. In its first year, PIE gave students "training and support to develop a new venture, culminating with the chance to pitch your new venture idea to alumni at Reunion Weekend in May," according to the inaugural PIE announcement. The student or group with the best idea would also receive funding to attend an entrepreneurial conference.

Faculty

With 115 faculty members, Pitzer boasts an enviable 10:1 student-to-faculty ratio. The college explains that the "faculty is organized by field groups instead of traditional academic departments. Scientists, sociologists, historians, writers and artists influence each other's work and often teach courses together." This kind of academic diffusion and integration is important when students decide that they want to create a Combined or Special major because the faculty they will be consulting with are already accustomed to thinking about their field beyond the boundaries of a specific department. Instead, faculty advisers are tuned into Pitzer's educational mission. "Intercultural understanding, social responsibility and interdisciplinary learning [become] apparent in the collaborations between faculty and students in designing their academic plan," the administration explained. Professor Purvis-Roberts, who also serves as the associate dean of faculty, told us, "The faculty are fully in control of the curriculum and educational philosophy at Pitzer College." This kind of control and flexibility allows the faculty to develop courses like the "Accelerated Integrated Science Sequence course," Professor Purvis-Roberts explained, "which combines a year of introductory Biology, Chemistry, and Physics into a double course. The purpose of the course is to introduce students to the intersections of the disciplines, and it has transformed other introductory courses in our department."

The administration gave us a behind-the-scenes look at their faculty search process, explaining, "When we hire new faculty, we are looking for excellent teacher-scholars who are gifted and innovative teachers and outstanding scholars in their field. During the 2013-2014 academic year, faculty authored or edited nine books, published forty articles and book chapters, and exhibited original work all around the world." And the search for dedicated teacher-scholars pays off. Professor Purvis-Roberts reported that "faculty care deeply about the students. In the Keck Science Department, every major is required to do a senior thesis. The majority of these theses involve working closely together

> **66 Students often present their research at scientific conferences and co-author papers with faculty members. 99**

in the laboratory setting on cutting-edge research. Students often present their research at scientific conferences and co-author papers with faculty members." Professor Purvis-Roberts said that professors "interact closely with students in the research laboratory, which is a great opportunity to mentor the students and also get to know them well." But in these close partnerships students begin to rub off on the professors as well. "I like how they apply concepts of social responsibility into the science classroom," Purvis-Roberts admitted.

Life after Pitzer

Alumni maintain strong ties to the college and the campus community, and nearly everyone we spoke with serves on the alumni board and mentors students. Pitzer graduates count among their numbers are a blend of writers and entertainers, including musician John Darnielle of The Mountain Goats and the Emmy Award winning writer for *Saturday Night Live* Max Brooks. There are just as many political leaders, including Hunter Lovins, a sustainability entrepreneur and writer who served as a North American delegate to the United Nations World Summit on Sustainable Development and was named a "Hero of the Planet" by *Time* magazine. When it comes to career, Pitzer College links up with rest of The Claremont Colleges in a joint On-Campus Recruiting Program that brings Paramount, Disney, Google, J.P. Morgan, and more to campus to tap into Claremont talent.

What does a Pitzer graduate, in particular, bring to the table? Dr. Suyapa Portillo, both an alumna and assistant professor at Pitzer, summed it up for us: "A graduating senior, a seasoned Pitzer student, has been engaged in some sort of project for a long-time (or the duration of their time at Pitzer and also while studying abroad), showing commitment and follow through. They are creative writers and researchers. There is a good balance between community work, and many understand the links between scholarship and societal concerns. They are probably going to apply and win a Fulbright, or Watson Fellowship, or end up going to work on something related to their course of study at Pitzer, from environment, to policy, to social justice, or healthcare." A 2012 English and creative writing alumna agreed. She said, "Their real world identities are diverse, but what they share is that they are life-long philanthropists."

Pomona College

333 N. College Way, Claremont, California 91711
Admissions: 909-621-8000
E-mail: admissions@pomona.edu
Website: www.pomona.edu
Twitter: @pomonacollege

Introduction

> **❝ Pomona attracts a student who is curious and passionate. ❞**

Located thirty miles from Los Angeles, Pomona College gives students the tight-knit feel of a small liberal arts school while providing them with the resources of a much larger university, thanks to The Claremont Consortium. According to one mathematics major, "Pomona is like an intellectually stimulating version of heaven." With roughly 1,600 students—and a student-faculty ratio of 8:1—Pomona offers small classes in a wide range of majors, with an emphasis on collaborative learning and seminar-based courses rather than large lectures. The majority of the professors, most of whom their students greet by first name, have an open door policy that they say actually stimulates discussion beyond just frantic questions in the days before an exam. One faculty member notes that, "One thing I love about Pomona students is that they come to office hours! They don't just come because they have a question about the upcoming exam but because they want to discuss the material. They are very engaged with their classes." In keeping with its liberal arts tradition, some of the most popular majors at Pomona—economics, biology, mathematics, politics, neuroscience, psychology, environmental analysis, and modern languages—show the school's wide variety of academic opportunities available to students. One French/pre-med major says that the "backbone of any school is the atmosphere created by the student body"—"Pomona attracts a student who is curious and passionate."

Settling In

One of the hardest transitions for college freshmen is the shift from living at home to living in a dorm. For Pomona first-years, Sponsor Groups help make this change a little easier. For one international relations major at Pomona, "The sponsor group . . . made the prospect of going to college less terrifying." A Sponsor Group is made up of ten to twenty Pomona first-year students who live in adjacent rooms in the same residence halls, along with two sophomore sponsors. These sponsors help their freshman charges get acquainted with everything from how to join a club on campus and how to buy books for various classes to how to navigate Los Angeles with—or without—a car and find the city's best local food joints. Sponsor Groups have been a Pomona tradition since 1927, and all first-year students are assigned a sponsor, who undergoes intensive training and is in contact with the school's other resident advisers, as well as Pomona's four other mentor programs—the Asian American Mentor Program (AAMP), Chicano/Latino Student Affairs (CLSA), Ujima (which is run by the Office of Black Student Affairs), and the Queer, Questioning and Allied Mentoring Program. Incoming students also have the opportunity to meet their fellow freshmen—and take advantage of some of the great nature activities around Pomona—during Orientation Adventure. These off-campus orientation programs, also chaperoned by trained student leaders, provide outdoor experience, bonding opportunities, and help new students develop important critical thinking skills that will serve them well during their academic careers at Pomona. In addition, each trip has a Community Engagement component—students participate in a service project specifically designed to help give back to the communities they visit. These include environmental service projects, civic and social justice projects, and educational sessions about students' impact on the natural world. There are twelve trips offered throughout Southern California, with locations ranging from the mountains and ancient Sequoia forests to inner city Los Angeles. Throughout their freshman year, Pomona students also get regular check-ins and informational letters as part of the 3-6-9 Steps for Success program, another way that the college helps incoming students adjust to their first year on campus.

Multiply the Opportunity

Pomona students can take advantage of all a small school has to offer—small classes and an intimate community feeling on campus—without sacrificing the tremendous opportunities that a larger university provides, thanks to the Claremont Colleges. Pomona is one of the five undergraduate colleges that are part of the consortium, along with Claremont McKenna, Harvey Mudd, Scripps, and Pitzer; there are two graduate institutions, Claremont Graduate Institute and Keck Graduate Institute, which round out the group. While each school is completely separate—if a student wants to take courses only at Pomona, there's no requirement to do otherwise—it's incredibly easy for students to sign up for courses at any of the participating consortium schools (and each college even saves spaces in many of their courses for students from the other Claremont Colleges). It helps that all the campuses border each other and it takes only a few minutes to walk from, for example, Pomona to Scripps—the consortium "mega campus" takes up one square mile. Alumnus Louis DiPalma, who is a Program Manager at Microsoft, told us, "Having a liberal arts education in combination with classes at Harvey Mudd (the tech focused school within the consortium) definitely primed me for [my] work" which is "quite technical, but also requires lots of writing, communication, and qualitative analysis skills." The choices available to Pomona students thanks to the consortium are jaw-dropping: nearly 2,000 courses with 230 English and literature options, 140 mathematics courses, and offerings in 12 languages. Pomona students also have access to the two million-volume Honnold-Mudd Library, which is shared with the consortium colleges. In addition to the academic offerings that the consortium offers to students from the five undergraduate colleges and two graduate institutions, the consortium also provides myriad social opportunities for students to get to know each other, with school-sponsored activities ranging from films, art exhibits, concerts, plays, readings, and lectures. Campus clubs are also open to students from consortium schools and students on the meal plan have the option of dining at any of the various dining halls throughout the campuses. As one biology major sums up, "Pomona is the best of both worlds: you get all the personal attention and small class sizes associated with a smaller school, along with the social scene and class choices of a larger university."

Sustainability and the Environment

"Pomona College," says one Spanish major, "is all about sustainability, diversity, and equality." The school strives to stay on top of the latest environmental issues, from sustainability to climate change, and adjust its policies accordingly. Pomona already had eight LEED certified buildings, and the under-construction Millikan Science Hall is being built to meet at least LEED Gold-certification standards. Instead of purchasing offsets (also known as renewable energy credits), Pomona plans to focus on behavior modification, conservation efforts campus wide, efficiency, and renewable energy sources. One molecular biology major says that Pomona's greatest strength is that the school and its student body is "environmentally, socially, and politically aware." In the dining halls, as part of the school's Sustainability Action Plan, the goal is to have 15 percent of the total food purchases qualify as sustainable by 2015 and 20 percent of total food purchases qualify as sustainable by 2020. That year is also the deadline for Pomona's objective to have 50 percent of produce purchased be local. Outside of the classroom—and the dining halls—students looking to get back to nature have the opportunity to join the Claremont Colleges' popular outdoor club, On the Loose, which helps organize backpacking, hiking, climbing, and rafting trips in California and the Southwestern states for interested students. According to OTL's website, the club "welcome[s] students of all ability levels, from the most hardened sherpas to the freshest greenhorns," so freshmen who want to take up a new sport, as well as those who are seasoned hikers, should join. As one international relations major puts it, "On the Loose, the outdoors club, is a huge part of campus culture. Most students will gladly work a Friday night to go climb rocks, surf, or hike early on Saturday with friends." Pomona also offers the resources of the Outdoor Education Center, one of the country's premier outdoor education programs. The Center provides hands-on opportunities for students in outdoor education and recreation and, as an added environmental bonus, the building where the Center is housed is Platinum-certified by LEED standards.

Language Immersion

66 *I am a freshman, and I am already working with a professor doing research.* **99**

While a foreign language requirement in college is nothing new, Pomona offers students a unique opportunity to immerse themselves in another language. The Oldenborg Center for Modern Languages and International Relations provides not only conversation courses in six major languages—Mandarin Chinese, French, German, Japanese, Russian, and Spanish—but also provides a select number of students the option of living in a language dorm, where not only will the students take the normal language courses but they'll be surrounded by the language all day long. One Spanish major praises the language programs at Pomona, saying that the school's "Foreign Language Resource Center has free tutoring from students in high-level language courses." The living requirements for Pomona's language dorms, which are supervised by language residents who are native speakers in the foreign language the students are learning, are fairly routine, with all residents needing to take a year of college-level language study and also be open to joining in Oldenborg's many extracurricular activities. These activities are open to all Pomona students, regardless of if they are residents in the Oldenborg language dorm. One popular gathering place at lunch are the language tables in the Oldenborg Center dining hall, where students congregate to practice their conversational foreign language skills with native speakers. Every day, tables are set up to accommodate the six major languages but for students who are interested in practicing a new language—or those international students who want to reconnect with a piece of their native country—the language tables also offer other options on a rotating basis, from Tagalog and Hindu/Urdu to Persian, Swedish, and Armenian. In addition to the language lunch tables, the Oldenborg Center also sponsors the Oldenborg Lunch Colloquium, and special events like the International Karaoke Klub Nite.

Science Facilities

Since Pomona students are all taught by professors, rather than teaching assistants or graduate students, opportunities abound to assist these professors in their lab or with other research projects. One philosophy, politics, and economics major notes, "I am a freshman and I am already working with a professor doing research," which seems to be the norm rather than the exception to the rule at Pomona. One member of Pomona's science faculty underscores that her fellow professors all mentor students for research projects. "Students (even first-year students) are able to participate in research at all levels," says this professor, "from study design, data collection, analysis, writing, presenting and sometimes publishing. Just recently [six] students from my lab presented their research at a professional scientific meeting on five separate research projects!" For students looking to pursue careers in the sciences, two key Pomona facilities where they can get more hands-on experience are the Table Mountain Observatory and the Scanning Electron Microscope. The Observatory, which is used primarily by the physics and astronomy department, includes instruments such as the Pomona College 1-Meter Telescope, which is housed at NASA JPL's Table Mountain Facility and located in the mountains above Wrightwood, California. This telescope is used to study dense interstellar clouds and star-forming regions. The Department of Physics and Astronomy, in conjunction with Harvey Mudd, also operates a Scanning Electron Microscope (SEM), the funding for which came from a grant from the National Science Foundation. Students, after attending a mandatory training session, are allowed to use the SEM for projects and research reaching beyond physics into fields such as chemistry, biology and geology. The Millikan Planetarium, also maintained by the Department of Physics and Astronomy, is undergoing renovations but will reopen in 2015 with a state of the art facility called the Digital Immersive Theatre. This new addition will include an "all-dome visualization capability that will enable us to fly through galaxies, land on planets, and to visualize datasets for all of the sciences, humanities, and art within [the] theatre."

Beyond Pomona

Even though one English literature major admits that Pomona's "great classes and great people" make it so that "you never want to graduate," the school does its best to prepare students for life after college. The Career Development Office is the place to go to get information about internships and job opportunities. One popular program among Pomona students is the Summer Experience Funding Program, where Pomona funds what would otherwise be an unpaid internship, which allows students to pursue opportunities in their career fields without the financial burden. It also gives community programs the benefit of employing eager Pomona students who otherwise might not have been able to accept a position. The Pomona College Internship Program provides internship opportunities in the greater Los Angeles area for Pomona students, while those students who are interested in working abroad are encouraged to use the Going Global resource, available through the Career Development Office. Taking full advantage of the advances in digital technology—and students' preferences to do as many things online as possible—the Career Development Office now offers access to Candid Careers, which provides information videos from professionals, including Pomona alumni, in a variety of fields. The topics range from the general ("What I wish I'd known as a student") to the specific ("Google wants to know if you're smart"). Pomona alumni are also encouraged to contact the Career Development Office and record their own short video segment to assist their fellow Sagehens in finding the best post-Pomona career paths.

As for career preparation, the alumni we spoke with told us that their extracurricular activities at Pomona were among their most valuable experiences there. Louis DiPalma described his involvement with the Associated Students of Pomona College (the student government) and serving as Junior Class President: "It gave me a really interesting look at the politics and inner workings of the school as well as helping me learn things like long-term planning, coordinating for an event, and finding funding for a project. In the end, some things I did were big successes, others were failures, but I took a lot of learning from what worked and what didn't that has helped me since." Alumna Jordan Pedraza, a Senior Program Manager at Google for Education, had been involved on campus as a mentor with the Office of Black Student Affairs, a student tutor, and a student technology consultant (among other activities). She told us: "Although it wasn't always clear during college how my trajectory would pan out, I was lucky to have wonderful mentors encouraging me to learn new skills and knowledge that would round out my background for the future. The writing, thinking, and analytical skills I developed at Pomona influenced my interest in becoming a professor; my classes tutoring and mentoring jobs influenced my passion for education and social justice; and my work with the technology department influenced my interest in technology." She continued, "The most valuable experience I had was developing my world view: All the readings, papers, discussions, and presentations inspired confidence to form an opinion, consider alternative perspectives, communicate my thoughts in a compelling way, and engage with response or feedback. . . . I find deep joy and fulfillment in thinking critically and sharing my viewed in my professional and personal lives, and Pomona has enabled me to experience that."

Princeton University

Undergraduate Admission Office, P.O. Box 430
Princeton, NJ 08542-0430
Admissions: 609-258-3060
E-mail: uaoffice@princeton.edu
Website: www.princeton.edu
Twitter: @ApplyPrinceton

Introduction

Students say Princeton University is "the perfect size (enough students that things never get boring, but a small enough student body that there's still a strong sense of community)." As the fourth-oldest institute of higher learning in the United States, Princeton University has long had a "sterling reputation" for quality academics. But students say Princeton's "unique focus on the undergraduate experience" gives incoming students an edge and helps prepare them for the future. The university is committed to undergraduate teaching, and all faculty teach undergraduates. Supporting these efforts are exceptional academic and research resources, including the world-class Firestone Library, the new Frick Chemistry Laboratory that emphasizes hands-on learning in teaching labs, a genomics institute, the Woodrow Wilson School of Public and International Affairs that trains leaders in public service, and an engineering school that enrolls more than 900 undergraduates. Princeton students can choose between more than eighty fields of concentration (i.e. majors) and interdisciplinary certificate programs, of which history, political science, economics, and international affairs are among the most popular. Among the sciences, molecular biology is quite popular. The school's excellent faculty-student ratio of 6:1 means that many classes are discussion-based, giving students a direct line to their brilliant professors, and "once you take upper-level courses, you'll have a lot of chances to work closely with professors and study what you are most interested in." All "unfailingly brilliant, open, and inspirational" faculty members also work closely with undergraduates in the supervision of junior-year independent work and senior theses. "Professors love teaching, and there are many fantastic lecturers," giving students a chance "to meet and take classes from some of the most brilliant academic minds in the world."

In particular, Princeton has a number of programs specifically designed to start freshmen off on the right foot, and some of these programs start before students even buy their books. The Bridge Year Program allows incoming freshmen to delay enrollment for one year while they participate in a two-semester community service program abroad. When they return, they will join "5,200 passionate, intelligent students" in classes taught by wonderful, captivating lecturers." And while the introductory lecture classes that provide the groundwork for future study are often large, Princeton offers Freshman Seminars that give newly matriculated students a chance to take an intimate, discussion-based class with some "really experienced and big-name professors, who actually want to teach undergraduates." Some students call these Freshmen Seminars the most rewarding and important experiences they have in college: "The discussions I have in seminar are the reason I get out of bed in the morning; after a great class, I feel incredibly invigorated."

All Princeton professors are "leading scholars in their field," including those who teach the freshman Writing Seminars, which are required as a component of the Princeton Writing Program. This program sets students up for success by providing them with in-depth writing and research courses that prepare them for the rigorous academic challenges ahead. After these seminars students agree that "academics that are fascinating and challenging, but nevertheless manageable."

But classwork and discussion are only half of the picture. Princeton hosts a huge number of research initiatives and community-based learning classes during the school year and in the summer that have allowed students to make a real world impact in areas like HIV research and Hurricane Sandy relief. Here are some of the programs and classes that Princeton offers its freshmen to get them off to the right start.

Freshman Seminars

These non-required but extremely popular classes give freshmen a chance to take a class that focuses on a narrow topic of inquiry in a way that is not typically available until junior or senior year, like "Japanese Monsters and Ghosts: A Social History," which examines everything from ancient religious texts to modern video games in order to trace how these figures interact with Japanese social, political, and economic life. In most cases, such a class would require previous study in sociology, history, or cultural anthropology, but the freshman seminars are designed for students to lean deeply into their subjects without relying on previous study. In this way first-years at Princeton have access to a great selection of classes, all taught within the university's six residential colleges, where they can discover new academic interests and develop a close relationship with a member of the faculty. That they are only open to freshmen lends these seminars a sense of comradery and makes it easier for students to speak up and be heard. In fact, the seminars are focused around discussion, presentations, and papers—rather than quizzes and tests. The freshman seminar gives students the benefits of small, intimate classes without the anxiety of taking classes with juniors and seniors on the first day.

The toughest part of the freshman seminar might be what one student describes as "the almost-maddening excess of opportunities." Oftentimes freshman seminar classes are arranged around a single, specific question, like "Can Entrepreneurial Innovation Cure What Ails America's Healthcare 'System'?" or "What Makes a Poem Endure," while other might explore a developing technology or industry, such as "The Smart Band-Aid," which peels back the science of healing soft tissue wounds and new ways to do it better. President Emerita and molecular biology professor Shirley Tilghman teaches a popular freshman seminar in genetics, "How the Tabby Got Her Stripes." Most freshman seminar classes also fulfill one of the school's general education requirements.

Bridge Year Program

Before they set their foot in the door, a select group of incoming freshmen are whisked away to Bolivia, China, Brazil, India, or Senegal for a tuition-free, nine-month community service mission that is sure to widen their perspective as well as to introduce them to Princeton's unofficial motto, "Princeton in the Nation's Service and in the Service of All Nations." And, let's be honest: High-achievers have been worked to the bone throughout their high school careers. The ability to defer enrollment for a year through the Bridge Program offers recent high school grads a well-deserved break and a chance to see the world and try something new. Through service, students can nurture some of their underutilized talents or discover new ones.

Bridge Year participants are called Bridge Year Volunteers, and they work with organizations that provide social services, like NGOs, schools or clinics. While abroad, Bridge volunteers study a foreign language through immersion and intensive language classes, develop an appreciation for another culture by attending or participating in cultural events, and gain insights into the broader international world through community service work. In the past, students have volunteered with organizations that work to prevent human trafficking in India and provide services to survivors; they have investigated the Daoist pillar of laguna—or "ecstatic perception"—in China; and they write regular updates about their experiences that are posted on the Princeton University website. These updates, which read like narrative essays, are well worth a read (at princeton.edu/bridgeyear/updates) because they are a terrific window into the unmatched experiences these students are having. Blog posts are dotted with images of farmers swinging pick-axes in a field beneath Peruvian mountain, recordings of the haunting call to prayer in Senegal, and the fine grain details of their day-to-day lives, like arriving at work with sixty-six bananas for the sixty-six people that the organization had just recovered from slavery.

Since its inception in 2009, nearly 160 students have participated, and during the 2015-16 school year the university expects to enroll thirty-five in the Bridge Year Program. These students come back from their work abroad reinvigorated, brimming with insights that will shape their work in college and contribute to the wealth of knowledge and experience on campus.

Writing Seminar

Not to be confused with the Freshman Seminar, the writing seminar is how Princeton lets first-years focus specifically on their writing skills in small, interdisciplinary classes of twelve students max. From specialized writing instructors, students "build a solid foundation for their later work at Princeton" by "[learning] to pose interesting questions, structure complex ideas, and make original claims that engage with a variety of sources and contribute to ongoing academic debates," according to the school. Students also learn the essential academic practice of peer review through small group and individual discussions with their professor and by providing feedback on one another's work. The class also provides students with an overview of the "important differences in disciplinary practices and approaches," so that they can write to a variety of audiences succeed in any academic field. Each writing seminar is organized around a single topics that gives purpose and direction to the semester's efforts. There are also a wide range of selections, so students are sure to find something that compels them among titles like "Living with Animals," "Apocalypse Now," "Mitigating Climate Change," and "Illusions, Delusions, and Neuroscience."

The diversity of these seminars is clear from the work students produce. In the second half of the class, students embark on an ambitious research project. In the following semester, a cadre of distinguished freshmen writers are selected to present their scholarly research at the Quin Morton '36 Freshman Research Conference. The spring 2015 roster features presentations that mix pop-culture with more traditional forms of analysis, like one called, "You Kill or You Die: An Examination of the Decision-making Framework in The Walking Dead," and others examine the different cultural meanings of the hijab or the state of India's pharmaceutical industry. Through "ten-minute presentations of their work in small panels, followed by question-and-answer sessions," these students get a sense of what it would be like to present scholarly research at a professional or academic conference, which many of them, in the course of their academic careers, will do. That first conference presentation can be truly nerve wracking.

But practice and experience in front of a crowd definitely helps, especially if that crowd is full of your friends and classmates. Programs like this are one of the reasons Princeton undergrads tells us, "I love the focus on undergraduates" and the "friendly people."

Community-Based Learning Initiative

The Community-Based Learning Initiative allows students to conduct research and interact with community organizations or government agencies that work in areas related to students' academic or career interests. These classes give students an outlet to test the theoretical frameworks they learn in class and an opportunity to serve the surrounding community. One previous class toured the New Jersey coast after Hurricane Sandy to assess the damage and rebuilding efforts. Then they developed methods to mitigate the effects of future storm surges and presented their findings to the Borough of Union Beach, along with resources like brochures for the borough to use. In another class students investigated HIV transmission between mothers and infants through the Robert Wood Johnson University Hospital and presented their findings to the hospital staff. Through these community-based learning initiatives, students engage in actionable research during their first year of college and interact directly with the organization that can put that research to use.

Undergraduate Summer Research

Princeton encourages students to think about summer research the moment they set foot in the door, and even offers a number of programs that are exclusively available to freshmen and sophomores. With so many research opportunities available, it is easy for Princeton to optimize some of its programs to specifically meet the needs and skills of novice researchers. In the end, this improves the experience for the freshmen while also making Princeton junior and senior researchers more effective.

Options like the Summer Programming Experience "offers novice programmers an opportunity to gain experience by working on a creative and substantive programming project" with the help of a faculty member or graduate student. The program is specifically billed for students who were totally new to programming before taking an introductory course in their freshmen or sophomore years. Students are provided with living accommodations on campus and given a stipend to cover living expenses so that they can devote themselves to a project full-time for six weeks during the summer. Student researchers usually work together in pairs, and their work has covered everything from 3D computer graphics, to computational biology.

Faculty

The Princeton University faculty are some of the world's most distinguished scholars, but they are also "dedicated to their students." Classes may be taught by Nobel laureates, but "the humility and accessibility of world-famous researchers and public figures is always remarkable." At Princeton, "there are so many chances to meet writers, performers, and professionals you admire." One literary-minded sophomore recalls, "The two years I've been here, I've been in discussions with Frank Gehry, David Sedaris, Peter Hessler, John McPhee, Jeff Koons, Chang-rae Lee, Joyce Carol Oates, W.S. Merwin, and on and on." In any field, Princeton is an "intellectually challenging place," but from the first day students are well prepared for an experience that will be "intense in almost every way" but also "magnificently rewarding."

Life After Princeton

Princeton University alumni hold the highest offices, and have made tremendous contributions to the overall store of human knowledge. The Supreme Court currently seats three alumni: Associate Justices Samuel Alito, Elena Kagan, and Sonia Sotomayor. The White House has seen three Princeton alumni, in the forms of James Madison, Woodrow Wilson, and Michelle Obama. Princeton alumni also find themselves in the highest ranks of the business community, like Jeff Bezos, CEO and founder of Amazon, or Eric Schmidt, executive chairman at Google, and Meg Whitman, president and CEO of Hewlett-Packard. Other well-known alumni include filmmaker Ethan Cohen, Teach for America founder and CEO Wendy Kopp, and *The New Yorker* Editor David Remnick. The extensive and well-connected Princeton alumni are also willing to give back and help current students with internships and job opportunities. As one student tells us, "Princeton is a place that prepares you for anything and everything, providing you with a strong network every step of the way." According to the university, more than 5,200 alumni volunteer advice and assistance through the Alumni Career Network—which is about one person for every current undergraduate student. The alumni network's global presence means that assistance is available anywhere in the world.

Rhodes College

2000 North Parkway, Memphis, TN, 38112
Admissions: 901-843-3700
E-mail: admininfo@rhodes.edu
Website: www.rhodes.edu
Twitter: @RhodesCollege, @RhodesAdm

Introduction

Whether on their beautiful Gothic style campus or in the surrounding metropolitan community, Rhodes College students like to keep busy. Situated in the middle of historic Memphis, Rhodes is across the street from Overton Park and the Memphis Zoo, and a short walk to many internship, and research opportunities, including institutions such as St. Jude Children's Research Hospital and the National Civil Rights Museum. The majority of students will participate in some form of hands-on learning experience before they graduate through service (80 percent), internships (75 percent), or study abroad (60 percent)—not to mention the fellowship experience that is the capstone of a Rhodes education. A small student body of 2,025 and an impressive 10:1 student-to-faculty ratio means every student at this private liberal art college has the opportunity to form meaningful relationships with a dedicated faculty. As a current student explained, "Rhodes offers a close, personalized environment where teachers and faculty are not just willing, but enthusiastic to help you find your unique path to achievement." With a dozen interdisciplinary programs that bring together faculty from different fields to "offer study opportunities that do not fit within the bounds of existing departments," a Senior Honors program that allows "more independent, intensive, and individual work than can be done in regular degree programs," and classes built around student-directed inquiry, Rhodes helps its students shape their own educational experience.

> ❝ Rhodes offers a close, personalized environment where teachers and faculty are not just willing, but enthusiastic to help you find your unique path to achievement. ❞

An Interconnected Community

Service is a strong part of the Rhodes culture, and it is even codified in the school's educational vision: "to inspire and involve our students in meaningful study, research and service . . . to graduate students with a life-long passion for learning, a compassion for others, and the ability to translate academic study and personal concern into effective leadership and action in their communities and the world." When Alison Lundergan Grimes, now the Kentucky Secretary of State, was looking at colleges, it was the Rhodes tradition of service learning that most appealed to her. As she put it, "Rhodes Colleges is a community that cares."

Fellowship programs like the Rhodes Learning Corridor, the Community Development Fellowship, and the Summer Service Fellowship, which partner with nearby public schools, encourage students to engage with local government and to address poverty, health and environmental issues in the Memphis community.

Dr. Elizabeth Thomas, associate professor of psychology, director of the Memphis Center and director of urban studies, told us that in her senior urban studies seminar, students often develop research around the community service activities that they had been involved in throughout their time at Rhodes. She told us about one student who is developing a "capstone project on community organizing and coalition building, specifically focused on efforts to build solidarity between communities in grassroots organizing in Memphis. The project grows out of the student's extensive experience as an organizer, and she is recognized by many as one of the city's most promising young leaders." Another student is using several years of experience as a volunteer, fellow, and intern supporting after school programs to examine the transportation and infrastructure needs of urban educational programs.

These programs help connect students to the community, but they also help students connect with one another. Alumnus Evans Falgoust told us that this sense of service and community impacted nearly every interaction: "I found it nearly impossible to walk across campus and not run into someone I knew well enough to have a 10 minute conversation. . . . At Rhodes, we worked hard but we always supported one another. I learned as much outside of the classroom as within it and I developed social skills and worldly perspectives that will serve me for the rest of my life. Rhodes was as much about interpersonal development as it was intellectual growth and the two became one in the same." Every member of the faculty we spoke to talked about the importance of service or community development in the educational ethos of Rhodes.

Undergraduate Research

At the end of every school year, Rhodes College showcases its stellar reputation for connecting students with internship and fellowship experiences when over 200 students wake up early on a Friday to present their year's research to the campus. The Undergraduate Research and Creative Activity Symposium, or URCAS, as the event is known, displays some of the best research opportunities, fellowships, and global study that Rhodes has to offer. In the morning, guests may hear from students conducting research at the Memphis Center describe "the human experience of the Memphis and Mid-South region, from the Civil War to civil rights," and in the afternoon watch Fellows at St. Jude Children's Hospital present the new cancer treatments and stem cell therapies they've been helping develop at the renowned hospital.

But the URCAS presentations do more than showcase student research accomplishments; they demonstrate a key component of the Rhodes educational mission: to produce skilled written and oral communicators. Evans Falgoust, a business major from the Class of 2011 who now works as a Strategy Manager at Dr Pepper Snapple Group, told us that, even among majors that typically involve less writing, Rhodes students are known for their writing skills. Rhodes students hardly ever see a multiple choice test, Falgoust explains, and even classes like accounting require papers. Dr. Mary E. Miller, professor of biology and director of the Interdisciplinary Program in biochemistry and molecular biology, echoed the sentiments of many of her colleagues when she told us that after four years of study, "the difference [in their communication skills] is remarkable, and we know that our students stand ready to articulate well their intentions and passions to the world after graduation." Secretary Grimes, too, credits Rhodes with setting her up for success when she went on to graduate study. She explained, "I learned to communicate there—both in writing and extemporaneously—which prepared me extremely well for law school at American University. Studying at Rhodes helped me know how to connect with others."

Senior Honors Program

In their senior year, students can devote up to eighteen academic hours to a research topic that they develop with a faculty mentor and work on independently throughout the year. The honors project "can be research culminating in a written report or thesis, or it can be a creative project as represented by an original production. An oral presentation of the final project is also expected. A copy of the final report or production is placed in a permanent file or on display in the library," according to the College. The Senior Honors Program is a great choice for students who think they may want to pursue a graduate degree in

66 *I attended three graduate schools and the preparation of Rhodes made graduate school a breeze.* **99**

the future. The intensive, individualized study with "the full resources of the library and laboratory" gives students in the Senior Honors Program a way to "test drive" graduate school. Plus, students who complete the program have a huge leg up when they actually enter graduate school programs. Dr. Barrett Haga, who graduated in 2001 with a double major in political science and Greek and Roman studies, told us, "I attended three graduate schools and the preparation of Rhodes made graduate school a breeze. For example, when completing my master's thesis, the senior thesis at Rhodes provided me with the research methodology necessary to write a 50-plus page analytical paper with ease. Many other big state school students struggled with such a long paper, but those of us with a Rhodes type background excelled."

St. Jude Summer Plus Fellowship

Many students come to Rhodes interested in pursuing a career in medicine, and the fellowship with St. Jude Children's Research Hospital is a huge pull. Evans Falgoust told us that "connections throughout Memphis with hospitals and research facilities" help make the sciences some of Rhodes' strongest programs. As Rhodes explains, the fellowship offers "students an intensive research experience that pairs students with St. Jude scientists and places them into the hospital's professional laboratories for a period of two semesters and the intervening academic year." The fellowship covers a wide range of research interests, including genetics, immunology, oncology, infectious disease, and developmental neurobiology, with "state-of-the-art research technologies and brilliant scientists from all over the world," according to one former fellow. Recent research collaborations with St. Jude scientists include a study of avian flu and development of new anticancer drugs, as well as studies that examine the "importance of cultural factors in reducing medication errors" and ways of improving Clinical Decision support in the Electronic Health Record. And there is no need to worry about a summer job or apartment. Fellows are paid a stipend for the forty hours a week they work during the summers and provided with housing on the Rhodes campus.

For students who want to add an international flair to their medical study, the Summer Plus Fellowship program has two slots available for students to do research at St. Jude's partner school, Calvo Mackenna Hospital, in Santiago, Chile. In the past, participants have elected to split their time in Santiago "between work in the hospital and Spanish classes through Español y Cultura en Latino America, followed by an academic year and second summer at St. Jude Children's Research Hospital in Memphis."

After two semesters and two summers, students have the option to extend their research into an Honors Research credit. But the St. Jude Fellowship experience often bleeds into other classes as well. Dr. Elizabeth Thomas, professor of psychology and director of the Memphis Center, told us about several students, in her senior seminar in urban studies, who were integrating research that they had conducted as interns and fellows during previous semesters into their senior capstone research project.

Faculty

The cliché of the lonely professor whiling away solitary office hours is unknown at Rhodes. Whether it is in their office, at a coffee shop, or in the lab, when they are not in the classroom Rhodes professors are usually found with their students. Dr. Timothy Huebner, chair of the history department, told us, "Relationships between students and faculty are what Rhodes is all about. I interact with students every single day of the week. Whether it is advising them about classes, answering questions about the requirements of the history major, discussing internship opportunities with students, or just helping students who are struggling with my class or who are studying for one of my exams, being with students is a huge part of what I do. It is what our institution does best. We direct and mentor students closely and continuously—through research projects, essay writing, internships, and co-curricular activities."

And all of this individualized attention gives professors a chance to really figure out what makes their students tick, and to develop individualized teaching strategies that will help their students most. Dr. David McCarthy, professor of fine art, explained, "I get to know my students really well. I know what I can say to them to motivate them; I know what their strengths and interests are, so I can tailor the examples that I use in the classroom or in office hours to what I know is of interest to them and that will hold their attention. That way I can make my point and we can continue to move forward together."

When we asked professors at Rhodes how they balanced the demands of teaching and conducting scholarly research, they all had the same answer: we combine them. Which makes sense because, as Dr. Miller explained, "Bringing students into [our] research and research into the classroom brings valued perspective to both worlds ... Faculty are actively engaged in their field and therefore able to integrate students into that work. In my experience, faculty interactions with students outside of the classroom take the form of one-on-one mentored research in the laboratory setting. I have mentored students in my research lab who have moved on to prestigious graduate programs and I have published multiple collaborative works with student authors. Mentored research is one example of how our faculty are able to provide perspective for our students that will prepare them to become the independent thinkers. Faculty understand that opportunities for independent thought and action on the part of our students will best prepare them for the challenges that they will face after graduation."

In fact, Rhodes professors develop long term academic relationships with their students and often end up as a senior adviser to students whom they have known for all four year. Dr. McCarthy tells all of his new advisees to "pick one professor each semester who you think is interesting and arrange to have either lunch or a coffee with them. Ask them how they got into this business and what their biggest successes and failures have been. We all have a journey or trajectory." Through this kind of exposure and dialogue, students come to understand what it takes to be a professional in their field. It also gives professors a chance to model the kind of behaviors that lead to success in a particular industry. And as a result of these enduring academic relationships, Dr. Thomas explained that "many of us present our research with students at conferences and publish with students. We routinely work with students in leadership positions on the campus to support our integrative education efforts in Memphis."

When working to integrate their current research into the classroom, it doesn't hurt that the faculty at Rhodes are at the helm of all things curricular. Dr. Miller told us that faculty control of the curriculum is key to the philosophy of the college. "We set policies for curriculum, drive curriculum reform, and regularly assess our curriculum. This creates a strong sense of personal investment in the educational philosophy of the school on the part of the Faculty," Dr. Miller explained. Dr. Huebner, who chaired the committee that oversaw the implementation of the College's general education curriculum, said that this kind of intense faculty involvement is "a great opportunity to get to know colleagues and their courses and to think broadly about what we do as professors and what we want our students to learn." This is one of the reasons that Rhodes College was just awarded a grant from the Mellon Foundation that allows faculty, students, and postdoctoral fellows to develop innovative pedagogies.

Life After Rhodes

Alumni maintain strong ties to the campus community and make an effort to give back. Dr. Barrett Haga, who currently works at the U.S. Department of Commerce, credits internships in the House of Representative and the Senate with helping to launch his career. Haga says that these internships and the strong political science department at Rhodes lead him "to positions with the State of Florida, the U.S. Department of Labor, then to my current position at the U.S. Department of Commerce." Today Dr. Haga hires a Rhodes intern to work at the Department of Commerce every summer.

Evans Falgoust agrees that the contacts he made through Rhodes gave him tremendous support in his field. "I had internships while attending Rhodes, mentors through the business department and alumni network, and exposure to the right companies when going through the recruiting process for full-time employment. My leadership experiences on campus, the rigor of the classroom, and the social/communication skills I built over the four years provided me the right tools for a successful professional career," Falgoust explained. And like many alumni, he is "a strong believer in paying it forward." Falgoust has returned to Rhodes multiple times to speak to classes, provide professional development, and participate in recruiting events. "I am also actively involved in assisting current students and other alumni individually by providing career feedback and being a mentor," Falgoust told us.

Rice University

6100 Main, Houston, Texas 77005-1892
Admissions: 713-348-7423
E-mail: admission@rice.edu
Website: www.rice.edu
Twitter: @RiceUniversity

Introduction

According to the students we surveyed, Rice University—located in Houston and home to just under 4,000 undergraduates—can best be summed up as an academically challenging yet nurturing school. "Rice has very good academic programs, and the overall atmosphere is very supportive," a computer science major told us. For alumnus Greg Marshall, an '86 graduate in managerial studies, his college admissions decision was swayed by "the university's reputation for academic excellence and a general quirkiness. (My high school counselor actually told me, 'It's a school for smart weirdos, you'd be perfect there.')" Rice has received high ratings from students both for student happiness and the overall quality of life at the school. "Even the squirrels are happy," an ecology and evolutionary biology major joked.

Students seem happiest with the residential college system, and the support of students that it offers. "Rice's greatest strengths are its seemingly endless support networks. Beginning with [orientation] week, every student is connected to their college's masters, RAs, peer academic advisers, college fellows, Rice health advisers, and orientation advisers. This system ensures that every new student has someone to whom they can go when they have problems and someone who will bake them cookies or a cake on their birthday," a bioengineering major explained. Within this supportive framework, Rice offers its students ample opportunities to shape the school and otherwise develop leadership skills, impact the community of Houston and the larger world, engage in cutting-edge research, and connect with distinguished faculty who are leaders in their field.

Residential College System

The vast majority of students we surveyed cited Rice's residential college system as the school's greatest strength as well as the number one reason students chose to attend the university. As one philosophy and sociology major explained, "I felt the residential college system would provide a positive, collaborative atmosphere and bring a small-school feel to a medium-sized research university (with all the resources that size brings)." A sociology and economics major agreed, stating, "I love the residential college system and the community it helps foster."

Alumnus Greg Marshall '86 explained how the system, which was the most important affiliation for him during his time at Rice, works: "Incoming undergraduate students are randomly assigned to one of these eleven on-campus housing and dining facilities before they matriculate, and each student remains affiliated with his/her assigned college until graduation. At Rice, there is no athlete's dorm, freshman dorm, etc., and you don't move to a new dorm every year during your academic career. Instead, each of the undergraduate colleges represents, in microcosm, a cross-section of all of Rice's diversity: both genders, all class years, all fields of study, and all of Rice's ethnic, geographic and demographic diversity. Each college is a self-governing entity (students pay college fees that are more than matched by Rice, then the students elect their own representatives within each college to decide how to administer the resulting college budgets). . . . Each college develops its own traditions and a strong sense of camaraderie, in some ways fulfilling the social roles of sororities and fraternities (which are not permitted at Rice, as these organizations tend to define themselves by whom they admit and whom they exclude). Instead, we have the college system, and in that system everyone—everyone—has a place where they 'belong.'"

This system is central to the sense of community that is prevalent at Rice. "My second home is my residential college at Rice University," one chemical engineering student said. Students also appreciate the greater connections to faculty that the system encourages. "Professors are definitely focused on the undergraduate experience, and that's brought even further to life by having some of them living in the residential colleges as masters and resident associates, which provides a wonderful opportunity to get to know the faculty and staff on a more personal level and to have a friendly, positive adult presence as a resource rather than a police force of RAs," a philosophy and sociology major explained.

Student Self-Governance

"Rice is heavily focused on student empowerment," a cognitive science major told us, a focus the school achieves largely as a result of the residential college system. A double major in biochemistry, cell biology, and Hispanic studies elaborated: "One of the greatest strengths of Rice is the amount of student leadership involved in running the campus.

66 *Rice is heavily focused on student empowerment.* **99**

The residential college system promotes student involvement, from coordinating activities to following university regulations." A physics and mathematics major provided even more specific examples of the governing role that she's been able to take within her residential community: "My dorm is being renovated. I decided to create a committee that works with the architects and engineers to advise them on the project. We have weekly meetings where we literally tell them what we want and they actually listen to us. Its incredible how much responsibility Rice gives to its students." Alumnus Judge Edward Emmett, the administrative county judge of Harris County, Texas, told us that he essentially got his start in politics as a student leader within the residential college system. He said, "I was president of my college my junior year. We had great arguments about things going on on-campus. The students really do get to make the decisions. The experience caused me to work with people from all stripes and come up with an arrangement that all people can agree to."

Beyond governing their residential colleges, students have a say in other university decisions. For example, the dean of undergraduates meets regularly with the presidents of the colleges and the president of the Student Association. The president of the university speaks at a Student Association meeting each fall to present a State of the University update and answer questions. The president also hosts open-office hours once a month to give students an opportunity to convey concerns, ask questions or just engage the president in conversation. Representatives from the Student Association and the Graduate Student Association also serve on some university committees, such as the Quality Enhancement Plan Steering Committee, and a student-elected Honor Council oversees the university's Honor Code and considers reported violations.

Leadership Opportunities

Aside from helping to run their own residential colleges and meeting with the university on other administrative matters, students at Rice have many other chances to develop leadership skills. In fact, many undergraduates we surveyed cited student leadership opportunities as one of the biggest strengths of the university.

The Doer Institute for New Leaders opened its doors in July 2015, thanks to a $50 million gift from alumni Ann and John Doer (who both have bachelor's and master's degrees in electrical engineering from Rice), and specializes in hands-on leadership training that extends for a student's entire college career. According to Rice, "The strengths of each student will be assessed and their potential will be developed in a four-year comprehensive, custom-made plan of classroom instruction, hands-on, real-world experience and guidance from personal coaches."

Another program, Leadership Rice, offers a mentorship experience combined with a summer internship. Before starting their internships, students attend training sessions that focus on leadership in professional contexts. For nine weeks over the course of the summer, students perform substantive work with recognized leaders in public, private and nonprofit organizations. Students also complete readings and written assignments that deepen their understanding of the personal and professional demands leaders face. Most significantly, each student is paired with a mentor who is responsible for overseeing the student's learning and personal development. Previous placements have been in Houston, New York City, Washington D.C., Paris, and Pune, India. Rice also offers a Leading Edge Workshop that prepares students to exceed expectations in experiences outside the university and then to leverage those opportunities for future leadership. During this two-day workshop, students learn how to make an impact in a professional setting, lead at any level in an organization and apply strengths and build skills to increase leadership capacities.

Engineering students have access to the Rice Center for Engineering Leadership (RCEL), which was established to educate and develop students into strong leaders, team members, and entrepreneurs. From academic courses and leadership labs to student discussion groups and structured learning experiences, RCEL program components provide students with opportunities to develop and strengthen their leadership abilities and prepare them to put these skills into practice in engineering and professional environments.

Beyond these programs, there are a number of student-run businesses on campus, such as the Coffeehouse, which offer students an opportunity to develop leadership and business skills. Rice also has a student-run newspaper, yearbook, radio station, and many student clubs to join.

Community Involvement

Rice students make their mark in the Greater Houston area as well. Students can earn a Certificate in Civic Leadership from the Center for Civic Leadership, whose mission is to foster engaged citizenship through integrated curricular and experiential learning opportunities. The center promotes and develops opportunities for members of the Rice community to engage directly with the city of Houston through collaborative, community-based research and design. The center hosts a number of courses, programs, and activities that allow students, faculty members, and community partners to work together on Houston-based civic projects. For example, Beyond the Sallyport is a program designed to introduce first- and second-year students to the city of Houston. The experience provides a pathway to civic leadership that guides participants toward engaged service experiences, a deeper understanding of social injustice, and a lifelong commitment to service resulting in the creation of sustainable change in the Greater Houston community and beyond.

During orientation (known as O-Week), there is an Outreach Day when freshmen can volunteer at a number of local nonprofit organizations. Rice's Community Involvement Center sponsors this event to enable students to make a positive impact on the Houston community by engaging in volunteer activities throughout the city.

Finally, Rice 360°: Institute for Global Health Technologies works in partnership with communities throughout the world to design and implement low-cost, high-performance health technologies that address major global health challenges. More than 60,000 people in twenty-eight countries have benefited from more than fifty new global health technologies and programs designed by over 400 students in Rice's global health initiatives.

Undergraduate Research

Participation in research is a fundamental part of the Rice undergraduate experience, one that many of the students we surveyed took advantage of. Research is defined very broadly as any opportunity to approach a problem in a critical and open-ended way; it ranges from the scientific experiments in science and engineering laboratories, to the design projects in engineering classes and architecture studios, to the fieldwork and original analyses of social scientists and humanists. Many students, including one anthropology major, appreciated the "opportunities for students to get into the 'real world' of research and work."

Rice makes it easy for students to get involved. The Office of Fellowships and Undergraduate Research helps Rice undergraduates, graduate students and recent alumni find additional academic opportunities beyond the classroom. On campus, students have access to research opportunities in various schools of study: engineering, natural sciences, social sciences, humanities, architecture, music and business. Rice also has more than forty institutes and consortia that offer interdisciplinary research experiences with faculty, visiting scholars, postdocs and graduate students. Off campus, the city of Houston provides an enormous landscape for independent research projects, collaboration with city government and internships with both the private and public sectors that make up the nation's fourth-largest city. Access to the world's largest medical center, NASA and twenty-six Fortune 500 companies makes Houston an extremely valuable resource for Rice undergraduates. It's not surprising then that one bioengineering major commented that "the opportunities for research are plenty."

Rice's Oshman Engineering Design Kitchen has all the "ingredients" for creative engineering students to tackle authentic design challenges or to experiment with their own building projects. The facility has 18,000 square feet of space that houses more than 66 work tables, conference rooms, a classroom, a wet lab, rapid prototyping equipment, large-format printers, 3-D printers, a designated woodworking area, a machine shop and access to a welding shop. It's the ideal place for hands-on experiential teaching, learning, experimentation and innovation.

Opportunities for Scholars

Students looking to push themselves beyond their coursework will find ample opportunity at Rice, depending on their majors and interests. All of the programs offered by the school give students a head start in shaping their careers. For example, for pre-med students Rice and Baylor College of Medicine select up to ten incoming freshmen each year to pursue a four-year bachelor's degree at Rice, followed by guaranteed admission to Houston's Baylor College of Medicine. Medical Scholars Program students are encouraged to explore the entire range of Rice undergraduate programs to expose themselves to a broad-based education. Ideally, students selected to the program will apply insight from this extensive exposure to the liberal arts and other disciplines to the study of modern medical science.

The Century Scholars Program matches select incoming freshmen with faculty mentors for a two-year period. During that time, the student and mentor collaborate on one of the mentor's research projects. Century scholars also receive a two-year merit scholarship and stipends for supporting research initiatives. Besides establishing a close relationship with an academic mentor, students also have the option of participating in exciting research endeavors. For example, the program has seen participants spend six weeks at the Fermi National Accelerator Laboratory studying physics while many others have accompanied their mentors to international conferences.

Finally the Undergraduate Scholars Program is designed for juniors and seniors from any department who are considering graduate school and academic careers. Undergraduates accepted in the program "act" as graduate students for an academic year, with a faculty member selected by the student who serves as a mentor and meets regularly with the student. During the first semester, students write a funding proposal, prepare oral and written progress reports, begin their research and learn about various aspects of academia through presentations. In the second semester, students focus on their research and writing and present their results orally and in the form of a scholarly manuscript. Some students attend a professional conference and present a paper.

Faculty

As you might expect of a premier research institution, Rice's faculty are all distinguished in their fields. Two Rice faculty members (one of whom is deceased) won the Nobel Prize in Chemistry. Another recently won the National Medal of Science. More than twenty current faculty members have been elected to the National Academy of Sciences, the National Academy of Engineering and / or the Institute of Medicine. Researchers at Rice are credited with pioneering the field of nanotechnology. They also collaborated with physicians at Baylor College of Medicine on early development of the artificial heart. Ninety-seven percent of faculty have PhDs or similar terminal degrees.

At the same time, the school offers an impressive 6:1 undergraduate student-to-faculty ratio, and the students we surveyed appreciated the accessibility of their professors. "The professors are amazing in class and even better out of class. They want to work with all the students to make sure that they succeed, and they want to know who you are, not that you just occupy a seat in their class," a sports management and economics major told us. A linguistics major agreed, stating, "The professors I have had at Rice are some of the most amazing people I have met in my life. They are experts in their field. They finely craft their courses but are incredibly flexible and approachable." They are also "unusually highly involved in teaching and learning outside of the classroom," John Hutchinson, the dean of undergraduates, told us. In addition to their informal interactions with faculty through the residential colleges, "a large fraction of [Rice] students engage in independent study, creative work, design, composition, research or other forms of scholarship under the mentoring of one or more members of the faculty."

66 *Rice students are very smart, and tend to have a funny, quirky quality which I'm glad to say has remained consistent for generations.* **99**

Life after Rice

According to Mayor of Houston and Rice alumna Annise Parker, "Rice grads are known for being smart, able to compete, and a little bit nerdy." (For those of you with political aspirations, Mayor Parker was a triple major in anthropology, sociology, and psychology.) Alumni are also deeply impacted by their undergraduate years at the university. Thirty years after he graduated, alumnus Greg Marshall still remembers the English classes he took with "legendary" professor Dennis Huston, and the public speaking course that, according to Mr. Marshall, is still so popular that Rice students camp out to register for it. Mr. Marshall credits these and other memorable courses, along with on-campus work experiences, with leading him down his career path, first to a position at an ad agency as Vice President of Director of Research and then ultimately back to Rice, where he works in the Public Affairs Office as the director of University Relations.

Rice alumni are a varied and successful bunch, making a splash in the world of sports (Lance Berkman, former pitcher for the Houston Astros), film (William Boyles, screen writer of *Apollo 13* and *Planet of the Apes*), business (Lynn Elsenhans, former chairperson and CEO of Sunoco), and technology (Shannon Walker, NASA astronaut), to name a few fields. Despite their diverse interests and career trajectories, Greg Marshall said that Rice graduates do have a few things in common: "Rice students are very smart, and tend to have a funny, quirky quality which I'm glad to say has remained consistent for generations. Creativity is intelligence at play, it is said, and I find Rice graduates to be intelligent, play-ful, creative people no matter what their fields of study or chosen careers." Rice comes in at number twenty one on The Princeton Review's 2015 ranking list for Best Career Placement and at number twelve on the list for the Top 50 Colleges That Pay You Back. Both rankings were reported in the 2015 edition of our book *Colleges That Pay You Back*.

Smith College

7 College Lane, Northampton, MA 01063
Admissions: 413-585-2500
E-mail: admission@smith.edu
Website: www.smith.edu/
Twitter: @smithcollege @presmccartney

Introduction

Smith was founded in 1871, and since then has grown into one of the most prestigious women's colleges in the country. With over 1,000 courses in over 50 areas
of study, Smith curriculum encourages women to develop a strong education on
their own terms, with the ability to explore and discover a varied education from
several diverse fields. Nestled in western Massachusetts in the scenic college
town of Northhampton, this private college boasts, "an education as unique as
you are." One of the cornerstones of a Smith education is the ability to design your
own academic experience within a plethora of curricular opportunities. There
are no required courses outside of the first-year, a writing-intensive seminar. In
addition, students have the added benefit of the larger academic community
of the Five College consortium, which includes Amherst, Hampshire, Mount
Holyoke, and the University of Massachusetts Amherst. Smith's strong liberal
background allows the college the freedom to nurture a variety of students and
interests. The high level of engagement set not only by faculty, but also by students, ensures that each woman who receives a degree from Smith does so with
a full understanding of who she is and what she wants to accomplish.

Smith College's students, affectionately known as "Smithies," are involved
with college search committees, discussions, and task forces. No major changes
occur on campus without student input and feedback. Smith students earn a
degree that covers all knowledge, not just the benefits and function of a spe-
cialization—literature, history, social science, natural science, math, analytic
philosophy, and the arts, in addition to a foreign language. According to a Smith
administrator, one of College's main goals is helping "women to understand the
complexity of human history and the variety of the world's cultures through
engagement with social, political, aesthetic and scientific issues."

With 2,500 undergraduate women (and a co-educational graduate program),
Smith College has created an incredible number of accomplished scholars across
all fields. Even so, after nearly 150 years of education, Smith continues to

develop and adapt to the global landscape. Two of the most exciting and striking endeavors at Smith are in research and sustainability. The school's growth and resources ensure that a Smithie not only leaves campus with an astonishing skill set, it allows their students the opportunity to decide how, and in what courses of study, they want to be prepared in their professional careers.

The Smithies

Writing-intensive courses and recommended first-year seminars ensure that Smithies express themselves well. The typical Smithie? As Kate Queeney, professor of chemistry, stated: "A student who's truly interested in learning. . . . Successful Smith students tend to be more internally driven—they

❝ Smith women are poised, efficient, straight-forward, and passionate.❞

want to do well for personal reasons, not just to earn a good grade. Smith is also a real community—it's a diverse community." Students are given the chance to explore across majors and interact with other students. And, for all of Smith's growth and development, it's still small enough to foster a community. No student is merely a number on an ID card.

Another administrator believes a Smith woman must be "smart, ambitious and creative . . . She is confident and secure in her opinions and isn't afraid to share them. Smithies work hard and are committed to their studies. They are passionate about social justice, fairness and equality, and want to use their education for the good of the world."

As a former intern at the Alumnae Association described, "Smith women are poised, efficient, straight-forward, and passionate. They model leadership after which I fashion my own style and it has worked incredibly well." Smithies go out into the world to discover their own purpose and yet are always connected to a life-long community that believes in the power and efficacy of women. When further asked what words she would use to describe Smithies, the alumnae offered, "Wicked smart, capable, authentic"—more proof that Smith College allows their students freedom to create their own paths.

The emphasis at Smith is to prepare women for the global landscape and to create "strategic problem solvers." Students aren't just told what they need to do to meet a certain goal; they are encouraged to set off on their own, armed with research, a sense of drive, and ambition, (plus the help of a faculty adviser). Greg White, professor of government, described a successful Smith student as "inquisitive, energetic, and open to uncertainty." Professor Queeney agreed: "The biggest difference I notice between incoming and outgoing students is the ability of the latter to tackle complex problems without a clear roadmap."

Campus Culture

Smith College doesn't only encourage students to find out how they want to spend their lives professionally. The positive culture lets students discover who they want to be, personally. Smithies in this tight community get to grow and learn with each other. When you ask a student about Smith, they'll often say something about finding their "best friends," about finding their "home," "ambition," and "balance." Students are involved in events on and off campus including a host of various student organizations. In addition to club sports and intramural programs, the Smith Pioneers also participate in thirteen varsity sports.

Old Smith traditions are still alive, like Mountain Day. Held since 1877, the president picks a gorgeous day in the fall and rings the bells in the morning for a surprise day off. Students can then continue to different activities on campus or to nearby parks. The Smith in the World Conference showcases student presentations and panel discussions, all based on how Smithies' off-campus activities benefited from their vast Smith education, and how those experiences later aided in their studies, as well. Professors nominate junior and senior students to participate.

"The campus is electric with all the ideas and programs and workshops and lectures—it is astounding all that you can learn in a single day at Smith both in the classroom and on your way to dinner, stopping off in the library for a lecture," a Smith alumna said. "At night after dinner for an inspiring reading by an internationally acclaimed poet sponsored by the Poetry Center or during January Term studying race and contemporary art with a world-famous alumna and curator and going to galleries in NYC for private tours." Another alumna described how she enjoyed dabbling in new ventures on campus, even yoga and horseback riding: "I would print out the newsletter of events every week with much excitement and circle all the events I wanted to go to." There are a variety of activities for students to create learning experiences, and a lot of fun, too.

Science and Engineering

In addition to Smith's storied history, liberal arts background, and strong collaborative culture, Smith's major growth has been in research and the sciences, including their engineering and sustainability programs. The Picker Engineering Program call Ford Hall home, a $473 million, 142,000-square-foot structure dedicated to science and engineering. A few proud Smithies told us, Picker is "the first and only all-women's engineering program in the country."

As the faculty note, you can't be at Smith if you aren't eager to learn. And there are plenty of opportunities for it. From internships, community service, and study-away programs, Smith offers their students the chance to learn from study outside of their campus, either domestic or international. SURF (Student Undergraduate Research Fellowships) fund research and let students explore projects of their own design. The AEMES (Achieving Excellence in Math, Engineering and Science) Program also gives opportunities to students who are historically underrepresented in STEM fields. SURF lets students have more leeway and a bit less faculty guidance in their studies. They are allowed to undertake "true research," according to an engineering student. Smithies are not only answering a question, they're discovering the varied answers and analysis that accompanies any in-depth research.

Smithies have a tremendous library at their fingertips, too, with over 1 million items to help their research. The library offers students a huge resource as they implement and advance their ideas. An assistant engineering professor said that this research "is an opportunity for students to investigate a subject that interests them with less faculty direction than is typical in the academic year and with less certainty as to what the outcome will be."

As Steven Williams, Gates Professor of Biological Science, said, "Nothing is more fun than when a student gets a great research result and comes bouncing into the lab because she's so excited about it." Smith faculty enjoys helping students succeed. An administrator also mentioned that Dr. Williams' lab "received a $100,000 Grand Challenges Exploration Grant from the Bill & Melinda Gates Foundation—one of only 81 grants awarded worldwide—for research on health issues in the developing world." So, while students are hard at work developing their ideas, professors like Dr. Williams are continually finding ways (and winning grants) to help students continue to flourish.

> ❝ Nothing is more fun than when a student gets a great research result and comes bouncing into the lab because she's so excited about it.❞

CEEDS

Smith is also wisely going green, with many sustainability classes among its course offerings. For example, students can receive an Environmental Concentration in climate change or sustainable food. To increase knowledge on the topic, the Center for Environment, Ecological Design & Sustainability also features "Green

Events" for students to attend, on and off campus. Environmental students also study at the MacLeish Field Station. A 240-acre plot of land in West Whatley, Massachusetts, CEEDS' mission statement lets students "pursue environmental research, outdoor education, and low-impact recreation." Smithies also study at the Bechtel Environmental Classroom, designed as one of the "greenest" buildings in the country, and Ford Hall, the science and engineering building, features a rooftop garden.

The Lazarus Center for Career Development

While students are at Smith and once they've graduated, the Lazarus Center provides a glowing opportunity for activities, resume workshops, and job preparation. The Center is currently hard at work on the Smith-Tuck Business Bridge Program, a collaboration between Smith and Dartmouth's Tuck School of Business. The program will host undergraduate women across the country, the first time Dartmouth's business courses will be available to different campuses.

Smith College prides itself on allowing students the freedom to create their own majors, but understands that Smith women aren't held to simply one standard and won't be tied down to the strict standards of a major. Women are encouraged, and required, to get involved in classes and projects across majors. The interdisciplinary aspects give students a chance to interact with more than people they share a major with. Professor White said he often advises his students to remember "the major you eventually choose is important, of course, but it only comprises basically a third of your college coursework." He says this lowers the anxiety over major selection and "opens up a conversation about a student's other goals: writing and communication skills, language study, quantitative training, study abroad" and more.

A 1998 history graduate, with a minor in women's studies, told us that while her business career may seem a departure from Smith's core liberal arts values, her alma mater prepared her "very well." She explains, "The Career Development Center was very helpful; all of my summer internships were through them. They helped me explore my various interests in nonprofits, government, and law. These helped me realize my real interest in business."

Community Engagement

Smith College may be private, but the students are frequently found off-campus involved with the community. An administrator described this as a "private college with a public conscience, where students use what they learn in the classroom to confront the challenges of the day. Placing community engagement at the core of the curriculum . . . equips students for their roles not just as learners but also as active and engaged members of society." The Lewis Global Studies Center encourages study and discussions on global issues. The college is also involved in projects with other schools and communities, which lets students explore other avenues. This connection among colleges also lets Smith work with Amherst, Mount Holyoke, and Hampshire colleges, along with the University of Massachusetts. Schools combine forces to help push initiatives like Smith's upcoming Data Science collaboration with Mount Holyoke. The Five College consortium provides each campus with student and faculty exchanges, various faculty appointments, increased course offerings, and access to the amenities of PhD programs. This includes the combined library catalogues and borrowing privileges between Smith and the other four schools for advanced research.

Faculty

Smithies are taught by 285 full-time and part-time professors in forty-one academic departments and programs, for a low student-faculty ratio of 9:1. Most of these educators and scholars hold a terminal degree in their field. The faculty is nearly split evenly between women and men, all dedicated to the Smith cause. These professors deal in more than education. Scholars in their own right, they pursue their own fields of study, and their accomplishments raise the bar for their students. The professors, described by their students as "top-notch," "engaged," "wonderful," "kind and helpful," go out of their way to include students on their scholarly research.

A sampling of Smith professors currently making waves globally include: Ruth Haas, the Achilles Professor of Mathematics and Statistics and professor of engineering, who was the 2014 winner of the Association for Women in Mathematics Humphreys Award for mentorship of undergraduate women in mathematics; Richard Olivo, professor of biological sciences, who was awarded for outstanding contributions to neuroscience education and training; Paula Giddings, the E.A. Woodson 1922 Professor of Afro-American Studies, who keynoted the Martin Luther King convocation at Jackson State University; and Joshua Miller, a professor in the Smith College School for Social Work who received a U.S. State Department grant to continue his conflict resolution work with nonprofit and government leaders in Uganda and Rwanda.

Alumnae

A Class of 2002 Smithie told us, "Smith chose me in a way that makes me smile to this day. I didn't know how much Smith would make me grow, intellectually, emotionally, and spiritually." Current students point out they were initially drawn to Smith through the accomplishments of other alumnae, especially in leadership positions. Smith has proven these women have a lot to brag about. Nearly 90 percent of Smithies go straight from graduation into jobs or to graduate schools.

In honor of one of their most famous alumnae, Julia Child (Class of '34), Smith College has hosted Julia Child Day since 2004. In grand Julia Child-fashion, the celebrations are full of food-related events, honoring the late chef, host, and author, and her contributions to the culinary scene. Other prominent alumnae include two first ladies; writers Margaret Mitchell, Madeleine L'Engle and Sylvia Plath; feminist and activist Gloria Steinem; and Rochelle "Shelly" Lazarus, former CEO and Chairman of Ogilvy & Mather.

As of early 2015, Smith has over 48,000 undergraduate and 7,000 graduate degree recipients in all fifty states and more than 100 countries. Once they graduate, Smithies aren't on their own. In addition to producing alumnae who lead lives of distinction, Smith tends to produce graduates with a degree of flexibility and multi-faceted interest. The Lazarus Center has published the results of survey sent to alumnae who graduated from Smith two, five, ten, fifteen, and twenty years ago, and the results show tremendous diversity in career outcomes across majors. "Alumnae who graduated with degrees in the natural sciences, history, humanities and the social sciences, for example, found professional success in fields ranging from agriculture to biotechnology to education," the school informed us. Over on the career website, the director of the Lazarus Center, Stacie Hagenbaugh, commented on the survey results that the Center has illustrated in an interactive chart. (You can view the chart at: http://www.smith.edu/news/alumnae-career-paths/). "It's a perfect visual response to the question of whether a liberal arts degree will take you anywhere," Hagenbaugh said. "It clearly shows that a degree from any of the divisions at Smith will lead to success in any field."

St. Lawrence University

23 Romoda Drive, Canton, New York 13617
Admissions: 800-285-1856
E-mail: admissions@stlawu.edu
Website: www.stlawu.edu
Twitter: @stlawrenceu

Introduction

Nestled in the small upstate New York town of Canton that's closer to Canada than it is to Manhattan, St. Lawrence is a liberal arts school with a strong sense of community and a dedication to academics. For one history major, St. Lawrence is "a university that pushes me to pursue my dreams," a place where "it felt like I was coming home, not leaving home." With roughly 2,300 students and a student to faculty ratio of 12:1, St. Lawrence prides itself on small classes and a tight knit environment where students and professors know their fellow Laurentians by name. With interdisciplinary studies encouraged, the most popular majors at St. Lawrence include economics, biology, government, psychology, and mathematics. Even though its location might be considered remote, the school's proximity to the Adirondacks is a huge draw and, as one anthropology major boasts, "St. Lawrence manages to be a place with countless opportunities and things going on despite being in the middle of nowhere."

First-Year Program

While orientation programs for freshmen that help new students settle into college are the norm, St. Lawrence's First-Year Program (FYP) is unique. All classmates who are part of the same FYP course live together (along with their FYP course faculty instructors) in a designated section of a residence hall, known as "residential colleges." When students live together and also share a common course, they're more likely to become comfortable exploring new avenues of academic discussion—

> **❝ The community building aspect of the FYP will make you friends for life. ❞**

when a philosophical discussion starts in class and runs over into a late-night talk over pizza in the dorm's common room, students thrive. One neuroscience major noted, "The community building aspect of the FYP will make you friends for life." Freshmen also live with two or so upperclassmen community assistants

(CAs), who function much like the traditional RA and help their charges navigate the various clubs, organizations, and opportunities on campus. During the spring semester of their freshman year, students choose a First Year Seminar, which helps hone their research skills. As students develop new critical thinking skills, they remain in close contact with their faculty advisers (one of the faculty instructors of the student's FYP.) It's up to the student to decide whether or not to continue working with this same adviser during sophomore year or find a new one; many students choose to stay with their FYP adviser simply because of the strong bond created during the program.

Heather McCauley, a 2006 alumna, told us, "My FYP was focused on health and medicine, and early on in our first semester, we had a guest lecture from a St. Lawrence alum who was a professor at Johns Hopkins Bloomberg School of Public Health. As he spoke about what public health was and how it could be applied, I remember thinking, 'Wow, I want to do this!'" Dr. McCauley, who is currently a social epidemiologist and assistant professor of pediatrics and psychiatry at the University of Pittsburgh School of Medicine, eventually declared a sociology major and "began to think about how I could combine my interest in health and medicine and my interest in sociology." Through FYP, students not only develop the writing, speaking, and research skills, they'll need to succeed in college, but they may uncover the interests that will sustain them throughout their academic careers and beyond.

Rhetoric and Communication Studies Program

The University President William L. Fox is vocal in his belief that "superior rhetoric and communication skills [are] a key differentiator for students who earn liberal arts degrees—skills employers that consistently identify as 'most important' in surveys conducted by the National Association of Colleges and Employers (NACE)." To that end, the "Writing Competency Requirement" is more than just a hoop to jump through at St. Lawrence—students graduate prepared to read, write, speak, and listen well. The school says that RCP "demands greater accountability for identifying students with serious weaknesses in their writing skills and getting a customized tutoring plan in place to help each student develop greater proficiency and skills as a writer." Beginning with the First-Year Program, the RCP offers seminars on how to deliver effective oral presentations. St. Lawrence's W.O.R.D. Studio further support students' communication skills by providing them with the space and resources they need to discuss and develop writing, oral presentations, research, and multimedia projects.

Majors You Won't Find Everywhere

St. Lawrence stresses flexibility when it comes to academics. Though it offers a wide variety of thirty-six majors and thirty-seven minors, students are encouraged to create their own majors—and meet the St. Lawrence course requirements in creative ways—through the school's multi-field options.

Business in the Liberal Arts

Embracing this multi-disciplinary approach one of the school's newest majors—business in the liberal arts—helps prepare students for careers in all types of business environments with courses in economics, marketing, accounting, and philosophy. This major requires that students combine it with one of the other offerings from the school, resulting in an automatic double major and helping students develop into dynamic business leaders who bring multiple perspectives to the table.

Conservation Biology

Another St. Lawrence major that combines two disciplines is conservation biology, which brings together economics and global studies, and encourages students to think about conservation on a local and global level. Students learn about the fundamentals of global biodiversity—the sum total of all living things—through a research project or an internship, which helps prepare them for a career in conservation biology or other related fields; course requirements include classes in biology, economics, geology, and chemistry.

Global Studies

St. Lawrence also offers global studies, an interdisciplinary major for students who are interested in subjects such as social movements, migration, and global inequality. The course requirements are a mixture of political economy and cultural studies courses, along with media studies and gender and sexuality courses. Students choose between three courses of study: a comparative area study of two geographic or cultural areas, which includes at least one semester of a second language; one area of intense study with a second language requirement, or an area-thematic study, which also includes courses in a second language. Geographical areas available for study are as varied as Canadian Studies and Middle East or Islamic Studies, depending on the student's interest. All global studies majors complete a research project during their senior year at St. Lawrence; these Senior Year Experience projects are often completed in conjunction with an off-campus internship or research opportunity, helping students take the lessons they learn in the classroom out into the real world and vice versa.

Multi-Language Program

> **❝ The Multi-Language Program that [St. Lawrence] offered is incredibly unique and fit my interests perfectly.❞**

In an effort to encourage students' development as citizens not just of St. Lawrence but also of the world, the school offers a multi-language major, where students are required to complete four credits in three different foreign languages offered at St. Lawrence (with one language chosen as their concentration language). Multi-language majors are strongly encouraged to study abroad. This is not difficult since, as one St. Lawrence professor noted, "Over 50 percent [of St. Lawrence students participate] in study abroad [and] the interest in connecting local and global issues is palpable across the St. Lawrence community." Each of the language majors and minors—Arabic, Chinese, French, German, Italian, Spanish, and Swahili—offer corresponding study abroad options. One multi-language major—whose focus is in Spanish, Arabic, and Chinese—said, "The Multi-Language Program that [St. Lawrence] offered is incredibly unique and fit my interests perfectly." The Modern Languages department also offers students the opportunity to sharpen their conversation skills in the new languages they're learning in the classroom in a more relaxed setting with a program called Modern Language Conversation Tables. Once a week at a designated spot on campus, students come together to converse in Spanish, Arabic, or Chinese—the other languages surely have unofficial gathering spots, too—with both fellow newcomers and native speakers. In addition to honing their conversation skills, the Conversation Tables also give students a chance to learn about different cultures, watch movies and television shows from the countries whose languages they're studying, and even swap study abroad stories The International Economics and Modern Languages and Literatures combined majors will afford students with enhanced opportunities to develop careers in the profit, not-for-profit and government sectors of the economy.

Kenya Semester Program

Since 1974, St. Lawrence has offered a semester-long experience for students in Nairobi, Kenya, where the school maintains a satellite four-acre campus. At over forty years old, the Kenya program is one of the longest-running study abroad programs on the African continent. Students who participate in the program get the chance to experience busy city living in Nairobi, as well as rural living outside the city and in Tanzania during home-stays with families. All students are required to study Swahili during their semester abroad. The Kenya Semester Program is an interdisciplinary one that encourages cultural immersion;

students take two required courses—Swahili and Culture, Environment, and Development in East Africa—and get to choose two elective courses that are in line with their individual areas of study. While abroad, St. Lawrence students have the chance to get hands-on experience with organizations like the African Wildlife Foundation and the Federation of Women Lawyers, helping prepare them for potential careers that encompass important contemporary social issues. Since the 1980s, St. Lawrence has offered two scholarships annually to Kenyan students to attend college in New York and many of these graduates now assist current St. Lawrence students during their semester abroad in Nairobi. Kenyan graduates of St. Lawrence have also gone on to hold key governmental positions in their native country.

Connecting with the Environment

In addition to having one of the oldest Environmental Studies Programs in the nation, St. Lawrence takes full advantage of its wilderness adjacent setting with offerings like the Adirondacks Semester, where students live off the grid in Arcadia, a yurt village in the middle of the Adirondacks. The goal of the unique program is for students to study nature while experiencing it firsthand, rather than simply reading about it in a textbook. Where traditional students have a separation between their coursework and their lives outside the campus, everything is integrated in Arcadia, where school, nature, and life blend together. Courses like "Knowing Nature" are interwoven with activities such as hiking and canoeing, and the knowledge that students gain during a session of Natural History will deepen their understanding of the biological and geological landscape around the yurt village. On the creative side, any number of experiences might be integrated into an art or writing project for one of the Expression courses. The sense of community is further deepened since all the students take the same classes so continuing a discussion from a morning course during an afternoon hike becomes the norm. Another off-campus program aimed at students interested in the natural world, and particularly environmental issues, is the Sustainability Semester Program, launched in 2013. St. Lawrence partnered with Cornell Cooperative Extension to lease a small farmhouse near the campus, along with roughly thirty four acres of farmland and several other small buildings. The Sustainability Program helps students study sustainability and conservation from a local and global perspective, as well as learning the best ways to assist their communities. During their time in the Sustainability Program, students study topics such as alternative transportation, food production and processing, community planning and design, green building, renewable energy systems, and ecology.

Life After St. Lawrence

Through the St. Lawrence University Fellows program, students get a head start on their future careers by pursuing particular academic topics that interest them during the summer, with the assistance of a faculty adviser. These lines of inquiry often lead to a future research project or course of study the next academic year. The Liberal Arts in New York City Semester gives students the chance to study and intern in New York City. Students are housed at the 92nd Street Y, and intern for institutions such as Credit Suisse, Christie's Auction House, MTV, *Cosmopolitan* and *Vogue* magazines, and Morgan Stanley. The Fellows program, open to twenty-five to thirty students each summer, provides a $3,500 stipend and pairs the student with a faculty member.

More than 96 percent of the Class of 2013 were either employed or attending graduate school within one year of graduation. In a joint effort, Career Services and the Student Alumni Association bring graduates back to campus in an ongoing effort called Laurentians in Residence. The program offers classroom presentations, panels, and networking and mentoring opportunities for current students looking to connect with alumni who were once in their shoes. One foreign language major summed up St. Lawrence as a "tight-knit community that translates into broad post-grad opportunities, thanks to the strong professor and alumni relationships." The Career Connections program offers a Career Boot Camp, which specifically targets sophomores who are on the cusp of declaring their major. Career Services also offers students the opportunity to participate in a program called Laurentians Investing Networking and Careers (LINC), which started in 2013 funded by a generous alumnus donation. The program helps match up current St. Lawrence freshmen and sophomores with participating St. Lawrence alumni with careers in the students' desired fields. The connection helps build the students' networking skills and lays the groundwork for a potential long-term mentoring situation. For students who are interested in getting a leg-up on the career search during winter break, St. Lawrence's Shadow a Saint program pairs student with alumni volunteers who work in the field that best matches the students' interest. The program allows students the opportunity to get to know their mentor, hopefully sowing the seeds for career guidance in the future, and also gives them an in-depth look at the industry they'd like to work in after graduation. And Laurentians make good use of these career resources. As journalist and St. Lawrence alumnus Ed Forbes put it: "Our people are extremely resilient, are fairly adventurous, and willing to take risks. We're great critical thinkers, great writers, great team players, and are ready to lead the charge."

Stanford University

450 Serra Mall, Stanford, CA 94305–2004
Admissions: 650-723-2091
E-mail: admissions@stanford.edu
Website: www.stanford.edu/
Twitter: @Stanford @ApplyStanford

Introduction

Stanford University always aims to impress. Founded in 1885 by Leland and Jane Stanford, the university was meant to stand out—the Stanfords planned an institution that would be co-ed, non-denominational, and would "promote the public welfare by exercising an influence in behalf of humanity and civilization." Today Stanford has grown to a current class of over 7,000 undergraduate students, who study at the three schools: Earth, Energy & Environmental Sciences; Engineering; and Humanities & Science (graduate programs include the schools of Business, Education, Law, and Medicine.) Stanford's campus was originally a stock farm and extends to over 8,000 acres. The charming nickname "the Farm" stuck, even as the university continued to expand into a major liberal arts and research school.

Smack dab in the middle of Silicon Valley, a student may get swept up in the tech world by sheer osmosis, but Stanford holds fast to its liberal arts roots, and the university's commitment to providing students with a well-rounded, rigorous education. For example, Stanford now offers ten joint majors, informally called "CS+X," so that students can study computer science along with English, music, philosophy, or the classics. Just like computer science students seem to speak in the language of CSS, Stanford offers their own helpful "Stanford Speak"—a quick reference to translating the lingo students often throw around on campus. From the ASSU (Associated Students of Stanford University) to The Zoo (KZSU, the radio station), Stanford wants to make sure that every student can fit in socially, even as they stand out academically.

Stanford students work together and play together. New students are required to live on campus, but this only increases the sense of community. An administrator described a student's first two years at Stanford as "intimate and personal." As a student stuying mechanical engineering said, "I came for the academics, but I stay for the people." Academically, they also enroll in the university's Thinking Matters program, aimed to help freshman students address problems and questions through critical analysis, close reading, analytic writing, and effective communication. The school encourages students to continue pushing their education as far as it can go. A computer science major said, "Stanford allowed me the most freedom to grow. I had no idea what I wanted to study, and at Stanford, that wasn't a problem considering it is phenomenal in all aspects." Academia isn't just test scores and getting the right answer without knowing why. Stanford's education allows students to get comfortable thinking for themselves. A 2015 grad told us he came to Stanford because it's "one of the most diverse and accepting schools in the nation. I can simultaneously major in engineering while receiving a world-class humanities education, something that I would never sacrifice."

Life on the Farm

Although on-campus housing is only required for the first year, 96 percent of all undergraduates live on campus, in a range of buildings and facilities. Students participate in 650 student groups and religious organizations. Stanford students may be smart, but they're quick, too. Stanford offers thirty-six varsity sports and holds 105 NCAA championships—that's one for almost every year the university has existed. Thanks to the California sunshine students are outdoors a lot. In addition to stylish fitness and recreation facilities, Stanford counts an estimated 13,000 bicycles on campus.

❝ I knew that not only would I be supported at Stanford, I would be encouraged to thrive. ❞

The students we surveyed steadfastly asserted, "There really is no typical Stanford student." And, thankfully, that "makes it easy to be an integrated and diverse student body." A student in urban studies called the African American community at Stanford "the strongest in the country. I knew that not only would I be supported at Stanford, I would be encouraged to thrive." Centers like El Centro Chicano, the Women's Community Center, the Black Community Services Center, and the LGBT Community Resources Center "serve as gateways to intellectual, cultural and leadership opportunities" for all students. Spaces like these not only help bring together people with similar interests or backgrounds, but their events are also open to students and the community, so any student can learn more about their peers outside of the classroom. An alum told us his classmates "further developed my innate curiosity until the pursuit of knowledge in myriad areas became a full-fledged passion." For the civic-minded students, the Haas Center for Public Service offers funded opportunities. The aim here is for "real-world experience and reflection." Students take part in programs for service-learning activities, public policy, and activism, among others. Stanford students come in with a strong sense of self, but still have a chance to not only decide what they want their professional careers to look like, but who they want to be as people.

Stanford students are also getting a global education. Stanford offers its own overseas programs in Australia, Barcelona, Beijing, Berlin, Cape Town, Florence, Istanbul, Kyoto, Madrid, Oxford, Paris and Santiago. And even though the school is surrounded by Silicon Valley, that doesn't alter the stellar arts and humanities programs. One senior boasted, "At Stanford, anything is possible; I've lived on a schooner with faculty studying sharks, snorkeled on the Great Barrier Reef, hiked in the Australian rainforest, studied Antarctic phytoplankton with world-class scientists, and spent countless nights discussing philosophy, politics, film, and art until sunrise." Some Integrated Learning Environments combine learning and living in the residences. Through programs like ITALIC (Immersion in the Arts: Living in Culture), students have more opportunities to spend time experiencing other cultures. The strong commitment to the arts is "a means of developing, honing and applying creativity."

In fact, the university recently finished a new building for the Department of Art and Art History, and a new "arts district" is taking shape on campus. Even while the largest majors are in the sciences and engineering, the university "considers exposure to the arts crucial to a liberal arts education." From the stunning acoustics in Bing Concert Hall to the presentation practices in the Hume Center for Writing and Speaking, students have a chance to receive a great arts education at Stanford, too. With twenty libraries, two observatories, and three art galleries, Stanford students can be much more than just their major.

Undergraduate Research

Stanford's huge research program ensures someone on campus is always making something new. With a sponsored research budget of over $1.33 billion, Stanford knows that great research comes from great resources. DoResearch is Stanford's online platform that helps student get organized and get started on whatever projects they can dream up. UAR (Undergraduate Advising and Research) connects students with faculty members studying or undertaking similar research or creative projects and provides $5.6 million to fund 986 student projects. With Stanford's faculty, students work to solve the world's toughest social problems.

Since Stanford pushes students to think for themselves from the first moment they step on campus, and provides them with opportunities to develop their own ideas and research, it's no surprise that students continue on this path after graduating. An administrator told us that the goal of a Stanford education is "to study a subject [the students] love, not one they think will assure them of a job right out of college, and we help them develop the critical thinking skills they will need over their lifetimes." Once a student gets started at Stanford, the university takes care of them. The "goal of a Stanford liberal education is the honing of a set of core abilities, including analysis of information and argumentation, the synthesis of information from multiple sources, and precise, persuasive communication, both oral and written."

Environmental Sustainability

Smart schools also know how to stay with the times. Stanford is proud of the developing environmental and sustainability courses and initiatives taking place on campus. In 2014, the school decided to divest from coal mining companies. This idea first came from a student organization called Fossil Free Stanford that petitioned the university to change their methods. Stanford's helpful Advisory Panel on Investment Responsibility and Licensing (APIRL) encourages students to make these kinds of suggestions to help Stanford live up to its name. APIRL includes faculty, staff, and students, who review all requests to determine their merit, broken up into subcommittees to cover important areas of content, especially Environmental Sustainability. This student movement was then presented to the Board of Trustees, who agreed with the students.

Elsewhere, in environmental news, over 200 undergraduates leave The Farm to go to Alternative Spring Break programs on actual farms in the Bay Area. "Beyond Organic" is just one of seventeen courses. A marine biology student called the university's way of combining disparate thoughts and ideas a great experience to bring "together sustainability, science and technology, humanities, and arts with the ingenuity and inventiveness." It should be no surprise that Stanford comes in at number twenty-two on The Princeton Review's 2015 ranking list for the Top 50 Green Colleges in our *Guide to 353 Green Colleges*.

Entrepreneurship

Many students realize that a college education is more than sprucing up a dorm room and going to class. Alumnus Christian Angulo said his "real education came from the daily interactions, conversations, and diverse experiences that gave me the foundation necessary to go out into the real world." Angulo now works for the university in undergraduate admission, helping to determine the quality of future Stanford classes. He originally picked Stanford because of what most students love about the university—he could choose any major and could live and study in beautiful California, halfway between San Francisco and San Jose. Plus Stanford's campus and amenities offer tremendous chances for collaboration. To describe his Stanford peers, he said that what drives them and defines them the most is entrepreneurship. Stanford students are "go-getters," he said, "known for putting their all into what they do and creating their own opportunities to achieve their goals." Students develop this sense of entrepreneurship and business-savvy from groups like Stanford Student Enterprises. SSE boasts businesses "for students and run by students." SSE's four enterprises now include over 100 employees. Small student businesses? Maybe. But their total assets now exceed $15 million.

Budding entrepreneurs "take advantage of programs, lectures, courses and mentorships," an administrator told us. The Stanford School of Engineering hosts the Stanford Technology Ventures Program, and students also work with an education nonprofit, StartX. Work like this "accelerates the development of Stanford's top entrepreneurs through experiential education."

Faculty

Students don't nurture this sense of ambition and drive on their own. Stanford's professors and scholars are talented in their own right. Stanford has found over 2,118 full-time and part-time faculty, engaged and dedicated to developing their students into future leaders. Most professors hold a terminal degree in their specialty. The highly regarded university also boasts a growing cross-section of minority and female professors, further expanding the outlook of research and academia. The enviable 4:1 student-to-faculty ratio means that nearly 70 percent of classes have fewer than twenty students. Every student has a voice.

In 2012, Stanford conducted a study with faculty and student recommendations on how to make updates to the curriculum. The faculty "extensively reexamined the university's approach through The Study of Undergraduate Education." At the end, faculty contributed fifty-five recommendations on how to update their required courses to "help students gain knowledge, but also develop the capacities for continued intellectual growth." Professors know that simply adding more courses doesn't necessarily increase the standard of a students'

❝ The professors are some of the most engaging I have ever seen . . . [they are] all superstars.❞

education. Who better to know about the commitment of these professors than their students? As a human biology major told us, "The professors are some of the most engaging I have ever seen . . . [they are] all superstars." A product design engineer said, "The professors at Stanford draw you into the material because they are so excited to share their passion for the subject with you, and because they're so eager to inspire us."

Stanford's current faculty include twenty-one Nobel laureates, four Pulitzer Prize winners, and twenty-seven MacArthur Fellows. Five assistant professors—Amin Arbabian, Michael Lepech, Marco Pavone, Manu Prakash and Sindy Tang—were awarded grants through the National Science Foundation's CAREER program. The grants allow new and junior faculty members to continue working on their own scholarly research, while continuing to teach and help their students test their own developing ideas.

Life After Stanford

Stanford alums are making a splash in virtually every field you can think of from art to athletics. Graduates can count among their ranks such prominent alumni as the first American woman in space, the late Sally Ride; Mozilla Firefox developer Blake Ross; and novelists John Steinbeck and Michael Cunningham. Stanford has graduated one U.S. President, four Supreme Court Justices, four current U.S. Senators, a National Security Advisor, two U.S. Secretaries, and the current U.S. ambassadors to China and South Korea. They've been instrumental parts of businesses like Hewlett-Packard, StubHub, LinkedIn, Yahoo, and PayPal and are the inventors of the microprocessor, the laser, and GPS.

Thankfully, networking with this prestigious group of 217,000-plus grads starts early. Along with standard services like job fairs and recruiting events, résumé critiques, and one-on-one counseling, Stanford's Career Development Center hosts CareerConnect, a job board that lists hundreds of alumni-posted jobs and internships. The Center also offers "career communities" in specific fields, including a special community devoted solely to the needs of underclassmen still a few years away from their post-grad job hunt. Most current students agree that Stanford "provides a great opportunity to pursue greater careers with a wide array of resources and support." A 2015 grad in bioengineering sums it up: "Stanford's given me the opportunity to go abroad three times as an engineer, to minor in modern languages, to explore classics and religious studies, while simultaneously excelling at the cutting edge of the world's finest bioengineering technology…with a relaxed and supportive social atmosphere. That's something that makes me feel incredibly lucky on a daily basis."

The State University of New York at Binghamton

4400 Vestal Pkwy E, Binghamton, NY 13902
Admissions: 607-777-2171
Website: www.binghamton.edu
Twitter: @binghamtonu

Introduction

It's impossible to talk about Binghamton University, located in upstate New York, without mentioning the low cost of attendance. In fact, the school's exceptional value combined with its high-caliber of academics was mentioned by almost every student we surveyed as their reason for attending. "It's practically half the cost of other private schools, has some of the best undergraduate research and publishing opportunities in the country, top-notch academics, and wouldn't put me over $200,000 in debt. Additionally, it has incredible campus resources, one of the most unique living systems in the country, and a renowned faculty and staff who interact personally with the students. It also has one of the highest returns on investment in the entire country," one English and history major told us. A psychology major summed it up more succinctly, describing the school as having an "Ivy League workload at a SUNY school price."

Binghamton is particularly well-known for its STEM program, and the business, engineering, and nursing majors are extremely popular. In the first edition of our book *Colleges That Pay You Back*, students praised Binghamton's great management program, strong science departments (especially in biology, pre-med, and psychology), and the pre-law program that yields high law school acceptance rates. But the school's great academic reputation attracts high-achieving students with diverse interests, all eager to make the most of their college experience. "The thing that really stands out to me is that our students are not only very bright; they are highly motivated to get the most out of their education. Many of them are first- or second-generation college students, and see higher education as the incredibly valuable opportunity that it is," Associate Professor of Philosophy Christopher Morgan-Knapp observed.

Though tuition is low, many of the students we surveyed commended the school for the amount of resources it makes available. Such features include innovative residential colleges; stellar academic support; abundant research, leadership, and volunteer opportunities; career guidance; and an active alumni network. Binghamton University must be doing something right: the school's 90 percent retention rate is well above the national average for comparable universities, and 20 percent of graduates also go on to receive graduate degrees from Binghamton.

Faculty Masters in Residential Communities

Through its residential college experience for freshmen, inspired by the Oxford University college system, Binghamton "build[s] smaller communities within the larger overall community of the school," a chemistry and mathematics major told us. "It has the small college feel thanks to the Oxford Community style of living on campus, and then it has all the opportunities of a large university from massive amounts of research to Division I sports," an industrial and systems engineering major added.

Under this system, freshmen are divided into five residential colleges, each of which has its own Faculty Master and affiliated faculty "Fellows." "Our role is essentially to be the academic leader of our community," the Faculty Master of Newing College, Mark Reisinger explained. In addition to his responsibilities at Newing, Associate Professor Reisinger is also director of undergraduate studies for geology. He told us: "In Newing College, we have approximately thirty-five to forty Fellows. . . . Once a month we hold a Students/Fellows Lunch where our residents can get to know faculty in a more relaxed atmosphere than the classroom. The fellows also participate in academic and social events within the community. This semester we started a new program, Faculty in Residence, to encourage even greater interaction between our residents and faculty. Newing College has a faculty in residence from our Graduate School of Education and from the Mathematics Department. Both are doing career-related events for their disciplines. They are also doing fun events such as movie nights. Of course, the movies are in some way related to education or math."

Faculty Masters, Associate Professor Reisinger told us, also have an opportunity to develop classes. "For example, I have been able to develop a course that has some of the students in my residential community participating, as well as a group of students in China that are part of our University Readiness Program. The class meets live twice per week for discussions via Web conferencing software. I feel this is a tremendous cross-cultural learning experience for both groups of students."

University Tutoring Services (UTS)

The first step toward preparing students to go on to successful careers is making sure that they succeed in their classes. To accomplish this, Binghamton provides access to free tutoring to all students through its Center for Learning and Teaching. "We know that students struggle in certain 'gateway courses' such as chemistry, biology, and economics. However, the Tutoring Center is willing to find tutors for other courses where there is a demand. Another good thing about the tutoring is that it is held within each of the residential communities," Associate Professor Reisinger explained. Currently UTS offers tutoring in eighty courses spread across twenty-eight departments. Tutoring is available by appointment, during walk-in hours, and online in certain subjects. Interested students can also apply to become tutors through UTS, thereby honing soft skills like communication and problem-solving and gaining valuable work experience all while helping their fellow students.

Research Opportunities

Binghamton doesn't believe that research experience should wait until junior or senior year. Through the Freshman Research Immersion, students in science and engineering programs have the opportunity to work directly with faculty on cutting-edge research projects. The research is done for course credit, and allows students to develop personal relationships with faculty. Binghamton sponsors a Summer Research Immersion Program for students majoring in the STEM fields as well.

Of course, students outside of the STEM fields also participate in research opportunities. "For instance, our Pell Honors Program runs a semester-long course for exceptional students writing their own research articles, puts on a conference at which they present their work to faculty and their peers, and edits a journal published by SUNY Press in which the best of these articles are published. This kind of engagement with students has really paid off, both in terms of the intrinsic rewards these students gain from such intense and high-level academic research, and in acceptances at top PhD programs and professional schools," Associate Professor Morgan-Knapp told us.

Beyond these more formal programs, students in all disciplines have opportunities for research, thanks to Binghamton's emphasis on faculty research. Associate Professor of Organizational Management Shelley Dionne explained the value of the school's focus: "The whole purpose of placing research faculty in the classroom is to keep the curriculum fresh and up-to-date and, I should add, to bring an aura of discovery into the classroom. Our faculty do this. They fashion courses that reflect both changes in the discipline and in their work, and they explore these with and through their students. Many also recruit students to assist in their research, in which case research and pedagogy blend rather seamlessly. "

Leadership Opportunities

❝ It's almost unheard of for a student not to be in charge of something in one form or another. ❞

With a Student Association, residential community governments, and almost 300 student-led organizations, Binghamton abounds with leadership opportunities for students. According to one industrial and systems engineering major we surveyed, "It's almost unheard of for a student not to be in charge of something in one form or another." For example, Off Campus College Transport—the transportation link between campus and the surrounding community—is student-run, as is Harpur's Ferry—the campus ambulance service—and the campus newspaper, radio station and television service. Student leaders have regular interactions with the school's administration and real responsibilities for running the school. The college informed us, "The president, vice presidents, and deans teach and mentor students, and they interact with student leaders in a variety of settings to discuss campus issues. The president and vice presidents meet regularly with the Student Association's elected officers, and a student participates in the University Council and monthly meetings of the vice presidents and deans. Each school has a student group that advises the dean. In our largest school, Harpur College of Arts and Sciences, students constitute 30 percent of the college council, which has final decision-making authority on curricular matters. The Student Association allocates funds that support student organizations, and each residential community has an elected government."

Students certainly recognize and appreciate these opportunities. "I was also attracted to the amount of clubs, student activities, and leadership opportunities available on campus," a human development major told us, while an English literature and history student cited "undergraduate leadership" as one of the strengths of the school. Lee Karchawer, who graduated from Binghamton in 2005 and went on to earn an MBA from the school in 2007 reported, "I would consider one of the most important experiences I had in college was when I started my own business with a fellow student, who is now one of my closest friends and for many years was my roommate in New York City post-Binghamton. We started a business called My Campus Promotions, which helped local businesses advertise to students including placing logos in the form of temporary tattoos on student's foreheads at campus events. Additionally, we started Bingmenus, which became a campus hit, by providing the students with a way to order food online for delivery from local restaurants. I pursued my MBA at Binghamton, while simultaneously running my business."

Center for Civic Engagement

According to one political science major we surveyed, "Binghamton University is all about serving the community." Much of this service originates with the Center for Civic Engagement, which employs both a full-time staff as well as Binghamton students. The CCE serves as a hub for coordinating engagement and academic service learning with communities within and beyond Binghamton's campus. The CCE website has updated listings of opportunities for Binghamton students to get involved in the community, including volunteer opportunities, speakers visiting campus, and activities like Alternative Spring Break, in which students volunteer during school vacation.

Through the website, students can also find service learning classes at Binghamton. These classes are organized service activities for students that connect what they're learning to the world, and meet the needs of a specified off-campus community. Students who take part in these service learning opportunities gain valuable real-world experiences, practical skills, and career guidance.

Fleishman Center for Career and Professional Development

The Fleishman Center is committed to helping students transition from students to professionals. According to the students we surveyed, the center accomplishes its mission. "[One of] the greatest strengths of my school [is] the career development center," a political science major told us. A human development major agreed, citing the "jobs and internships" as two of the best aspects of the school. The center provides students with help choosing a major and career path, locating and securing internships, preparing a résumé, and networking with alumni. In addition to the Fleishman Center, each of the undergraduate schools at Binghamton has its own career development centers that help students translate their academic work into career opportunities. In Harpur College for instance, select students can take part in Liberal Arts to Career Externships (LACE), which gives them three to five job shadowing sessions over winter break. The university reports that the top destinations for employed recent graduates include PwC, Teach for America, and the U.S. Government, among others.

The Fleishman Center relies in part on the strong alumni network to provide these services to students. For example, Rick Krisburg, who holds both a bachelor's in political science and an MBA from Binghamton, described his participation in organized events at the school. "I've participated in the Metro Career Night for at least the last ten years. I do hire alumni, when possible. My door is always open to network with fellow alumni. I recently placed an ad through the Fleishman Center for a position within my company."

Faculty

As Binghamton is a research university, it is perhaps not surprising that 94 percent of full-time faculty have a PhD or other terminal degree. The faculty have distinguished themselves beyond their credentials as well, winning the Pulitzer Prize, Guggenheim and Fulbright Fellowships, major National Science Foundation and National Institutes of Health grants, and the Barnes and Noble Writers' Award, to name a few. They testify before Congress, write op-ed pieces for the *New York Times* and *Wall Street Journal*, appear on national television, and invent things such as the lithium ion battery.

While Binghamton is a research university, faculty do strive to balance their research with their teaching. "In my department, for instance, we have a policy of having tenured or tenure-track professors teach our introductory courses, rather than leaving that to graduate students or adjuncts. And I have often been impressed in the Harpur College's monthly meeting of chairs and directors how much time and concern is dedicated to the educational portion of our mission," Professor Morgan-Knapp told us. Professor and chair of the chemistry department Wayne Jones detailed further the interactions between students and faculty at Binghamton: "From open office doors for office-hour conversations, to research labs bulging with multiple undergraduate and graduate students on teams, faculty see students as the life of the university. Often this extends beyond the campus. I have enjoyed hosting students at my home for dinner, joining them for science demos or discussions in the residence halls, working with students on outreach activities for local kids in the K–12 community, and bringing students to present at national and regional meetings in my discipline. These experiences are not unique as many faculty engage with students in this way."

Faculty also appreciate the resources provided to them by the university. "Binghamton provides an environment where faculty can engage with students individually in the classroom and laboratory to create deep learning and teaching opportunities. At the same time, faculty have the resources and support to create deep scholarship, research and creative work in their discipline to create new knowledge for the community," Professor Jones explained. Associate Professor

Dionne elaborated on the university's support for its teachers. "Throughout Binghamton University there are teaching centers, mentoring programs, leadership development programs and variety of classes and seminars offered regularly to improve teaching effectiveness. Administration actively rewards outstanding teachers, as well as faculty who balance strong performance in both teaching and research."

Alumni/ae

With over 120,000 alumni in all fifty states and around the world, the Binghamton alumni network is certainly extensive. Among their ranks are Scott Krug, the chief financial officer of the Yankees; singer-songwriter Ingrid Michaelson, and New York Congressman Hakeem Jeffries (with respective degrees in accounting, theatre, and Afro-American/African studies). Beyond the numbers, many alumni are actively engaged in networking with current and former students. For example, Gary Kibel, who graduated from Binghamton in 1990 and went on to earn his MBA in 1992 told us, "I am active in the Binghamton University Alumni Association. I attend many Binghamton-sponsored events in the NYC metropolitan area. I also return to campus at least once a year. I seek out and connect with other Binghamton alumni in my personal and professional life, both online and offline," while Lee Karchawer reported, "I have attended alumni events in NYC and still maintain many personal and business relationships with former students. I also have hired students/alumni for business ventures as well as helped many pursue their own business ventures or careers."

Stevens Institute of Technology

One Castle Point Terrace, Hoboken, New Jersey 07030
Admissions: 201-216-5194
E-mail: admissions@stevens.edu
Website: www.stevens.edu
Twitter: @FollowStevens

Introduction

With a fantastic engineering reputation and its close proximity to New York City—the Manhattan skyline twinkles just across the Hudson—Stevens Institute of Technology is a small university that offers its students big opportunities. Since it opened its doors in 1870, Stevens, known as The Innovation University®, has been committed to technology and technological innovation, both in the classroom and preparing Stevens alumni for careers in the ever-changing world. But just because the school excels in providing students with top-notch science and engineering courses, doesn't mean that it lacks a solid foundation in business or the arts and humanities. In addition to the expected majors like civil and mechanical engineering, students at Stevens can also choose to pursue a degree—or even a double major—in fields as diverse as history, literature, and philosophy. It's often the intersection of art and science that sets Stevens apart: students have the opportunity to major in interdisciplinary fields such as music & technology, visual arts & technology, and science communication. With thirty-four possible majors to choose from, students will certainly find something that piques their interests, as varied as those may be.

The school itself is small enough, with roughly 2,900 undergraduate students, to feel close-knit and, as one mechanical engineering major puts it, "People assume students at an engineering school would be very anti-social, but it's quite the opposite. It is very easy to make friends and fit in at Stevens." With a 10:1 student faculty ratio, students can expect one-on-one help in the classroom from professors who "are truly here for the students and want to give them the best opportunities they possibly can whether through internships or research opportunities within their own labs," as one biomedical engineering major sums it up. In fact, the schools says that more than 90 percent of undergraduates participate in some form of hands-on education, and average two to three internships prior to graduation.

Starting Off on the Right Foot

Starting college is daunting, whether you're coming from across the country, the ocean, or even just from a neighboring New Jersey town. At Stevens, in addition to the typical orientation activities, incoming freshmen may sign up for Pre-Orientation, a chance to meet other new faces, as well as faculty and staff, while participating in fun, stress-free activities. There are five Pre-Orientation options, offering something for everyone: Outdoor Adventure, which includes canoeing, backpacking, mountain biking, and rock climbing; Performing Arts Experience; Sports & Fitness; City Life Experience; and Flavors of New York. In order to help guide freshmen academically, both at Stevens and in preparation for their

66 *There's always someone there to get me on the right path . . . where I am now is all thanks to Stevens.* **99**

lives after college, the school assigns every student a career counselor and counselor within the student's department. It's this "open door policy" that a 2014 mechanical engineering alumna cites as one of the school's greatest strengths: "There's always someone there to get me on the right path . . . where I am now is all thanks to Stevens." For students across all four schools— the College of Arts and Letters, the Schaefer School of Engineering and Science, the School of Systems and Enterprises, and the Howe School of Technology Management— two core classes offer a common foundation starting during freshman year. All students take Writing and Communication and CAL Colloquium: Knowledge, Nature, Culture during their first year at Stevens; these courses help sharpen students' written and oral skills using humanities-based texts. In the Schaefer School of Engineering and Science, students are now required, as a new addition to the engineering curriculum, to take Introduction to Entrepreneurship as part of their freshman course load. Even for students who don't foresee careers as entrepreneurs, the class emphasizes the importance of problem solving in the real world and using your imagination to tackle problems, both of which are vital when it comes to the constantly changing world of technology, one where the only guarantee is that it will change radically between the time a student enters Stevens and the time he or she graduates.

Another, less conventional way that Stevens takes a hands-on approach to meeting student need and helps prepare its students for tackling real-world problems that will inevitably pop up in any working environment is the popular event known as "Pancakes with the President," where twenty students—there's an application process in place to participate—have the opportunity to sit down with the university's president in an informal setting to discuss a wide range of issues, from foreign language options available to students to proposed construction of new buildings on campus. In addition to getting their voices heard by the school's president, this forum also educates students on the best avenues and resources for solving other problems that may arise on campus.

Unique Majors

Stevens first opened its doors during the Industrial Revolution, and the family for which it's named was on the forefront of technological innovation from the beginning—John Stevens not only pioneered the development of the steamboat but also designed the first American-built steam locomotive. So it's no surprise that a century later, in 1982, Stevens became the country's first major educational institution to institute a personal computer requirement for its students. There are ten engineering majors available for students—biomedical, chemical, civil, computer, electrical, engineering management, environmental, mechanical, naval and software—and many choose to double major, coupling engineering with a business- or technology-based major (or often something in the humanities). As a cutting edge technical institution, Stevens also offers courses, majors, and minors that aren't available at other schools, particularly ones such as cybersecurity, naval engineering, and quantitative finance. At the School of Engineering and Science (SES), undergraduates can pursue a major in cybersecurity through the department of computer science, which pulls together pulls together coursework in math, cryptography, networked systems, and IT administrations. Also at SES, students can take advantage of the Davidson Laboratory, a nationally recognized center for maritime design research, while they pursue a degree in Naval Engineering. Having such a prestigious center at their fingertips allows students to mix hands-on learning—often with projects from private companies and the US government—with more traditional classroom learning. This allows students to make connections that can help launch their post-college careers, as well as round out their experience as Stevens students. In the School of Technology Management, undergraduate students have the unique opportunity to pursue a degree in quantitative finance, which prepares them for careers in financial risk management and analysis, structured finance, financial modeling, financial strategy, and financial engineering, not to mention graduate school. One quantitative finance major cites the "innovative quantitative finance program that isn't offered as an undergraduate degree at any other college" as a key reason for choosing Stevens.

The Cooperative Education Program

It's one thing to generally encourage students to pursue internships and stop by career fairs during their college years. It's another create a program specifically designed to give students the opportunity to leave the classroom for a semester and experience life as an engineer, a software designer, or any number of other career options they might be considering. At Stevens, the Cooperative Education Program, known as the Co-op, alternates full-time semesters in the classroom with full-time semesters in the workplace. Says one mechanical engineering major, "the cooperative education program at Stevens does wonders in finding students great experience in the field they hope to work in after they graduate." Co-op positions are directly related to students' career and academic goals, and the companies partnered with Stevens included industry leaders from ExxonMobil and Colgate Palmolive to the Panasonic Corporation of North America and Merck. For incoming students still undecided about their major, the Co-op

> 66 The cooperative education program at Stevens does wonders in finding students great experience in the field they hope to work in after they graduate. 99

program is the perfect opportunity to get hands-on experience in a potential to see if a particular line of work is interesting and fits your particular skill set; the off-campus experience is also a time to discover new talents and new interests that you can turn around and use in the classroom, perhaps even to send you down a new path in your studies. Unlike internships, which students fit in around their class schedules, the Co-op program's unique structure of five increasingly productive work terms—for which the student is paid—means that students get to experience what it's like working in corporate offices or laboratories with some of the foremost experts in their fields, forging connections that could lead to permanent positions following graduation. The Co-op office, located in the Howe Center, is an integral part of getting students prepared for their time in the Co-op program, from running mandatory résumé review sessions to conducting senior exit interviews, where graduating seniors sit down with a Co-op office staff member to discuss their experience in the program. In fact, staff members are there to support students every step of the way: each student's progress through the program—both on and off campus—is monitored by the Co-op office through a series of regularly submitted documents.

Senior Capstone Projects

Similar to a senior thesis, all seniors at Stevens, regardless of their major, are required to complete a Senior Capstone Project. All of these projects are shown at the annual Senior Design Exposition, an event that's open to the Stevens community and the general public. Just like the relationships that students who participate in the Co-op Program build with their bosses and mentors during their semesters off campus, seniors are encouraged to develop their Capstone Projects with the collaboration of an industrial sponsorship, providing another route for students to secure post-college employment. The Capstone Project, whether you're a Naval Engineering major or a Visual Arts and Technology major, should be seen as the culminating experience of a student's in his or her particular program and stem both from personal interest and future career goals; students are assigned Capstone advisers to help guide them through the process of writing their reports and presentations and preparing their projects for exhibition. For one 2014 graduate, who pursued a dual bachelor's/master's degree in mechanical engineering and engineering management, respectively, her senior Capstone Project consisted of the rigorous solar decathlon, which spanned two years. "Anyone can learn math calculations and science information," she says, "but being able to get that information across within a group and have it be successful and optimized is another skill."

Prep for the Real World

One of the key elements of an engineering education at Stevens is an integral part of the curriculum called the Design Spine. Made up of eight courses—students take one each semester—the Design Spine teaches creative thinking, problem solving, teamwork, the economics of engineering, project management, communication skills, ethics and environmental awareness, all vital skills needed for the engineers of the future. The first five core courses are taken by all engineering students, regardless of if they're biomedical or naval engineer, while the last three, which consist of a class taken during the junior year and a two-semester senior Capstone Project, are taken within a student's particular discipline. Instead of focusing on one isolated piece of the puzzle, Design Spine encourages the importance of systems thinking and the idea of total design and approaching a problem from every possible angle.

As an institution, Stevens also goes to great lengths to prepare its students for life after college. As one civil engineering major puts it, "the Career Development Office and the Cooperative Education Office are great at getting students internships and co-op positions during the summers/semesters." One important distinction between the Career Development Services at Stevens that sets it apart from many other universities is its proactive approach to reaching students from the moment they enroll at Stevens as freshmen. Instead of waiting until a panicked junior, or even a senior, comes knocking on the door with no idea what to do after graduation, Career Development takes the first step. As a 2014 mechanical engineer graduate notes, even though it might seem strange to talk to a Career Development counselor as a freshman ("I just got into college. Why are they talking to me about jobs already?), once students meet with one of the members of the career development team "you really understand how they're willing to help you, whether it's with a co-op where you alternate semesters with school and work, or if it's an internship."

The strategy seems to be a hit. According to the school's most recent career outcomes report, within six months of graduation, 96 percent of the graduating class had secured their intended outcome in fields of their choice. In fact, Stevens comes in at numer three on The Princeton Review's 2015 ranking list for Best Career Placement, reported in the 2015 edition of our book *Colleges That Pay You Back*. Prominent alumni include such innovators as the physicist Frederick Reines, winner of the Nobel Prize in Physics; sculptor Alexander Calder, known as the originator of suspended "mobiles"; and Alfred W. Fielding, the inventor of Bubble Wrap. Three career fairs each year attract employers like Google, Microsoft, JPMorgan Chase, and even Victoria's Secret to campus, and Fortune 500 companies, as well as start-ups, participate in the Stevens professional development and recruiting programs.

Swarthmore College

500 College Ave, Swarthmore, PA 19081
Admissions: 610-328-8300
E-mail: admissions@swarthmore.edu
Website: http://www.swarthmore.edu
Twitter: @swarthmore

Introduction

Founded in 1864 as a co-ed college by the Religious Society of Friends, Swarthmore College has always touted the benefits of adhering to simple, classic values. Swarthmore is a private liberal arts college with dedicated research and engineering courses and faculty. The school aims to "facilitate discovery and foster social responsibility" in its students. From the Oxford-style of its outstanding Honors program to the stunning Scott Arboretum, Swarthmore (and its students, known affectionately as "Swatties") are surrounded by history and culture at every turn. Valerie Smith, former Dean of the College at Princeton University, became president of the college in July 2015.

The college sits on 425 acres of "rolling lawns, a creek, wooded hills, and hiking trails" settled eleven miles south of Philadelphia. The Scott Arboretum nicely frames the campus. The scenic gardens with over 4,000 plants and trees, illustrate Swarthmore's commitment to its past. The arboretum was created in 1929 as a living memorial to Arthur Hoyt Scott (Class of 1895), a horticultural enthusiast. Its goal is to educate the public, and plant and grow a variety of vines, shrubs and perennials native to the Philadelphia area and suitable for the local climate. Everything is meant to grow hardy here, and that goes the same for Swarthmore's students.

The small, but impressive community of 1,534 students is nearly split evenly between men and women. Ninety-three percent of students live in the seventeen residence halls. Students can choose from over forty majors and more than 600 courses, or they can design their own independent major. As part of the Tri-College Consortium, students work with and study with students at Bryn Mawr and Haverford Colleges, and are allowed some cross-registration privileges with the University of Pennsylvania.

Amy Cheng Vollmer, professor and chair of the biology department, said her students "leave here having developed a sense of their own identity as scholars. What I mean by that is they've identified a disciplinary area or area of inquiry in which they have a passion and in which they have developed a set of skills." Swarthmore wants their students to be involved and civically engaged, not solely concerned about receiving a grade but about receiving an education. The school emphasizes learning about cultures and community and pushes students to explore to learn more about the world around them. This kind of commitment doesn't only happen in the classroom. Over 60 percent of Swarthmore students volunteer, and students are involved in over 100 clubs on campus—quite a few for an enrollment smaller than many high schools.

First-Year Seminars

One of the first times students are given the chance to express themselves are in first-year seminars. These small academic discussions are limited to twelve students each. New students get involved in one particular field and develop their learning skills from the very first day. The classes allow for "analytical thinking, critical reading, construction and presentation of sound academic arguments, academic writing, information literacy" among other tasks.

As an administrator explained, the global outlook at the college allows for a "diversity of perspective" which "contributes to the community's strong sense of open dialogue and engagement with ideas and issues." Swarthmore's intimate community allows for a much tighter learning experience than at larger schools. Students are given a true opportunity to express themselves when they are allowed to openly voice their opinion and easily contribute to important discussions.

Swarthmore students are also given instruction on the best use of their library, which will further help them with research and collaborative learning. As Dr. Vollmer said, "It should be liberating for a student to learn that life is not linear because then it's not like there is one decision you make and everything else depends on that. . . . The students really are in the driver's seat for their own learning."

> 66 The students really are in the driver's seat for their own learning. 99

Research and Development

Once a student is interested or intrigued by a topic, then they get to start putting some of their ideas into action. Swarthmore's driven students are always working on something big. Sixty-six percent of students participate in undergraduate research or creative projects, and the school proudly provides more than $800,000 in grants to support their students' endeavors during these summer research periods. Swatties undertake research in engineering, the social and natural sciences, and the humanities and drive social action projects with the support and mentorship of faculty members. Students who recently received grants were working on projects like toxicology work in Ghana or analyzing exploratory data from a research study on HIV/AIDS.

Dr. Timothy Burke, professor and chair of the history department said, " It's something of a cliché at Swarthmore that students have a chance to participate in research at a high level, to work with faculty closely in many settings, to drop in and see faculty at their office hours frequently, but that's because this is largely the truth." It's rare for most students to have this kind of unfettered research and analysis time. The summer is the best for these research periods because it allows students a chance to explore their ideas without dealing with the typical semester's constraints of other coursework and extracurricular activities.

Once a student has a more solid idea of what they want their career to look like, they can participate in Extern Week. Swatties have the opportunity to get as close as they can to a hands-on experience in what they want to do for the rest of their lives. Some students interested in the environment and gardening spent time at Ground Floor Farm. "I thought it would be interesting for Swatties to get a glimpse of a career choice that is probably pretty far away from what most of them would imagine they will do with their lives," said Jackie Vitale '09, who manages the farm (quoted in an article about Extern Week published on Swarthmore's communications website). "They helped us with seeding, planting, harvesting, and market prep."

Students like Christine Yao heard the benefits and downfalls of becoming, and working as, a physician. "Hearing the downsides of a career in medicine helped me grasp a better sense of my future," she told Swarthmore's communication office. "It was nice to hear about the career in an un-idealized, unfiltered way." Extern Week provides students with the opportunity to test drive their intended careers to see if they'll like the jobs once they graduate. Swarthmore isn't only about helping students succeed, the school also wants its students to be fulfilled and happy, too.

Lang Center for Civic and Social Responsibility

The Lang Center works "to prepare and motivate students to understand and engage issues of civic and social concern [and] to set their own paths towards shaping a more just and compassionate world." This is a high aim, but Swarthmore endeavors to exceed these goals at every turn. The Lang Center is supported by an endowment created in 2001 by Eugene Lang (Class of '38). Lang connected with Swarthmore's aim to push students into "lifelong leadership in civic engagement and positive social change."

The Lang Center provides funds for students to work with community service and activist groups. Joy Charlton, Executive Director at the Lang Center, is especially proud of the Opportunity Scholarship Program, which provides up to $10,000 for a student to continue research or work in the community. The emphasis is particularly on "social action projects" or volunteering. Students have the chance to develop and attend courses for CBL (community-based learning), from dance and music, to water quality and pollution control, or an LGBTQ Linguistics course. If students have a larger project in mind, they can also apply for grants through the Swarthmore Foundation.

Swarthmore students like Aarti Rao developed a Lang Project to "understand the root cause behind the high infant mortality rate and poor standards of health in Churu, India." In addition to survey work and interviews, Rao looked up published information about birth practices and access to emergency contact information. These projects help the students even more once they're finished— Rao is using this for her senior thesis, as well.

Dr. Vollmer pointed out that the typical Swarthmore student is "self-motivated" and "does not mind being pushed out of their intellectual comfort zones."

Honors Program

Lots of schools have Honors Programs, but the unique program at Swarthmore might just be its most distinguishing feature. About one third of Swarthmore students work towards Honors distinction throughout their junior and senior years, in a program, which "emphasizes independent learning and dialogue." The program was first introduced in 1922, and "features small groups of dedicated and accomplished students working closely with faculty; an emphasis on independent learning; ongoing dialogue between students and their peers, teachers, and examiners; and an examination at the end of two years' study by outside scholars."

Honors candidates create a program for themselves made up of four "preparations" (i.e. a seminar, thesis or research project) in at least two disciplines. One of the fantastic things about the program is that it's entirely defined by the students. At the end of the program, external examiners who are experts in their fields, such as theater professionals from the Tisch School at NYU and Google software engineers, come to evaluate them through written and oral examination. Dr. Vollmer explained, "During one weekend in May, hundreds of honors examiners arrive on our campus. All of the oral exams take place in a matter of two days." Seniors who have been creating and nurturing groundbreaking ideas, get to then demonstrate what they've been learning and doing—to an expert. Their ideas are expressed and analyzed in a full discussion usually reserved for a graduate thesis defense, which can be a daunting yet exhilarating experience for students. Dr. Vollmer continued, "The Honors Program puts the student and the faculty on the same side. The faculty member is helping the student prepare for this exam through rehearsals, mock orals, or reading over drafts. The level of learning is very high."

Dr. Vollmer said that the program is unique in the way that experts in the field are introduced to Swarthmore's best and brightest. The reputation for Swarthmore scholarship returns with them to their home institutions, a very useful rep to have when students are later applying to graduate school. Still, she said truly "the only priority at Swarthmore is undergrad." There's no "this will be useful later" mentality. Swarthmore students' work is always useful and relevant, right now.

Campus Culture

The diverse campus includes an intercultural and an interfaith center, as well as a large number of clubs and cultural activities on campus for students. Students relax in McCabe Library (one of four libraries on campus) in the Popular Reading Room, dubbed by some intrepid students as the "McCave." They pile in at "10 p.m., when the free coffee-and-snack bar opens for business and people from all floors, majors, and politics stream into the McCave," a student told us. Swarthmore students also do silly, fascinating activities like passing around Ninjagrams on Valentine's Day. Students dressed as ninjas and pirates hand over candies and cards to unsuspecting students and professors in the name of romance and goodwill. All proceeds from the Ninjagrams go to a charity.

❝ The defining feature among us is that each person is brilliant at something: maybe dance, maybe quantum physics, maybe philosophy. ❞

Overall, students are "not sure if there is a typical Swattie," but suspect that "the defining feature among us is that each person is brilliant at something: maybe dance, maybe quantum physics, maybe philosophy." One undergrad summarizes, "While it is tough to generalize [...] one word definitely applies to us all: busy." Swarthmore's small size combined with its vast number of clubs and organizations provide opportunities to participate in pretty much whatever you want, and if not "you can start your own club." "There are student musical performances, drama performances, movies, speakers, and comedy shows," along with all kinds of school-sponsored events, so "there is almost always something to do on the weekend." When they can spare a couple of hours, many Swatties like to blow off steam in nearby Philadelphia, which is easily accessible by public transportation, including the train station located right on campus.

Faculty

Swarthmore's flexible faculty teach courses, lead seminars, advise individual students through their projects, and still continue their own research. Swarthmore employs 178 full-time and tenure-track faculty of which 98 percent hold terminal degrees in their fields. The 8:1 student to faculty ratio ensures that class sizes are small, to maintain Swarthmore's comfortable atmosphere. We asked Dr. Vollmer to describe her students, and she told us, "The kind of student who does well at Swarthmore is the self-motivated student who does not mind being pushed out of their intellectual comfort zone. An athlete who really strives to be excellent is going to train with a coach who pushes them out of their comfort zone. In the classroom or in a laboratory we're just saying, 'You've shown me what you can do. Now try this.'" Dr. Carina Yervasi, professor of French and Francophone studies echoed this sentiment: "Being a good teacher and a good student requires that both engage in knowledge creation. As a teacher, it is not merely that I guide students through the materials, but that we, as a class, develop a practice around the texts, bringing understanding and critical thinking into play."

The faculty understands that their students don't exist in a bubble, and as professors continue their research, they happily bring in their students. Swarthmore levels the playing field. It eliminates the barrier between what it takes to be a "scholar" by allowing students an incredible amount of leeway and respect to begin challenging ideas and beliefs. One of the most impressive aspects of Swarthmore faculty is the amount of trust and openness they express with their students.

Life after Swarthmore

Swarthmore alumni are doing pretty well, too. Dr. John Mather, a senior astrophysicist at NASA's Goddard Space Flight Center and co-recipient of the 2006 Nobel Prize in Physics, told us, "Swarthmore gave me a complete education in the basics. They promised me that when I went for my first interview before I even chose the place. They said, 'We're going to be sure we'll give you everything you need and that the fundamentals will be sound.'" He described how the physics faculty made it a simple process for him to jump ahead to sophomore level courses as a freshman student: "That was the most important message of being at that school which is that if you work hard at something, maybe you can win. And that I was actually going to be able to win occasionally. This is the sort of thing that shapes a person's self-image. I thought, 'I'm just going to do what I want to do here: study and learn.'" Patrick Awuah, Jr. (Class of 1989) was set on choosing engineering at Swarthmore, but wound up with a double major in engineering and economics. He also found time "outside of academic work" to learn martial arts, which he still practices today. And because of the interactions he had at Swarthmore, his education allowed him "to return to Ghana and help with economic development here through education." He is the founder and co-president of Ashesi University College, "whose goal is to educate African leaders of exceptional integrity and professional ability. By raising the bar for higher education in Ghana [Ashesi aims] to make a significant contribution towards a renaissance in Africa." He credits this career path to "the people I met [at Swarthmore]. The education I received through economic seminars greatly influenced me."

A sampling of other notable Swarthmore graduates include the philanthropist Eugene Lange (of the aforementioned Lang Center for Civic Responsibility); Cynthia Leive, the Editor-in-chief of *Glamour*; Evan and Andrew Gregory, producers of Auto-Tune the News, National Medal of Science recipient Sandra Moore Faber; and novelist Jonathan Franzen.

Swatties find that their liberal arts education is a boon whether they work in education or in research labs, write novels, or start companies. As Dr. Yervasi said about her students' future careers: "Graduating students will have gained intellectual flexibility, a sense of social responsibility, and an understanding of the ways in which they can participate in democratic engagement."

University of California— San Diego

9500 Gillman Dr., La Jolla, CA
Admissions: 858-534-4831
E-mail: admissionsinfo@ucsd.edu
Website: http://ucsd.edu
Twitter: @UCSanDiego

Introduction

Mathematics and the sciences reign supreme at the University of California—San Diego, and the school has an excellent reputation, huge research budgets, and an idyllic climate that have helped it attract the sixteen Nobel laureates who have taught at the university in the last fifty years. Offering what a probability and statistics major calls a "world-class education and a sense of community amongst students," UC San Diego is a public university with an ambitious mission. Simultaneously student-centered, research-focused, and service-oriented, UC San Diego aims to help its students attain not only greater knowledge and successful careers, but become better citizens of the world. When its founders established the school in 1960, they hoped to create a new kind of campus and a new kind of educational experience, melding the advantages of a small liberal arts college with the vast resources of a larger, public research university.

UC San Diego comes in at number thirty-one on The Princeton Review's 2015 ranking list for the Top 50 Colleges That Pay You Back, which was reported in the 2015 edition of our book *Colleges That Pay You Back*. The university is also recognized as one of the top fifteen research universities by the Center for Measuring University Performance. Yet the emphasis on an intimate, personalized education remains. The division of the undergraduate program into six smaller colleges helps take some of the edge off UC San Diego's big-school vibe (roughly 23,000 undergraduates) and allows students easier access to administrators. A quarterly academic calendar also keeps things moving.

Located in the beautiful La Jolla community of San Diego, California, the UC San Diego campus was described to us by a cognitive science major as "the most beautiful place on Earth, and it attracts the most interesting people I've ever met." An environmental systems major concurs: "It is a great location, has excellent services, is one of the top research universities in California, has made tremendous green efforts, and is full of sun!" Besides offering easy beach access, friendly SoCal culture, and all that picturesque San Diego has to offer, at UC San Diego, the campus amenities are even more attractive than its aesthetics. First and foremost is the centerpiece Geisel Library, the school's foundation for research and for what alum calls "the leading edge work we were exposed to in our regular classes." The new 1,000-bed Village at Torrey Pines, built especially for transfer students, is one of the most environmentally sustainable student housing structures in the nation. UC San Diego also offers 24/7 study spaces on campus, as well as a writing center where undergraduates can take advantage of hands-on academic assistance. A hands-on approach is also practiced in the classroom; UC San Diego's six-college system helps keep classes small and interactions with staff personal. "It's a great way to not feel like a small fish in a huge ocean," according to a communications and political science major. Yet the school has placed a premium on affordability and accessibility, with more than half of UC San Diego's undergraduates receiving financial aid.

As one human development major tells us, "UC San Diego is a very strong academic school that takes pride in its research, diversity, and sustainability." Professor Melissa Famulari, who is the vice-chair for undergraduate education in the economics department, sums up the school's mission for us: "By the time they leave UC San Diego, [students] tend to have a deep understanding of what they are passionate about learning and where their talents lie. Not only have our students acquired the tools of a specific major, but they have also learned to apply those tools in diverse settings." And the university provides students with a wide variety of tools and programs to explore their areas of interest and achieve personal and academic success.

Public Health

The school offers a new public health major in association with the UC San Diego School of Medicine, which places health into a context of both human rights and cultural understanding. With students developing and applying knowledge from multiple disciplines—including biological sciences, social and behavioral sciences, and quantitative skills—the program benefits not only student on a conventional medical school track, but those seeking to enter legal, business, and other health-related professions. One alumnus tells us that access to graduate school resources like these was a key in skill-building for his future career. "Since I was interested in technology and applied physics, the practical laboratory work in graduate school was certainly very valuable. This taught me the techniques that I would use later in starting a company."

Marine Science

Through the campus's world-famous Scripps Institution of Oceanography, UC San Diego offers a thrilling marine science minor, providing the school's science majors the opportunity to complement their own training and knowledge with this fascinating and environmentally focused interdisciplinary program.

Education Initiative

UC San Diego recently launched the Education Initiative, emphasizing that this not merely a school where professors lecture at students and leave it at that; instead, its administration and instructors seek out strategies, whether originating in their own classrooms or worldwide research, to support students' intellectual, academic, cognitive and social development. As part of this initiative, the campus launched a New Teaching and Learning Commons, which will focus on changing the inside of the classroom, preparing the students.

Evolving Curriculum

In fact, evolution is the name of the game at UC San Diego. The curriculum is a work in progress, constantly shifting and reinventing itself based on the needs of both students and the world they're entering. Professor Famulari gives one example: "Recognizing that UC San Diego's strengths in STEM disciplines attract many mathematically strong undergraduates to our campus, the Economics faculty designed the Management Science major. Management Science applies rigorous mathematical analysis and economic models to study the complex decisions that businesses and governments must make." Though patterned somewhat after a similar major at MIT, the UC San Diego program fuses management science with econometrics, a field of economics where faculty are highly ranked. Professor Famulari tells us there are now over 800 management science majors at UC San Diego.

Adaptability isn't confined to the classroom, either; an international studies major was particularly impressed by the school's numerous "community- and student-initiated programs like the Cross Cultural Center, LGBT Center, Women's Center, [and] SPACES [the Student Promoted Access Center for Education and Service.]" Centers like these join the Black Resources Center and Raza Resource Centro as student support networks on campus.

Research Library

A communication and political science major aptly describes UC San Diego as "a research and theory school that gives students access to cutting edge technology and theories." And countless students sing the praises of the UC San Diego Library, which plays a critical role in advancing and supporting the university's research, teaching, patient care and public service missions, while providing the foundation of knowledge needed to advance cutting-edge discoveries in a wide range of disciplines.

The Campus

An important element of that challenging academic load is the opportunity to relax. "Students work hard," a bioengineering major tells us, "but they also have a lot of opportunities to hang out. There are events almost every night, whether that be a concert, movie, or free rec class." Or, as another bioengineering major explains it, "Study, study, study, sleep, FUN!" "The area is beautiful!" a psychology major says. "It's the best of both worlds: quiet and peaceful for studying with so many places to discover. Plus the beach is very close by!" (The beach is a popular destination: a human biology listed several campus pluses before adding, "Of course, being five minutes from the beach is a nice perk too.") But there's much more to do than lounge on the beach. UC San Diego has 575 registered student organizations, with ninety-two of those organizations naming community service as their primary focus. A total of 14,275 students are engaged in a form of community service and in 2013, the university's students completed 2,138,760 hours of community service. And in taking such an active role, UC San Diego students serve as tutors, mentors and positive role models. Or, as a human development major puts it, "UC San Diego is a great place to find balance with school, work, opportunities, adventure and play!"

Faculty

> 66 **Professors are key to UC San Diego's success as a university.** 99

Among the UC San Diego students we surveyed, the most frequent praise was for the school's faculty, which a psychology major describes as "passionate, articulate, helpful," and "super friendly." Their enthusiasm is understandable; they learn from an impressive staff of leading researchers, authors, and scholars (sixteen Nobel laureates have taught at UC San Diego in the past five decades). "Professors are key to UC San Diego's success as a university," a human biology major explains. "An all faculty-taught undergraduate education—so rare!"

"My professors are incredibly knowledgeable about their material, and many of them are actively doing research in their field," notes a molecular biology major, echoing a popular sentiment among students: that the UC San Diego faculty isn't just teaching, but doing. "The professors are always doing research and writing books and have great insight into what it's like outside in the real world," says a communications and political science major. "They are incredibly intelligent."

UC San Diego doesn't just seek instructors—they seek innovators and thinkers, interested in conducting complex, question-driven research in an interdisciplinary environment, and in contemplating big questions and important issues. And with over 1,000 full-time faculty members, the school's 19:1 ratio allows professors to work closely with students, and vice versa. "The professors here are truly amazing," a literature of the world major told us. "In the Literature Department, professors work to make sure that students get what they need out of class time, usually spending the majority of the time focusing on getting students to participate in intellectual discussions rather than spending the whole hour lecturing. It helps to make us start thinking more critically about what we are studying so we will be prepared if we choose to take our studies to the next level. They are also always available outside of class and extremely friendly and helpful." Alumnus Sheldon C. Engelhorn agrees. Engelhorn, a 1972 graduate in biology who went on to co-found the biotechnical research tools company NOVEX, recalls, "I really enjoyed and benefited from the research experience . . . The excitement and passion for discovery that professors brought to the classroom was inspirational."

The school also offers several mentorship programs, including the Faculty Mentor Program; California Alliance for Minority Participation in Science, Engineering and Mathematics Program (CAMP); Health and Medical Professionals Preparation Program (HMP3); McNair Program; and the Marshal Mentor Program, which specifically connects transfer students with a faculty mentor.

Alumni/ae

Notable alumni of UC San Diego include prominent researchers, CEOs, computer designers, scientists, authors, journalists, artists, activists, musicians, athletes, actors, a Congressman, and two Nobel Prize winners. Business relationships often begin at UC San Diego; the aforementioned Sheldon C. Engelhorn began NOVEX with 1974 graduate Richard Chan, and UC San Diego alumni Bob Akins and Richard Sandstrom founded Cymer together. Cymer is an industry leader in developing lithography light sources for the semi-conductor industry. "Both my wife and my business partner are UC San Diego alums, and our company has hired over 100 UC San Diego graduates," Sandstrom tells us. "We maintain many contacts with professors so that we can get first dibs on the best students. We have endowed various chairs and student scholarships on campus."

Career Opportunities

> **❝ Employers know that graduates are capable of handling difficult, challenging, and creative environments.❞**

Cymer isn't the only company with an eye on UC San Diego students. As Engelhorn explains, "It's recognized as one of the most challenging schools in the country, so [employers] know that graduates are capable of handling difficult, challenging, and creative environments." To help facilitate these relationships, the school offers an Academic Internship Program, which allows students to merge their academic theory with real world applications, using research tools to explore the relationship between them, and gain hands-on professional experience while earning school credit. A psychology major speaks highly of the "many internships, labs, and other opportunities outside of the classroom." With shared-space centers, incubators and accelerators across campus, and a curriculum that places emphasis on education, career preparation and social responsibility, UC San Diego fosters a culture of collaboration and sense of community while strongly embracing the principles of diversity and equity. "The coursework is challenging," an electrical and computer engineering major tells us, "but the academic atmosphere is friendly and supportive. The sense of competition is minimal, but this doesn't mean that students don't study hard. It just means that the students are more willing to support their classmates and help each other out."

Professional success is practically synonymous with UC San Diego. Indeed, according to PayScale.com, the average starting salary for San Diego grads is $50,600. Students looking to jumpstart their search can easily turn to the Career Services Center. Here undergrads have the opportunity to meet with advisers to explore the breadth of career options, conduct assessments and research various industries. Most importantly, the Center hosts job fairs and networking events every quarter. These present great opportunities for undergrads to learn about internships, part-time gigs and full-time positions. Companies that have recently attended include Amazon, Boeing, Apple, Chevron Corporation, California State Auditor, Hulu, Groupon, Intel Corporation, and the Peace Corps.

Looking Ahead

Home to what a human biology major dubs "an intelligent student body passionate about community and global issues and each other," the University of California San Diego is the very model of a 21st century university: research-based yet practical and personal, academically traditional but constantly evolving, emphasizing community and diversity, and creating exciting new opportunities in the classroom and beyond. "I am proudly attending one of the top public universities in the nation," a communication and sociology major tells us. "But what I am most excited about is where UC San Diego is going. This university will undoubtedly set the new standard of what it means to be a public university in the years to come."

University of Dayton

300 College Park, Dayton, OH 45469
Admissions: 937-837-7433
E-mail: admission@udayton.edu
Website: https://udayton.edu
Twitter: @univofdayton, @daytonflyers

Introduction

As a Catholic, Marianist university, the University of Dayton states its mission as "We educate for service, justice and peace." According to its students, a spirit of "servant leadership" pervades the "faith community" of the school, and indeed, UD's values of community, diversity, and ethical grounding all strongly guide its educational imperative. UD has a fantastic track record for sponsored engineering and sponsored STEM research, and more than 140 patents have been assigned to the university—including the boxes that keep your Domino's Pizza hot. Within the university's four academic units—the School of Engineering, School of Education and Health Sciences, College of Arts and Sciences, and School of Business Administration—undergraduates may choose from a wide range of over 80 majors. UD's STEM programs are particularly strong, and feature prominently in students' reasons for choosing the school. A "close-knit community" within its mid-sized (about 8,000 undergrads) Dayton campus enables students to enjoy a 14:1 student-to-faculty ratio.

The University of Dayton is likely to suit students who want to put their education to work for the greater good. It makes helping students build networks for life a major priority, bringing them into close contact with faculty, alumni, and peers through its research opportunities, faculty mentorships, service projects, and love of the front porch conversation: The UD student neighborhood is studded with front porches to facilitate casual intellectual dialogue among its constituents. Its Marianist educational philosophy major states, "You are not alone at the University of Dayton . . . We believe we learn best in community." Indeed, "community" is the word that most dominates students' depictions of the UD experience: "the focus on community and service," according to many undergraduates, is the hallmark of a UD education. This servant leadership extends not just locally to the Dayton area, but through a prolific number of international learning and fellowship programs facilitated by UD. The university devotes a sizable measure of its resources to building global citizens out of its students, and those who demonstrate a sense of geographic adventurousness along with deep social conscience will thrive on UD's global opportunities. As one alumna, who entered college convinced she was going to be a lawyer, describes: "When I got to UD and discovered through class work that there was this career path in international development and that it allows you to combine service and learning—that was a whole new concept to me. Not only did UD introduce me to those ideas, which I never would have known about otherwise, but they made it possible for me to take the initial steps that got me on this pathway. They didn't just put me on the path, they supported me at every stage along the way."

> **66** *They didn't just put me on the path; they supported me at every stage along the way.* **99**

Below are a few of UD's crown jewel programs and community-building opportunities for students of all academic passions.

Common Academic Program

Beginning in Fall 2013, the implementation of the Common Academic Program, or CAP, revitalized the UD undergraduate educational mission. Under development by key members of the UD faculty for about a decade, the university calls CAP "an evolving, flexible curriculum" meant to touch on topics across a wide array of disciplines and combine "traditional learning with life experiences, theory with application, and practicality with creativity" all the while rooted in Marianist ideals of scholarship, faith traditions, diversity, community, practical wisdom, critical evaluation of our times, vocation. Programming begins freshman year with a cadre of courses in the "humanities commons" and builds from there, culminating in a capstone experience in the major. Deborah Bickford, professor and associate provost for Academic Affairs and Learning Initiatives, explains CAP's value: "Only in higher education do we think that problems only present themselves in one area. The world's greatest problems cut across academic boundaries. We think of the education we're providing as helping students traverse those boundaries." Interested prospective students can read about CAP's philosophy in great detail at udayton.edu/provost/cap.

University Honors Program

The University Honors Program offers UD honors students from all majors and programs the opportunity to pursue an honors diploma with or without a six-hour honors thesis. Each honors thesis writer has a faculty mentor who oversees their thesis project over the course of three semesters, creating deep connections between students and professors within their major. According to Carissa Krane, associate director for Honors Thesis Research and professor of biology, these "thesis mentor" relationships often vastly enrich students' preparation for graduate school by enabling faculty to write well-informed recommendation letters: "These letters that the faculty mentors writes about the student's aptitude to research are usually the strongest the student will ever get as an undergraduate ... We have a very high number of students going into graduate programs using their undergraduate thesis as their baseline." Dr. Krane detailed some of the exceptional research related to UD's focus on human rights. Past thesis topics, related to the university's human rights focus, have included projects related to war crimes, human trafficking, immigration, local refugee resettlement and access to health care. Other projects have related to stroke rehabilitation and the use of the fruit fly to better understand the development of Alzheimer's disease.

The Center for Social Concern

The Center for Social Concern (CSC) calls UD students to "hope and action. Feed the hungry. Shelter the homeless. Care for the sick. Tutor the kids who need help. Protect the vulnerable. Care for God's creation." The CSC sends its students' commitment to community service outward in many directions, organizing both short- and longer-term immersions in service work, especially through its BreakOut Trips and Cross-Cultural Summer Immersion Trips. Recent International Summer Immersion destinations have included India, Zambia, Guatemala, and Cameroon, and more locally, UD students serve communities in Erie, Pennsylvania and Nazareth Farm, West Virginia. Short BreakOut Trips are available every season of the year, for terms varying from about three to seven days, whereas participating students will commit most of their summer to an International Summer Immersion. What's more, the CSC also invites students to devote their Saturday mornings to SERVICE Saturdays locally in Dayton, hosts one-day Plunges, or discussion-based immersion experiences in big topics like race and immigration, and oversees over thirty service clubs for students. The CSC's dynamic wealth of service opportunities makes it impossible for students to claim they can't find the time to give back.

Intensive English Program

UD's commitment to diversity manifests itself not only in calling its students to global service, but in making a UD education accessible to global learners. As a measure to attract international students to UD and facilitate seamless integration of the China Institute into UD's educational milieu, the non-credit-bearing Intensive English Program serves both part-time and full-time students of every English proficiency level from absolute beginner to advanced. IEP students attend class on the main campus and become "part of the tapestry of campus life." For ambitious international students who wish to pursue an accredited UD education, the university offers conditional admission options, including full undergraduate or graduate admission to UD upon successful completion of the IEP.

China Institute

UD's state-of-the-art China Institute is located in the Suzhou Industrial Park, where a third of the world's Fortune 500 companies are located. The China Institute benefits UD graduates' professional opportunities in business, research and technology, and also makes a UD education available to Chinese students through "degree programs, continuing education courses, leadership training and intensive English programs for all who want to learn." UD's growing list of Chinese educational partners includes Nanjing University, Nanjing University of Science and Technology, Nanjing Medical University, Nanjing University of the Arts, Nanjing University of Finance and Economics, University of International Business and Economics, Shanghai Normal University, and Zhejiang University.

Engineers in Service

With projects in twenty countries, and collaborations with thirty-eight project sponsors and partners, Engineers in Technical Humanitarian Opportunities of Service Learning (ETHOS) facilitates ten-week summer immersions and ten-day breakouts for UD engineering students. By connecting science to UD's community imperative, ETHOS "seeks to provide service-learning experience through technical immersions, student activities, research, and hands-on projects . . . Participating students have been able to use their engineering skills for humanitarian purposes, serving others through practical engineering knowledge. Our alumni learn about the world, different cultures and themselves." As Dr. Bickford notes, these projects tend to draw in other students from across the university: "Often these projects need not only engineering students, but marketing and legal students. We have good connections between our professional schools and the college."

Flyer Enterprises

For those who are entrepreneurially inclined, hands-on programs run out of the School of Business have undergraduates making major decisions in everything from running campus businesses to investing millions of dollars of the University's endowment. Flyer Enterprises is a network of ten businesses across campus that are entirely student-run, meaning undergraduates are responsible for everything from hiring and firing to purchase orders and market research.

The ArtStreet Café, The Blend (a coffee shop), and FE Storage are all student-run enterprises that answer to a Board of Directors. Dr. Bickford, who sits on the board, tells us, "They've learned things in the classroom, and they've applied them beyond the classroom. But there is no textbook in the world that can prepare you for the types of things that happen in life." Not every business succeeds either, which is another lesson. "The students in this business have more than one product. One is that they have to provide a service and make a profit. But another product is the learning experience they get," Dr. Bickford says.

The Davis Center for Portfolio Management

❝ There is no textbook in the world that can prepare you for the types of things that happen in life. ❞

In a similar vein, the Davis Center is another student-run venture, this time tasked with providing "the quality market and equity research needed to effectively manage the University's student-run undergraduate portfolio." You read this correctly: The Flyer Investments, housed in the Davis Center, is a group of fifteen undergraduates who make all buy, sell, and hold decisions for a dedicated fund and report semi-annually to an Advisory Board. The Davis Center runs a leadership development program for a group of forty to fifty undergraduates interested in learning the ins and outs of real-world portfolio management tools. Flyer Investments is the capstone experience seminar that is responsible for decisions on more than $20 million of the University's investments. Dr. Bickford tells us, "I remember one year the students did better than the university did! They are really challenged to do a good job at this." As a result of all their hands-on experience, including in-depth analysis of the economy as well as equities themselves, Dr. Bickford says that alumni of the program "do really well getting jobs on Wall Street and in investment banking and other areas."

Faculty

The University of Dayton's distinguished faculty includes 526 members on its central campus, 40 percent of which are women. As its 14:1 student-to-faculty ratio suggests, 96 percent of UD's classes have fewer than fifty students. Notable UD faculty include Susan Brenner, cybercrimes expert and the NCR Distinguished Professor of Law and Technology; Mark Ensalaco, director of human rights research; Panagiotis Tsonis, a biology professor and director of the Center for Tissue Regeneration and Engineering at Dayton; and Bob Taft, a former two-term governor of Ohio and the great-grandson of President William Howard

Taft. UD students offer near-unanimous praise for their professors; one student appreciates that "professors are personally invested in their students' successes," and another calls her UD professors the best she's had "throughout my academic career, especially the professors associated with my major." Students feel close to professors, saying they're "always willing to help you learn regardless of how long it takes," and "they become a wonderful support system."

Life after Dayton

UD's most famous alumni include humorist and journalist Erma Bombeck, cartoonist Chip Bok, pitcher Jerry Blevins, David J. Bradley, the inventor of the Control-Alt-Delete computer keyboard function, Super Bowl-winning coach and sports commentator Jon Gruden, and Nobel Prize winner Charles J. Pedersen. Students name UD's "alumni connections" as among the school's greatest strengths: "The connection . . . fostered between students, faculty, and alumni creates a strong base of people who are more than willing to help the school in any way they can." By encouraging community, service, integrity, and ethical commitment as well as academic excellence in students, a UD education builds pathways to the future for its graduates.

Ann Hudock, who has both a bachelor's in English and a master's in international affairs from UD, details beautifully how her transition from a UD student to a UD alumna has led her to her current position as Vice President of International Programs at Plan International USA: "I was involved in the student newspaper called the Flyer News, and I became the managing director. The president of the university at that time, Brother Raymond Fitz, had arranged a breakfast with the different student leaders, and I had a chance to meet him through that. When I was talking to him, he asked me what did I want to do here at UD. I told him that I wanted to go to Sierra Leone, and I wanted him to send me. He was pretty floored, but through a couple years of conversations, networking, and lots of arrangements we worked it out. He bought the ticket and the Marianists funded me the airfare. They helped me make connections to another local organization of Sierra Leoneans living in Dayton. They gave me a living stipend. Then they connected me to a Dayton Peace Corps volunteer who had just come back from years working in Sierra Leone with the Catholic Relief Services, and he connected me with a local NGO I could volunteer with. That was the life-changing event that happened for me."

Hudock continues: "These people make an investment in students because they're invested in our careers at the university and in the mission of the university, the values, and the community."

University of Florida

201 Criser Hall, Box 114000, Gainesville, FL, 32611
Admissions: 352-392-1365
E-mail: freshman@ufl.edu
Website: ufl.edu
Twitter: @UF, UFAdmissions

Introduction

The University of Florida is the prototypical large, state school that current undergraduates say "provides its students with a well-rounded experience: an excellent education coated in incomparable school camaraderie." With a total enrollment of nearly 50,000, this school is among the five largest universities in the nation, proffering "first class amenities, athletics, academics, campus, and students." Those students, who hail from all fifty states and more than 150 countries, are looking for more than your standard academic fare. UF certainly doesn't disappoint, as the school has "a great reputation and...great academic programs for the tuition price." The campus is home to more than 100 undergraduate degree programs, and undergraduates interested in conducting research with faculty can participate in UF's University Scholars Program. One unique learning community, Innovation Academy, pulls together students from thirty majors who share a common minor in innovation. The Career Resource Center (CRC) is a major centralized service that helps students prepare for their post-graduation experiences—UF "seeks to graduate academically ahead and 'real-world-prepared' alumni."Organized career fairs are conducted regularly, and the university is very successful in attracting top employers nationally to recruit on campus.

❝ The University of Florida is all about innovation and working to better the lives of all Americans. ❞

Commitment to Innovation

University of Florida tells us that Gators have "an altruistic drive to change the world for the better." To support these proactive students the University itself has made "a comprehensive commitment to innovation and entrepreneurialism that is championed throughout our sixteen colleges and more than 150 research centers and institutes." And students agree: "The University of Florida is all about innovation and working to better the lives of all Americans." Three new building projects epitomize this focus: "We've created and developed the novel Innovation Square," the university says, "an adjacent campus with facilities for startup companies whose technologies emanated from laboratories at the university." The university is building Infinity Hall, an undergraduate living/learning community and residence hall near the Square, themed around entrepreneurism, in addition to a learning center for both undergraduate and graduate students. Innovation Square is part of the UF culture of "preparing students to be innovative leaders in and outside of their profession," while "challenging students to innovate and solve the world's greatest problems all while having an immense amount of fun," students say.

Innovation Academy

Other programs on campus shepherd student research and entrepreneurialism from the moment they walk in the door to the moment they find they need new office space. The Innovation Academy is, according to the university, "the nation's first live/learn entrepreneurial based academic community." This dedicated UF undergraduate program allows students to collaborate with other entrepreneurial-minded students, develop their own products and ideas, meet business leaders and venture capitalists, and participate in co-op learning during the fall. During spring and summer semesters, students takes classes and get to interact with the Innovation Square startup community. In the fall, instead of taking classes students can find co-op employment, complete internships, study abroad, or use their time in any other way that customizes their education.

Majors and Minors in Innovation

Students in the Innovation Academy can choose from a wide array of UF programs and majors that have been carefully curated to align with the academy's mission. Students are provided with a sample program plan that suggests what classes they should take and when, and it also provides them with details about the kinds of careers that program could prepare them for. This allows students to focus and specialize their educational pathways toward a specific career from the start. For example, one program plan for the College of Agricultural Life Sciences provides students with career paths in entomology and nematology that include biosecurity, ecotourism, and plant protection. In each program students are provided with a step-by-step guide that takes them from freshman to senior year. There are equally detailed plans and career options for students in the diverse fields in six different colleges, such as information systems, accounting, journalism, political science, and mathematics.

Students also pursue a minor in innovation that helps them develop practical skills in their field. The minor focuses on ways that students can enhance their careers through interdisciplinary and creative approaches to problem-solving. In a pair of interlinked classes, "Creativity and Context" and "Creativity Practicum," students learn "theoretical groundwork and evolution of psychologically-based research on dimensions of the creative person, process, product and press," according to the university. They then get practical experience and develop "problem-solving strategies through completion of an innovative project." By the end, students have developed, refined and tested a prototype creation in their chosen field. Students then present their work to the academy and guests from the business community, including patent attorneys and venture capitalists.

The Gift of Time

Another huge benefit to the academy is getting the fall semester off. As most students head to class, academy students "place themselves ahead of the competition" by pursuing co-ops or internships that most students are too busy to exploit. This also puts students nearing the end of their college careers with an opportunity to study for exams like the GRE, MCAT and LSAT. And, as applications to the most prestigious graduate and professional schools are often due near the end of the fall semester, seniors in the academy have a perfect opportunity to make their application materials really shine as their peers are pulling their hair out trying to find the time.

The Innovation Hub

When students have finished their time at the academy, they can take their initiative straight to the marketplace through the Innovation Hub, the flagship program and facility of the Innovation Square. The Hub is a 48,000-square-foot facility on the Innovation Square campus with whose "main objective is to enable companies accepted into the program to devote their limited resources to technology and market development, rather than [the] operational infrastructure," that takes a long tenured business savvy to get right, and often stymies new technologies and business ventures that are otherwise sound. These budding business leaders don't have to worry about securing office technology and facilities—the Hub provides office space for UF entrepreneurs and their startups to share. They also have access to the kinds of fully equipped, modern labs that they are used to finding on campus. Student researchers in the Hub also gain "access to venture capital firms" ready to give them advice about the market prospects, feasibility, and funding structures and—most importantly—to provide them with the capital they need to get their ideas off the ground. Residents also find pro-bono service providers are provided in the form of legal advice, accounting, and help with product design. While the best of schools offer these kinds of services through different entrepreneurial initiatives and programs on campus and through alumni networks, the University of Florida has them all in one place, which has the unexpected advantage of getting many of UF's entrepreneurial students together. To maximize the exposure these groups have to one another, the Hub arranges "programs and events to enhance collision and collaboration between tenants."

Bob Graham Center for Public Service

Students in almost any field can benefit from taking part in the Center for Public Service. The university told us that the Center "is a community of students, scholars and citizens who share a commitment to training the next generation of public and private sector leaders for Florida, the United States and the international community." The center provides UF students with research opportunities, internships, and a lecture series.

Graham Civic Scholars

The Graham Civic Scholars program help students develop an understanding of public policy issues and develop "practical skills needed to be aware and active participants in our communities," according to the university. Each year the program selects a topic that its fifty scholars will pursue. Scholars help to develop and organize the programs activities, complete service learning activities and research projects, and conduct "in-depth interviews as part of their investigation," of the year's topic, according to the university. Past topics have included food insecurity and the aging infrastructure in Florida. Scholars are assigned different tasks within the organization; for example, in the spring of 2015 ten students were "selected to plan and implement a service learning project," and three were given "financial support to write a senior thesis or public policy proposal on the issue" of food insecurity. This is a great opportunity for students to take charge in the implementation and design of projects, developing great leadership and problem solving skills.

Internships in the Public Sector

The Center for Public Service also offers a number of different internship opportunities that engage students with local government and civic service, while providing them with important contacts and future job prospects. The Local Government Internship Program places students in city or county manager's offices across the state. Students gain valuable on-the-job training in " business/ finance, engineering, landscape design, and public administration. Interns will receive on-the-job training to help them move forward on their career path and attain valuable work experience in the competitive economy." In the Florida Cooperative Extension Service and Graham Center Public Service Internship Program, students create educational programing in collaboration with county extension faculty. Programing areas include agriculture, water resource, environmental quality, and economic development. This is a perfect experience for any student interested in community development, sustainability, or environmental studies as these fields often interact with government personnel.

Faculty

UF students have the benefit of learning beside a world-class faculty. The school reported that "UF has more than 4,000 faculty members with distinguished records in teaching, research and service, including thirty-four Eminent Scholar chairs and forty-two faculty elections to the National Academy of Sciences, Engineering, the Institute of Medicine, or the American Academy of Arts and Sciences. Awards include two Pulitzer Prizes, NASA's top award for research, Smithsonian Institution's conservation award, and two Guggenheim Fellowships." Students praise the "truly incredible faculty and staff" and appreciate that "one of the greatest strengths of UF is the fact there is always someone to turn to for help." Vasudha Narayanan, Distinguished Professor in the religion department, tells us that she enjoys teaching her "bright and open-minded" UF students who she believes grow to have a "better understanding of global and local cultures historically" and "better ways of critiquing materials, and communicating ideas logically and creatively" by the time they graduate.

Preparation for Careers Ahead

University of Florida provides "experiential learning opportunities in every field, including internships, service learning, research and leadership opportunities." And through programs sponsored by the Career Resource Center, such as the "Certified Gator Professional workshop series, students are taught about the job and internship search, résumé preparation, networking, interviewing and professional development in the workplace." First generation college students are offered additional support "through unique scholarship programs, such as the UF McNair Scholars Program and the Machen Florida Opportunity Scholars Program," which provide students with financial resources and one-on-one support and mentoring throughout their college careers. In addition, the university told us that the "Early Connections event (sponsored by the Target Corporation) allows students from underrepresented backgrounds to polish their networking skills and access valuable social collateral in the form of discussion and advice from recruiters." And to top it off, the UF Career Resource Center "[hosts] the largest career fair in the southeast." There are also great deal of programs that offer students with particular interests or career goals with professionals in those fields. On Gator Shadow Day students are "matched with a Gainesville based employer for a day of insight and industry exposure." And for students who aren't sure what industry they would like to work in, there is Explore Lab, where students "discuss action steps [they] can take to help make the most out of [their] time at UF."

University of Houston

4800 Calhoun Road Houston, TX 77004
Admissions: 713-743-2255
E-mail: admissions@uh.edu
Website: www.uh.edu
Twitter: @UHouston

Introduction

Set against the shimmering, bustling backdrop of our nation's fourth biggest city, the University of Houston is a real up-and-comer on the higher education scene. In 2011, it was declared a prestigious Tier One public research facility—making it only one of three in Texas—and today the school annually brings in $141 million in funding for academic research, with dozens of participating labs and centers around campus. So if you're looking for an education that fuses traditional in-class instruction with ample opportunities to roll up your sleeves, UH may be just the ticket.

Established in 1927 as a junior college and formalized as a university in 1934, UH now boasts more than 30,000 undergraduates pursuing 120 majors across thirteen different colleges and schools. While its roots are in serving the greater Houston area as a commuter college, the rapidly expanding university has started attracting students from all over—including 137 different nations. These days, it enjoys a fantastic reputation as the second-most diverse university in the country. This status is a real point of pride among its students: "I hear over ten different languages walking to class!" a history major exclaimed. "No matter what you do in life, the interaction with people of other cultures cannot be overemphasized, and thus it is a huge perk to UH," a political science/electrical engineering student told us.

In fact, the university itself seems to be a major source of pride for UH's Cougars (or Coogs, as the cool kids say). Maybe it's some of that celebrated "don't-mess-with-Texas" swagger, but UH students seem thoroughly pumped to be here. "The greatest strengths of UH are our school spirit and the every-one-can-be-involved mentality. Whether it's in the classroom, doing research, or participating in student activities, everyone has a place. Everyone belongs here," relayed a student in the elementary education program. And a petroleum engineering major said, "The University of Houston is very big on school pride... They encourage students to get involved on campus, meet new people, wear red at any given chance, and overall just have fun." In fact, faculty, staff, and students don the school's signature bright red color every Friday to show their spirit!

Also high on the list of students' favorite features is affordability (an attribute UH shares with the other institutions profiled in our book *Colleges That Pay You Back.*) An industrial design student dubbed it "great value for a great education" and an electrical engineering student declared it the "best bang for the buck," while hundreds of students stressed its important ties to the local Houston job market. Ultimately, this gateway to Houston and its many career opportunities can't be overstated when it comes to describing what UH brings to the table. "Houston is the energy capital of the world, it has the [second] largest port in the world! ... [It's] home to the #1 medical center in the world! And it also has the [second]-most theater seats in the U.S.—second to only New York. It has everything, whether you are going into engineering, business, fine arts, or into the healthcare . . . field. And the University of Houston is the perfect path to get access to all these great things," gushed a kinesiology student.

The Honors College

UH may be big, but with fifteen to thirty-five students per class, its Honors College is downright cozy. "The Honors College can provide a bit of camaraderie and a 'small-school feel,'" reported one psychology major. A physics student enthusiastically added: "It's like your own mini Ivy League without the high cost!" The program kicks off with the Human Situation, a requisite two-semester course that takes freshmen on a high-octane expedition through major literary, philosophical, and political texts, encouraging thoughtful and stimulating dialogue and initiating students into academic discourse. As the college said, "It's a big, long welcome to the world of ideas." The Honors program continues with students fulfilling coursework in their majors via Honors sections and culminates in a senior thesis; along the way, they receive mentorship and dozens of opportunities, including study abroad programs, leadership training, and research programs.

❝ The research opportunities afforded to me as an undergraduate have been incredible. ❞

Office of Undergraduate Research

Talk with any student for five minutes, and they'll proudly tell you of UH's coveted Tier One public research school ranking—and share with you how research has tremendously shaped their educations.

"The research opportunities afforded to me as an undergraduate have been incredible. I've published multiple papers as a first author and a textbook chapter—all of which have helped me to not only grow as a scientist but also get into my dream graduate school," a physics/mathematics student said. A biology major added, "At UH, I not only prepared for medical school by taking challenging classes and labs, but [I] also had many opportunities to do research." Sample opportunities in the recent past include working on an interface that allows the brain to control a prosthetic hand, exploring cell-phone sensors in early earthquake detection, and developing the next generation of high-efficiency rechargeable batteries.

These wonderful, career-starting experiences begin in the Office of Undergraduate Research. Identifying itself as a "clearing house for mentored research opportunities," this program pairs students up with faculty members to collaborate on large-scale original scholarship. Students are usually entrusted with one component of the project, which means they really get their feet wet—and get some good resume or grad-school application cred, too! Of students who engaged in research at UH, a staggering 97 percent reported to the school that it upped their game when it came time to find jobs or pursue higher learning.

Opportunities are great, but what about the funding many students need to be able to participate? UH has that covered, too, with the Provost's Undergraduate Research Scholarship—which provides support for a semester-long study with a faculty mentor—and the Summer Undergraduate Research Fellowship, a ten-week, full-time program that allows students to dig into a topic of their choosing with a faculty adviser.

Student Life

While only about 8,000 UH students technically live on campus, that doesn't mean it doesn't feel like home. With 500-plus student organizations, there's something for everyone at this lively institution, and the school really goes the extra mile to make sure attendees feel the love—and get outside of their comfort zones. "There's … a really neat program called Cougar Cards that promotes events and encourage[s] students to stretch and attend more of a range … than they might on their own," said a computer science major. "Many events give out a Cougar Card for attending—if you collect twenty unique cards, you get a free T-shirt; if you collect all fifty-eight cards for the year, you get a $1,000 scholarship." The cards all feature the faces of prominent faculty and alumni, almost like baseball cards, which is great for instilling school pride. Dr. Simon Bott, chair of the undergraduate chemistry program, told us, "Last year there were 3,800 events at which card were handed out and 1,600 students collected at least twenty of the cards and thousands more collected at least some of them. It goes back to the idea that since Houston is such a huge city with so much going on off-campus that it's very easy for students to come here and got to class and go away again. There are so many studies out there that demonstrate the importance of student involvement and engagement with the university towards student retention and graduation. A lot of our award winning faculty have trading cards of themselves that they'll hand out in class and encourage kids to go to more events in that way."

This school also really knows how to throw a party. Each spring, UH students organize and host the Frontier Fiesta, a full-blown re-creation of western life in the 1800s—complete with variety shows, carnival booths, and brisket cook-offs. "[UH has] traditions, like Frontier Fiesta, that are nothing like any other university has," reported a public relations student. There's also The Cat's Back, the annual party that kicks off the fall semester.

Beyond the plethora of clubs and events put on by the Student Program Board, most UH students can't get enough of their state-of-the-art Rec Center (rock climbing, anyone?), and tailgating before football games seems to be as classic here as it is at most other American universities. And, of course, there's always Houston itself, the fourth largest city in the country: "You can never be bored in the city of Houston," one health communications major told us. "If you are, you're doing something wrong."

Bauer College of Business

For students looking to get exemplary educations in the highly practical, immediately useful realms of finance, marketing, taxation, and more, the Bauer College of Business is a fantastic choice. For nearly a decade, it has dominated the top slots on our ranking list of the nation's best entrepreneurial programs. It seems the students overwhelmingly agree with this assessment: "The University of Houston's Bauer College of Business is all about innovation, entrepreneurship, a go-getter attitude, and moving the world forward," said one enthusiastic supply-chain management student. "The College of Business is nationally recognized, has significant alumni, and career placement and opportunities seem endless," offered a management information systems major. One marketing student declared, "I believe we have the #1 business school in the world"—clearly already putting those marketing chops to good use!

So what's so buzzworthy about Bauer? For starters, its Wolff Center for Entrepreneurship helps students develop and implement business plans with tailored coursework, industry-specific roundtables, weekly Lunch and Learns with expert businesspeople, coaching for mock negotiations, and business plan competitions, to name a few. MBA and master's students can also get firsthand experience with capital via the Cougar Investment Fund, where they team up to manage a $10 million equity mutual fund. Meanwhile, the award-winning Program for Excellence in Selling gives students the opportunity to make sales presentations, sell sponsorships, and attend the PES career fair—where they can mingle with scouts from more than 100 companies. There are also tons of leadership opportunities at Bauer. For instance, students can apply to the prestigious Ted Bauer Leadership Certificate Program—a year-long endeavor that grooms the next generation of bright young things in business—and the LeaderShape Institute, which seeks to create business leaders with a focus on ethical solutions.

A supportive and responsive faculty cap off the experience. Dr. Richard Scamell, the associate dean of Student Affairs, told us, "I like to think of Bauer faculty and staff as 'builders' who make an effort to encourage students, who believe in them, and who build them up." And associate professor, Dr. Norm Johnson agreed when he described the relationship between faculty and students at Bauer: "It is characterized by a high level of support. This support often comes in the form of faculty members working with students as they prepare for local and regional competitions. Faculty members also act as mentors to students who are engaged in research." University of Houston comes in at number two on The Princeton Review's 2015 ranking list for the Top Entrepreneurial Programs for undergraduates. The ranking is based on administrator surveys conducted in 2014.

> **❝ I like to think of Bauer faculty and staff as 'builders' who make an effort to encourage students, who believe in them, and who build them up. ❞**

Interdisciplinary Research Clusters

Sure, you've read a ton about how UH is all about research. But the university is also set on providing multifaceted, integrated educational experiences for its students—crucial for today's job market, in which skills and ideas collide to make successful careers. To this end, the school has created six "clusters" to promote the cross-pollination of ideas. There's the Arts and Human Enrichment cluster, which explores different cultures and histories through visual art, music, dance, literature, and media. Students interested in hacking human health (for the better!) can study within the Bio-Med Sciences & Engineering cluster, while those who gravitate toward fostering cultural sensitivity and economic development through social work and education can select the Community Advancement & Education track. The Energy & Natural Resources cluster allows students to focus on environmental issues and alternative energy and the Nano-Materials students get to geek out on the material sciences (very hot right now!).

Finally, the Complex Systems/Space Exploration cluster aims for the stars—quite literally—by working on artificial intelligence, high-performance computing, neuron scattering, and advanced materials for use in space. "There's a wide range of majors and many interdisciplinary systems, and many ties to local business and industry," a computer science major shared with us. "There is [actually] a space architecture program in the College of Architecture, building on the synergy with NASA." Impressive!

Conrad N. Hilton College of Hotel and Restaurant Management

Students after real-world experience in the field of hospitality can do no better than the Hilton College, an internationally top-ranked learning institution initially funded by—wait for it—the owner of the global Hilton Hotels and Resorts chain, Conrad Hilton. Amenities include a state-of-the-art teaching hotel; a wine-tasting lab; Barrons, the student-run restaurant; and Cougar Grounds, the student-run coffee shop. Whether you dream of opening up your own spa, becoming a master sommelier, or masterminding the global expansion of the next boutique hotel craze, the Hilton College is a fantastic environment for hands-on, experiential learning. "I have learned that hospitality encompasses so much more than just a restaurant and [a] hotel; there's lodging, spas, tourism, resorts, gaming and casinos, and event coordinating," said one student in the program. "Under Conrad Hilton College, I am able to explore these interests through organizations, volunteering, and other activities outside of the classroom."

Cougars After College

The University of Houston has tons of amazing alumni—and what an inspiring, motley crew they make! There's Carl Lewis, winner of nine Olympic Gold Medals in track and field; Julian Schnabel, noted visual artist and filmmaker who created Basquiat; legendary country crooner Kenny Rogers; popular contemporary novelist Alice Sebold; celebrated liberal firebrand Elizabeth Warren; and acclaimed rapper Lil' Wayne. That's not to even mention the two astronauts that graduated from UH, Bonnie J. Dunbar and Bernard Harris. More than 255,000 graduates make up the school's spirited alumni base, and an active network in the Houston community and beyond helps students land first jobs once they've completed coursework. "Within the greater Houston area, there are hundreds of thousands of alumni from my college, which means a greater number of opportunities to find employment," said a finance major.

Faculty

Many noted scholars have made the University of Houston their home, including three-time Pulitzer Prize–winner Edward Albee, who penned the eye-opening play "Who's Afraid of Virginia Woolf?"; physicist Paul Chu, whose groundbreaking work in conductive materials garnered him a National Medal of Science; and Jody Williams, an activist awarded the Nobel Peace Prize for her efforts in clearing the world of landmines.

Despite the school's large size, the student to professor ratio is a healthy 22:1, with 56 percent of all classes containing fewer than thirty students. Plus, professors work hard to make students feel welcome. Dr. Scamell told us that how that over his forty-three years at the University of Houston he had worked with many faculty members across the University who conduct themselves both in and out of class in such a way that students with whom they work feel that they are important to them as persons and not solely faces in a crowd. And Dr. Bott added, "For [a] university of this size and research level, involvement [between] the faculty [and] the student body is much closer to what you'd expect for a small liberal arts school." There's also Profs with Pride—a 300-strong faculty group that helps students know what's going on all over campus, be it lectures, concerts, plays, or athletic events.

As for student reviews of the faculty, the results are in—and they're highly positive. "I have been very impressed with the quality of the professors and the material presented ... in the courses," said a computer science student. "The professors I have had have generally been excellent teachers, very understandable in class ... and have very open door policies for helping students." A vocal performance major echoed the sentiment: "It's really quite remarkable to be involved with such a talented pool of teachers as well as students. The expectations—as well as the work on the part of the teachers—is really quite high."

University of Michigan— Ann Arbor

515 E. Jefferson St Room 1220, Ann Arbor, MI, 48109-1316
Admissions: 734-764-7433
Fax: 734-936-0740
Website: umich.edu
Twitter: @umich

Introduction

The University of Michigan—Ann Arbor is a big school with big opportunities, and we do mean big. The university has a multibillion-dollar endowment and one of the largest research expenditures of any American university, also in the billions. It's physical campus includes more than 34 million square feet of building space, and its football stadium is the largest college facility in the country. With more than 28,000 undergraduates, the scale of the University of Michigan's stellar offerings truly is overwhelming. With "an amazing honors program," a "wide range of travel-abroad opportunities," and "research strength" all available "at a low cost," it's no wonder students tell us that UM "provides every kind of opportunity at all times to all people." Academically, Michigan "is very competitive, and the professors have high academic standards for all the students." In fact, some here insist that "Michigan is as good as Ivy League schools in many disciplines." Undergraduates can apply to one of thirteen undergraduate schools. According to current students, standout offerings include business ("We have access to some of the brightest leaders" in the business world), a "great engineering program," and "a good undergraduate program for medical school preparation." UM is also home to one of the largest liberal arts schools in the world. Those seeking hands-on academic experiences here will find "a vast amount of resources. Internships, career opportunities, tutoring, community service projects, a plethora of student organizations, and a wealth of other resources are just the beginning: The Third Century Initiative, supported by the president and provost with $25 million, seeks to encourage student experiences that are global, engaged, action-based, multidisciplinary and innovative (the university says: Stay turned for more to come). Of course, while the following list reflects some of the ways this is happening already at UM, it doesn't encompass all experiential learning that is taking place in Michigan's nineteen schools and colleges.

Welcome to Michigan

New-student orientation at UM is a campus-wide affair. The Welcome to Michigan Program is a campus tradition designed to help student feel connected to their new community from the start. The school says, "Large events such as New Student Convocation, Artscapade, Pre-Class Bash, and Meijer Mania actively engage a large part of the Campus community, while smaller events held by student organizations, Academic Units, and University offices highlight many of the opportunities and resources available." The week is orchestrated by the Office of New Student Program, which also offers a University Mentorship Program that connects first-years with an upper-level peer mentor and one faculty or staff mentor. (They even offer mentoring programs for parents, too!)

Student Organizations

Current students say the Michigan student body "is hugely diverse," which "is one of the things Michigan prides itself on." "If you participate in extracurricular activities and make an effort to get to know other students in class and elsewhere, you'll definitely end up with a pretty diverse group of friends," undergrads assure us. Although varied, students tend to be similar in that they "are social but very academically driven." Students here also have a reputation for political activism. In fact, a University of Michigan student movement, which contributed to the establishment of the Peace Corps was initiated on this campus following a speech given by President John F. Kennedy. There is a place for everyone here because "there are hundreds of mini-communities within the campus, made of everything from service fraternities to political organizations to dance groups." With more than 1,400 registered student organizations, "if you have an interest, you can find a group of people who enjoy the same thing."

Learning Communities

For students who want that big campus to feel a bit smaller, Learning Communities in the residence halls bring together students and faculty with similar interests. The Health Sciences Scholars bond over their love of medicine and their pre-professional aspirations. Writers and artists unite in the Lloyd Hall Scholars Program, which pulls in students with a creative flair from diverse academic interests. These communities have faculty partnerships as well. Each year the Lloyd Hall Scholars sponsor a Writer-Artist In Residence to lead workshops, readings, and art installations for a term. And every incoming first-year student in the Michigan Research Community is offered a research partnership with a faculty member in a field that appeals to them. Other options include the Michigan Community Scholars, for those interested in service, the Women in Science and

Engineering program, for those thinking about majors or careers in science, technology, engineering, mathematics or pre-health; an Honors Program; and the Residential College, known as the RC.

Honors Program

> **❝ Current students and alumni, alike, share that [the thesis] is a defining moment, preparing them for graduate schools and careers. ❞**

Over four years, students in the LSA Honors Program (within the College of Literature, Science, and the Arts) take courses in almost every department. They can live together, too—Honors Housing functions as another Learning Community for honors student who opt in. You can also choose to live in one of the other living learning communities!) During their final two years in school, honors students work on a capstone project by writing a thesis under the mentorship of an adviser. The school says, "Current students and alumni, alike, share that this project is a defining moment, preparing them for graduate schools and careers." Facilities like the Perlman Honors Commons, make for a great place to relax between classes, and a program called "Lunch with Honors" gives student direct contact to the fascinating thinkers that visit campus. Michigan's College of Engineering has an honors program too, so you don't have to choose between an honors program in the liberal arts and sciences, and engineering.

Undergraduate Research Opportunity Program (UROP)

First- and second-year students across schools at Michigan can utilize UROP to link with faculty research scientists. (According to the school, the program includes more than 1,300 students and 900 faculty researchers.) Every student working with a researcher is also assigned a peer adviser and attends regular seminar meetings to get the most out of the experience. Students learn how research is conducted in any academic discipline of interest to them; how to work through a problem; and they gain insight into potential career paths. In fact, the university says that studies of this unique research program show that more students who participate in UROP go on to earn law, medical, or doctor of philosophy degrees than their peers who do not.

Matthaei Botanical Gardens & Nichols Arboretum

The botanical gardens in northeast Ann Arbor and the arboretum, located where the central and medical campuses meet, are more than places to relax and enjoy nature. They both offer volunteer, work-study, and internship experiences for future environmentalists, and scientists—or just casual nature lovers. A docent program trains students to guide school-age children through educational programming. There is a Campus Farm, located at the botanical gardens site, that the university says "is as much laboratory as classroom." Hands-on experiences like these, they say, "provide invaluable lessons in small-scale food production for students who . . . will play a role in food production and delivery systems in many of their future careers." Students can also join gardening teams, run campaigns with the marketing department, or run their own project through the Summer Internship program.

Innovate Blue

Budding entrepreneurs take note: Michigan comes in at number eighteen on The Princeton Review's 2015 ranking list of the Top 25 Undergraduate Programs for Entrepreneurship. The ranking is based on administrator surveys conducted in 2014. Innovate Blue is the UM umbrella for entrepreneurial activities that take place all across the university such as in Ross School of Business, the School of Information in LSA, the College of Engineering and beyond. If you have a great idea, then the Center for Entrepreneurship, with a home base in the College of Engineering, will help you make it a reality. A popular "Ask an Entrepreneur" program puts students in a room, one-on-one, with entrepreneurs who can talk about their path, give advice, and help undergraduates connect with the right people in their area. For students a little further along, the Center offers one-on-one startup advising. The Center also offers what they call "innovation training." Startup Treks, for instance, take students away from Ann Arbor to get a feel for the entrepreneurial landscape in another community. During a recent trek to Detroit, about an hour from campus, students interacted with startups and tech companies as well as met with Michigan alumni in the area. The school says, "Treks are not for the passive, the tired, or the uninspired: they are intense immersions into the cultures, companies, and communities, that ignite innovation. They are platforms from which students can launch relationships with potential investors, professionals, executives, leaders and peers." Annual competitions on campus like 1000 Pitches, the Michigan Business Challenge, MHacks, or Entrepalooza Symposium well help get the creative juices flowing.

Barger Leadership Institute

Barger Leadership Institute's signature program is the Leadership Fellows Program, which is open to undergraduates on campus no matter their year or major. Students are nominated into the program for their first fellowship year and graduate to be ambassadors. Benefits of participation are faculty-facilitated workshops, peer coaching and other events and projects. The Institute also sponsors a Global Internship Award where student can "explore the practice of leadership in a global context." Recent recipients studied in Cusco and Tanzania.

Wolverines Abroad

Ranging from traditional intensive language study to global health and development projects, more than 3,600 wolverines are abroad each year. The Center for Global and Intercultural Study (CGIS) is geared toward undergraduates who want to study abroad for a summer or even a year. Through the Global Intercultural Experiences for Undergraduates, CGIS offers learning opportunities that allow a team of students and faculty to travel to field sites as close as Detroit and as far away as Oaxaca, Mexico; Lushoto, Tanzania; and Cusco, Peru. Students learn how to lead in a group, work very closely with a faculty member, and see first-hand some of the "national, political, social, and economic issues" they've been studying. International Programs in Engineering offers programs tailored to the needs of their students, with some 500 engineering students engaged each year, and Ross Global Initiatives supports more than 800 business students engaging in action-based projects all over the globe.

Wolverines in the World

The Career Center offers a wealth of resources to students learning to be advocates for themselves post-graduation. The massive fall Career Fair jumpstarts the process for job-seekers (the Career Center even offers a smartphone app for navigating the floor plan), and the semester schedule is packed with programs and workshops like Career Crawls, which focus on themes such as choosing a major, or Immersions, a program which hosts half-day visits to an organization's workplace. Career Center Connector lists tons of job and internship opportunities while Alumni Profiles provide glimpses into grad's career choices and job search strategies. Other structured programs, like the Public Service Intern Program, link students with internship openings in the U.S. and abroad. The alumni network is massive with more than 545,000 members. Famous Michigan alumni include actors James Earl Jones and Lucy Liu, football player Tom Brady, Google co-founder Larry Page, and writers Arthur Miller and Susan Orlean.

University of Notre Dame

220 Main Building, Notre Dame, IN, 46556
Admissions: 574-631-7505
E-mail: admissions@nd.edu
Website: nd.edu
Twitter: @NDadmissions

Introduction

School spirit is always high on the grounds of the University of Notre Dame, and a huge percentage of the approximately 8,300 undergraduate students live on campus. Notre Dame is near South Bend, Indiana, but 90 percent of its students are from out-of-state, and ninety countries are now represented throughout the student body. Notre Dame is one of the most selective colleges in the country, and nearly all who join its ranks were in the top 10 percent of their high school classes earning top test scores. Because so many students live on campus, students say that the "dorms on campus provide the social structure" and supply undergrads with "tons of opportunities to get involved and have fun." Beyond residential life, sports, volunteering, "religious activities, campus publications, student government, and academic clubs round out the rest of ND life."

The University of Notre Dame is well known nationwide for its athletics program, its high academic standards, and its Catholic mission. And, while a lot of weight is usually put upon the first two, ND students know that "combining athletics and academics in an environment of faith" is what really makes their school distinctive. And for some students on campus, that mission is huge: "As an Irish Catholic, Notre Dame is basically the equivalent of Harvard. I've always viewed the school as an institution with rigorous academics as well as rich tradition and history—and a symbol of pride for my heritage." While not every student is Catholic, many undergraduates "have some sort of spirituality present in their daily lives" and lead a "vibrant social and religious life." Additionally, the Catholic mission plays a big role in the tremendous amount of service learning opportunities the school offers. ND has a long and storied history of experiential learning programs that seek to understand and combat poverty throughout the world.

If you only know Notre Dame as "the fighting Irish," you might be surprised to learn that the school's many traditions include a dedication to undergraduate research and an extensive array of programs with long and successful histories of educating students through thoughtful and considered service to the world. There are Notre Dame students who travel every week to prisons to engage in Inside-Out education, where, the university explains, students' at the Westville Correctional Facility and 'outside students' from the Notre Dame campus learn with and from each other and to break new ground together." Notre Dame students also intern around the country, helping microfinancing companies fund impoverished communities, and they travel the world to understand and combat poverty in developing and industrialized countries. Here are several ND programs that help students get valuable, hands-on training in a variety of fields while pursuing social justice and servicing communities pushed to the margins of society.

Exchange Programs

Guided by its Catholic mission to provide service to "the human family," ND has "ninety different courses [that] engage students in an experiential or community-based learning" every year. Some of the community learning courses focus on the communities near campus, like the "Rethinking Crime and Justice" class that examines the U.S. prison system. Each week Notre Dame students learn about the causes and costs of criminal behavior, the efficacy of the criminal justice system and its responsibility to different stakeholders, restoration justice, and the different ways prisons are used by society. And each week Notre Dame students discuss these topics with student from Westville Correctional Facility who have read the same texts. This "inside-out" model is now well established in the US, supported by efforts of The Inside-Out Center, which describes this kind of exchange program as "education through which we are able to encounter each other, especially across profound social barriers, is transformative and allows problems to be approached in new and different ways." The program also teaches students to investigate problems through collaboration and dialogue and to explore many alternative perspective simultaneously. Dialogue, collaboration, and alternative analysis: These are the essential skills of leadership and problem solving vial to any career.

Learning in the Community

While some of the classes explore social issues close campus, many others offer students the opportunity to explore wider communities: They include destinations like the U.S.-Mexican border, the Appalachian Mountain region, and world climate change advocacy organizations in Washington, D.C. In these classes, students spend a significant amount of time carefully studying the many dimensions of an issue over the course of a semester before traveling to the site during a school break.

In these service projects, students are exposed to a broad range of social, political, and institutional elements that affect the communities they serve. Students often assume a lifestyle change during their service immersion that gives them added insights into the communities in which they work and study. For example, during their service learning immersion, students studying rural health care, food justice, housing, education, and energy issues in the Appalachian Mountain live in relatively sparse quarters with limited showering arrangements and few amenities. They prepare "meals which will be enough to eat simply and be well nourished," according to the university. Similarly, while working with humanitarian agencies in southern Arizona, students observe legal proceedings, visit a U.S. Border Patrol detention facility, "travel through the desert and ports of entry," and visit Nogales, a Mexican border town. They also discuss border activism with area faith leaders and visit the border wall to study its environmental impacts. In doing so, students develop a first-hand appreciation of the cultural, moral, political and physical realities of the U.S.-Mexico border.

International Service Learning

These community based learning courses also include international opportunities, like "Approaches to Poverty and Development in Chile," where students travel to Santiago to study at the Jesuit University Alberto Hurtado and work with local service agencies. Notre Dame is great at preparing students for the opportunities and responsibilities of service learning abroad. All students are required to take a one-credit class that helps them prepare for the experience before participating, and students are encouraged to talk to professors in their major before their travel to discuss any reading or areas of inquiry that might prove useful in their overall degree and career plans. Before they arrive, students are well-versed in the cultural, economic, and political realities in Chile, and they have devoted thoughtful consideration to the theological concerns that they will be addressing as well. This way students don't have to spend their precious time abroad with experts learning the basics that they can pick up anywhere. In addition, because the students have all spent a whole semester together at home, they have already bonded as a group and can avoid the additional strain of getting to know one another in a foreign country.

The class is divided into two sections that deal with perspectives on poverty and approaches to development, respectively. Students are given a multidisciplinary understanding of the social, economic, moral, and theological issues surrounding poverty and development through a series of lectures by Alberto Hurtado faculty and guest lecturers, who often work in organizations that provide social resources. Throughout these lectures, students are encouraged to add insights and ask questions that have arisen from their weekly work with social service organizations in Santiago. This sense of collective engagement and collaborative inquiry is enhanced as each session a few of the students make a simple meal and the group dines together. Students also get the benefit of a total language immersion, as all lectures, presentations, readings, and papers are in Spanish.

International Summer Service Learning Program

The primary purpose of the International Summer Service Learning Program is to educate students about the causes and consequences of endemic poverty throughout the world and "to create links of solidarity across borders." These service learning programs grant students international perspective and cross-cultural understanding while training them to cipher through complex problems, just as they gain insights into "the multi-dimensionality of poverty in the developing world," and "analyze root causes, and identify strategies for social development" to help alleviate and prevent it. This international education is also vital to understanding the social issues that affect a huge portion of the world's population and developing a sense of global citizenship. This experience is great for anyone interested in development, sustainability, international affairs—or any career that requires dynamic, creative thinking and a willingness to take risks. In the past, students have taught children in Bangladesh; worked with women in prison, helped with nutrition programs, and conducted environmental research in Bolivia; and worked with various HIV/AIDS related issues in Cambodia.

Before they travel, students take a semester-long course that prepares them for the experience with weekly classes, public lectures, special training, and a weekend retreat to develop cross-cultural skills. Students also have to option to integrate their experience into a senior thesis, independent study, or research with a member of faculty. The early start that students get helps with the planning and logistics of these kinds of arrangements.

Social Enterprise and Microfinance Internships

The Social Enterprise and Microfinance Internships (SEMI) offer sophomore and junior business majors (or any student who has taken the prerequisite enterprise and microfinance courses) a chance to work with organization that either provide social welfare service (combating poverty, providing access to healthcare, reducing recidivism) or provide "high impact" financial services to communities, small businesses and individuals. The organizations that Notre Dame partners with operate throughout the United States in urban and rural areas. Depending on the organization they are placed with, students might learn how microfinance operations structure their loans, help research startups and conduct market research, or help develop business plans and economic models. Interns are expected to develop academically and follow a syllabus of reading and writing during their eight-week assignments that are designed to help them engage with the development and service organization they work for. Students who are selected for one of the internships are awarded a stipend to cover the cost of housing, food, and transportation, and, in addition, receive a substantial scholarship for their effort.

Students who participate in the internships don't necessarily have to hold a burning desire to go into non-profit work, though many of them are inspired by the work they do and develop a strong interest in social services. However, these microfinance companies and micro-entrepreneurs require the same kinds of skills and techniques that big, for-profit corporations need, so interns get the pride and satisfaction of engaging in a social justice cause without losing out on any of the financial or business experience of their corporate corporate-intern counterparts. For example, Mission Markets, Inc., a New York based firm that "makes it easier to learn, source and move capital into investments that have a positive social and environmental impact," explains in their SEMI site description that "past projects have included specific market research reports, impact sector development reports, and mapping particular impact ecosystem stakeholders and the relationships between them." During the first week, Mission Markets teaches interns about impact investing and the specific markets it works with. And CleanTurn, a SEMI partner in Columbus, Ohio, says that it "will ensure the student has exposure to every aspect of the business, operations, business development, etc. The student will understand the dynamics involved in starting and stabilizing a social venture in a service based company."

Faculty

An 11:1 student to faculty ratio means that students can develop intimate relationships with ND's internationally acclaimed faculty. Their awards include an average of two awards for excellence in research from the National Science Foundation per year (and an astounding eight in 2014), and IBM's "Big Data

66 *Our President (a priest), as well as both of our Presidents emeritus, makes it a point to interact with the students in a variety of ways—teaching a class or saying mass in the dorms, etc.* **99**

and Analytics Faculty Awards for top-rated curricula and research that mix business and technical skills." Professors at Notre Dame are, by all accounts, "wonderful": "Not only are they invested in their students," they're "genuinely passionate about their fields of study," "enthusiastic and animated in lectures," and "always willing to meet outside of class to give extra help." Wary that distance might breed academic disengagement, professors ensure "large lectures are broken down into smaller discussion groups once a week to help with class material and...give the class a personal touch." For its part, "the administration tries its best to stay on top of the students' wants and needs." They make it "extremely easy to get in touch with anyone." Like the professors, administrators try to make personal connections with students. For example, "our president (a priest), as well as both of our presidents emeritus, make it a point to interact with the students in a variety of ways—teaching a class, saying mass in the dorms, etc." Overall, "while classes are difficult," "students are competitive against one another," and "it's necessary to study hard and often, [but] there's also time to do other things."

Life after Notre Dame

Prominent alumni include notable voices in the fields of government, politics and foreign policy, including former Secretary of State Condoleezza Rice, political analyst Mark Shields, and U.S. Senator Joe Donnelly. Notre Dame alumni maintain the dedication to service they learned in college throughout their extensive alumni networks. Alumni continue to be service leaders and stewards of their communities through programs like the Hesburgh Service Initiative's Month of Service, which bring alumni and current students together. According to the university, the initiative celebrates the 16th President of the University of Notre Dame, Rev. Theodore M. Hesburgh, C.S.C., "who spent his life championing major social issues," by announcing a service theme every year that "is an invitation to celebrate, through continuing his pursuit of peace and stalwart promotion of human dignity." Many of the service learning initiatives on campus trace their roots to Father Hesburgh's tenure as president of the university. Students can visit Go IRISH, the careers center's primary recruiting database, for information about interviewing opportunities, employer information sessions, or opportunities that specifically seek a Notre Dame student or alum.

University of Pennsylvania

1 College Hall, Philadelphia, PA 19104
Admissions: 215-898-7507
E-mail: info@admissions.upenn.edu
Website: www.upenn.edu
Twitter: @Penn, @PreviewingPenn, @PennCareerServ

Introduction

The University of Pennsylvania is both steeped in tradition and decidedly forward-thinking. Founded by Benjamin Franklin, Penn is the fourth-oldest institution of higher learning in the United States, and the first Ivy League institution to elect a woman as its president. Its leafy Locust Walk serves as the main artery on the 279-acre campus (and is often lined with flyer-wielding students promoting performances, clubs, and causes) with West Philadelphia and Center City right next door. A 2008 grad reminisces about "that vibe" she got from Penn on her campus visit: "Walking around campus, people seemed happy to be there. There were tons of students out and about, saying hi to each other . . . it felt like a vibrant exciting place." With approximately 10,000 undergraduates, Penn is composed of four undergraduate schools: College of Arts and Sciences, School of Engineering and Applied Science, School of Nursing, and the Wharton School, home to the undergraduate business program. One alumnus says of his college application process, "I felt like I had to make a hard decision in striking a balance between the size of the school being large enough that it would offer a lot of opportunities to explore different careers and find exceptional mentors in many fields, yet wasn't so large that I didn't get the opportunity to meet and engage with my professors. Penn seemed to strike that balance well. "

Penn is obviously a fantastic choice for STEM majors. Wharton and Penn Engineering are internationally recognized and have appeared on PayScale.com's lists of the best schools by salary potential for business and engineering majors, respectively. In our book *Colleges That Pay You Back*, we described the pre-professional atmosphere on campus for those students who already have major

66 *Some of my best friends are working as game designers, doctors, writers, environmental scientists, entrepreneurs, and artists.* **99**

and career goals in mind. But rest assured: Penn is a place that actively encourages exploration. The students most at home here are those who are intellectually curious, so don't feel that you have to have your future mapped out before you apply. A political science and history double major explained to us, "While Penn is more pre-professional than most schools to be sure, it's a false stereotype that we all know what we're going to do, or even what degree we're going to get." And an alumnus agrees that he "spent a lot of time . . . sampling classes in different departments" when contemplating his major. "One of the things I loved about Penn is that there were so many different paths that you could take," said an alumna. "Some of my best friends are people that I met at Penn, and they are doing all kinds of things now, working as game designers, doctors, writers, environmental scientists, entrepreneurs, and artists."

Whether you major in business or Slavic languages, here are a few programs, centers, and facilities on campus that welcome students of all sorts. Any of these gems could be a gateway to discovering new interests (some of which may not be what you were expecting!).

Interdisciplinary Study

The curriculum for every student at Penn, no matter his or her school, is built around collaborative study. Students in the Schools of Engineering, Nursing, and at Wharton are all required to take some courses at the College of Arts & Sciences—Wharton says that up to 43 percent of classes its undergrads need to graduate can be taken outside of Wharton—and a communications major in the College tells us that "you can take courses in any of the schools, including graduate level courses." In fact, it is not uncommon for a student to pursue degrees from two schools at the same time. A student can pursue a bachelor's in psychology from the College while working on a BSE in computer science from the School of Engineering. Penn calls this arrangement a coordinated dual degree, and there are a number of these formalized programs in place. The Huntsman Program in International Studies and Business, for one, combines a BS in economics from the Wharton School with a BA in international studies from the College of Arts & Sciences. Plus, a handful of students in any given year create individualized majors by working with a faculty mentor to develop a "coherent set of courses," and a research project.

Having students from different academic backgrounds in one classroom can only enhance the experience there. "The cool thing is that the nature of everyone's experiences and accomplishments is different," one double major explained, "so you can learn a lot from others." In fact, one recent alumnus credits the collected experience of learning from friends and classmates as his most valuable experience at Penn: "Being inspired by them helped me figure out what I wanted most from my future and motivated me to actively seek it out. Without that motivation I wouldn't have worked hard to put myself on projects that engage my passion of exploring the social determinant of health."

Center for Undergraduate Research & Fellowships

CURF helps students find, land, and fund the research projects that fuel their intellectual and career interests. The Center starts by making the case for the value of research across all fields and schools (high on the list is the practical training in critical thinking and problem-solving that will serve any student after graduation), and then supports undergrads every step of the way in coming up with an idea, finding a faculty mentor, applying for grants, and publishing the results. A user-friendly research directory helps undergrads find faculty projects already underway. In one history major's experience, "Almost every professor is open to having undergraduates assist in their research." Students often tout experiential learning—like research—as a defining experience in their college careers.

Benjamin Franklin Scholars

The Benjamin Franklin Scholars (BFS) program within the Center for Undergraduate Research & Fellowships is another incarnation of the academic flexibility that students praise. It gathers students from all four undergraduate schools into one community that takes small, interdisciplinary seminars together (in an addition to their other classes) on a broad variety of topics. The best part is that students can tailor their seminar choices to whatever they find interesting and can be assured that a single seminar will relate to a wide array of topics. "Food in the Islamic Middle East," a past BFS seminar, delved into politics, economics, environmental studies, literature, religion, and public health—all as lenses for examining "the cultural dynamics of food" in the region. Scholars are invited as high school seniors or can apply as freshmen. Penn says, "We look for spirited, independent people who find their own passions, and are predisposed to explore their own ideas, wherever they might lead." The program may be just the ticket for students who are interested in, well, everything.

Public Service

Two spaces come to mind when students talk about Penn's avenues for service and community engagement: Civics House and the Netter Center for Community Partnerships.

Civic House

Civic House is the service hub on campus for students with extracurricular and career aspirations in community engagement. Programing like Alternative Spring Break and the West Philadelphia Tutoring Project are House staples, and lots of the student-led social advocacy groups on campus are supported in some way by Civic House with funding, meeting space, or publicity. Workshops and career panels at Civic House help student seeking public interest careers find their way, plus their internship program places undergrads in summer- or semester-long gigs at Philadelphia nonprofit organizations (and funds positions that would otherwise be unpaid or lowly paid).

Netter Center for Community Partnerships

The Netter Center's mission is based on the concept that "Penn's future and the future of West Philadelphia/Philadelphia are intertwined" and a host of programs work toward the goal of improving the quality of life in West Philadelphia as well as the Philadelphia community at large. One graduate we interviewed cites Netter's Penn Program for Public Service, in which she participated during the summer between her junior and senior year, as one of her most valuable college experiences. She reports: "I spent my summer teaching at a Children's Defense Fund Freedom School at an elementary school in West Philadelphia and writing a group research project on how to increase student engagement in school through a culturally relevant and peer-assisted reading model. It was an incredible learning experience because it completely broke down the 'ivory tower' paradigm. I experienced first-hand how universities can engage in action research that is driven by and directly intending to solve a real social problem."

Though this graduate majored in literature, her experience with the Netter Center, along with her other extra-curricular experiences at Penn, was the impetus that led her to a career in education. She eventually went on to pursue a Masters of Public Administration with a focus on nonprofit program evaluation.

Kelly Writers House

The inclusive, homey vibe at this Philadelphia institution is not due solely to its location in an actual house, complete with comfy couches, an open kitchen, and dining room table, but rather the people you'll find inside. Built in 1851, the structure has become the gathering place of an eclectic group of writers, yes, but also "wild freethinkers" and "voracious readers" from every academic discipline. On any given afternoon, this place is buzzing with book clubs, workshops, tutoring programs, and, in the repurposed parlor, weekly events with "poets, fiction writers, editors, composers, publishers, painters, musicians, literary agents, screenwriters, essayists, playwrights, journalists." An Alumni Mentors Program connects students interested in writing-related careers with some professional guidance, and each semester the Writers House funds special projects (like blogging your way down the Mississippi River) through fellowships and prizes. If you are a writer of any kind, this may be where you find your people, but students across schools often find a piece of home here, too. Budding journalists take note: Students regularly rate *The Daily Pennsylvanian* quite highly as well.

Weiss Tech House

Another unexpected place to find your niche, the Weiss Tech House is a student-run hub of innovators entrepreneurs, and tech enthusiasts. Inventors can compete in the annual PennVention competition, social activists can teach science and technology in local after school programs (baking soda and vinegar volcanoes!), and aspiring marketers can hone their communications chops via outreach and promotion efforts. Anyone with an idea can apply for a sizable grant through the Innovation Fund, a mini venture-capital fund that has supported commercial launches of projects like "edible marketing" and motion technology. Weiss House says they welcome students of any major and skill-set, so this could be a great place to embrace your tech side outside of your field of study.

Student Clubs

A majority of the alumni we interviewed were involved in campus clubs and student organizations during their time at Penn. One alumna wrote passionately about her experience with Penn Dance Company, a student-run modern dance group ("It was really important to me to have a creative and artistic complement to the science I was getting curricularly") and another described her sustained involvement with the West Philadelphia Tutoring Project, a Civic House program, of which she ended up joining the executive board. A Wharton alumnus with a BS in economics told us, "I was very involved in the finance clubs on campus, especially the Pennsylvania Investment Alliance. This club invested about $30,000 of club member money in stocks that we discussed in weekly meetings. It was an amazing experience to debate the merits of investing in certain companies alongside other students who had a passion for it."

Penn alumni advised: Don't discount the value of club experiences toward your life in the professional world. A dancer detailed beautifully how her involvement with Penn Dance translated to soft skills: "I had the opportunity to serve as co-chair of the company, which meant that I coordinated all the details of scheduling rehearsals and theatre space, running company meetings, managing show budgets, and generally spearheading the company. It was probably the experience that prepared me more than any other for managing projects in the 'real world.'"

Faculty

❝ [My professors] taught me that I didn't have to sacrifice things that I wanted out of potential careers, and I could work to build my own path. ❞

Faculty at Penn are about 4,500 members strong, and the student-faculty ratio is stellar at about 5:1. Past and present instructors include recipients of the MacArthur Award, National Medal of Science, Nobel Prize, Pulitzer Prize, and Guggenheim Fellowship. They are members of the Institute of Medicine, the Academy of Arts and Sciences, National Academy of Sciences, American Philosophical Society, and the National Academy of Engineering. They also happen to be great teachers. As a criminal justice major reports, "I have not always had professors I liked, but I have ALWAYS had professors who had a passion for what they were teaching and were able to challenge and stimulate me in a new way." One alumnus credits his fieldwork under a mentorship of a Penn professor as the experience that helped him "understand what is was like to be an anthropologist, both functionally and academically." He is now pursuing an MD-PhD program in medicine and anthropology, also at Penn. He tells us, "Without the exposure to faculty who were willing to take on undergraduate ethnographers to get that kind of exposure I may have never discovered the field. They also taught me that I didn't have to sacrifice things that I wanted out of potential careers, and I could work to build my own path."

Life After Penn

With so much cross-pollination between departments at Penn, it should be no surprise that Penn alumni are involved in plenty of field-bending enterprises. Grammy winner John Legend famously served as musical director of the jazz and pop a cappella group Counterparts while he was a student a Penn (English degree with a concentration in African-American literature and culture, if you're curious!) and plenty of other graduates as well are acting on passions they discovered or nurtured on campus. One young alum, Omar Maskati, who recently made his off-Broadway debut, is a graduate of Penn Engineering, but also acted during his time there with the musical comedy troupe Mask and Wig. And a 2008 grad, who studied environmental science and political science while maintaining a major commitment to Penn Dance Company, found a career path that merges those interests. From graduate school to a stint in digital communications for the U.S. Environmental Protection Agency to her current position, this young alumna explains the effect Penn has had on her overall career trajectory, thus far:

"I see myself as equal parts scientist and artist, but until recently, I have pursued these two prongs of my interests and identity separately. . . . I became interested in how I could integrate both in my career, and while doing communications work at EPA, I realized that I combine my love and knowledge of both ecology and art to educate and inspire people to change their perspective and behavior on environmental issues. . . . I now work at the Schuylkill Center for Environmental Education, a 340-acre nature center in Northwest Philadelphia, where I run the environmental art program. I finally found a way to bring my science and creative sides together! Everything I did at Penn informed this trajectory and prepared me for where I am now. I even took an arts management class through Wharton, which I draw from regularly in my job."

A current student in the environmental studies department told us that "networking and alumni connections" are among Penn's greatest strengths. Penn comes in at number twenty on The Princeton Review's 2015 ranking list for Best Alumni Network and number fourteen on the Best Career Placement list. Both rankings were reported in the 2015 edition of our book *Colleges That Pay You Back*.

University of Pittsburgh— Pittsburgh Campus

4227 Fifth Avenue First Floor Alumni Hall, Pittsburgh, PA 15260
Admissions: 412-624-7488
E-mail: oafa@pitt.edu
Website: www.pitt.edu
Twitter: @pittadmissions

Introduction

On August 20th, 2014, nearly 3,800 new students gathered on the University of Pittsburgh campus, each armed with an LED glow stick. At the start of every year, the incoming class tries to break a world record, and the class of 2018 was trying to create the largest torch-lit image formed by people. Their image? A globe. As a powerhouse research institute in a major city, Pitt boasts international connections and study abroad programs in seventy-five countries and every world region; state-of-the-art labs, and professors who are world-class scholars, researchers, and specialists. Through its Innovation Institute and the Mascaro Center for Sustainable Innovation, Pitt offers two major programs devoted to innovation, where Pitt students have access to everything from basic research to real world application, development and commercialization. Programs like Guaranteed Admission, which allows freshmen to lock in admission to one of Pitt's top professional or graduate schools and an Honors College that confers a Bachelor of Philosophy degree that will have graduate schools clamoring are just a few ways Pitt sets students up for success after graduation. Here are examples of how Pitt students earn their reputation for innovative thinking, hands-on experience, and a global perspective.

Student Communities

Audrey Murrell, the associate dean for the undergraduate College of Business Administration, told us that Pitt students "are comfortable working in teams, sharing knowledge with their classmates, actively engaging in our various . . . student organizations and value what it means to be part of a broader university community." It's no accident that Pitt has a number of programs that help cultivate collaborative skills. While these abilities help make fun and engaging learning environments, they are also key to launching a successful career. This skill set "is an attractive asset for our corporate recruiters who look at students who can balance a strong academic program with healthy involvement in activities outside classrooms," Dr. Murrell told us. Pitt's Living Learning Communities and its Outside the Classroom Curriculum help create engaged student learning communities while preparing students for careers in a globally interconnected world.

Living Learning Communities (LLC)

LLCs at Pitt allow students to join one of twenty residence halls that are built around a particular theme. Some LLCs focus on student interests and enrichment, like the Global Village, which "helps its community members become more globally educated citizens," or One Pitt, One Planet, which focuses on sustainability initiatives, including the intersection of sustainability and profit. Other LLCs are built around a particular area of study, such as nursing, and offer perks like sophomore and junior resident assistants from the major who serve as guides and mentors. In the Engineering LLC, as well, "dedicated Swanson School of Engineering faculty and staff provide time, attention and resources to help each resident achieve success as a Pitt engineer," according to the school.

The LLCs are shown to increase academic success, graduation rates, and overall satisfaction while creating ways for students to connect with like-minded peers. They make it easy to find study partners, explore a field, and create networks that can come in handy, especially in terms of career development. Having students with common interests in one place also makes it a snap to bring in guest speakers or develop themed events. And being around other motivated students can simply make it easier to maintain your own motivation. Dr. Murrell told us that, for every Pitt student, it's "a desire to perform well academically that motivates them to hit the ground running as freshmen," and the Living Learning Communities provide that energy with a direction and purpose. "Students who were early adopters of the opportunity to be part of this enhanced experience and who have taken advantage of curricular and co-curricular opportunities within the residence hall are showing themselves to be top performers among the freshman class," Associate Dean Murrell explained.

Outside the Classroom Curriculum (OCC)

Pitt's Outside the Classroom Curriculum offers an expansive array of opportunities and experiences divided among ten different goal areas, including leadership, career development, wellness, appreciation of the arts, and others, all with the express purpose of helping students "gain a competitive edge for graduate or professional schools, internships, and the job marketplace," according to the university. Students who complete the Outside the Classroom Curriculum by participating in all ten categories are able to graduate with distinction and are eligible for a Pitt Advantage grant, which provides funding for students to continue "extra-curricular involvement in the form of an experiential learning activity such as a study abroad experience, an unpaid internship, or a volunteering project."

The OCC works under the assumption that 80 percent of a student's time will be spent outside of the classroom during their undergraduate education and that the school should create out-of-the classroom experiences and opportunities that complement educational and career goals. For example, to complete the global and cultural awareness goal students must participate in a diversity or social justice program, participate in an international program, and attend a seminar about ecological issues. Dr. Murrell told us that they are discovering how students "are engaging and progressing in terms of key competencies that are developed by [OCC]."

Global Perspective

According to Dr. Murrell, one of the most exciting parts of the Pitt Business educational journey is taking students "from the classroom, to the city, to the world." For decades Pitt has been cultivating international relationships and developing curricula with a global perspective. "Our global focus as a university," Dr. Murrell explained, "also helps to make sure I have the opportunity to equip students for the real nature of business today, which is global in nature. Teaching at Pitt Business allows me to have a living laboratory that helps students inside and outside the classroom come face to face with real business challenges and the opportunity to apply the knowledge they have gained to solving them."

Study Abroad

The best place to see this global reach in action is through Pitt's extensive study abroad programs. With more than 1,700 students in 2013–2014 able to include a study abroad experience on their résumés, Pitt is a global studies dynamo. Its programs are grounded in specific, hands-on study, and they run the gamut from social policy issues in Cuba to bioengineering a better environment in Brazil. Pitt is practically guaranteed to have a study abroad program for every academic interest and career field. Students can select programs that last anywhere from a few weeks in the summer to a full academic year, but the programs that impressed us the most were the Plus3 Program and Pitt MAP, which show how powerful a truly global education can be.

Plus 3

For any business or engineering student wanting to make a big splash on the international stage, the Plus3 Program is a must. It offers students exposure to a range of developed and developing countries, each with its own unique engineering and business opportunities, and access to industry insiders. "Designed for undergraduate students in the summer after their freshman year," the University explained to us, "the Plus 3 Program allows students to travel to foreign countries to examine issues related to business and engineering from a global perspective. Jointly sponsored by Pitt's Swanson School of Engineering and the College of Business Administration, the two-week, three-credit program features industry-specific company tours, Q&A sessions with executives, and academic lectures." For the 2015 summer session, students can choose from studying the smartphone industry in China, automobiles and manufacturing in Germany, development in Vietnam, or coffee in Costa Rica. In the Plus3 Program, students stand at the intersection of culture, environment, history, engineering and international trade in some of the most dynamic and promising world markets. There is no better way to understand the forces that shape globalization than to step into the global marketplace.

Pitt MAP

In contrast to Plus3, in which students take a microscope to a single market in a single country, study in the Pitt MAP program spans three continents during a whole semester. Pitt MAP is designed to be interdisciplinary and incorporates broader topics and different study tracks, making it flexible to accommodate the research and professional goals of any student from conflict resolution to pre-med. A recent semester had MAP students focused on health, migration, and society through study in Spain, Morocco and China.

Prep for Graduate School

Pitt has several ways to help students get a leg up on graduate school—or even get them a guaranteed spot from day one of college. Through the University Honors College, Pitt is one of the only schools in the country to offer a Bachelor of Philosophy, or BPhil, a unique undergraduate degree which is awarded jointly by the Honors College and a student's home school. In addition to the requirements of the major, students propose a program of study that must be approved by the university and that culminates in an undergraduate thesis. A BPhil candidate completes an oral thesis in front of a panel of professors, just like a graduate school thesis defense. In fact, the school said that "students should strive to have the same research experience—and produce the same caliber of thesis—as that of a graduate student at the master's level within your academic discipline." And there is no better training for graduate school. Mary Ellen Callahan, who graduated with a BPhil in political science and Russian/Eastern European studies, told us that "because of the Honors classes, tailored advising, and the ability to receive a Bachelor of Philosophy degree with an undergraduate thesis, I was much better prepared, and had a more comprehensive education, than my Ivy League peers at the University of Chicago Law School."

Pitt also offers guaranteed admission to nineteen of its prestigious graduate and professional schools, including law, medicine, and business, through the Freshmen Guarantee. For exceptionally qualified freshmen with a clear career trajectory, Pitt will guarantee admission into the appropriate graduate or professional school when the student is accepted as an undergraduate. That is certainly one way to avoid the nerve-wracking worry of graduate admission four years down the line. Beyond senior year stress relief, the Freshman Guarantee provides students with a sense of encouragement and reassurance about their career goals throughout their undergraduate careers. Several of the students we surveyed said that the Freshman Guarantee was what brought them to the University of Pittsburgh.

Any Other Guarantees?

Rest assured: Students who don't plan on attending graduate or professional school don't miss out on these types of opportunities. Pitt offers an Internship Guarantee to any student who completes the internship prep program. The program isn't just a hoop to jump through, either. It provides students with invaluable career advancement tools that aren't often covered in the classroom, like workshops on networking and using social media, mock interviews, and individual appointments that train students in interview follow-up etiquette.

Faculty

With a student to faculty ratio of 14:1, Pitt students get plenty of face time and individual attention from their instructors. Pitt faculty know that "complex issues . . . are all better understood when we can couple learning inside the classroom with experiential learning outside of the classroom," according to Dr. Murrell. One problem that can plague professors, especially ones at a large research institution like Pitt, is how to balance their teaching and research responsibilities. Here's where the Pitt Business focus on experiential learning and career preparation comes in. Dr. Murrell, who is also an associate dean, explained, "We have a number of faculty who are successful in leveraging what they do inside the classroom with their writing and research interests. The use of experiential learning inside of the classroom is actually supportive of these types of efforts. Faculty are able to utilize case studies or engage students in project work that is related to their research agenda while providing an opportunity for students to apply classroom knowledge to real-world problems." And at a University where world class research is conducted, getting in on the action is a huge boon. "Thus, there is no need to see teaching and writing and research in conflict . . . the work of faculty inside and outside of the classroom—or their teaching and research and writing activities—work in synergy."

Life After Pitt

Pitt counts Nobel Prize winning scientists and Pulitzer Prize winning writers among its alumni, as well as pioneers in nuclear energy and biotechnology. Yet Pitt also has a real penchant for producing entrepreneurs, industrialists and global leaders, like Wangari Maathai, '66, who founded the Green Belt Movement, or industrialist William S. Dietrich, '80 and '84.

We had the chance to talk with a more recent alum who is already making big waves. Mark Visco, a 2014 double major in marketing and psychology, is a good test case in what Pitt's career support can do for its students. Visco spoke to us about how Pitt helped him to shepherd his post-graduate entrepreneurial venture into an award winning start-up. Visco credits an early marketing internship he had on campus with giving him a leg up in the business and marketing world. "I was offered a lot of responsibility," Visco told us, "which helped me get a paid internship at the biggest ad agency in Pittsburgh." Then, in his junior year, Visco developed a business idea through the Randall Family Big Idea Contest, which is now run by the new Pitt Innovation Institute. Even more important than the 100k in prize money, Visco explained, were "the mentoring and business coaching sessions, the practice giving pitches, and the learning experiences in each round of the contest." The business idea that Visco first developed at Pitt is now, less than a year after graduation, Suitable LLC, a startup that "helps college students chart a career path to the best internships and entry level jobs upon graduation," according to the Suitable website. Visco's startup has worked with Dick's Sporting Goods, the University of Pittsburgh Medical Center, the Community College of Allegheny County's business program, and now has developed a pilot program with 300 students at the University of Pittsburgh's campus in Pittsburgh, where it all began. Visco told us that there are even current Pitt business and computer science undergraduates working on his team: "I try to get Pitt students on my team however I can because I want to give back to Pitt however I can."

> **❝ I try to get Pitt students on my team however I can because I want to give back to Pitt however I can. ❞**

University of Southern California

John Hubbard Hall 700 Childs Way, Los Angeles, CA, 90089-0911
Admissions: 212-740-7311
E-mail: admitusc@usc.edu
Website: usc.edu
Twitter: @USCAdmission

Introduction

❝ Even though it's a big school, it definitely has a small school feel. ❞

With eighteen professional schools, 150 undergraduate majors and 150 minors, University of Southern California offers plenty of options for students to get exactly what they want from their education. Students say USC "wants its students to do what they love without any restraint" and that the school "is all about tailoring an education to the individual, and not vice-versa." Unique double majors or major-minor combinations allow students to explore diverse interests, supported by "the millions of opportunities . . . to get involved on campus" (there are more than 850 student organizations on campus). A fine arts major says, "I personally love how small the campus is in proportion to the number of students there are. You can walk anywhere in ten minutes and bike anywhere in five." Fellow students agree, "even though it's a big school, it definitely has a small school feel." Programs in journalism, engineering, music, architecture, and business are particularly strong—USC comes in at number eight on The Princeton Review's 2015 ranking list for the Top Entrepreneurial Programs for undergraduates. (The ranking is based on administrator surveys conducted in 2014.) Here are just a few of the resources on campus that keep students on their toes.

Renaissance Scholars

In keeping with USC's flexible approach to education, all USC undergraduates can apply to join the Renaissance Scholar Program, which honors students who are pursuing two widely different fields (a major in enginnering with a minor in cinema, for instance). In the model of Leonardo da Vinci, who is equally well known for his work in the arts as well as the sciences, students are able to see what happens "when two widely separate fields of thought are brought together in the same mind." Graduating seniors in the program are in the running to receive $10,000 in Renaissance Scholars Prizes.

Iovine and Young Academy

The school told us that USC students have a "distinct advantage" whether they are entering the job market or moving on to graduate school, "through the Schools' global reach, state-of-the-art facilities, opportunities to conduct original research or develop creative works, and opportunities for networking and mentorship within their respective industries." Nowhere is that advantage more clear than in the Iovine and Young Academy for Arts, Technology and the Business of Innovation.

Near Hollywood and Silicon Beach, USC seems the perfect location for an academy that bridges art, computer science and business. First of all, the school points out, the program is believed to be the first of its kind. As the Academy's expansive title suggests, the goal is for students "to think outside accepted boundaries and become the next generations of innovators, entrepreneurs and inspired thinkers, across the fields of technology, the fine arts and business." The inaugural class of twenty students has just enrolled, and the academy provides these students, who will spend their undergraduate career moving through the academy's carefully curated curriculum, with a multidisciplinary education that focuses on "art and design; engineering and computer science; and business and venture management," according to the university. The open, collaborative environment invites students, professors and mentors in a variety of fields to work together in the academy's state of the art, custom built facility. At the heart of this ambitious curricular effort is the confidence that multidisciplinary approaches and broad collaboration uncover new ways to examine old problems and create disruptive innovations.

Hands-on Curriculum

Teaching innovation starts with innovative coursework. The fields of design, computer science, and venture management all have specific, insider languages, so the academy starts with a core curriculum of "team-taught interdisciplinary courses" to bridge these gaps and allow students to "think seamlessly across multiple disciplines, and to apply a vast array of relevant technologies and techniques toward innovative problem solving." All students study the fundamentals of design, computer programing, sound and audio, and business software. In this way, students can collaborate in every aspect of each other's projects. During their second and third years, students continue with the core curriculum while focusing on two curricular emphases (technology, audio design, visual design, venture management, and communications). This allows students to personalize their education, and, as a result, students will carve out a niche of specialty within this intimate academic group. They also gain advanced skills in "2-D graphic design, including typography, and motion graphics; 3-D design in both actual and virtual spaces." And with the help of high-powered computer software and hi-tech 3-D printers, students work with advanced coding and rapid prototyping.

The Garage

In their fourth and final year, students enter "The Garage," the academy's lab and collaborative space. With members of the faculty as well as outside mentors and industry leaders, teams of students develop self-directed projects that utilize all of the manufacturing and computer technology the lab has to offer. These newly minted experts can create projects "for new products, ventures, art forms, technologies, or services." The advanced technology available in the garage include state-of-the-art rapid prototyping tools and production grade machines that "produce durable, thermoplastic prototypes with moving parts . . . Fused power 3-D modeling allows for complex forms at high resolution, and laser cutting enables a high quality surface finish to products."

Research Spaces

The academy isn't the only place on campus with state of the art technology. USC has advanced research equipment and laboratories "that often rival those found in professional settings. From our fMRI scanner to motion capture stages to computer and multimedia labs, students find they have all the resources they need without ever leaving campus." Two distinctive research programs, the Summer Undergraduate Research Fellowship (SURF) and Student Opportunities for Academic Research (SOAR) allow students to conduct research in the top labs with USC's world-renowned faculty. Any student on the USC campus can apply for SURF funding "to pay for travel, equipment, living expenses, fees, or other costs related to the research effort" in conjunction with a faculty member's summer research project, and SOAR provides funding for students who want to work as a research assistant for USC faculty members during the academic terms. Through these programs USC students can gain access to any of these diverse resources, like the Loker Hydrocarbon Research Institute, the Space Sciences Center, or the USC Stevens Center for Innovation.

Institute for Creative Technologies

The Institute for Creative Technologies combines computer science, psychology, interactive media and other academic fields in a number of different labs to "[explore] and [expand] how people engage with computers through virtual characters, video games, simulated scenarios and other forms of human-computer interaction." The Academy Award-winning developers in the Graphics Lab have been developing new ways of rendering photo-realistic "people, objects and environments." Their light stage is capturing and storing a vast library of objects for programmers to manipulate, while a "low-cost 3D display system with form factor . . . for displaying 3D images in 3D" could make interactive holograms a home and office staple. Other labs examine medical virtual reality, computer simulations of human interaction, and virtual humans that "use language, have appropriate gestures, show emotion and react to verbal and non-verbal stimuli."

In addition to the potential for SURF and SOAR funding opportunities, the Institute offers a huge number of internships in different labs. These opportunities give student researchers direct interaction with the research team and provide mentorship opportunities. The institute also "offers a ten-week summer research program for undergraduates in interactive virtual experiences." Because of the interdisciplinary mission of the institute, "students in computer science, as well as many other fields, such as psychology, art / animation, interactive media, linguistics, and communications," find a home in this project-based program. The undergrads who are selected are teamed up with research staff, faculty, and other students in labs "focusing on different aspects of interactive virtual experiences." The program also includes seminars and social events, and students prepare a final written report to present to the institute along with their final project. And the best part: The experience is funded by the National Science Foundation.

More Research Options

The Institute for Creative Technologies is just one among scores of research centers and institutes at USC, and only one kind of research. USC offers research opportunities in the form of study abroad, service learning, leadership opportunities, conservatory and creative projects. And students aren't limited to assisting in faculty research. Directed Research "is student-proposed, faculty-supervised research" available in every academic field from theatre to Slavic languages. Students can count their directed research as elective credit, or, depending on the major, student-directed research may be a requirement for graduation. This offers students control over their research topic while benefiting from the mentorship of a USC faculty member. Students who conduct original research are also eligible to become Discovery Scholars, a distinction the university grants to recognize "students who excel in the classroom and display the ability to create exceptional new scholarship or artistic works." The commendation is an official honor from the university and looks great on a résumé or academic CV.

Career Prep

The university takes career planning seriously. From a student's first day on campus, "our Undergraduate Planning for a Career initiative integrates professional development with academic course selection," the university told us. "Students work with faculty, academic advisers and the Career Center to match their academic interests to possible career paths or graduate studies," and there are specific initiatives in many individual departments or programs that offer additional resources to particular students. Student can take courses with an internship component as well as career courses tailored to their particular school like "Planning Your Engineering Career" for Viterbi Engineering students or "Choosing and Planning a Future Career in Business" for Marshall School of Business students. The Career Center runs continuous workshops, counseling, information sessions, and events to help students discover and progress on their careers. An Internship Week and CareerFest (including career panels, networking mixers, and Employer Résumé Review) are held every fall and spring, as are Explore@4 Career Panels where students can interact with alumni and industry professionals.

First-Generation Success

The McNair/Gateway Scholars program provides resources for "low-income and first-generation college students as well as students from historically underrepresented ethnic groups" to pursue grad school and a career in academia. McNair Scholars receive stipends and scholarships as well as "mentorship experiences, graduate school preparation, research training, career development, and a series of academic skill-building initiatives." Scholars start the program by taking a research methods class to prepare them for advanced research, and they participate in the college's Summer Research Institute and receive academic advising throughout the school year from professors and USC PhD students. These students are carefully groomed for academic success, and the college strengthens its network of academics and industry experts around the world.

The university operates a program with similar aims for students who are looking into careers outside of academia. "Through the First-Generation Mentors program," the university tells us, "first-generation college students can take advantage of academic and career guidance from alumni who were first-generation students themselves." And this program isn't just a casual meeting over coffee or a few email correspondences. Students and mentors commit to a one-year relationship and meet every month for a professional activity. The career center also holds two to four events, which students and their mentors are required to attend, to help cultivate these relationships. After they graduate, the mentee becomes a mentor in the program.

Trojans Hiring Trojans

Students say one of the best perks about USC is its "large and enthusiastic alumni network." Becoming "part of the Trojan Family" is a great way to jumpstart your career because USC graduates love to hire other USC graduates. "Almost everyone talks about getting job offers based solely on going to USC," a student confides. According to the school, "The Trojans Hiring Trojan program gives students chance to forge key relationship with our alumni network around the world. A solid career network aside, these grads are talented in their own right. The school says that USC students are "curious about the world" and "natural leaders." USC has gradated the likes of director and producer George Lucas, opera singer Marilyn Horne, astronaut Neil Armstrong; Warren Christopher, the former U.S. Secretary of State; architect Frank Gehry; symphony director Michael Tilson Thomas; and the founder of Kinko's Paul Orfalea.

Faculty

The school tells us that the faculty at USC are "leaders and innovators in their respective fields." They are "Nobel laureates, Pulitzer Prize winners, Emmy and GRAMMY award winners and numerous members of the National Academies. They receive more than $645 million in annual research funding and continue to push the forward edges of medicine, science and technology, and the arts and humanities." Success doesn't go to their heads though. "Most of my professors insist that we call them by their first names," a fine arts major tells us. And a kinesthesiology major says, "The professors are very passionate about their field of study and always incorporate their personal experiences. The academics at USC are taken very seriously." Overall, students report professors "make the subject matter come alive" and make themselves "very available" outside the classroom. "My academic experience at USC is fabulous," gushes an aerospace engineering major. "I would not choose any other school."

❝ My academic experience at USC is fabulous. ❞

The University of Texas at Austin

1823 Red River Street, Austin, TX 78701
Admissions: 512-475-7440
Fax: 512-475-7475
Website: www.utexas.edu
Twitter: @UTAustin

Introduction

With roughly 39,000 undergraduate students, The University of Texas at Austin is the largest school in The University of Texas System and one of the largest public universities in the world. That size comes with a lot of opportunities, and plenty of Texas pride. "Attending The University of Texas at Austin isn't just about seeking higher education but also about incorporating oneself into Longhorn culture," an English major told us. "Learning to adapt to the size of the student body and acclimate to the "40 Acres" campus . . . played a huge role in defining my career opportunities. The more general experience of adapting to a new environment offered critical lessons that have been applicable throughout my business career," said alumnus Al Sommers, owner of Sommers Marketing + Public Relations.

The size of the school also means that it's difficult to define the typical undergraduate experience at UT Austin, or the typical student. "The University of Texas at Austin is all about bringing diverse groups of people together, and giving them the chance to successfully thrive while pursuing higher educations," explained a public relations major. "Everyone here has his or her own niche," another student advises. With over 1,300 student groups, state-of-the-art laboratories, and a wide array of opportunities to gain leadership and entrepreneurial experience, here are a few ways UT Austin's motivated and hard-working students find the support they need.

Support For First-Year Students

Helping students to adjust to life at college, 360 Connections are small-group communities, assigned during orientation, of about twenty first-year students. Each group attends a weekly seminar led by a peer mentor and a staff facilitator. Students develop a sense of community as they attend classes, study, and participate in various activities and events with their mentor and fellow first-year students.

UT Austin also offers Signature Courses that introduce first-year students to the university's academic community through the exploration of new interests. A variety of courses match student interests with faculty expertise from every college and school at the university. The result is a common intellectual experience for all first-year students that crosses disciplinary boundaries and explores societal issues from a variety of angles.

"These courses are interdisciplinary, are focused on contemporary social concerns, emphasize writing and communication skills, and introduce first-year students to at least one of the 'gems of the university,'" Associate Professor of American Studies Julia Mickenberg told us. Professor Mickenberg went on to explain more about the Signature Course she teaches, which is part of an interdisciplinary honors program. "I teach a Plan II Signature Course on 'College and Controversy,' in which we discuss the history of higher education, discuss fiction and films focused on college life, and get into contemporary controversies facing higher education (the corporatization of the academy, pressures that come from online education, the high cost of college, etc.), and then students do a group research project on a current or past controversy here at The University of Texas."

Liberal Arts Honors Program

In fact, students looking to push themselves beyond the standard curriculum will find a variety of options at UT Austin. For example the Liberal Arts Honors Program provides students with the personalized attention of a small liberal arts degree, and the resources of a major research university. Almost 500 students participate in the program each year, taking small classes with top professors and following an individualized course of study. In addition to taking honors coursework focusing on reasoning, research, and writing, Liberal Arts Honors students are encouraged to study abroad and become global citizens. Nearly all participate in internships to help them build professional networks, and define themselves.

Research Opportunities

One education major we surveyed summarized life at UT Austin as "research, education, and service." Involving undergraduates in research is a core aspect of the faculty's mission, according to Associate Professor Mickenberg: "It's very important [for] undergraduates [to] recognize the value of working with professors who are doing cutting-edge research, because this is partly how they can fully comprehend that knowledge is itself constructed and always evolving, and they are learning not just information but how to build knowledge. I'm also modeling an attitude of inquiry for the students . . . I've found that they're very interested, and also excited to know that they're learning from teachers who are also scholars. I'm also constantly trying to get students themselves into the archives, and to find way for them to get a sense of the thrill that comes from discovering new material and/or finding new connections between things that had always been seen as unrelated."

The Freshman Research Initiative, which offers first-year students the opportunity to initiate and engage in authentic research experiences with faculty and graduate students in areas such as chemistry, biochemistry, nanotechnology, molecular biology, and computer science, is one such research opportunity for UT Austin students. Each year more than 750 students participate in the program, which guides students through the process of producing independent, potentially publishable research projects.

Faculty are involved with student research in other ways. For example, "I participated in a research mentoring program in which I worked with a sophomore American Studies major and continued working with her through the time she wrote a senior thesis," Professor Mickenberg told us. "Affording students additional research opportunities, the Brackenridge Field Laboratory is an urban research station on eighty-eight acres on the banks of the Colorado River with a national reputation as a premier site for research on invasive species, evolution and behavior, biodiversity, climate change, and drought. The field lab plays a strong role in undergraduate teaching in the life sciences and is a valuable magnet for attracting top faculty and graduate students to UT Austin."

Cutting-Edge Technology

UT Austin puts its resources to work for students, providing them with access to new technologies and innovative curriculum. For example, at the Satellite Design Laboratory undergraduate and graduate students work on everything from designing software to building and testing hardware for satellites that actually get launched into space. Students in 2013 who built a small satellite called ARMADILLO won first place in the national University Nanosatellite Program competition. At the Longhorn Maker Studio, students can make use of cutting-edge technology to build, create, and invent for class assignments and personal education. The maker space inspires students, expands courses, provides hands-on learning opportunities and spurs both innovation and entrepreneurship. The studio has 3D printers, laser cutters, 2D routers for manufacturing printed circuit boards, plasma cutters, and a three dimensional CNC milling machine. Finally, UT Austin's Idea to Product program is an international, student-led competition for early-stage technology commercialization. Students from across disciplines come together to create new products that solve problems and fill a market need. Today it's an independent entity that hosts specialized competitions across the country. Teams from sixty-three universities have participated in I2P competitions on five continents.

Leadership Training

UT Austin also offers several programs designed to help students build leadership skills. The University Leadership Network (ULN) helps 500 economically disadvantaged students from each class develop leadership skills while also setting them up for academic success. The program includes a comprehensive four-year plan that involves training, experiential learning opportunities, and community and university service. ULN participants attend weekly Leadership Speaker Series and small group application sessions, complete community service and specialized coursework, and attend ULN events, and can earn up to $5,000 each year in financial assistance.

The University of Texas Leadership and Ethics Institute (LEI) is a centralized, comprehensive leadership-training program coordinated by the Office of the Dean of Students. LEI provides students with leadership training and workshops, opportunities for leadership positions, and resources and programs to help build leadership skills. In addition to LEI, the Office of the Dean of Students offers several workshops and programs focusing on leadership skills including conflict resolution, ethical leadership and decision-making, goal setting, inclusive leadership, recruitment and retention, values based leadership, and team building.

Entrepreneurship

UT Austin encourages entrepreneurship and fosters a startup community within the university. To do so, the student government recently launched the Longhorn Entrepreneurship Agency, which connects and coordinates all UT Austin entrepreneurship organizations. The agency, which is student-run, hosts an annual UT Entrepreneurship Week each March and annually awards the UT Austin Student, Faculty and Alumni Entrepreneur of the Year awards, made possible through the sponsorship of the university's president.

UT Austin is also home to the IC2 Institute, an interdisciplinary research unit that works to advance the theory and practice of entrepreneurial wealth creation. Among its programs, the IC2 Institute runs the Austin Technology Incubator (ATI), which helps startup companies successfully compete. ATI collaborates with faculty from the university and hires thirty to thirty-five UT

Austin undergraduate students each semester, providing students with valuable learning experiences during the undergraduate careers.

For Al Sommers, real-world business experiences—as a sports reporter for *The Daily Texan* and for the student radio station and through sports writing and marketing internships with the Austin American-Statesman and the Dallas Cowboys—led him to a career working on public relations campaigns for professional sport organizations and finally to the communications agency that he now manages today: "The basic tenants of taking on a challenge, mapping out a game plan, collaborating with a team and executing to the best of your ability carry through to all levels of experience. And having the opportunity to serve in these work and intern environments as a student also afforded a valuable opportunity to observe the habits and work ethics of some very successful businesspersons along the way."

Service-Learning

66 UT Austin's motto is 'What starts here changes the world.' 99

UT Austin's motto ("What starts here changes the world") is particularly realized in the school's commitment to community service. Through the Longhorn Center for Civic Engagement, 75 percent of students volunteered over a million hours of service in 2013, according to the Center's website. The center runs an events page listing larger events students can volunteer at, as well as linking students with other student organizations with whom they can serve. Additionally through the center UT Austin offers academic service-learning courses, which offer course credit for community involvement. To create these service-learning opportunities the center works with UT Austin faculty to either modify existing courses to include a service component, or to create new courses from scratch. In these courses, students work with a community partner, and are responsible for generally twenty hours of service over the semester in addition to engaging in reflective learning. Alumnus Al Sommers told us that UT Austin alumni have "a reputation for loyalty, hard work, uncompromised ethics, independent thinking and a passion for making a difference in the lives of those around us."

Faculty

The University of Texas at Austin is one of the world's leading research universities. Its faculty and research staff generated more than $628 million in federal and corporate funding last year. This research funding and the graduate students it attracts help contribute about $2.8 billion and about 16,000 jobs annually to the Texas economy. Current faculty at the university include a Nobel Prize Award winner; two Pulitzer Prize winners; two faculty who have received the National Medal of Science; two faculty who have been awarded Prix de Rome Awards; more than a dozen faculty who are currently serving as members of the National Academy of Engineering; and approximately a dozen faculty members who are fellows of the American Association of the Advancement of Science. "The quality of my engineering education was impacted greatly by the professors and facilities that were available to me. Because they were well prepared and ready to interact with the students, I feel that I was able to learn everything easily and smoothly," an electrical engineering told us.

While faculty are focused on their research, they are also invested in their students. "Overall though all of the professors are professionals in their departments—not just teachers. They are always willing to meet you outside of class and they try their best to encourage students to speak up during class," a public relations major explained. Students may find, though, that at such a large university they have to take the initiative to reach out to their professors. "I especially appreciate the students in larger classes who make an effort to come to office hours and get to know me," Professor Mickenberg said.

Texas Exes

It would be an understatement to say that the UT Texas alumni network is extensive; with over 100,000 members the Texas Exes—UT's Ex-Students Association—is one of the largest alumni networks in the world. The alumni association aims to improve the lives of both students and alumni. Members of the association benefit from networking events around the country, an online jobs board, and continued access to the UT Library System, among other advantages. In addition to his role on the marketing committee for Texas Exes, alumnus Al Sommers described how he supports his fellow Longhorns via the alumni network: "I serve as a guest lecturer on occasion to students in the public relations program, sharing stories from my career and offering perspectives on the role of public relations in today's marketplace. . . I have also created internship opportunities for current University of Texas students at my marketing agency." Notable UT Austin alumni include journalist Walter Cronkite, the longtime anchorman for CBS news; former first lady Lady Bird Johnson; Michal Dell of Dell Computer Corporation; mezzo-soprano Barbara Smith Conrad with the Metropolitan Opera, and Abdullah Tariki, the co-founder of OPEC. Competitive academic programs, legendary athletics, a huge sprawling campus, the eclectic allure of Austin, and a strong sense of Texas pride are the hallmarks of an education at University of Texas at Austin.

Vassar College

124 Raymond Ave., Poughkeepsie, NY 12604
Admissions: 845-437-7300
E-mail: admissions@vassar.edu
Website: www.vassar.edu
Twitter: @vassar

Introduction

Ask any Vassar undergraduate to describe a typical student at the school, and you might find yourself on the receiving end of a friendly eye roll: This is one student body that prides itself on being anything but typical! "There is no typical Vassar student because we are all so individual," a psychology and economics major confirms. "[Everyone] on campus brings in their own uniqueness. Vassar is a puzzle and each student provides a piece that puts it together."

Even still, some key traits seem to pop up again and again among the student body. "Vassar College is a place where left wing, artsy, intelligent students thrive," a sociology major tells us. An environmental studies student remarked that most students are "philosophical and [strive] to be as politically correct as possible." And a psychology student chimes in with some humorous real talk: "There are a lot of hipsters, indie kids, people who shop only at thrift stores."

Vassar College has long enjoyed a reputation as a prestigious and very selective haven for eclectic, highly liberal, and fiercely smart students. The school opened its doors in 1865 as the first comprehensive women's college and soon thereafter adapted an educational philosophy that they call "going to the source": encouraging students to challenge perceived notions and to engage directly with primary materials, rather than accepting the information presented to them as fact. Pioneered by Lucy Maynard Salmon (the school's first history professor), the approach still resonates across the current curriculum—from biology to art, from chemistry to history.

Today, Vassar offers degrees in fifty majors to just shy of 2,500 students. Situated on a gorgeous, 1,000-acre campus studded with exceptional architecture and first-rate utilities, the college has a surprisingly hands-off approach to curriculum. "Vassar has very few requirements, so helping students ... figure out how they are going to wander their way through the curriculum [comes up] a lot [in] conversations between faculty advisers and the students," says a psychology professor. But Vassar students love and seek out this open curriculum approach: "What I really appreciate about Vassar was the level of academic freedom they gave me. No one told me it was crazy to minor in physics while pursuing English," an alumnus reports.

This nontraditional, choose-your-own-adventure style of education means Vassar grads are uniquely primed to forge ahead with confidence and independence after graduation day. And it's definitely working: We wrote about the success of Vassar grads in the first edition of our book *Colleges That Pay You Back*. But don't just take it from us. Instead, take it from the real experts—current students and alumni—who describe Vassar's wealth of high-quality programs and resources to demonstrate the school's many merits.

Freshman Writing Seminar

Students start off strong with the required Freshman Writing Seminar, an enriching, concentrated round table that gets first-year attendees writing up a storm. Taught by professors from all departments and capped at under twenty students, each session is focused on a fascinating topic—say, "From Gold Rush to Dust Bowl: Writing the American Frontier," "Dynamic Women: From Bachelet to Ugly Betty," or "Ecological Ghandi." Beyond boosting writing skills to the college level, these seminars are also known for sparking interesting classroom dialogue and establishing a sense of community early on among incoming students. When asked what distinguishes freshmen from graduates, a professor of psychology doesn't hesitate: "They certainly learn how to write... They have a lot of intensive experience writing here and learn how to write in different styles, depending on the area of study they are involved in. They learn to be much more analytic and reflective and ultimately willing to say 'I don't know, but I want to find out.'"

Student Life

In the words of one English major, "Extracurriculars eat up a lot of time, but they're so fun." And if you're hoping to book up your calendar with loads of dynamic organizations, Vassar is brimming over with them. For the musically inclined, there are nine a cappella groups—including the Night Owls, the nation's longest-running all-female group, who have sung at President Clinton's inaugurations and appeared on Comedy Central. There's also the Philaletheis Society (founded in 1908), and other entirely student-run theater groups, several comedy and dance troupes, Ultimate Frisbee and figure skating teams, and a circus arts group called—what else?—the Barefoot Monkeys. With twenty-three NCAA Division II teams ranging from golf to basketball, athletics are also alive and well on Vassar's campus. Politically minded and socially conscious students will also find a wealth of like-minded clubs to join, including the Vassar Greens and chapters of Habitat for Humanity and Amnesty International, as well as the Vassar Student Association, whose members function as student representatives at major administrative committee and trustee meetings—honing leadership skills that will certainly come in handy in their careers. As for good times on campus, the college's ViCE (Vassar College Entertainment) regularly books awesome musical talent, such as the Flaming Lips, TV on the Radio, Girl Talk, Wyclef Jean, and more.

Multidisciplinary Curriculum

66 I have been able to take a wide range of classes that has broadened my perspectives. 99

Vassar was one of the first schools to make interdisciplinary studies a reality—and at Vassar, what a collaborative, multifaceted reality it is. Students can choose from thirteen vigorous existing majors: Africana, American, Asian, environmental, international, Jewish, Latin American and Latino/a, media, Medieval and Renaissance, urban, Victorian, women's studies, and a fascinating three-way mashup of science, technology, and society. Typically, a multidisciplinary degree involves coursework across many departments—dipping into history, literature and the arts, sociology, methodology, economics, popular culture, race, gender studies, religion, and more. Students also work closely with a professor to create original scholarship and study abroad or pursue a practical internship component. An environmental studies major says of the program, "I have been able to take a wide range of classes that has broadened my perspectives." Janet Gray, the director of the science, technology, and society program (STS), stresses that the multidisciplinary degrees excel at providing flexibility for students looking to branch out: "I like to think of STS as the quintessential undergraduate liberal arts major. It explicitly looks at the bridges between natural sciences and social sciences and the dialogue between science and technology. Within that there are specified requirements, but there is lots of flexibility in meeting many of the requirements. It's all so visible when [students] write their theses[—]the topics are all over the place."

For students looking to forge something completely fresh (and at Vassar, that's often the case), there's the independent program, which allows students to work with a faculty member to design their own interdisciplinary major.

Field Work

Internships may be all the rage these days, but Vassar's been doing its own version of practice-meets-theory coursework since the '40s—in fact, its popular Field Work program is one of the oldest in the nation. Every year, 500 students engage in internships off campus, lending their talents to and gaining hands-on experience at nonprofits, government agencies, human services organizations, and businesses as far away as NYC. A sponsoring professor consults with each student to guarantee the educational merit of the internship and provide it with structure, such as writing a final paper or maintaining a journal throughout. "It's a real opportunity for students to get out in the larger community and get some experience," says a psych professor. "But it also explicitly links back to [the] academic program."

In the summertime, the Field Work Office lands students at local institutions that promote social justice for ten weeks of full-time paid work. Potential placement includes the awesome Spark Media Project, which teaches filmmaking to inner-city youth, and the Grace Smith House, a shelter for women and children in danger of domestic abuse. And outside of the Field Work Office, there's the Undergraduate Research Summer Institute, a ten-week program for burgeoning scientists looking to make a difference—whether stimulating nematodes with blue light or designing robots to simulate evolution, there are lots of good projects to get involved with. Meanwhile, students with a zeal for the humanities or social sciences can opt to create original scholarship in the Ford program. Sample projects include studies of Russian sci-fi cinema, the corporatization of America, and the relationship between the ailing oceans and twenty-first century Caribbean art.

The Class of 1951 Observatory

Built in 1997 with funds gifted from the class of 1951, the state-of-the-art observatory is an incredible spot for physics and astronomy students to get real-world experience researching supernova, quasars, and objects in our solar system. The observatory boasts two big telescopes (the thirty-two-inch is one of the two largest research scopes in New York) and several other smaller viewing tools. A bonus for local residents: The observatory is open to the public for viewing every Wednesday night while school is in session. The Class of '51 structure is a replacement for the beloved Vassar College Observatory, first erected in 1864 for Maria Mitchell—the world's first widely recognized female astronomer in the United States and Vassar's first hired professor. (Today the building is an official National Historic Landmark and houses the Education Department.)

Frances Lehman Loeb Art Center

Another real campus gem is Vassar's own dedicated art center, housed in a stunning building designed by celebrated architect César Pelli, that houses an astonishing 20,000 artworks by masters such as Picasso, Rembrandt, Dürer, Bacon, Calder, O'Keefe, and Pollock. The Center hosts several major exhibitions annually—from early daguerreotypes to contemporary abstract works. For students of studio art and art history, there's no better way to understand a particular technique or period than to experience the art directly, and the art center goes out of its way to do just that. Professors from any department can request artworks be displayed in the Project Gallery for the purpose of student inquiry, and students can get up close with works by the masters in the Print Room. Enthusiasts who'd like to be more involved—possibly as preparation for a career in museum work—can even become student docents or curatorial assistants.

Faculty

Vassar's 2,400 attendees enjoy an "insanely small student-professor ratio," according to an American studies major. At 8:1, it's one of the lowest in the nation, and of more than 1,100 classes sections, a mere eight have more than forty enrolled students. In fact, more than half have fewer than twenty! A biology/English student cites Vassar's commitment to intimate learning as one of the school's main draws: "The class sizes were smaller than other schools, which was really important because it meant that there were more opportunities to meet classmates and interact with professors."

❝ I've never had a professor who didn't know me by my first name. ❞

Another phrase that came up when we asked students about their teachers was "absurdly accessible." Students report a faculty that regularly makes themselves available—whether it's extending office hours to be more convenient for a student to even loaning out their cars! (Pro tip: Don't ask—let them offer.) Plus, unlike at some large, research-based institutions where the faculty is more invested in their research than in the classroom, "professors at Vassar are here to teach students," a philosophy major states. "I've never had a professor who didn't know me by my first name." As for caliber and instruction style: "I adore all of my professors here. Recently, in a women's studies class, our professor asked us permission to give a lecture. It's quite out of the ordinary to have a professor talk at you for seventy-five minutes. As a student, you are expected to participate in class discussions, so you definitely have to prepare before class," an English major shares with us.

Prominent faculty include Robert Brigham, the first U.S. scholar given access to the Vietnamese archives on the war, acclaimed pianist/composer Richard Wilson, and Debra Elmegreen, the first liberal arts college professor elected president of the 110-year-old American Astronomical Society. But more often than not, students find themselves enthralled with a staff member they've maybe just discovered—for instance, Michael Joyce (one of the first writers to create hypertext works) or Mia Mask, a go-to source on African American cinema.

Life After Vassar

Vassar's legacy has turned out numerous exceptional graduates over its 150-plus years in operation. Interestingly, the school has especially appealed to remarkable female poets, including Edna St. Vincent Millay, Elizabeth Bishop, Muriel Rukeyser, and Mary Oliver, and talented actors, such as Meryl Streep. Other highlights on the alumni list include computing pioneer Grace Hopper, astrophysicist and MacArthur "genius" John Carlstrom, comic and novelist Greg Rucka, public health innovator Dr. June Jackson Christmas, Flickr co-founder Caterina Fake, and indie film darling writer-director Noah Baumbach.

Beyond the illuminati, however, are more than 38,000 living alums who do much to make their alma mater proud. An impressive two-thirds of Vassar graduates go on to pursue a further degree, and the school routinely appears among the top ten producers of Fulbright Scholars. Their alumni association provides students with a directory of 30,000 other graduates, which is no doubt a boon when job-hunting or just seeking a little career advice.

Villanova University

Austin Hall, 800 Lancaster Avenue, Villanova, PA, 19085
Admissions: 610-519-4000
E-mail: gotovu@villanova.edu
Website: www.villanova.edu
Twitter: @VillanovaU, @NovaAthletics

Introduction

❝ If you want to succeed, the community will do everything in its power to make sure you can do so. ❞

Villanova University was founded in 1842 by the Order of Saint Augustine, and the rich Augustinian tradition creates a real sense of community there, stemming from solid academics, a dedication to service, school spirit, and a perennially good basketball team. Located just twelve miles west of Philadelphia, the University is composed of 6,554 undergrads across four colleges: the College of Liberal Arts and Sciences, the Villanova School of Business, the College of Engineering and the College of Nursing; there's also the Villanova School of Law and College of Professional Studies. Current students told us, "Everyone actively [pursues] their own area of academic interest," and "if you want to succeed, the community will do everything in its power to make sure you can do so." Another student said that, at Villanova, "students definitely run the show!" This student pointed out that New Student Orientation, Special Olympics, and the Blue Key Society (made up of over 200 student tour guides) are all student-run and "some of the most popular activities on campus." A great support system of professors, advisers, tutors, and both math and language learning centers prepare students for success while they're in school and "lots of projects across majors that have real-world applications . . . are designed to help students in the long run." Villanova's "emphasis on service" is a point of praise for the student body, and everyone here embraces a sense of duty to make the world a better place (spring break is a "service break" for many students at this university who go on Habitat for Humanity trips and other service-related exeprience all across the country and internationally). "We are the Nova Nation, built upon an unbreakable foundation of community," said a student. Here are a few ways Villanova students are building up communities and doing some good, too.

Augustine and Culture Seminar Program

Community-building starts right away with New Student Orientation, and a continues through the first year as each freshman takes the unique two-semester Augustine and Culture Seminar sequence. These small discussion and dialogue driven classes pull in students across colleges (Arts & Sciences, Engineering, Business, and Nursing) to be educated "in Augustinian inquiry through a great-books curriculum and an intensive program of critical reading, writing, and discussion," according to the university. Additionally, first-year housing is tied to your ACS seminar ensuring that you'll get to know some of your fellow first-years really well from class and in the residence halls. "Each new student makes twenty new friends off the bat," a student explained. "The orientation program is fantastic," another gushed. "You will feel like part of the community right away."

First-Year Learning Communities

Students can also choose a First-Year Learning Community, where freshman students live, study, and work together. Each learning community has a specific theme, and students are grouped together based on the themes they select, which include Arts and Culture, Creativity on the Page, Environmental Leadership, Global Citizenship, and Caritas: Service Learning. In addition to living together, students in each Learning Community come together for their Augustine and Culture Seminar, a course specially designed to address topics related to each Learning Community's theme. They also take a one-credit workshop, called "4th Hours" that meets in their residence hall and explores their chosen theme through discussion and small group work. Students in these Learning Communities benefit from a collective college biography: Their shared experiences and class work helps bond them together and their common interests give them a sense of collective identity and purpose. And it helps that the ethos of the Villanova student body is "based on community, service, and friendship. Villanova is a school where everyone is kind, helpful, and dedicated to work as well as fun," one student told us. The Learning Communities are a bit of both. Students get "special opportunities to attend plays, concerts, lectures, and dinners off campus, with their professors, classmates, and hall mates," according to the university, and they benefit from increased attention from professors, who "seek to create meaningful educational experiences both in and out of class."

Caritas: Service Learning

Predictably, students hold the Service Learning Community in high regard. "The Service Learning Community is so popular you actually have to apply to be part of it," one student said. In addition to the other benefits of the First-Year Learning Communities, students in Caritas make weekly trips to tutor students in a Philadelphia high school. Students love that "Villanova offers great service experiences" and look forward every week to "driving into Philly to play with kids and help them with their studies."

The popularity of Caritas among first-years has spawned a sophomore level group, one that expands upon the activities of its freshman counterpart. Students in the sophomore Service Learning Community, or SLC, work with one of the group's community partners—which provide services like adult literacy and youth education—for at least three hours a week while they continue to take the "4th Hour" class. In addition, these students undertake a Community Action Project at the community site where they work. Students are challenged with a problem or issue that is of vital concern to the organization's efforts and then devise a plan to address it. These projects provide students with an opportunity to troubleshoot real-world problems and develop cooperative solutions while working in small groups. Past projects have included organizing and running a talent show to raise the self-esteem of elementary school students, developing a leadership camp at a nearby high school, creating a volunteer manual for the Graterford Prison Literacy Program, and translating adult literacy manuals into three languages.

Service Learning Classes

66 What I have learned through the different service opportunities offered by Villanova truly has made me the person I am today. 99

In addition to other requirements, like attending certain lectures and completing a reading series, student in the SLC also are required to take one of the university's Service Learning Classes, which cover a broad range of topics and academic fields. One example is Urban Education, a course that explores the social, political, and economic factors that shape urban education. Students work with high school seniors to "explore what it is that urban youth truly want and need in their educational experiences, and . . . deliberate collectively on the reform agenda best suited to meeting those needs and aspirations," according to the university. Another example is a studio art class in mural painting, which gives students an idea of what a real commissioned gig feels like. In one such class, students were tasked with painting murals in a home for children with multiple disabilities. A current undergraduate told us, "Service is probably the largest highlight of what Villanova has to offer. What I have learned through the different service opportunities offered by Villanova truly has made me the person I am today."

Villanova Engineering

Not every engineering program in the country offers service learning opportunities to its students, but in the College of Engineering at Villanova, service forms the "cornerstone of the engineering curriculum, and in many cases students participate by applying the engineering skills they learn in the classroom to help benefit communities around the world," according to the university. It also has an extensive STEM outreach program that gets middle and high school students interested in STEM—with special programs that focus on populations that have historically been underrepresented in STEM fields. In fact, the College of Engineering "is believed to support more active outreach programs than any other engineering school in the country," which reflects the high value that the student body places on service learning and community support. Many of these service programs involve an application process because of their popularity. However, Villanovans agreed that "this level of competition reflects well on the student body and . . . it prepares us well for interview processes for jobs after we graduate."

Career Prep

Villanova's Career Center and internship offices focus on getting students into jobs after college, and "the opportunities outside of the classroom really complement your education." The Career Center hosts career fairs in the spring and fall to help hook students up with internships and jobs, and there are small industry-based fairs—for fields like nursing or teaching—held throughout the year. There is a "great presence of recruiters on campus," and potential employers collect student résumés and conduct on-campus interviews via the Career Center. Hundreds of alumni also take part in the Career Connection Advisor Program. According to students, Villanova does an impeccable job coordinating employment and volunteer opportunities for students. "Villanova is full of resources for my success now, as a student, and will continue to be after I graduate as an alum," said a student.

Internships at Home

Villanova comes in at number nine on The Princeton Review's 2015 ranking list for Best Schools for Internships, reported in the 2015 edition of our book *Colleges That Pay You Back*. And options abound in each of the Colleges, regardless of major. In the School of Business, for instance, the Spring Accounting Internship Program gives junior accounting majors the chance to work full-time at accounting firm during tax season. Students who intern through the program can then stay on track to graduate in four years by taking courses in the summer. In the College of Liberal Arts and Sciences, rising juniors should check out an internship placement (for credit!) with the Catholic Relief Services. The office is a mere ten minutes from campus and the perfect place to solidify your commitment to peace and global justice. If law school is in your future, internships with Villanova's Law School Clinical Program lets undergrads work with current Villanova law students, "who represent real clients with real legal issues." Six law clinics run the gamut from Refugee and Emigrant Services to Juvenile Law. And in the College of Engineering, the Joseph DiGiacomo Internship with the Center for Advanced Communication is geared toward students interested in signal processing and wireless communications.

Internships Away

If you have your eye on the entertainment industry, then The Los Angeles Internship, offered in conjunction with Philadelphia's Temple University, could be your induction into the field. A program in Vatican City lets students take courses in Rome while interning in the Pontifical Council for Social Communications, the Internet Office of the Holy See, and the Rome Bureau of the Catholic News Service. A longstanding relationship with The Washington Center links students to internships in the D.C. area. Plus, there are plenty of study abroad options in London, Ireland, Australia, South America, and Europe that incorporate internships into the travel experience.

Faculty

Classes at Villanova average twenty-two students. Small class sizes combined with a stellar student-to-faculty ratio of 12:1, mean that student really get to know their professors well. Students said their "passionate" professors are "true teachers and scholars," and they "go above and beyond their office hours." They are "easily accessible," says a student, and "if you want to succeed, the community will do everything in its power to make sure you can do so," says another. Classes are often a mixture of "lecture, discussion, individual/group projects, [and] field trips." According to the school, 90 percent of full-time faculty hold the highest degrees in their fields. And freshmen don't have to wait until senior year or graduate school to learn from prominent faculty members. The school said, "Even nationally renowned endowed chairs have taught our freshman Augustine and Culture Villanova Seminar."

Wildcats in the World

Villanova alums are entrepreneurs and inventors, CEOs and nonprofit leaders, professors and Broadway producers. Notable Wildcats among their ranks are Madeline M. Bell, '83 NSG, President and Chief Operating Officer of Children's Hospital of Philadelphia; John L. Hennessy, PhD '73 ENG, President of Stanford

University; and Alexander J. Martins '86 VSB, Chief Executive Officer of the Orlando Magic. Current students can reach out to alumni for career advice and mentorship through Career Connections, a contacts database, or through their handy Alumni Student Mentoring LinkedIn page. A recent alumni posted a testimonial there: "After joining this LinkedIn subgroup, I posted a discussion asking for help making connections for my career, not exactly sure what to expect. Within one week, I have been contacted by over ten alumni with offers of advice, job leads, and connections to their companies and contacts." Wildcats continue to grow together long after graduation.

Wagner College

1 Campus Rd, Staten Island, NY 10301
Admissions: 718-390-3411, 800-221-1010
E-mail: admissions@wagner.edu
Website: wagner.edu
Twitter: @WagnerCollege

Introduction

Founded in 1883 in Rochester, New York with just six students, Wagner College now sits on Grymes Hill on Staten Island and boasts 2,000 students in more than thirty academic programs. The campus, consisting of 104 acres of park-like greenery, overlooks the New York Harbor, Manhattan, and the Atlantic Ocean. Wagner takes full advantage of not just the views, but the opportunities afforded by its proximity to New York City's business and cultural capital. In addition to a foundation in the liberal arts, Wagner students receive real-world experience and connections that will help them succeed after graduation. Wagner College is known for its "Wagner Plan for the Practical Liberal Arts" program, which "combines the traditional liberal arts with integrative learning, reflective practice, and the incredible professional opportunities offered by New York City." The plan emphasizes problem-solving, adaptability, and the "flexible leadership abilities necessary to adapt, lead, and succeed in an ever-changing world."

While there are over thirty programs to choose from, the highly regarded theater major and selective physician assistant major are currently the most popular, followed by nursing, childhood education, biology, business administration, English, nursing, psychology, and sociology. Wagner is known for its impressive student to teacher ratio, and the experiential instruction encouraged by the Wagner Plan is definitely appreciated by current students. As a theater major notes, her largest class had only fourteen students. Theater majors also have access to two dedicated theatres: The Main Stage, a proscenium theatre that seats approximately 300 and regularly "sells out to students, family, staff and the greater Staten Island community;" and Stage One, a black box theatre. It's easy to see why the theater major is so well loved. In addition to a performance concentration, the theater major also offers concentrations in design, technology, management, and theatre studies, as well as a dual major in theater and education. But it's not only theater majors who benefit from small classes, great faculty, and resources. "The professors are *all* some of the best in their fields, teaching subjects that are important to them," says a psychology major. And "Wagner really tries to do whatever it can for its students."

A Case for Experiential Learning

Wagner College is a great choice for students of all majors who are interested in engaging with their community and applying their education to real-world projects and applications, whether their aspirations are in business, science, or the arts. Theater majors benefit from the proximity to Broadway's bright lights, while students in professional programs such as business, nursing, and social work benefit from early professional training. Students most at home at Wagner College are intellectually curious, notes Amy Eshleman, professor of psychology. Students "work actively in and outside of our community," says Margarita Sánchez, associate professor of modern languages, and she adds that Wagner students "are well-rounded citizens who do research projects, participate in creative ventures and volunteer in the community." Community engagement is integral to the Wagner experience with over 80 percent of Wagner students participating in community-based projects. And Wagner admissions officers know that intellectual curiosity and engagement doesn't always show up on standardized test scores. Nick Richardson, associate professor of chemistry says that though some of his students may not have been the best performers on standardized tests, they are "engaged, intelligent, and hard-working" and continue to "excel after graduation." And this ethos comes from the top down: Richard Guarasci, president of Wagner College and founder of the Wagner Plan, says, "At Wagner College, we believe that true leadership has less to do with power, rank, or authority, and more to do with the ability to bring together diverse groups in common purpose and inspire a shared vision of a better world. This is exactly the kind of leader the Wagner Plan prepares students to become."

And for his part, sociology professor John Esser says, "I believe our seniors have a much more realistic understanding of the world outside the college gates than those in other colleges" and "a heightened awareness of their obligations to the community around them." Whatever major you choose, here are some of the programs that help Wagner students excel in college and after.

Learning Communities

Wagner believes that Learning Communities are integral to the success of Wagner students, and they are a key component of the Wagner Plan for the Practical Liberal Arts. The learning communities are a set of thematically linked courses in which students stay with the same cohort, learning and growing together. Students complete three Learning Communities prior to graduation: the First Year, Intermediate, and Senior Learning Communities. The first and last Learning Communities also include a "reflective tutorial."

First Year learning Community

The First Year Learning Community consists of two general education courses, and a Reflective Tutorial (RFT), which share a common theme like "The Love-Hate Relationships Between Human, Microbes, and Chemicals" or "Exploring the Hispanic World through Language and Film." Courses share common readings and assignments, allowing students to engage with the material in multiple ways. The intimate Reflective Tutorials, which are generally capped at twelve to fourteen students, allow students to focus on their writing skills while working on course work. Professor Eshleman notes that the First Year Program "creates a strong connection between faculty members and students." Teachers in the program advise twenty-four new students in the first semester. The small group size and consistent contact create a bond between students and faculty that "carries through the undergraduate experience," she says. Amanda Bailey, a 2007 graduate in English, tells us, "You're set up for a really great relationship with your adviser for the next four years."

Students who have this kind of initial support are less likely to flounder during their first year, and feel more engaged with the academic community. And that engagement goes beyond the academic community. Experiential learning is also a big part of the Learning Communities, which link coursework to fieldwork. Students are placed in field sites where they are able to gain hands-on experience by researching, engaging with, and analyzing various projects and organizations. Donald Stearns, professor of biology, told us about his class's hands-on approach to research into water pollution in Toms River, New Jersey: "In Toms River, students interviewed cancer victims, relatives of cancer victims, officials of corporations named in the lawsuit, attorneys, developers, and other citizens concerned about the Toms River situation. In Trenton, the students interviewed Toms River experts from the New Jersey Department of Environmental Protection; they also toured a water analysis facility used by the state to chemically analyze drinking water. In Manhattan, they interviewed the U.S. Environmental Protection Agency federal experts overseeing the cleanup operations at the two Superfund sites in Toms River….By bearing witness to the drama unfolding in Toms River, the students came to understand the complexity of a real environmental/human health issue in the community."

As you can see, the courses cover a variety of topics and offer something for every student.

Intermediate/Senior Learning Communities

The Intermediate Learning Community may be taken at any time between the first and final year, and emphasizes "learning by doing." Students advance their writing skills, engage in challenging research, and complete a final project that includes a written or an oral presentation.

The Senior Learning Community includes a 100-hour experiential learning component—which gives students invaluable experience in their discipline in a professional setting and professional contacts—and a substantive written project and presentation, in addition to coursework. The Learning Communities frequently participate in off campus activities ranging from community engagement to research. These opportunities for "real-world" involvement and career exploration are known to correlate with career success. The typical graduating seniors is "remarkably more comfortable engaging in thoughtful discussions about complex ideas," and is a "notably more confident writer within the major discipline," says Professor Eshleman, in no small part due to the Learning Communities.

The New York Connection

Wagner College offers its students the full advantage of one of the world's greatest cities: New York. Students are encouraged to engage with projects and organizations in all of five boroughs. Because New York City is an epicenter of business, art, and culture, the opportunities are endless. Students have interned with the Clinton Foundation, been featured in the Tribeca Film Festival, and landed major music industry jobs. They have also given back to their local community by helping with Hurricane Sandy support and engaging in the Port Richmond Partnership, the goal of which is greater civic engagement between Wagner students and the surrounding Staten Island community.

Intercultural Opportunities

Wagner values its role in the melting pot that is at the heart of New York City's (and the country's) success, and offers courses such as "International Perspectives" and "American Diversity" that allow students to "critically examine their own and other cultures, promoting their ability to understand and work well with diverse peoples."

Faculty members are engaged in New York City's multicultural community and encourage engagement in their students. For instance, an English professor teaches a course on film and media in developing countries alongside a teacher in Ethiopia who holds her class at the same time. Though on different continents, students in these two classes are able to work on projects together and learn from each other. Wagner's Center for Intercultural Advancement works with faculty and students to encourage intercultural dialogue, cross-cultural learning, and "strategic initiatives to internationalize and diversify the campus." The Center also provides support for international students and students of color.

Expanding Your Horizons Program

Students are also able to get out of the classroom and out from behind the computer to study abroad via Wagner's Expanding Your Horizons program, which offers students the opportunity to take a course that incorporates short, ten- to twelve-day international or domestic faculty-led trips. The courses prepare students before the trip and allow them to process and apply what they have learned afterward. Rose Tobiassen, a 2012 graduate in anthropology, tells us that experiential learning opportunities like the Expanding Your Horizons program "was a big draw" when it came to deciding between colleges. She explains, "I knew that I wanted a hands on educational experience, and while I didn't know exactly what I wanted to study when I started college, I knew that I wanted to be exposed to a lot of different places and experiences. Specifically, the Expanding your Horizons program interested in me in that it offered experiences abroad in unique places." In 2015, students went to Bangladesh, where they studied environmental health; Mexico, where they studied art and culture in San Miguel de Allende; Germany and Poland, where they studied Nazism and the Holocaust; and Senegal, where they studied the "Transatlantic Triangle: From Harlem Renaissance, Paris' Negritude Movement To Nationalism & Independence of Africa."

❝ My experience in Kenya was what inspired me to pursue international development.❞

At Wagner, 26 percent of students have studied abroad by their senior year. For Rose Tobiassen, who is program and operations coordinator with the Clinton Global Initiative, study away in Kenya was a future-making experience. "I was unsure of what I wanted to study when I started college, and my very first anthropology class changed all of that. The discipline fascinated me and it was an area of academics that catered to all of my strengths. I had a fantastic supervisor, who was also my anthropology professor, who helped expose me to so many of the different facets of the discipline, and she helped me look at the many ways I could translate my anthropology degree and skills into exciting careers that I would be passionate about. My experience in Kenya was what inspired me to pursue international development," she explains.

Center for Leadership and Community Engagement

As you may have noticed by now, civic engagement is integral to the Wagner experience. The Center for Leadership and Community Engagement (CLCE), which supports student and faculty engagement, offers programs including the Bonner Scholars and Leaders program, whose participants perform 150 or more hours of community service each semester, and meet on a weekly or bi-weekly basis for reflective seminars; the IMPACT Scholars Civic Network; and Project Pericles, which features conferences such as Debating for Democracy. Former student body president Tad Bender tells us that Student Government was by far one of his most valuable Wagner experiences. "During my time there, we brought the level of professionalism and ability to get things done much higher than seen previously and it earned great respect on campus. Being part of building that, managing it, and driving its strategic path going forward showed me how much I enjoyed building and managing a business (solving problems, working with people, etc.) which I use as I continue to advance my career."

Faculty

Wagner has a student to faculty ratio of 14:1, and boasts 221 faculty members, including ninety-eight full-time and 128 part-time faculty members. And 90 percent of full-time faculty members have the highest degree in their field. Students find faculty members to be engaged, approachable, and helpful. "My professors are all willing to help out the students in and out of the classroom," says a nursing major. "It is comforting that I can go to my professors whenever I need assistance with work." Professor Stearns can attest to the close relationship that Wagner students and faculty share. He explains: "As the experiential coordinator for environmental issues, I serve as a mentor for students, regardless of major, who want to somehow include their interest in the environment within their academic program, or who wish to pursue an off-campus experience such as an environmental internship. Far from serving as a mere referral agency, I meet with each student individually, discuss his / her interests and work with the student to shape together the experience that approaches his / her personal goal."

And at Wagner College the faculty are very involved in the curriculum. Nick Richardson, associate professor of chemistry, says that "the faculty is highly involved in the creation of majors and program, with the administration giving support when needed. In fact, all changes to programs, or the creation of new programs comes from the faculty." Faculty members are also very engaged with the community, modeling the very type of civic engagement they seek to instill in their students. For instance, Dr. Margarita Sánchez, an associate professor of

Modern Languages, created an afterschool program for children of Hispanic immigrants, and encouraged her students to volunteer (and many of them did!). She also developed a relationship with El Centro del Inmigrante in Port Richmond and has volunteered at the Center and recruited students to work as volunteers. Faculty members also regularly collaborate with students on research that leads to presentations at international conferences and publications. In fact, 41 percent of students will conduct research with a faculty member outside of class assignments, giving them access to invaluable hands-on experience.

❝ You're not doing it on your own. Whether it's learning from the other people in your Learning Community or taking a tour of Wall Street, Wagner steers you in the right direction. ❞

Wagner College alumni love to stay involved, as evidenced by the school's unique alumni travel program. The program lets small groups of Wagnerians travel the globe while bonding and seeing new cultures. The fall 2014 trip went along the Yangtze River in China. Every fall semester, alumni flock to campus with parents and students to participate in the Fall Festival. At the festival, Wagnerians connect, reconnect, cheer on their beloved Seahawks, and even brave the "Tower of Terror." Amanda Bailey, a 2007 graduate in English, attested to Wagner's "great reputation" in NYC: "A lot of people intern [in New York City], and there are so many networks. If you want to work in the city, everyone knows our college, everyone knows how capable we are and how great our business program is or our theater program is." Wagner College's NCAA Division I athletics have helped the college produce professional athletes, including MLB pitcher Andrew Bailey, NFL kicker Piotr Czech, and NFL linebacker Julian Stanford. Other notable alumni include former Texas Rangers owner Brad Corbett, CSI: NY actor Carmine Giovinazzo, and Boardwalk Empire star Sophie Tucker. Andrew Bailey, who majored in business administration with a minor in finance, spoke fondly of his overall experience there: "You're not doing it on your own. Whether it's learning from the other people in your Learning Community or taking a tour of Wall Street, Wagner steers you in the right direction."

Wake Forest University

1834 Wake Forest Road, Winston-Salem, NC 27106
Admissions: 336-758-5201
E-mail: admissions@wfu.edu
Website: wfu.edu
Twitter: @WakeForest1834

Introduction

Balancing the wide scope and personalized approach of a liberal arts college with the resources, opportunities, and academic focus of a top research university, Wake Forest is an iconic institution retaining the openness and edge of a new kid on the block—encouraging students to ask why, to pursue new ideas and new approaches, and to find the best way rather than the conventional way. Founded in 1834, Wake Forest has a tradition of excellence and comes in at number forty on the The Princeton Review's 2015 ranking list for the Top 50 Colleges That Pay You Back. (The ranking was reported in the 2015 edition of our book *Colleges That Pay You Back*.) As one health and exercise science major tells us, "Wake Forest works to ensure that its students receive the highest quality education possible while simultaneously enjoying a vibrant campus life outside of the classroom." The advantages offered by the school are multifold: "A very friendly student body, amazing academics and a big-school sports feel at a small school," according to a communications major. The beautiful campuses in Winston-Salem, North Carolina offer a host of invaluable facilities. Chief among them is the Z. Smith Reynolds Library, which provides the foundation for undergraduate research endeavors and serves as a hub of campus social life. Students also award high marks to the university's excellent Writing Center and Mentoring Resource Center.

Though equipping its students with the tools to pursue career success, the liberal arts curriculum allows them to sample a variety of disciplines, subjects, and ideas before locking in to a major. Students are accompanied on that journey by a peerless faculty, working in small classes and one-on-one sessions to promote a teacher-scholar ideal. Intimacy and individual attention are the name of the game at Wake Forest, whether in the classroom or the research lab. "Wake Forest is a beautiful and challenging school with a good reputation," according to an elementary education major. "The professors are intentional, the classes are engaging, and the student life vibrant. It has everything I could ever want in a school." A mathematical business major concurs: "Not only does the education focus around each individual, but also every student here is incredibly involved in events, organizations, clubs and community service on campus."

In fact, the university's motto, "Pro Humanitate," is most often translated as a call to service "for humanity." To that end, Wake Forest students contributed more than 140,000 hours of community service last year to more than 150 community partners locally, nationally and globally, via tutoring, hunger relief programs, construction, and environmental work. More than half of undergrads incorporate volunteerism into their educational experience. As a psychology major tells us, "Wake Forest prepares students to lead lives that matter."

❝ We want our students to have a particular skill set so that no matter what they choose to do...they are able to motivate others. ❞

According to Dr. Michael Sloan, assistant professor of classical languages, "Wake Forest University enjoys a student body who are not only intelligent and well-trained, but are cognizant of the University's mission to be the premier liberal arts university. They value and expect a first rate educational experience, and they reward the professors with a conscientious attitude and diligent work ethic." And Evelyn Williams, professor of practice for the Business School and associate vice president of leadership development, adds, "We want our students to have a particular skill set so that no matter what they choose to do—whether it's graduate school or going right into the workplace—they are able to motivate others, influence outcomes, and build and maintain relationships to be a leader in the field."

First-Year Seminars

The mission to make those leaders begins right away, with the school's program of first-year seminars. These invigorating sessions are known for their intense intellectual interchanges, both oral and written, which bring students and faculty from all disciplines together in a seminar setting to engage in critical thinking and analytical argument. The topics are stimulating and eclectic; recent seminars grappled with everything from literature to ancient civilizations to the latest Beyoncé album.

Leadership Courses

"Wake Forest fosters an environment of critical thinking, self-evaluation, and self-development," a religious studies major tells us, and much of that work is done in the school's excellent leadership courses. Take, for example, a course called Design Thinking and High Performance Teams, where students work in groups on consulting projects with high-profile clients. "We use design-thinking as the structure for problem-solving," Professor Williams explains, "but we pull in the richness of liberal arts to get better depth in each of the steps of the design thinking process." The setting is in a classroom, but the experience is real-world; previous teams have worked on projects with executives from Apple, Cisco Systems, Google Education, and Deloitte.

Also noteworthy is Catalyst Scholars, an immersion leadership course that takes high-potential sophomores on an intellectual journey to develop creative and critical reasoning, problem analysis and problem solving, design thinking, team building, communication, and presentation skills. The aim is to make each student's skill set adaptable to their circumstance. Professor Williams learned this from her own experience; graduating as an English major, she had to learn "how to translate this wonderful liberal arts experience and use all those great processes and readings in the everyday world. That's what Catalyst Scholars program is doing."

And when students are ready to get out of the classroom—way out of the classroom—they can try Individuals and Dynamics in Global Organizations. This summer abroad experience sends students around the world, to destinations like London, Paris, Edinburgh, and Barcelona, to meet and learn from those who are prospering and leading from the global stage. This focus on leadership is deliberate, particularly for 21st century students. "As millennial students graduate," Professor Williams says, "they are entering a place in the world where it's not good enough to just have great ideas—you have to be able to implement them."

Real Opportunities

Most impressively, Wake Forest doesn't just walk students through hypotheticals; they make connections that open doors. For example, career coaches at Wake are divided by major and industry. Dr. Katharine S. Brooks, executive director of the Office of Personal and Career Development, explains that this is "so that students who come in for a specific major or are interested in a specific industry will know they have a coach they can go to that is specialized in that area (nonprofit field, education, business, etc.)." She tells this story: "Our STEM majors coach focuses exclusively on students studying in the science, technology, math areas—at Wake, that's over 900 students. He ran a program this year for the first time that was a STEM Slam—an informal gathering of employers and students in the STEM fields that was a chance for students to ask individual questions. It was not like a formal career fair where you have to go in prepared to ask the right questions. This was meant as a conversation. Out of that event came sixty different job opportunities from companies we had not previously dealt with in our recruiting process. Some students were given interviews immediately."

Faculty

"The positive relationships between faculty and students are a hallmark of the Wake Forest University education," says Professor Sloan. "Students enjoy a suite of opportunities to embrace mentored research and learning beyond the classroom." Indeed, the most common comment among the students we surveyed was praise for the "fantastic professors—devoted to their students, very accessible, and passionate about what they do," according to an English major. Much of that accessibility is thanks to Wake Forest's student to faculty ratio: an astonishing 11:1. "The classes are small in size," a health and exercise science major explains, "So the academic setting feels very intimate, making it easier to connect on a personal level with professors." In fact, 57 percent of undergraduate classes boast fewer than twenty students—and a mere 1 percent of Wake Forest's classes have more than fifty students on the attendance rolls. That's an extremely low percentage among top tier schools. And in those classrooms, professors, not graduate students, are the primary instructors. In fact, all classes (with the exception of health classes and some laboratory sections) are taught by faculty members rather than teaching assistants. At some schools, this would be exceptional; for Wake Forest's faculty, it's part of the job. "It would be hard to imagine professors who cared more about their students both inside and outside of the classroom," a business and enterprise management major tells us, and a communications major sums up much of the feedback we received about the faculty: "They love what they do and it shows."

Career Prep

"Students are starting as first years and sophomores and building their own futures," counseling professor Heidi Robinson explains. "They are entrepreneurs of their own careers." A communications major we talked to confirms the school's focus on the future: "The career center is nationally known to be one of the best, and for a school this size, that's incredible. The resources that are available there almost guarantee you the best internships and jobs."

This is not hyperbole: by six months after graduation, 98 percent of the class of 2014 were either employed or in graduate school. And it's not an accident either. Throughout their Wake Forest education, students learn how to connect their academic disciplines to possible careers, while faculty connect them to experiential learning opportunities like internships and academic research. Students at Wake Forest don't just get a great education; personal and career development is a mission-critical component of their college experience.

The school's radical rethinking of the college to career experience, veering from the outdated notion of "career services" into a comprehensive and holistic four-year approach, has made it a national leader in this field, enthusiastically covered by national news and higher education media. The program of for-credit College-to-Career courses better prepares students for life and work after college, in a variety of ways. Students interested in launching a business are provided support and resources via the Center for Innovation, Creativity and Entrepreneurship. The Mentoring Resource Center supports a culture of mentoring on campus. Personal and professional relationships are facilitated with Wake Forest alumni, who can provide guidance for post-collegiate success. And the University Employer Relations office uses state-of-the-art recruiting facilities to build bridges from students in all disciplines to the employers who can make their careers happen.

And those bridges are built by faculty coaches who know how and where to construct them. According to the school, these career coaches "can help you identify your strengths and talents, create the stories you will tell at interviews and in your 'elevator pitch', refine and improve your résumé and cover letter, get you ready for your upcoming interview, assist you in clarifying your career plans and job search, and help you find an internship or other ways to gain experience."

The program offers countless opportunities for self-assessment—of one's values, interests, personality, and skills, via a potent combination of research and exploration. In the process, Professor Robinson says, the two most frequently posed questions are tackled and answered: "What are the options? How do I get real information that's helpful to me?" Wake comes in at number ten on The Princeton's Review's 2016 ranking list for Best Career Services, reported in 2016 edition of *The Best 380 Colleges*, and number twenty-three on the 2015 ranking list for Best Schools for Internships, reported in the 2015 edition of *Colleges That Pay You Back*.

Life After Wake

Wake Forest alumni excel both in and out of the classroom. Among students going on to graduate programs, nine Wake Forest students have been named Rhodes Scholars in the past twenty years (thirteen have been so honored since 1986).

66 *The Wake alumni network is strong, robust, and wants to help.* **99**

Eighty-nine Wake Forest graduates or students have been named Fulbright scholars since 1992; in the last year alone, seven Wake Forest students and recent grads were awarded Fulbright Scholarships or Fulbright English Teaching Assistantships to go abroad during the 2014–2015 academic year. Notable alumni include Dish network co-founder and CEO Charlie Ergen; Vimeo co-founder Zach Klein; Standard Oil founding partner Jabez A. Bostwick; Volvo Logistics President and CEO Susan Alt; VF Corp. President and COO Eric Wiseman; Senators Richard Burr and Kay Hagan; political journalist Melissa Harris-Perry, golf legend Arnold Palmer; and Sopranos creator David Chase. "The Wake alumni network is strong, robust, and wants to help," says Professor Robinson, who helped develop Wake's College-to-Career Courses. "Networking isn't a scary thing. It's an opportunity to let people know you."

The Last Word

"One of the nicknames of Wake Forest is 'Work Forest,'" Dr. Brooks tells us. "We are known for having a very hard working student body. Our curriculum is hard, our students work hard to attain their grades—we don't have the level of grade inflation that might be seen at other schools. As a result, the students are seen by employers as very professional, hardworking, energetic, bright, and interested." But for all of the applauded attentiveness to life after school, the college experience at Wake Forest is just as noteworthy; it's a time for students to become their best selves and to engage that self with the world around them.

"Wake is steeped in Southern traditions and hospitality but is also home to students from around the country and the world," a business and enterprise major tells us. "It has the resources of a large research institution but the personal attention of a small liberal arts college. . . . Wake Forest is perfect."

Washington University in St. Louis

One Brookings Drive, St. Louis, MO, 63130-4899
Admissions: 800-638-0700
E-mail: admissions@wustl.edu
Website: www.wustl.edu
Twitter: @WUSTL, @WUSTLcareers

Introduction

Washington University in St. Louis provides its students with a total educational experience designed not only to prepare each student to find success in whatever career path he or she chooses, but also to make a contribution to society. Current students say the school is "rich with great people, amazing extracurricular opportunities, an underrated city just down the street, and an education that will challenge you." Academic flexibility allows students to study across academic disciplines in the university's five undergraduate schools, and these co-curricular programs "are flexible enough to allow students to pursue academic interests in business, arts and sciences, art and architecture, and engineering all at once." Students at Washington University have the benefit of working alongside some of the brightest students in the world as they learn from world-renowned faculty who love to work with undergraduates. "There's a level of approachability from the dean down to professors that does seem like people are there to support you. If there's something you wanted to do there, there's a pretty good chance that you'll be able to do it," one alumna tells us. Professors "are engaged and lively," and faculty interactions can include research and mentoring, not only in the natural sciences, but in all fields, including through freshman programs. "You can tell everyone just loves to be here," says a student.

> **❝ There's a level of approachability from the dean down to professors that does seem like people are there to support you. ❞**

As for life on campus, boredom is practically nonexistent. There's never a day that passes without some form of exciting entertainment. For example, "the carnival on the swamp and a visiting orchestra are just a few things to look forward to each year." Certainly, extracurricular options abound and "anyone can find organizations on campus that pursue his/her interest." A freshman strongly agrees: "Everyone gets involved with different student groups on campus, from environmental awareness groups to improv groups to butter-churning groups." Plus, hometown St. Louis is a "really cool city for the people willing to explore it." The university even issues every student a UPass which "covers [all] of the public transportation in the area." Undergrads can enjoy everything from "art galleries and museums to exquisite restaurants (like the Peruvian 'Mango') and a well-frequented stadium for the Cardinal's baseball games." The spaces on campus are pretty spectacular, too. Not only does WashU come in at number two on The Princeton Review's 2016 ranking list for Best College Dorms, but it also comes in at number seventeen on the Best Science Lab Facilities list.

❝ WashU students are obviously known for being smart, but also for being willing to go out there and try things and do things, and be leaders.❞

Cheryl Perlmutter, who returned to WashU for her MBA after receiving her undergraduate engineering degree there, sums up the reputation graduates have out in the real world: "WashU students are obviously known for being smart, but also for being willing to go out there and try things and do things, and be leaders. So many of the activities that I did on campus, a lot of them were extracurricular, they really taught you leadership skills. That support as you're developing into an adult is very important. That coupled with the people the university attracts, who are doers, who are socially responsible, who want to make a positive impact on the world, is a really good combination." Here are a few undergraduate programs that are sure to impress.

IQ Curriculum

WashU works to ensure that every student's education is distinctive and unique to his or her particular interests. Here's where the IQ Curriculum comes in. Using the plan, students devise a sequence of classes that take care of some core requirements, explore a range of academic fields (from humanities to the natural sciences) and demonstrate how different disciplines overlap and interact. The latter is accomplished by taking what the school calls "integrations"—three integrations in at least two areas of study. One type of integration is your major or minor, similar to most schools. But for the others, students can turn to a variety of intriguing programs to fulfill their integrations requirement:

FOCUS

Freshman FOCUS programs are small, yearlong seminars that are built around a particular professor's area of expertise and often include extensive out-of-classroom activities. You might take Women in Science, for instance, and run a two-day STEM workshop for ninth grade girls. Or you might take a course in literary Ireland and travel with your class to Dublin and the Aran Islands over spring break to visit the Abbey Theater and hear traditional storytellers.

WU-Led Away Programs

Unlike some schools where students must be creative to get their study abroad experiences to count toward college requirements, WashU builds these experiences into the curriculum. According to the school, a whopping 50 percent of graduating seniors in Arts & Sciences reported having a study away experience at some point during their college career. With over one hundred programs in fifty countries, students have plenty of options. Plus, WashU follows a unique system of establishing a study abroad adviser in each academic department. This ensures you are getting advice tailored to your study interests which makes for a more meaningful experience.

Integrated Inquiries

Lastly, Integrated Inquires (or IQs) are multidisciplinary courses that ask big, timeless questions. How do we perceive, remember, and think? asks the Mind, Brain and Cognition course. Or, as the Environmental Issues course asks, how should humans interact with the natural world? The school says these courses are meant to complement a student's major, "enabling them to better fulfill the broader educational goals of a liberal arts education."

Pathfinder Program in Environmental Sustainability

Although the Pathfinder Program was officially founded in the early 2000s, it can trace its origins back to 1995, when Ray Arvidson took over a freshman seminar on environmental science and decided to focus more on actual environmental case studies rather than reading from the textbook. His approach struck a chord with his students, who persuaded him to organize a group field trip for spring break. Because Dr. Arvidson, the James S. McDonnell Distinguished University Professor in earth and planetary sciences in Arts & Sciences, was working with NASA and the jet propulsion labs in Pasadena, they went to the Mohave and studied land use there. When the students decided they wanted to keep going, Dr. Arvidson organized a trip to Hawai'i, where he'd been doing some work as well. Dr. Arvidson ran his class like this for several years before it became its current formalized iteration: an intensive program for eighteen students interested in environmental issues. Dr. Arvidson serves as his students' freshman adviser and their four-year adviser. (He says he set the class size at eighteen because that's how many students you "can fit in three vans.")

Pathfinder is a one-and-a-half year program, including a writing course taught by an environmentalist, sometimes with a senior capstone trip. It's called "pathfinder" because, as Dr. Arvidson says, "It's a way to find your path through a research university. These eighteen students have at least three courses together in the fall: they become social friends, and they become academic support friends. Even the best students academically sometimes have a difficult transition from high school to college."

Besides fulfilling an IQ integration and jumpstarting students' adjustment to their new "high-powered" environment, Dr. Arvidson says the course instills a mode of problem-solving, "an ability to attack problems using diverse directions and skills they build up in their majors, all while folding in the revelations that problems tend to be multi-variant. In order to solve them you can't just use biology or geology. We encourage a combination of approaches." This is the philosophy behind the courses' reliance on case studies as well, starting with Mono Lake in Northern California, due east of San Francisco. "It's all about approaching things from different disciplines," says Dr. Arvidson. "What's really neat is that the students come with drastically different interests and perspectives. As they begin to take courses and develop their skills, they bring those skills back into our classes and our discussions."

StEP

There are over 700 different entrepreneurship programs in the United States. But only a handful of universities offer students the ability to operate businesses with allocated, subsidized storefront locations. The Washington University Student Entrepreneurial Program, or StEP, provides a unique opportunity for students to own and operate a business on campus. They take what they are learning in their classes and apply it to a real business venture. WashU gives student business owners a leg up by giving them access to university mailing lists, web space, and mentorship from an advisory board of local business owners and WashU faculty. A loan fund even allows students to borrow the capital to get up and running or to purchase a business already established on campus. Eight businesses on campus run the gamut from a bike rental and repair shop to a water delivery service (and there's always the option to propose a new business idea to the board).

Summer Research Early Identification Program

WashU has a rock-solid summer research program with over twenty programs (and counting) across business, the sciences and humanities, at home and away. One program on campus comes out of WashU's partnership in the Leadership Alliance, an academic consortium of colleges and universities, whose mission is "to develop underrepresented students into outstanding leaders and role models in academia, business, and the public sector." The Summer Research Early Identification Program (SR-EIP) is open to undergraduates across the nation who have an interest in pursuing a PhD, or MD-Phd after graduation. They work for eight to ten weeks over the summer with a faculty research mentor learning research methods and conduct (with the added benefit of providing fodder for an amazing grad school application). The best part is that the program covers travel expenses, room and board, plus a stipend. The school says that SR-EIP is "principally designed to encourage students from groups traditionally underrepresented in the sciences, social sciences, and humanities including students who identify as African Americans, Hispanic Americans, Native Americans (including Alaska Natives) and U.S. Pacific Islanders, to consider research careers in the academic, public, or private sectors."

Real-World Experience

In addition to hands-on research and business experiences, WashU has a vibrant co-op program that gives students authentic career experiences. Offered to students of the School of Engineering & Applied Students, the Engineering Co-op Program places students with employers for full-time work that lasts at least a semester and a summer, but could last for a full academic year if a student wants to continue. To complete the program, students take time off from their academic course load. At work they are assigned entry-level duties and paid a salary. Cheryl Perlmutter, who completed her co-op experience at Boeing, tells us that the hiring process was "a mini version of what seniors have to go through when they're looking for full-time employment. You had to interview just like it was a normal job to get a position." Once there, Cheryl explains, "I definitely got to directly apply the things I learned with CAD (Computer-Aided Design) and design at Boeing, and saw how it was really done in the real world." After completing her co-op at Boeing, Cheryl was hired there full time. Cheryl tells the story: "Basically, it's hard to get hired at Boeing from the outside. But once you make it through that as a co-op, they have a career fair with all the different departments who want to hire co-ops full-time. I really hit it off with the hiring manager. I had some special skills that he was looking for that actually WashU incorporated into their curriculum. It was really directly related to something that I had learned at WashU."

Real world experiences are, of course, not exclusive to the co-op program. For example, Dr. Ron Cytron, professor of computer science and engineering, explains, "Our discipline is all about the engineering of software in context, so we take lots of problems from the real world, and almost all of our students have internships that develop that sense of practice in computer science. Our university has a nice push toward the entrepreneurial, which interests many of our students."

Faculty

Many of the faculty feel that their "real teaching happens outside the classroom, when [we] interact with students in labs, office hours, and in research. Most of us are also involved with students as advisers, faculty mentors/associates in the dorms." Professor Cytron states emphatically that "we [the faculty] are partners in their education." The alumnae we talked to spoke highly of the guidance they received from faculty mentors. Alumna Nicole Kaplan, founding president of Telesto LLC, a Florida-based consultancy, admits that when enrolled at WashU as a first-year coming off of a career-ending gymnastics injury, she was a bit out to sea. "I got to school and had no idea. I had no particular academic interests." She tells us: "I got really lucky in that the course in macroeconomics I took was taught by a fellow named Laurence Meyer, who was a professor at the university, and ran a firm where he advised Wall Street firms and other entities." Professor Meyer went on to become a member of the Board of Governors of the Federal Reserve System.

Kaplan found she had a talent for economics and continued taking courses with Professor Meyer. She says, "He basically became fairly critical in all of this—he was very much a mentor. I interned at his forecasting firm. I was the teaching assistant for his macroeconomics class my junior and senior year. And he was my thesis adviser. So I think that when you look at college experiences, you can't get a better story than that." When Kaplan, a former Director on Wall Street, began the job hunt her senior year, Professor Meyer guided her toward finance and counseled her through the intense recruitment process. She credits Professor Meyer with giving her the academic and professional opportunities that laid the foundation for her career in finance and investment banking and adds that this is "a very real dynamic at WashU. With mentorship from world-respected professors, students go on to notable careers."

Similarly, alumna and chemical engineer Melissa Holtmeyer, who received her bachelor's, master's and PhD degrees from WashU, tells us, "I went into college wanting to design cars. I haven't lost that dream, but since leaving WashU I have worked at the intersection of science, technology and policy for the U.S.

Senate and the U.S. Department of Defense. These positions never crossed my mind when I first started college. Good professors and great advisers that supported me helped me figure out a fit for my skills and led to me where I am today."

Alumni/ae

Every faculty member and administrator we asked about career preparation at WashU could easily rattle off the success stories of their former students. Dr. Arvidson told us about adventurer Steve Fossett (a graduate of WashU's Olin Business School MBA program), who enlisted the help of the Pathfinder class to run some of the support stations during his quest to be the first person go around the world in a balloon. When he crashed off of New Caledonia, an incoming Pathfinder used her high school French to coordinate with search and rescue and evacuate Fossett safely. Dr. Arvidson keeps close tabs on his former advisees: "They're professors at Caltech, at Berkley, at Georgetown. They are vice president for Teach for America, they're the CEOs of the Missouri Coalition for the environment. They're physicians all over the world. They're in the EPA. It's a lot of fun to track these folks." Similarly, Dr. Cytron says his computer science students "go on to Facebook, Amazon, eBay, Google, to graduate studies at top universities. Some don't practice computer science—one of my advisees is now a successful photographer." And Dr. Philip Bayly, the Lilyan and E. Lisle Hughes Professor in Engineering, told us that WashU's mechanical engineering graduates "go to diverse careers in the industry (large and small; established and start-up companies), government, law, medicine and academia. We have a disproportionately large number of alumni in smaller, advanced engineering companies like SpaceX and Tesla Motors. Our students are also in demand at larger, established companies like Boeing and ExxonMobil. Deanne Bell (2002) is a TV science program host. Andrew Brimer (2013) co-founded his own company. Bob Behnken (1992) is a NASA astronaut and Chief of the Astronaut Office." A chemistry major sums it up: "WashU prepares you for a variety of different careers. It's not just good at being a pre-Med school. You have options in business, art, architecture, and engineering. . . . It prepares you to think critically and handle a variety of situations. " Washington University comes in at number thirty-four on The Princeton Review's 2015 ranking list for The Top 50 Colleges That Pay You Back, which was reported in the 2015 edition of our book *Colleges That Pay You Back*.

Worcester Polytechnic Institute

100 Institute Road, Worcester, Massachusetts 01609
Admissions: (508) 831-5286
E-mail: admissions@wpi.edu
Website: www.wpi.edu
Twitter: @wpi

Introduction

For students looking for a place to jumpstart future careers building spacecrafts that could one day take humans to Mars and beyond, Worcester Polytechnic Institute could be the perfect place to start. A STEM-focused school that doesn't skimp on its humanities education, WPI emphasizes hands-on learning, and its relatively small campus and enrollment numbers help create the feeling of a friendly community of thinkers and technological innovators. Since many of its graduates will be looking at careers that may take them far from the Massachusetts campus, WPI maintains a strong global presence through its Global Project Centers; there are currently forty-four centers on six continents, and more than half of WPI students choose to complete a project at one of the off-campus locations.

With its prime New England location, WPI is close to several other universities and only an hour away from Boston, though historic Worcester, Massachusetts boasts great dining, museums, and nightlife in its own right. Inside the classroom, WPI professors—91 percent of the full-time faculty hold PhDs—are dedicated to both teaching and bringing their students up to speed on their latest research projects. Since so much of the learning takes place outside the classroom, on an authentic, experiential level, many students get the opportunity to work alongside their professors in top-notch research labs. There are more than sixty majors available to WPI undergraduates, and since the school also offers master's degrees, postdoctoral certificates, and doctoral degrees, interested students have the opportunity to fulfill a long-term academic career at WPI.

Project-Based Learning

WPI's founding motto of "theory and practice" continues to drive its educational philosophy 150 years after the school's founding in 1865. All students at WPI, regardless of their majors, participate in project-based learning. This gives them unique professional and social advantages when it comes to applying the skills they learn at WPI to careers in the real world, in whatever discipline they might choose. Integrative projects, which students engage in throughout all four years, are an integral part of the undergraduate curriculum at WPI. As one robotics engineering major (a self-described "hands-on learner," who finds it "much easier … to

66 *WPI has an amazing project system that really sets it apart from any other school.* **99**

understand something if I can visualize it") puts it, "WPI has an amazing project system that really sets it apart from any other school. Early in my freshman year I was working on projects my friends at other schools didn't even hear about until their junior year."

Great Problems Seminar

While the major projects are embarked upon during junior and senior years, project-based learning is a through-line for the entire academic experience at WPI, beginning with the Great Problems Seminar, a two-course introduction to university-level research that students may take in their first year. It focuses on issues of global importance and is tied to current events, helping students develop the skills they'll need—not only for the more extensive projects they'll work on during junior and senior year but also for their post-WPI lives. In an effort to make sure that all WPI students, regardless of whether they're planning to major in something as technical as robotics engineering, receive a well-rounded education that includes immersion in the arts, the university requires that all students essentially "minor" in the humanities. Students take six courses of their choosing, ranging from philosophy to art to foreign language.

Interactive Qualifying Project

The Interactive Qualifying Project (IQP) is a nine credit-hour requirement that most students complete during their junior year. Since it's not a course, the IQP is not related to a student's particular major; instead, students are organized into small teams, guided by various faculty members, and tasked with conducting research to solve a particular problem or need. Results are presented through oral reports and formal presentations to faculty advisers and project sponsors, which often include nonprofits and local or national government agencies. With WPI's focus on global issues, many of the IQPs are completed off campus at one of the numerous project centers around the world through the university's Global Perspective Program. This program gives students the opportunity to experience a new culture while helping to solve real-world problems in the field rather than in the classroom. One common theme that unites many IQPs is the idea of sustainability, which can be addressed through the lens of education, environmental studies, technology, energy, cultural preservation, or any number of combinations of those fields.

Major Qualifying Project

For their senior year, WPI students work on the equivalent of a senior capstone project known as the Major Qualifying Project (MQP). These are high-level design or research-based projects that students complete in their chosen field of study; just as in the IQP, many students work in small teams to complete their MQP, under the advisement of a faculty member. One industrial engineering major notes that working in teams "encourages cooperation among students rather than cut-throat competition." In keeping with WPI's emphasis on hands-on learning and the fact that MQPs are focused on design and research, students often get the opportunity to work alongside faculty members in these advisers' state-of-the-art research labs. It's not uncommon for students to complete their MQP at one of WPI's many centers away from the main Massachusetts campus and, because of the students' reputation for exemplary performance on-the-job, a good number of these projects are completed with corporate sponsorship. One alumna from the class of 1992 told us that her major qualifying project on grinding wheels, sponsored by Norton Manufacturing, made for excellent fodder during interviews for her first job post-college. She laughs, "My first boss used to kid me about that fact that I had a grinding wheel in my purse during the interview (note: I used to run labs in between WPI classes to get more test results.) It was a quirky but compelling trait during the interview for certain!"

Classic New England Feel on a Term System

Not only is Worcester, Massachusetts about as picturesque as New England college towns get, it's also home to nine other colleges and roughly 36,000 college residents. The WPI campus itself, however, manages to evoke feelings of a small, close-knit community, where students recognize each other on the quad and greet professors by name on the way to class. One benefit of having so many neighboring colleges in town is that WPI is a member of the Colleges of Worcester Consortium, which gives WPI students the opportunity to take courses at other colleges, and to take advantage of cultural offerings at other institutions. Instead of the traditional semester system, where students spend roughly 15 weeks taking four or more classes, WPI operates on a five-term system, four during the traditional academic year (August-May) and a summer term. The academic terms consist of each student taking three courses for seven weeks. An alumna tells us that this accelerated course schedule makes WPI "very similar to the real world where individuals do not get half a year to grasp concepts and translate them into action. The experience not only helped me in both grad classes to quickly assimilate information, but also in the working world. You must make tangible impact quickly."

Since the quarter system can make for some intense weeks of studying, WPI developed Insight, an advising program to help freshmen adjust to life on campus. Each incoming student is assigned three advisers, which make up their Insight Advising Group: a community adviser and a resident hall adviser (both students), and a faculty adviser. Organized by residence hall, these groups help guide new students through their first year at WPI, both by helping stimulate social interactions and by encouraging students to participate in educational programming that covers topics like time management—an important skill when each course runs just seven weeks—healthy living, and community service. The advising program also helps students develop relationships with upperclassmen and faculty, both of which are beneficial not only for a more enjoyable overall college experience but also because students can count on assistance and support when they embark on their more complex projects down the road.

Majors You Don't See Every Day

Worcester Polytechnic Institute is the place to study if you want to be on the cutting edge of technology, or, even better to be one of the people who tells the world what's cutting edge because you designed it. WPI offers students some of the most varied options when it comes to engineering majors, particularly robotics engineering. In 2007 WPI became the first university in the country offer a bachelor's degree in robotics engineering, with a master's option following in 2009 and a PhD program debuting in 2011. WPI is currently the only university to offer all three levels of education in the field of robotics engineering. Since the need for a variety of robots—from defense and security to medical and hospital uses—continues to increase, the robotics engineering program at WPI is a popular major and one with constantly applicable real-world situations. It also stresses WPI's belief in interdisciplinary studies, as many of the uses of robots in the real world—as opposed to the vacuum of a college laboratory—occur at the intersection of engineering and other branches of science and even the arts.

Another popular and unique major at WPI that falls directly into the category of interdisciplinary

66 We hear from so many employers that our graduates are self-starters.**99**

studies with real-world applications—ones that are in very high demand—is interactive media and game development (IMGD), the first undergraduate degree program of its kind in the country. Launched in 2004, IMGD at WPI began offering a master's degree in 2011. The faculty is a mixture of professionals from the computer science, social science, and policy studies departments, as well as WPI's Robert A. Foisie School of Business. Both the undergraduate and graduate programs give students the opportunity to design immersive, interactive games; at the graduate level, game industry professionals can use the education to make the transition into leadership positions.

For students looking to pursue a joint bachelor's/master's degrees, WPI offers a five-year BS/MS program in fire protection engineering. As under-graduates, students in this program pursue a degree in one of the engineering disciplines (such as mechanical, electrical, civil, or chemical) and then a master's degree in fire protection engineering, which can lead to consulting jobs in places as varied as engineering firms, the petrochemical industry, insurance companies, healthcare facilities, and code enforcement agencies. Fire protection engineers also investigate explosions and fires, assess safety in the NASA space program, and conduct fire experimentation and research. Another popular engineering program at WPI is architectural engineering, which the school began offering in 2012. A multi-disciplinary program—it draws faculty from the civil, environmen-tal, electrical, computer, mechanical and fire protection engineering departments as well the arts and humanities—the architectural engineering program at WPI is one of only seventeen such offerings in the country and the only one in the Northeast. Aerospace engineering, like robotics engineering, draws students from around the world who are keen to get the opportunity to design and build airplanes, helicopters, and rockets. WPI has resources such as wind and water tunnels, space simulation chambers, autonomous aerospace vehicles and robot-ics systems to help students get the most out of their experience, particularly the chance to work hands-on in a lab with professors who build rockets for a living.

Internships and Volunteer Opportunities

With all the hands-on experience WPI students gain in the classroom and alongside their professors in labs and at various WPI centers across the globe, the university also stresses the importance of getting work experience. One way to do this is through the myriad summer internships the university helps set up through its Career Development Center, the place to go to polish your résumé, look for job and internship openings, and ask all manner of questions about interview techniques and even what career trajectory might be right for you. As one 1988 business management/industrial engineering graduate puts it, after struggling through a difficult class and being unsure of how to proceed academically, "The Career Counseling Office had all sorts of aptitude tests available that helped me identify where my academic focus should be, and I never looked back except to appreciate the life lessons." High students ratings of the Career Development Center earned WPI a spot on the Best Career Placement list in the 2015 edition of our book *Colleges That Pay You Back.*

Another popular option for students looking to gain valuable experience is the Cooperative Education Program. In Co-op, which is non-credit, paid work experience, students get a chance to put the skills they've been developing in the classroom, along with their growing technical skills, to use in the business world. Students learn valuable lessons about how the concepts and practices that they're reading about and carrying out in a laboratory environment work in the day-to-day world of their chosen industry. There are several Massachusetts-specific opportunities that WPI students can take advantage of, including the Massachusetts Clean Energy Internship Program, for students interested in a career involving clean and sustainable energy; the Mass Life Science Intern Program, where students interested in life sciences are placed with institutions matching their particular interests around the state; the MassTech Internship Partnership, which matches students who are interested in careers in high-tech with various companies around Massachusetts; the MassDiGI Summer Innovation Program (SIP), a digital games institute that gives aspiring video game designers a chance to help design the next big game; and the Tech Generation, which hooks students up with tech start-ups in Boston that might not otherwise have the resources to find and hire interns.

Life after WPI

We've described just a handful of the hands-on opportunities open to Worcester Polytechnic Institute students. It should be no surprise that alums have found that WPI has a terrific reputation in the working world. A 1988 alumnus, who double majored in biology and biotechnology, tells us: "WPI students are well-known for being exceptionally prepared, motivated and ready to perform impactful work in the real world. I am happy to report that I recently hired a WPI graduate into my group. As expected for a WPI grad, he is a wonderful member of the team, has the skills to run with complex projects, and has already been tagged as a strong scientist with leadership potential." From the faculty perspective, an associate professor of mechanical engineering tells us, "We hear from so many employers that our graduates are self-starters." She explains, "During four years at WPI they not only become highly knowledgeable in a discipline, they develop skills and competencies related to teamwork (they work in a variety of teams and most learn to identify and manage conflict in teams); problem solving (they're able to ask the right questions, scope problems, manage complex projects and get things done); and 'learning to learn'—figuring out what they need to learn and jumping right in." The schools says that it consistently has a 90 percent job and/or graduate school placement upon graduation with students receiving job offers from Amazon, Microsoft, Bose, Dow Chemical, Google, Pfizer, Sikorsky, EMC Corporation, and ExxonMobil, to name a few.

Indexes

Index of Schools By Location

Index of Schools By Tuition

Index of Schools By Enrollment

About the Author

Rob Franek, Senior Vice President-Publisher at The Princeton Review, is the company's chief expert on education and college issues. Over his 22-year career, he has served as a college admissions administrator, test prep teacher, author, and lecturer. He is lead author of The Princeton Review's annual books, *The Best 380 Colleges* and *Colleges That Pay You Back: The 200 Best Value Colleges and What It Takes to Get In*. He is also co-author of *If The U Fits: Expert Advice on Finding the Right College and Getting Accepted*. Follow his Tweets at @RobFranek.